Fodor's

MADRID

Welcome to Madrid

Little did we realize that the emergence of a novel coronavirus in early 2020 would abruptly bring almost all travel to a halt. Although our Fodor's writers around the world have continued working to bring you the best of the destinations they cover, we still anticipate that more than the usual number of businesses will close permanently in the coming months, perhaps with little advance notice. We don't expect things to return to "normal" for some time. As you plan your upcoming travels to Madrid, please confirm that places are still open and let us know when we need to make updates by writing to us at this address: editors@fodors.com.

TOP REASONS TO GO

★ **Electric nightlife:** Let loose to bassy DJ sets, Latin jazz, or feisty flamenco.

★ **Artistic treasures:** Ponder prized Goyas, Picassos, El Grecos, and Velázquezes.

★ **Multiculturalism:** Senegalese lunch counters, Chinese hot pot, Venezuelan bars.

★ **Raucous festivals:** Feel the pulse at Madrid Pride, outdoor festivals, or a verbena (outdoor fair).

★ **Sporting events:** Bellow ¡goooooool! like a Spaniard at a rollicking soccer match.

★ **Epic tapas crawls:** Embark on a gastronomical adventure.

Contents

Fodor's Features

El Prado: Madrid's Brush
with Greatness 112

Alhambra: Palace-Fortress. 273

Chapter 1

EXPERIENCE MADRID

20 ULTIMATE EXPERIENCES

Madrid offers terrific experiences that should be on every traveler's list. Here are Fodor's top picks for a memorable trip.

1 Parque del Buen Retiro

Leafy trails, outdoor cafés, and French gardens aren't just within reach of the city center—they're at the very heart of it in this park that spans nearly 300 acres in the heart of old Madrid. *(Ch. 7)*

2 Puerta del Sol

There's never a dull moment in this semicircular plaza, where friends gather, buskers perform, and bar crawls begin. *(Ch. 3)*

3 Museo Nacional de Reina Sofía

A towering sculpture by Roy Lichtenstein greets you at the door to Spain's preeminent modern art museum; beyond it, works like Picasso's *Guernica* await. *(Ch. 8)*

4 Museo del Prado

Spain's premier museum houses a treasure trove of 12th- to 19th-century European art and masterpieces by the Spanish greats including Velázquez, Goya, and El Greco. *(Ch. 7)*

5 Tapas

While there's still plenty of baguette and *jamón*, tapas today are usually far more intriguing. Sample Madrileño standbys on Cava Baja or eye-popping *nueva cocina* numbers on Calle Ponzano. *(Ch. 6, 8, 9)*

6 Botín

Guinness World Records calls this creaky local favorite the world's oldest restaurant, opened in 1725. Order the suckling pig, roasted in the original wood-burning oven. *(Ch. 8)*

7 Palacio de Liria

The stunning abode of the late Duchess of Alba finally opened to the public in 2019. It contains what some experts say is the finest private art collection in Spain. *(Ch. 5)*

8 Parque del Oeste

For a sunset stroll, there's no place like this charming park with a rose garden, fountains, dogs galore, and—drum roll—a transplanted 2,200-year-old Egyptian temple. *(Ch. 4)*

9 Plaza Mayor

Steeped in four centuries of history, Madrid's most famous square has Flemish-style spires, endless arcades, and busy sidewalk restaurants. *(Ch. 3)*

10 Food Markets

A curious new way to dine has emerged in Madrid in recent years with the transformation of old-school markets into experimental (and affordable) tapas emporiums.

11 Museo Thyssen-Bornemisza

Bridging the gap between the classical Prado and modern Reina Sofía, this private collection presided over by a baroness spans seven centuries and countless artistic movements. *(Ch. 6)*

12 Shopping

Hand-sewn espadrilles, colorful painted ceramics, haute couture garments by avant-garde local designers—there's a souvenir for every type of traveler if you know where to look.

13 Real Madrid

In Spanish, *real* means royal, and to the network of Real Madrid devotees around the world, the team is nothing short of that. Bow with locals at Santiago Bernabéu stadium. *(Ch. 10)*

14 Flamenco

You don't have to go to Andalusia for traditional flamenco—Madrid is awash with outstanding performance venues that cater to all tastes and budgets.

15 Coffee Culture

The third-wave coffee revolution is sweeping the city, and there's no shortage of award-winning cafés serving complex brews alongside pastries and snacks.

16 Palacio Real

Welcome to the largest palace in Western Europe, nearly double the size of Versailles with 2,800 rooms. Visitors swoon over the only surviving Stradivarius quartet and the 18th-century Royal Kitchens. *(Ch. 4)*

17 Nightlife

As revelers around Europe tuck themselves into bed, the party in Madrid has barely begun. After a *primera copa* at a chic wine or cocktail bar, hit the *discoteca* and groove till the wee hours.

18 Churros at Chocolatería San Ginés

San Ginés is to Madrid what Café du Monde is to New Orleans: a national sensation that for generations has been frying spirals of piping-hot churros and *porras* (churros' larger cousins). *(Ch. 3)*

19 El Rastro

Merchants and shoppers have been congregating at this legendary open-air market every Sunday since 1740. Its 3,000-plus stalls brim with unique finds and tchotchkes. *(Ch.8)*

20 El Escorial

Take a day trip to Felipe II's imposing castle on a hill, a veritable labyrinth of gilded halls, grand frescoed chambers, and manicured Renaissance gardens. *(Ch. 12)*

WHAT'S WHERE

1 Sol. After a stroll through the Plaza Mayor, settle in for some chocolate con churros at a legendary chocolatería or snap up handmade Spanish wares at a centuries-old crafts shop.

2 Palacio and Moncloa. Time-travel to Madrid's noble past in these districts defined by their palaces, French gardens, awe-inspiring religious sights, and stately plazas.

3 Chueca and Malasaña. Trendy tapas bars, packed nightclubs, fabulous vintage shops, and plenty of LGBT+ pride—the epicenter of Madrid's countercultural revolution of the 1980s hasn't lost its rakish edge, even if Airbnb and international chains are quickly encroaching.

4 Barrio de las Letras. Come nightfall, it doesn't get much livelier than Letras, home to the pedestrianized Calle Huertas, Plaza de Santa Ana, and one of Europe's most coveted private art collections at the Museo Thyssen-Bornemisza.

5 Retiro and Salamanca. Taking in the sprawling Retiro Park, unparalleled Prado Museum, and miles of boutique-lined side streets, these abutting barrios drip with old-world charm and class.

6 La Latina, Lavapiés, and Arganzuela. Lavapiés, an graffitied multicultural hub with steep cobblestone streets, is a quick walk from the timeless taverns of La Latina and the rambunctious El Rastro flea market.

7 Chamberí. Once a sleepy residential neighborhood, Chamberí is a culinary hot spot with gastro-markets and a tapas corridor (Calle Ponzano) so popular it commands its own hashtag, #Ponzaning.

8 Chamartín and Tetuán. Come for the *fútbol*—Real Madrid's home stadium is situated here—and stay for the down-home restaurants and locals-only nightclubs.

9 Carabanchel, Usera, and Latina. Explore Madrid's next frontier in these blue-collar barrios across the Manzanares that mix cutting-edge art studios with international restaurants, no-frills abuelo bars, and tranquil parks.

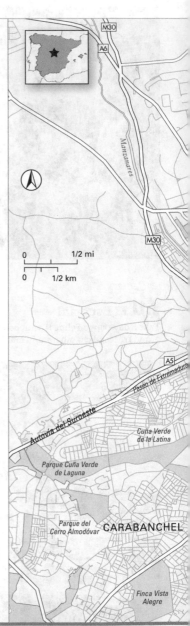

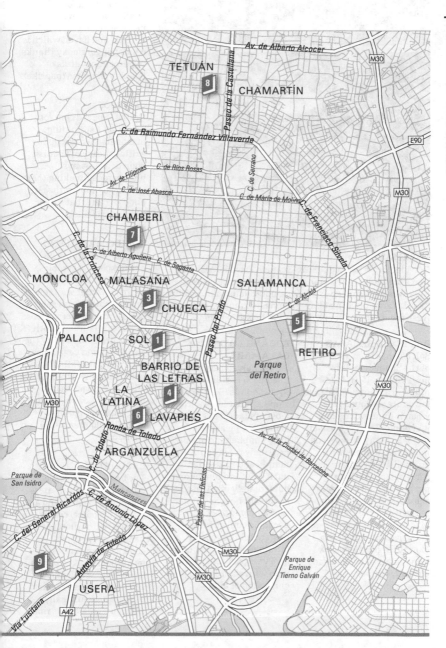

TETUÁN

8

CHAMARTÍN

M30

Av. de Alberto Alcocer

Paseo de la Castellana

C. de Raimundo Fernández Villaverde

E90

Av. de Filipinas   C. de Ríos Rosas

C. de José Abascal

C. de Serrano

C. de María de Molina   C. de Francisco Silvela

M30

CHAMBERÍ

7

C. de Alberto Aguilera   C. de Sagasta

C. de la Princesa

MONCLOA   MALASAÑA

3

CHUECA

SALAMANCA

C. de Alcalá

5

2

PALACIO   SOL **1**

Paseo del Prado

RETIRO

BARRIO DE
LAS LETRAS

Parque
del Retiro

M30

LA
LATINA

4

6 LAVAPIÉS

M30

Ronda de Toledo

ARGANZUELA

Av. de la Ciudad de Barcelona

Parque de
San Isidro

C. de Toledo

Manzanares

Paseo de las Delicias

C. del General Ricardos   C. de Antonio López

9

Autovía de Toledo

M30

M30

Parque de
Enrique
Tierno Galván

USERA

Vía Lusitana

A42

What to Eat and Drink in Madrid

CALLOS A LA MADRILEÑA

Madrid-style tripe stew has long been a national sensation, both for its quality (you'll never perceive so much as a whiff of funk) and flavor, which is comfortingly smoky thanks to heaped spoonfuls of Spanish *pimentón* (paprika).

CHURROS

Unlike Mexican churros, which get a sprinkling of cinnamon-sugar upon exiting the fryer, Spanish *churros* are always unsweetened, making them the perfect foil for the rich hot chocolate that's their requisite sidekick.

TORRIJAS

Don't let locals hear you call it "Spanish French toast," but that's basically what *torrijas* are. A favorite treat during Holy Week, these deep-fried cinnamon-dusted pillows ooze like custardy bread pudding. The finest examples are plated fresh from the skillet and drizzled with warm honey.

COCIDO MADRILEÑO

This soul-satisfying stew of chickpeas, vegetables, and various meats is the ultimate winter warmer. Traditionally it's presented in three courses, or *vuelcos*: the rich, gelatinous broth comes first, followed by the garbanzos and vegetables, and finally the fall-off-the-bone meats, which generally include beef shank, ham hocks, pork belly, and hen, plus sausages like *morcilla* (blood sausage) and chorizo.

BATTERED BACALAO

Salt cod has been a fixture of the Spanish table for more than half a millennium, so it's no surprise that locals are seasoned pros when it comes to cooking it *al punto*. Though bacalao can take many forms—you might find it *al pil-pil* (in an emulsified garlic sauce), *a la vizcaína* (with melty peppers and onions), or in countless other newfangled variations—the classic Madrid rendition is battered and fried and served as a gloriously greasy *pincho*, a one-bite portion impaled with a toothpick.

BOCADILLO DE CALAMARES

Sure, a halved baguette filled with nothing but fried squid sounds like a dry, bland affair, but as with most of Madrid's celebrated dishes, the pleasure lies in its simplicity: rings of pristinely fresh squid are floured and flash-fried until juicy and tender and immediately piled into a cloud-soft hoagie—*y ya está*. Enjoyed as is, the *bocadillo* could be the poster child of gastro-minimalism, but no one will give you grief for zhuzhing it up with some lemon juice or a dollop of aioli.

CROQUETAS

The best Spanish-style croquettes have a shatteringly crisp exterior and a molten béchamel center flavored with whatever's handy: chopped ham ends, sautéed porcini mushrooms, flaked bacalao, leftover roast chicken—you name it. They're one of those hedonistically delicious "a-ha" tapas that

Tortilla española

you'll find yourself ordering at every opportunity.

GAMBAS AL AJILLO
Always a flamboyant spectacle, *gambas al ajillo* (garlicky shrimp) arrive sizzling in an abundance of olive oil. After fishing out each plump, briny morsel, indulge in the primal pleasure of dunking crusty bread into the garlic- and chili-infused oil.

JAMÓN
Madrid's proximity to Spain's principal ham-producing regions, Andalusia and Extremadura, make it ground zero for some of the best porcine products money can buy. Sweet and subtle *jamón serrano*, the industry standard, is a gateway drug to the more complex—and expensive—stuff, *jamón ibérico de bellota*.

PATATAS BRAVAS
Madrid's famous "angry potatoes" are fried in olive oil until crisp and blistered and blanketed in fiery chili-vinegar sauce, making them optimal bar food.

SPANISH GIN-TÓNIC
Order a gin and tonic (*gin-tónic* in Spanish) in Madrid, and you'll be presented with a fishbowl-size goblet filled with ice, tonic, over-the-top garnishes (think cardamom, pink peppercorns, basil, or berries), and more gin than you'll care to remember the next morning. Note: in Madrid, cocktail hour is traditionally after dinner, so don't be caught off guard when the waiter offers a round of *copas* upon clearing the dessert plates.

SPANISH WINE
You might know your Rioja from your Priorat and your cava from your albariño, but Spain's most famous

wines are a fraction of the enological treasures you can find in Madrid. Try a Manchegan airén aged in *tinajas* (amphorae), or a rosé txakoli from the Basque Country, or a local raspy red garnacha or apricot-scented white albillo from the Sierra de Gredos, an hour from the city.

TORTILLA ESPAÑOLA
How can a simple omelet of potatoes, eggs, and onions taste so sublime? Buckets of fruity Spanish olive oil may have something to do with it. *Tortilla española* (aka tortilla de patata) is the most ubiquitous dish in Spain—Spanish kids grow up eating it at least once a week—and its joy lies in its countless variations.

Best Nightlife Spots in Madrid

CAFÉ CENTRAL

Madrid's best-known jazz venue hosts an enviable roster of international artists. Performances are usually 9–11 nightly, and tickets can be bought at the door or online (the latter is advisable if traveling around holiday time).

LA CANÍBAL

Welcome to Madrid's newest hot spot for wine geeks. Pull up a stool in the warehouse-like bar area, with massive concrete pillars and long wooden tables, and choose from dozens of boutique bottles or some 15 small-production Spanish wines on tap.

CORRAL DE LA MORERÍA

Corral de la Morería is the ultimate soup-to-nuts *tablao* (flamenco cabaret) experience. Opt for an elegant meal in the main hall or at the adjacent four-table Gastronómico restaurant. The no-photography policy and whisper-quiet staff keep you focused on the passion-packed music.

CAFÉ BERLÍN

For a space so small and unassuming, Café Berlín packs quite the acoustic punch and draws an international, eclectic crowd. Before midnight, catch nightly live music acts in a panoply of styles (flamenco, swing, soul, and more); from around 1 am on, drop in for the disco-inflected DJ sets that ooze good vibes until 6 am.

FABRIK

World-famous megaclub Fabrik is so far from the city center that you have to take a 30-minute charter bus to get there (€3; departures Friday and Saturday every 30 minutes from Plaza de España 11 pm–6 am). But those who make the schlepp—up to 7,000 people on a good night—are rewarded with euphoria-inducing DJ sets by big-name artists. You can thank the 44 Tecnare speakers for the ringing in your ears on the hazy ride back into town.

KAPITAL

Perhaps Madrid's most legendary nightclub, Kapital has seven floors—each of which plays a different type of music spun by top local and international DJs—plus a small movie theater and rooftop terrace. Dress to impress for this one: no sneakers, shorts, or tanks allowed. VIP tables overlooking the dance floor (approximately €170 for four people) are a worthwhile splurge if you can swing it.

Café Berlin

MACERA TALLERBAR
The age-old technique of maceration rules at Macera, where bartenders treat spirits like blank canvases, imbuing them with surprising flavor combinations. Gin, for instance, is steeped with fresh cilantro, lime, and jalapeño until it achieves a grassy piquancy that shocks and pleases the palate all at once. Dark spirits more your speed? Choose a whiskey cocktail infused with almonds, fresh cherries, mint, or vanilla bean.

PAVONEO
Tourists have yet to discover Chueca's buzziest new gay bar, which caters to well-dressed creatives, selfie-snapping influencers, and models on their nights off. Bartenders may not know what a Negroni is (even if they have all the requisite ingredients), but their sigh-worthy looks make them easy to forgive.

TACONES MANOLI
A clandestine "gastronomical flamenco experience" (their words, not ours) akin to New York's Sleep No More, Tacones Manoli is dark, edgy, and moving with soulful ballads and up-tempo *bulerías*. Guests wander with a tarot card and mask to take in various scenes as they play out over two hours in the rooms of three stories of a historical building. Literature buffs will pick up on allusions to works by Federico García Lorca. A high level of Spanish is a must.

SALMON GURU
Regularly featured on best-of lists, Salmon Guru is Madrid's—and perhaps Spain's—most innovative *coctelería*. The *nueva cocina* tapas are almost as impressive as the eye-popping concoctions. Try the Chipotle Chillón, made with mezcal, absinthe, and chipotle syrup.

What to Buy in Madrid

ESPADRILLES
Nothing screams summer in Spain like a pair of colorful rope-soled *alpargatas*, or espadrilles. Antigua Casa Crespo, in business since 1863, still makes them the old-fashioned way, using top-quality rope and hand-sewing the seams.

ÁBBATTE TEXTILES
The mother-and-daughter duo behind Ábbatte combines the former's hands-on expertise in textile construction with the latter's academic background in Spanish design history. The result? Plush, pillowy perfection with a nod to the past in every handmade piece, from blankets to bedspreads to cushions and rugs. All wares are woven in the Cistercian abbey of Santa María de la Sierra, an hour north of the city.

CAPES
Travelers who like their souvenirs on the zanier side should check out the merino wool capes at Seseña, the world's oldest cape maker. Seseña has outfitted the likes of Picasso, Hemingway, and Michael Jackson—and the fourth-generation owners are ever more experimental when it comes to newfangled fashions.

CERAMICS
The Moors brought exquisite ceramic craftsmanship to the Iberian Peninsula in the 8th century with their florid mosaics and azulejos, and the art form reached its apogee in Spain during the Renaissance. Though you won't find specimens that old outside museums, the hand-painted jugs, bowls, and pitchers that grace the shelves of Cocol are a close approximation; alternatively, see how the new generation of ceramicists is interpreting this age-old tradition at Guille García Hoz's intimate boutique.

CUSTOM THREADS
Like many European cities, Madrid has a rich tradition of craftsmanship when it comes to custom-made apparel. Bespoke leather shoes, designer gowns, meticulously tailored suits—the art of individualized, timeless couture is alive and well in Madrid; the only hitch is whether you can afford to shell out the euros for it. If so, make a beeline to Oteyza, whose expert tailors dress Madrid's upper crust with hand-stitched garments that fit like a glove.

FAN
Summer visitors are often surprised to see locals—mostly women—fanning themselves as if they stepped straight out of a Goya painting. But unlike during Spain's glory days, today's *abanicos* are seldom brandished for show—they're simpler in design, lightweight and practical and ideal for stuffing into a purse for use on the metro or restaurant *terrazas*. Splurge on an attractive yet sturdy one at Casa Diego, the legendary old-fashioned boutique at Puerta del Sol that makes each fan by hand.

GUITAR
Whether you're a seasoned *guitarrista* or are still wrapping your fingers around the main chords, you'll no doubt appreciate

Fans

the artistry of a sleek handmade Spanish guitar. Try one on for size at Juan Álvarez, the luthier made internationally famous by Eric Clapton in 1992, when the blues artist chose one of its guitars to play the now-mythical "Tears in Heaven" on MTV's "Unplugged" concert.

JAMÓN
No offense to Italy, but even the best prosciutto doesn't hold a candle to real-deal *jamón ibérico de bellota* (acorn-fed ham), made from semi-wild black-hoofed pigs that roam the scrubby forests of southern Spain. To savor this delicacy at home—FDA regulations be damned—purchase vacuum-sealed envelopes of jamón at any traditional market (e.g., Mercado de la Paz, Mercado de la Cebada) or at specialty vendors like Cinco Jotas.

KITCHENWARE
To set yourself up for culinary success at home, you'll need (ok, want) some specialty cookware: earthenware *cazuelas* come in all shapes and sizes; you'll use these for all-day stews and gratins. A paella pan is a must—you won't achieve optimal levels of *socarrat* (that blissfully burnt bottom layer of rice) without one. And then there's all the attractive dinnerware, from ceramic plates to olive-wood boards to glass oil dispensers (*alcuzas*). The lauded kitchen store Alambique carries all of these items and more.

OLIVE OIL
Olive oil is the lifeblood of Spanish cooking, and even the standard supermarket stuff in Madrid is usually an echelon above what most Americans are used to. Spring for cold-pressed *aceite de oliva extra virgen* sold in opaque

bottles—clear glass, though admittedly more attractive, exposes the oil to too much light, turning it rancid.

SOCCER SWAG
Even if you don't make it to the bleachers of Santiago Bernabéu stadium, you can flaunt your Real Madrid spirit by sporting a jersey with your favorite *futbolista's* name on the back. Avoid counterfeit merch by shopping at the stadium or at an official store in the city center.

WINE
Stock up on oddball varietals, limited-production releases, and cult natural wines at upmarket Lavinia, in Salamanca neighborhood, or the more alternative Bendito Vinos y Vinilos, in Lavapiés. Fringe perk: you can sip while you shop, since both stores double as wine bars.

Under-the-Radar Things to Do in Madrid

MADRID RÍO

Madrid Río, the city's most ambitious urban planning initiative in recent history, solved the space conundrum of Parque del Buon Retiro by laying nearly 30 km (19 miles) of green space and bike-friendly paths along the Manzanares River.

CASA DE CAMPO

More than five times the size of Central Park, the Casa de Campo is Madrid's largest park and a nature-lover's paradise, complete with bike trails, picnic tables, and pine forests. Strike out on a walk or jog and see how many hares, foxes, red squirrels, and hawks you can spot.

CHAMBERÍ FOOD SCENE

Fusion tapas spots, cheffy gastro-markets, timeless seafood restaurants, newfangled Basque pintxo bars—the district of Chamberí is Madrid's new culinary north star. After grazing on international bites at Mercado de Vallehermoso, meander over to the bar-lined Calle Ponzano for one of the city's most memorable tapas crawls.

CHINATOWN

Most visitors come and go without hearing so much as a murmur about Usera, one of Europe's most vibrant Chinatowns that established itself in the early 2000s. Situated across the Manzanares east of the Carabanchel district, its streets are lined with hot pot restaurants, dumpling stalls, dimsum parlors, and more—all punchy antidotes to the (sue us!) minimalist spiceless-ness of traditional Spanish cooking.

MATADERO MADRID

Once an industrial slaughterhouse complex, El Matadero reopened in 2007 as Madrid's most avant-garde creative arts and exhibition center. Thanks to its diverse roster of restaurants, bars, and day and evening events—which include plays, concerts, poetry readings, and movie screenings—the surrounding district of Arganzuela has gotten a new lease on life.

MUSEO DEL ROMANTICISMO

To catch a glimpse of how the Spanish bourgeoisie lived in the early 19th century, step into this marquis' palace decked out with ornate period furniture, evocative portraits, and other historical artifacts culled from the height of Spanish Romanticism. It's worth spending a few minutes admiring the flamboyantly decorated fans and backlit lithophanes. You only need an hour or two to take in the permanent collection, but don't rush out: the plant-filled interior patio is a gorgeous, tranquil place to enjoy tea and pastries.

NATURAL WINE BARS

You're never far from a *bodega* or *taberna* in Madrid, but the wine served in these old-school haunts is almost always one-note, over-oaked plonk from industrial wine factories up north. To taste small-production Spanish wines that have personality and *terroir* for days, seek out natural wine bars like Bendito Vinos y Vinilos, La

El Matadero

Caníbal, or—the newest arrival on the scene—Tribunal Supremo de Vinos.

NONTOURISTY FLAMENCO

As any seasoned traveler to Spain will tell you, there's flamenco, and then there's *flamenco*. To experience the Andalusian art form at its purest and most vivacious, it pays to go where the tourbus crowds don't. Consider Teatro de Flamenco, a newcomer situated in Malasaña, which hosts concerts by professional dance troupes, or the more intimate La Quimera, far enough from the city center that you'll be surrounded by local aficionados.

RAYO VALLECANO

Most sports fans are familiar with Spain's powerhouse soccer team Real Madrid, but to enjoy a spirited match with locals and without the long lines

and inflated price tag, step up to Rayo Vallecano's box office. The team's second-tier status doesn't make the games any less thrilling (think college ball vs. NBA), especially when you catch them on their home turf a short metro ride from the city center, in the southeastern Madrid neighborhood of Vallecas. Known as Madrid's third team, *Los Franjirrojos* (The Red Sashes) are a club with a great story and active, class-conscious supporters (in 2014, the players joined fans to save a local 85-year-old fan who was being evicted from her home). They are also one of the last of the teams in Spain to represent a Barrio or neighborhood.

REGIONAL SPANISH CUISINE

Thanks to Madrid's diverse makeup, you don't have to catch a train to sample top regional specialties.

Even the staunchest paella purists rave about Aynaelda's saffron-scented paella valenciana, studded with garrofón beans and tender chunks of rabbit and chicken. For a culinary journey to Asturias in the mountainous north, head to Casa Mingo, a lively *sidrería* (cider house) that's been ladling *fabada* (bean soup) and splashing cider since 1888. Other regional restaurants worth marking on your map include El Rincón de Jaén, for Andalusian fare like salmorejo and shrimp fritters; El Chacón, for hearty Galician octopus and smoked ham; and Gofio, for experimental Canarian tasting menus.

What to Watch and Read Before You Go to Spain

HOMAGE TO CATALONIA
BY GEORGE ORWELL

Orwell's journals directly document his time at war in Catalonia, and his first-person narrative provides a view of war-torn Barcelona that today may seem wholly foreign.

THE SHADOW OF THE WIND
BY CARLOS RUIZ ZAFÓN

Daniel Sempere is 10 years old when his father, a bookseller in post–civil war Barcelona, takes him to a mysterious labyrinth filled with treasured but forgotten tomes and tells him to pick one that he will then dedicate his life to preserving. What follows is a tale of a young man who discovers a mysterious person—or perhaps creature—is destroying all remaining works of Julián Carax, the author whose book he now protects. The Shadow of the Wind's story of life, death, and history may be fictional, but its setting in a war-torn Spain is forceful, and the fact that it's sold more than 15 million copies hints at its compelling universe.

THE BEST THING THAT CAN HAPPEN TO A CROISSANT
BY PABLO TUSSET

Pablo "Baloo" Miralles is the lazy, debaucherous scion of a well-to-do Spanish family. When his elder (and more accomplished) brother inexplicably disappears, Baloo suddenly finds himself pulled into the dealings of the family's powerful financial firm, a turn of events which inspires him to try to locate his missing sibling. Within this satirical quasi-detective story is a modern-day tale about the city of Barcelona.

FOR WHOM THE BELL TOLLS
BY ERNEST HEMINGWAY

All the typical Hemingway elements are present in this fictional account of the Spanish Civil War: romance, bravado, glory, death, and tragedy. It's an incredibly evocative slice of historical fiction that is almost impossible to put down once started.

MARKS OF IDENTITY BY JUAN GOYTISOLO

A searing masterpiece from Spain's greatest living novelist describes the return of an exile to Barcelona. Goytisolo comes to the conclusion that every man carries his own exile about with him, wherever he lives. The narrator (Goytisolo) rejects Spain itself and searches instead for poetry. This is a shocking and influential work, and an affirmation of the ability of the individual to survive the political tyrannies of the last century and the current one. Marks of Identity was banned in Spain until after Franco's death.

MONSIGNOR QUIXOTE
BY GRAHAM GREENE

This novel provides a wonderful journey through Spain in the company of Monsignor Quixote, an aging village priest, and his friend Sancho Panza, the communist ex-mayor. It's a contemporary reimagining of Miguel Cervantes's classic Don Quixote but set in Spain in the 1980s rather than the 1600s.

THE NEW SPANIARDS
BY JOHN HOOPER

How was the transition from dictatorship to democracy accomplished so smoothly? How did a country noted for sexual repression find itself in the European vanguard in legalizing gay marriage? What's the deal with the Spanish royal family? Read Hooper's fascinating study, considered one of the clearest insights into the sociology and culture of modern Spain.

¡AY CARMELA! **DIRECTED BY CARLOS SAURA**
This 1990 film portrays the ethical and personal dilemmas a group of nomadic comedians face during the Spanish Civil War. The film features a scene where Carmela, played by Carmen Maura, tries to teach a Polish prisoner, an International Brigadist, how to pronounce the /ñ/ sound in the word "España."

BIUTIFUL **DIRECTED BY ALEJANDRO GONZÁLEZ IÑÁRRITU**
Alejandro González Iñárritu's first feature since *Babel*, and his fourth moving film is the story of a single father of two (Javier Bardem) in Barcelona who finds out he has terminal cancer and tries to find someone to care for his children before his death. While melancholy, this is also a story of redemption as a father seeks a better life for his children.

TODO SOBRE MI MADRE (ALL ABOUT MY MOTHER) **DIRECTED BY PEDRO ALMODÓVAR**
After Manuela's 17-year-old son Esteban is killed before her eyes she decides to move to Barcelona in order to find his father, a transvestite named Lola who doesn't know that Esteban exists. It's a brilliantly directed tale which sensitively examines a variety of complex topics such as bereavement, addiction, gender identity, and the impacts of HIV. It also earned director Pedro Almodóvar the Best Director award at the 1999 Cannes Film Festival and the Academy Award for Best Foreign Language Film in 2000.

WOMEN ON THE VERGE OF A NERVOUS BREAKDOWN **DIRECTED BY PEDRO ALMODÓVAR**
This Academy Award–nominated black comedy was Pedro Almodóvar's international breakthrough and secured his place at the vanguard of modern Spanish cinema. Madrid-based Pepa resolves to kill herself with a batch of sleeping-pill-laced gazpacho after her lover leaves her. Fortunately, she is interrupted by a deliciously chaotic series of events.

BELLE EPOQUE **DIRECTED BY FERNANDO TRUEBA**
It is 1931 in Spain and the country's monarchy is facing its final days. During this time of confusion and conflicting loyalties, Fernando, whose allegiance is to the republic, deserts from the army and goes on the run into the beautiful Spanish countryside. There, he meets Manolo, a painter with the same political beliefs and four young, beautiful daughters.

A GUN IN EACH HAND **DIRECTED BY CESC GAY**
Catalan director Cesc Gay recruited some top-notch Spanish actors and actresses for this comedy. Told through a series of vignettes, *A Gun in Each Hand* explores how changing gender roles in Spain affect modern relationships and speaks to how Spanish ideas about masculinity and relationships are changing, and how the an evolution can benefit women in Spain.

PAN'S LABYRINTH **DIRECTED BY GUILLERMO DEL TORO**
Set in the early years of Franco's dictatorship, this film follows an imaginative kid, Ofelia, who moves with her pregnant mother to her future stepfather's house. In her new home, she meets the faun, Pan, who tells her she might be the lost princess of an underground world. While she faces mythological creatures and terrifying beasts, a rebellion is taking place in her stepfather's military post.

FAMILY UNITED **BY DANIEL SANCHEZ AREVALO**
Combining two of Spain's greatest passions—football and family, this Spanish comedy takes place at a family wedding in a mountain-village near Madrid during the 2010 World Cup soccer final.

Madrid Today

"A breakwater of all the Spains" is how poet Antonio Machado described Madrid nearly a century ago, referring to its patchwork quilt of residents hailing from every corner of the Iberian Peninsula. Today, you could call Madrid a breakwater of the world. This, after all, is Europe's third-largest city—a place where, in the span of a single block, you might find a century-old tavern, a Senegalese textile supplier, a Sichuan hot pot restaurant, and a glitzy boutique hotel. In other words, the Madrid of Ernest Hemingway—of bullfights and siestas and sherry wine and frilly fans—has largely faded into the past. Expect instead a cosmopolitan, open-minded, modern metropolis with enough youth-driven verve to keep you on your toes but enough history and old-world charm to remind you that you're on vacation.

THE ARTS

The "Golden Triangle" of museums (Prado, Thyssen-Bornemisza, and Reina Sofía) play host to an ever-rotating repertoire of world-class exhibitions, so it's worth looking past the permanent collections. Up-and-coming local artists have found a new home across the river in scruffy Carabanchel, where converted industrial spaces come alive during Artbanchel, an "open studio" festival held each May. Alternatively, you can get a taste of Carabanchel's cutting-edge art scene year-round at Sabrina Amrani Gallery.

Traditional Spanish *artesanía* is experiencing a renaissance with locals finding new appreciation for the painted ceramics, woven baskets, blown glass, and handmade textiles of their forebears. Boutiques selling such "Made in Spain" treasures are popping up left and right; Cocol and Hijo de Epigmenio are two examples.

GASTRONOMY

In the last five years, Chamberí has become Madrid's culinary nerve center, thanks to a glut of buzzy restaurant openings like Arima, Charnela, and Tripea and the sudden popularity of Mercado de Vallehermoso, a once-endangered market that lures trendsters with envelope-pushing tapas bars and international food stalls. Like any other international city, food fads here change on a dime: 2019 was the year of ramen and over-the-top burgers, and 2020 saw a huge uptick in fancy-pants Italian food and designer pizzerias; what's next—especially post-pandemic—is anyone's guess.

NIGHTLIFE

Madrid has been synonymous with dusk-to-dawn nightlife for as long as dusk has turned to dawn. There's no excuse to head back to the hotel early, whether your definition of a great night out involves remixed reggaeton tracks (try Oh My Club), live jazz (check out Sala Clamores), a live flamenco show (Teatro Flamenco Madrid is a notable newcomer), or simply a few *vinos* or cocktails at a hot spot like Macera, La Caníbal, or Viva Madrid.

TRANSPORTATION

Since 2019, much of the historic center is a low-emission zone (known as "Madrid Central"), meaning the bulk of rental cars aren't allowed entry. Beyond the dependable metro (subway system), there are dozens of new BiciMAD bike-share docks with electric-powered bikes available for rent. In spring 2020, a completely free (and emission-free) bus service called Línea Cero ("Line Zero") was unveiled connecting Atocha railway station to Moncloa via Gran Vía. For trips farther afield, Madrileños rely less on regional trains and buses and more on the affordable Blablacar ridesharing app.

Chapter 2

TRAVEL SMART

Updated by
Joanna Styles

👫 POPULATION:
Just under 3.3 million

💬 LANGUAGE:
Spanish

$ CURRENCY:
Euro

📠 AREA CODE:
34

⚠ EMERGENCIES:
112

🚌 DRIVING:
On the right

⚡ ELECTRICITY:
220v/50 cycles; electrical
plugs have two round prongs

🕐 TIME:
Six hours ahead of New York

✈ AIRPORT:
MAD

🌐 WEB RESOURCES:
www.esmadrid.com/en
turismomadrid.es/en
www.spainisculture.com

Know Before You Go

While you might get side-eye for ordering a café con leche in the evening (a cortado is the standard afternoon pick-me-up), for the most part Madrid isn't big on hard-and-fast rules. Minor cultural foibles won't get you into any serious trouble but it's still worth knowing what to expect to ensure a frictionless trip.

TAPAS TIPS

Tapas are Spanish bar snacks, and in Madrid, they can be complimentary or charged, depending on the establishment. Most traditional taverns will offer a free tapa—a handful of olives, a bit of cured sausage, or whatever the bartender feels like feeding you—with each drink. If you think you're due a tapa but it got lost in the shuffle, don't fret. Simply ask the (often flustered) bartender for el aperitivo, por favor. Note that many upscale bars and restaurants don't serve free tapas. If a tapa is a small aperitif geared toward individual barside consumption, a ración is a larger portion designed for sit-down sharing; these are always charged. Note to the less famished: "Medias raciones," or half-portions, are often available even if they're not on the menu, so ask your waiter.

MANY MUSEUMS ARE FREE—IF YOU KNOW WHEN TO GO

The Prado, Madrid's most legendary museum, offers free entry 6–8 pm Monday to Saturday and 5–7 pm Sunday, while the Reina Sofía (Spain's preeminent modern art museum) welcomes guests at no charge 7–9 pm Monday, Wednesday, and Saturday, and 1:30–7 pm Sunday. Many other museums and sights have complimentary days and times as well, so check individual websites for details. A number of smaller museums, such as Museo de Lope de Vega and the Madrid History Museum, are always free.

YOU CAN DRINK FROM THE TAP

The water quality is excellent in Madrid, but that doesn't keep many bars and restaurants from trying to upsell the bottled stuff, particularly to unsuspecting tourists. If you want tap water, the term to remember is agua del grifo (as opposed to agua mineral or agua con gas). Unlike in the United States, you always have to ask for it, and the default is sans ice. Most establishments will happily pour you a glass from the tap, but, vexingly, aren't obligated to do so by law.

GETTING FROM A TO B

It's not worth renting a car in Madrid as the entire city center is a low-emission zone (called "Madrid Central"), off limits to all but the greenest vehicles. Besides, Madrid is extremely walkable anyway. The metro system, the most convenient and environmentally friendly way to get around, is exceptionally clean and reliable and runs 6 am–2 am. City buses are a fine alternative; night buses (locally known as búhos, "owls") run 2–6 am. Uber and Cabify are the most popular ride-hailing apps; the latter is both cheaper and (marginally) better when it comes to workers' rights. Official taxis are ubiquitous (the green light up top means it's hailable) and not nearly as expensive as those in, say, Paris or Berlin. Unless you're accustomed to biking in traffic, skip BiciMAD, the local bikeshare system—Madrid has a dearth of designated bike lanes.

NAVIGATION NOTE

Numbers in postal addresses come after street names (i.e., it's Calle Fuencarral 10, not 10 Calle Fuencarral), so that's how you should communicate where you're going, whether you're talking to a cabbie or using a navigation app.

"SPANISH TIME" IS A THING

Lunch at 3, dinner at 9—by American standards, Spain is on a pretty wacky schedule when it comes to mealtimes. Most restaurants don't even take reservations before 2 and

8 for lunch and dinner, respectively, and the vast majority are closed Sunday night. Standard commercial hours are equally enigmatic: family-owned establishments often close 2–5 pm for the siesta (afternoon "nap"), while others, especially international chains, operate straight through the day. Always check online or call ahead to ensure you don't wind up staring at a "cerrado" sign.

THERE'S A WRONG TIME (AND PLACE) FOR PAELLA
You're in Spain and you want to eat paella; no judgement here. Paella is one of Spain's most famous dishes but you should know that it is original to Valencia, not Madrid, so it is (obviously) best sampled in Valencia, or even neighboring Catalonia. That said, you can find any regional Spanish cuisine in Madrid, so if you want paella, you can have paella (try Arrocería Casa de Valencia, alongside Parque del Oeste). Note: If you notice a look of disapproval when you order paella at dinner, it's because this dish is traditionally lunch fare.

SOME OF THE BEST FOOD ISN'T "SPANISH"
You didn't come all the way to Spain to eat pad thai and pizza, but visitors who limit themselves to Spanish food while in Madrid are missing some seriously thrilling bites. The city boasts one of Europe's best (and least-known, at least for now) Chinatowns, Usera, where you can satisfy cravings for dim sum, wokked noodles, and shao bing. A sizable West African community whose nucleus is in Lavapiés translates into hearty, exuberantly spiced dishes, perfect for when jamón fatigue sets in. And a recent influx of Venezuelans means hot and gooey arepas, tequeños, and cachapas for all.

TIPPING ETIQUETTE
At upscale sit-down restaurants, tip up to 10% of the bill. At more casual spots, €1 per person is about right, though many Spaniards simply leave loose change or don't tip at all. At bars and nightclubs, don't tip the bartender, even if you've ordered food—it's not a faux pas, per se, but it's not common practice. In nice hotels, slip the bellhop a euro or two per bag and leave a few euros in the room each day for housekeepers; €5 to €10 euros is the norm for helpful concierges. In taxis, just round up the bill, unless you're schlepping particularly heavy (or numerous) bags, in which case a couple extra pavos (local slang for euros) go a long way.

AVOID HOT TOPICS
Spain's politics are quite polarized at the moment, and you can never be sure about new acquaintances' sympathies. Hot-button topics best avoided (unless you're prepared for battle) include Catalan and Basque independence, the monarchy, bullfighting, Franco, and the Church. It's also worth noting that the Spanish flag means different things to different people: for some on the left, it is viewed as a nationalist symbol that harks back to Franco's dictatorship, while for others, it's brandished as a symbol of national unity.

AVOID FINES
Drinking in public is prohibited, and if you're caught boozing in the street or on the metro, you could be hit with a €600 fine. Exceptions to this rule include designated outdoor dining areas and street fairs. That said, it's not uncommon to see locals flouting open container laws altogether. Cannabis is illegal but decriminalized.

ALLOW TIME FOR SIDE TRIPS
Sandwiched between the two Castiles (Castile and León to the north and Castile-La Mancha to the south), Madrid is a fantastic jumping-off point for jaunts to those rugged historical regions. Toledo and Segovia are the most popular daytrip destinations from Madrid with their stunning architectural monuments, soulful cooking, and fairytale churches and castles, but Cuenca, Salamanca, Sigüenza, and a number of other intriguing towns and cities are also well within reach. For more natural escapes, nearby mountain ranges such as the Sierra de Guadarrama and Sierra de Gredos have hidden mountain villages and well-marked trails for hiking.

Getting Here and Around

Air

Flying time from New York to Madrid is about seven hours; from London, it's just over two hours. Most flights from North America land in, or pass through, Madrid's Barajas Airport (MAD).

From North America, Air Europa flies to Madrid; American Airlines, part of the Oneworld Alliance, and Iberia fly to Madrid and Barcelona; Delta flies direct to Barcelona, Madrid, and Málaga (June–September). Note that some of these airlines use shared facilities and do not operate their own flights. Within Spain, Iberia is the main domestic airline and also operates low-cost flights through its budget airlines Iberia Express and Vueling. Air Europa and Ryanair both offer inexpensive flights on most domestic routes. The earlier before your travel date you purchase the ticket, the more bargains you're likely to find. Air Europa, Iberia Express, Vueling, and Ryanair also have flights from Spain to other destinations in Europe.

Bicycle

BiciMAD is Madrid's public bike-share service with 208 docks scattered around the city center. The bikes are electric, meaning you hardly have to pedal, and are an excellent alternative to the metro and buses, provided the weather is good and you're comfortable riding in traffic (separate bike lanes are virtually nonexistent). Avid urban cyclists staying for a month or more may wish to purchase a €25 yearly membership, which drastically lowers the cost of individual rides to €0.60 for up to one hour, but occasional users can pay €2 per 30-minute ride, buying a ticket at each service station. The bikes can be borrowed from, and returned to, any station in the system.

Bus

Within Spain, a number of private companies provides bus service, ranging from knee-crunchingly basic to luxurious. Fares are almost always lower than the corresponding train fares, and service covers more towns, though buses are less frequent on weekends. Smaller towns don't usually have a central bus depot, so ask the tourist office where to wait for the bus. Spain's major national long-haul bus line is ALSA.

ALSA has four luxury classes in addition to its regular seating. Premium, available on limited routes from Madrid, includes a number of services such as à la carte meals and a private waiting room, while Supra+ and Supra Economy include roomy leather seats and onboard meals. You also have the option of *asientos individuales,* individual seats (with no other seat on either side) that line one side of the bus. The last class is Eurobus, with a private waiting room, comfortable seats, and plenty of legroom. The Supra+ and Eurobus usually cost, respectively, up to one-third and one-fourth more than the regular seats.

Car

Driving around Madrid isn't for the faint-hearted; access roads tend to be very congested and in the center, strict Madrid Central antipollution measures (see below) prohibit entry by private cars to many areas. Add to this the locals' impatience with drivers who don't know exactly where they're going plus the lack of parking lots, and you have the potential for a stressful time behind the wheel.

Hiring a car while you explore Madrid isn't necessary because the city has excellent public transportation as well as taxi and Uber services. If you plan to explore beyond Madrid to Andalusia, for example, you may wish to rent a car particularly if you want to add some side trips along the way. In this case, choose to hire a car at the end of your stay in Madrid—some hired car companies bring the vehicle to your hotel.

PARKING

Madrid has private and public parking lots where charges typically start at €2.50 an hour with lower rates for 24-hour stays. Street parking in the center is very limited and restricted to hourly rates. Most hotels offer parking, but it is rarely included in the room rate. Expect to pay at least €20 a day.

RULES OF THE ROAD

Spaniards drive on the right and pass on the left, so stay in the right-hand lane when not passing. Children under 12 may not ride in the front seat, and seat belts are compulsory for both front- and backseat riders. Speed limits are 30 kph (19 mph) or 50 kph (31 mph) in cities, depending on the type of street, 90 kph (56 mph) on national highways, 120 kph (75 mph) on the autopista or autovía. The use of cell phones by drivers, even on the side of the road, is illegal, except with completely hands-free devices.

 ## Public Transport

To ride the metro, you must buy a refillable Tarjeta de Transporte Público (Public Transportation Card), which costs an unrefundable €2.50 and can be obtained at ticketing machines inside any metro station. Each journey costs €1.50–€2, depending on how far you're traveling within the city; you can also buy a 10-ride Metrobus ticket (€12.20). There are no free transfers between the metro and bus systems. The **Abono Turístico** (Tourist Pass) allows unlimited use of public buses and the metro for one day (€8.40 for Zone A, €17 for Zone T) to seven days (€35.40 for Zone A, €70.80 for Zone T); buy it at tourist offices, metro stations, or select newsstands. The metro runs 6 am–1:30 am, though a few entrances close earlier. *(See the metro map in this chapter.)*

 ## Ride-Sharing

Blablacar is Spain's leading rideshare app in intercity travel with more global users than Uber. Its free platform allows you to book ahead using a credit card, and message with the driver to set meeting and drop-off points. Blablacar is the most affordable way to travel to Madrid's outlying cities and beyond as drivers aren't allowed to make a profit (you essentially help the driver offset the price of gas and tolls).

Taxi

Taxis work under several tariff schemes. Tariff 1 is for the city center 7 am–9 pm; meters start at €2.40. There is a fixed taxi fare of €30 to or from the airport from the city center. Supplements include €3 to or from bus and train stations. Tariff 2 is for the city center 9 pm–7 am on weekdays (and 7 am–9 pm on weekends and holidays); the meter starts at €2.90 and charges more per kilometer. Besides reserving a taxi by phone, you can also do it through mobile app MyTaxi, which works with local official taxi drivers. As of mid-2019, Uber and Cabify are back in operation after a hiatus due to legal restrictions; in 2017, UberONE, Uber's premium service, added 50 Teslas to its Madrid fleet.

Getting Here and Around

🚆 Train

The chart here has information about popular train routes. Prices are for one-way fares (depending on seating and where purchased) and subject to change.

DISCOUNTS

If you purchase a ticket on the REN-FE website for the AVE or any of the Grandes Líneas (the faster, long-distance trains, including the Talgo) you can get a discount of 20%–60%, depending on how far ahead you book and how you travel: discounts on one-way tickets tend to be higher than on round-trips. Discount availabilities disappear fast: the earliest opportunity is 62 days in advance of travel. If you have a domestic or an international airline ticket and want to take the AVE within 48 hours of your arrival but haven't booked online, you can still get a 10% discount on the AVE one-way ticket and 25% for a round-trip ticket with a dated return. On regional trains, you get a 10% discount on round-trip tickets (15% on AVE medium-distance trains).

■TIP➔ If there are more than two of you traveling on the AVE, look for the word "mesa" in the fare column, quoting the price per person for four people traveling together and sitting at the same table. If you select the price, it tells you how much the deal is for one, two, and three people. You have to buy all the tickets at the same time, but they're between 20% and 60% cheaper than regular tickets.

Train Travel Times

Madrid to Barcelona: €45–€181	High-speed AVE trains make the trip in 2 hours 30 minutes
Madrid to Bilbao: €20–€65	Semi-express Alvia train time is 5 hours 4 minutes
Madrid to Málaga: €24–€135	Fastest AVE trains take 2 hours 25 minutes
Madrid to Seville: €26–€128	Fastest AVE trains take 2 hours 20 minutes
Madrid to Granada: €35–€80	Fastest AVE trains take 3 hours and 5 minutes
Madrid to Santander: €18–€80	Semi-express Alvia is 4 hours 5 minutes
Madrid to Valencia: €33–€115	Fastest AVE trains take 1 hour 42 minutes
Madrid to Santiago de Compostela: €27–€75	Fastest time about 5 hours

Essentials

⚡ Activities

BASKETBALL

The Spanish are avid basketball fans and the country has several world-class players, many of whom such as Pau and Marc Gasol, and Ricky Rubio play in the NBA. The national men's team have won the World Championship twice (the latest in 2019) and the women's team took bronze position in 2018. In the last decade, Spain has won the highest number of FIBA basketball medals in the world. The Spanish league, ACB, runs from late September to early May and includes the Copa del Rey championship play-off. Madrid has three basketball teams: Real Madrid, Estudiantes and Fuenlabrada. Real Madrid and Estudiantes rank among the best in Spain and play at their home stadium, the WiZink Center.

SKIING

In the winter, the locals turn their attention to the snowy slopes in the three resorts to the north of the city. All are within an hour's journey of Madrid and offer skiing and snowboarding. The ski season runs from late December to late March when the resorts open daily.

SOCCER

Madrid is home to two big players in Spain's national obsession, often referred to as "not a matter of life and death, but more important." Both Real Madrid and Atlético de Madrid regularly finish at the top or near it in the national soccer league (La Liga) and play at international level. They're also among the oldest teams in the country, founded in 1902 and 1903, respectively. The capital also has three other soccer teams, Getafe and Leganés (both in the top league) and Rayo Vallecano, in second division.

The Spanish soccer league runs from mid-August to the end of May and all teams play each other twice during the season. Matches usually take play at weekends and tickets sell out fast. Those for the local 'derby' matches between Real Madrid and Atlético de Madrid, twice a year, are the most expensive and you need to book as soon as sales open.

TENNIS

Since Manolo Santana won Wimbledon in 1966, Spanish tennis has gone from strength to strength and produced world-class players. Rafael Nadal is considered the greatest Spanish player of all time and one of the best in the world. Spain has produced several other world number one players including, Arantxa Sánchez Vicario, Garbiñe Muguruza, Carlos Moyá, and Juan Carlos Ferrero. Spain has one of the best, most comprehensive schedules of national junior, International Tennis Federation junior and professional circuits of events of any country in the world. This cluster of high level junior and professional tournaments is a tremendous developmental advantage. Rising Spanish stars to look out for include Roberto Bautista Agut and teenager Carlos Alcaraz.

The Caja Mágica, designed by French architect Dominique Perrault, hosts the annual Madrid Open, part of the ATP Masters 1000 and Premiere Mandatory, in May. The championship brings together the world's best players on its clay courts.

🍽 Dining

As Spain's most vibrant melting pot, Madrid is home to countless regional Spanish restaurants serving everything from Valencian Paella to Basque *pintxos,* but the most classic fare closely resembles that of Castile. International fare has its best representation in the capital

Essentials

where dietary preferences (e.g., vegetarian, vegan, and gluten-free) are also widely available. You'll find the widest range of dining venues in the country, from upmarket Michelin-starred restaurants to "cheap and cheerful" tascas or taverns with just about everything in between. Prices tend to match the venue and expect a good value for money at many. Most are open six days a week for lunch and dinner (Monday is the most popular day to close) and many close during the month of August.

When it comes to traditional local fare, the climate described as *nueve meses de invierno y tres de infierno* (nine months of winter and three of hell) plays a major role and it's no surprise to discover that most typical dishes are comfort food. Garlic soup, stewed chickpeas, and roast suckling pig and lamb are standard complements of Madrid feasts. *Cocido madrileño* (a meat-packed winter stew) and *callos a la madrileña* (stewed tripe) are favored local specialties, although most restaurants also serve lighter dishes. Fish and seafood feature on most menus and despite its inland location, Madrid has some of the best in Spain.

MEALS AND MEALTIMES

Mealtimes in Madrid are later than elsewhere in Europe, and even later than those in the rest of Spain. Lunch starts around 2:30 or 3 and dinner after 9 (as late as 11 or midnight in the summer). Weekend eating times, especially dinner, can begin upward of an hour later. In areas with heavy tourist traffic, many restaurants have an all-day kitchen or open a bit earlier.

PRICES

What it Costs in Euros			
$	$$	$$$	$$$$
RESTAURANTS			
under €16	€16–€22	€23– €29	over €29

 Health

COVID-19

A new novel coronavirus brought all travel to a virtual standstill in the first half of 2020. Although the illness is mild in most people, some experience severe and even life-threatening complications. Once travel started up again, albeit slowly and cautiously, travelers were asked to be particularly careful about hygiene and to avoid any unnecessary travel, especially if they are sick.

Older adults, especially those over 65, have a greater chance of having severe complications from COVID-19. The same is true for people with weaker immune systems or those living with some types of medical conditions, including diabetes, asthma, heart disease, cancer, HIV/AIDS, kidney disease, and liver disease. Starting two weeks before a trip, anyone planning to travel should be on the lookout for some of the following symptoms: cough, fever, chills, trouble breathing, muscle pain, sore throat, new loss of smell or taste. If you experience any of these symptoms, you should not travel at all.

And to protect yourself during travel, do your best to avoid contact with people showing symptoms. Wash your hands often with soap and water. Limit your time in public places, and, when you are out and about, wear a cloth face mask that covers your nose and mouth. Indeed, a mask may be required in some places, such as on an airplane or in a confined space like a theater, where you share the space with a lot of people. You may wish to bring extra supplies, such as disenfecting wipes, hand sanitizer (12-ounce bottles were allowed in carry-on luggage at this writing), and a first-aid kit with a thermometer.

Given how abruptly travel was curtailed in March 2020, it is wise to consider protecting yourself by purchasing a travel insurance policy that will reimburse you for any costs related to COVID-19 related cancellations. Not all travel insurance policies protect against pandemic-related cancellations, so always read the fine print.

🛏 Lodging

The Spanish government classifies hotels with one to five stars, with an additional rating of five-star GL (Gran Lujo) indicating the highest quality. Although quality is a factor, the rating is technically only an indication of how many facilities the hotel offers. For example, a three-star hotel may be just as comfortable as a four-star hotel but lack a swimming pool.

All hotel entrances are marked with a blue plaque bearing the letter *H* and the number of stars. The letter *R* (for *residencia*) after the letter *H* indicates an establishment with no meal service, with the possible exception of breakfast. The designations *fonda* (*F*), *pensión* (*P*), *casa de huéspedes* (*CH*), and *hostal* (*Hs*) indicate budget accommodations: these are no longer official categories, but you'll still find them in Madrid. In most cases, rooms in such buildings will be basic but clean, although they can be downright dreary.

When inquiring in Spanish about whether a hotel has a private bath, ask if it's an *habitación con baño*. Although a single room (*habitación sencilla*) is usually available, singles are often on the small side. Solo travelers might prefer to pay a bit extra for single occupancy of a double room (*habitación doble uso individual*). Make sure you request a double bed (*cama de matrimonio*) if you want one—if you don't ask, you will usually end up with two singles.

The Spanish love small country hotels and agritourism. Rusticae (⊕ *www. rusticae.es*) is an association of more than 170 independently owned hotels in restored palaces, monasteries, mills, and estates, generally in rural Spain. Similar associations serve individual regions, and tourist offices also provide lists of establishments.

A number of *casas rurales* (country houses similar to B&Bs) offer pastoral lodging either in guest rooms or in self-catering cottages. You may also come across the term *finca*, for country estate house. Many *agroturismo* accommodations are fincas converted to upscale B&Bs.

PARADORES
The Spanish government operates nearly 100 paradores—upscale hotels often in historic buildings or near significant sites. Rates are reasonable, considering that most paradores have four- or five-star amenities, and the premises are invariably immaculate and tastefully furnished, often with antiques or reproductions. Each parador has a restaurant serving regional specialties, and you can stop in for a meal without spending the night. Paradores are popular with foreigners and Spaniards alike, so make reservations well in advance.

Essentials

FACILITIES

You can assume that all rooms have private baths, phones, TVs, and air-conditioning, unless otherwise indicated. Breakfast is noted when it is included in the rate, but it's not a typical perk at most Madrid hotels. There are a few hotels with pools, though some are indoors.

PARKING

Most large hotels in Madrid have dedicated parking lots or access to secure facilities within easy walking distance of the hotel. Hotels without parking will usually recommend the best place to leave your car. Expect to pay at least €20 a day (24 hours or less).

PRICES

By law, hotel prices in Madrid and the rest of Spain must be posted at the reception desk and should indicate whether the value-added tax (I.V.A. 10%) is included. Note that high-season rates prevail not only in summer but also during Holy Week and local fiestas. In much of Madrid, breakfast is normally *not* included. As a general rule, you'll get a better room rate if you book via the hotel website directly than through a booking platform.

RESERVATIONS

Reservations are always a good idea and essential if you travel to Madrid during high season (spring, Easter, and Christmas). Weekends are usually busy at any time of year especially during events such as World Pride and sporting events.

What it Costs in Euros			
$	$$	$$$	$$$$
HOTELS			
under €125	€125–€174	€175–€225	over €225

Nightlife

Unlike in other European cities, where partying is a pastime geared only toward the young, there are plenty of bars and discotecas with mixed-age crowds, and it's not uncommon for children to play on the sidewalks past midnight while multigenerational families and friends convene over coffee or cocktails at an outdoor café. For those who don't plan on staying out until sunrise, the best options are the bars along the Cava Alta and Cava Baja, Calle Huertas near Plaza de Santa Ana, and Calle Moratín near Antón Martín. Those who want to stay out till the wee hours have more options: Calle Príncipe and Calle De la Cruz, lined with sardine-can bars lined with locals, and the scruffier streets that snake down toward Plaza de Lavapiés. But the neighborhood most synonymous with *la vida nocturna* is Malasaña, which has plenty of trendy hangouts along Calle San Vicente Ferrer, Calle La Palma, and all around Plaza de Dos de Mayo. Another major nightlife contender is is Chueca, where tattoo parlors and street-chic boutiques sit between LGBT+ (yet hetero-friendly) bars, dance clubs, and after-hours clubs.

Packing

Pack light. Although baggage carts are free and plentiful in most airports, they're rare in smaller train stations and most bus stations, and you will not want to drag a big case around on side trips. Madrid has a continental climate and can be bitterly cold from late fall to early spring and seering hot in summer. It makes sense to wear casual, comfortable clothing and shoes for sightseeing, but you'll want to dress up a bit in the city for fine restaurants and nightlife.

🎭 Performing Arts

Madrid is a thriving center for performing arts and is home to Spain's most important venues and companies. The capital offers a year-round calendar of music, theater, and dance, indoor in the winter and open-air in the summer heat. You'll find entertainment for all tastes and genres from baroque chamber music and Wagner opera to Indy pop and flamenco fusion; classic Lope de Vega and Lorca theater to avant-garde Ernesto Caballero and Cristina Colmena; traditional ballet to modern dance; plus concerts from the world's top artists and musicals—Madrid has the most in the world after New York and London.

💲 Tipping

Aside from tipping waiters and taxi drivers, Spaniards tend not to leave extra in addition to the bill. Restaurant checks do not list a service charge on the bill but consider the tip included. If you want to leave a small tip in addition to the bill, tip 5%–10% of the bill (and only if you think the service was worth it), and leave less if you eat tapas or sandwiches at a bar—just enough to round out the bill to the nearest €1.

🇺🇸 U.S. Embassy/Consulate

All foreign governments have embassies in Madrid (some also have consular offices in other Spanish cities), and most offer consular services in the embassy building.

Tipping Guides for Madrid

Bartender	Not necessary, just enough to round out the bill to the nearest €1
Bellhop	€1 per bag per bag, depending on the level of the hotel
Coat Check	€1 per coat
Hotel Concierge	€5–€10 for exceptional service
Hotel Maid	€2–€5 per day (in cash, preferably daily since cleaning staff may be different each day you stay)
Hotel Room Service Waiter	€1 per delivery, even if a service charge has been added
Porter at Airport or Train Station	€1 per bag
Restroom Attendants	€0.50
Skycap at Airport	€1 per bag checked
Spa Personnel	10% of the cost of your service
Taxi Driver	About 10% of the total fare, plus a supplement to help with luggage
Tour Guide	€2 per person
Waiter	5%–10%, but not necessary

📍 Visitor Information

The largest tourist information office is on Plaza Mayor. There are two smaller offices located in Terminal 2 and Terminal 4 at the airport, and at Plaza de Callao, the Reina Sofia and Prado art museums, and the Royal Palace.

Helpful Phrases in Spanish

BASICS

Hello	Hola	**oh**-lah
Yes/no	Sí/no	see/no
Please	Por favor	pore fah-**vore**
May I?	¿Me permite?	may pair-**mee**-tay
Thank you	Gracias	**Grah**-see-as
You're welcome	De nada	day **nah**-dah
I'm sorry	Lo siento	lo see-**en**-toh
Good morning!	¡Buenos días!	**bway**-nohs **dee**-ahs
Good evening!	¡Buenas tardes! (after 2pm)	**bway**-nahs-**tar**-dess
	¡Buenas noches! (after 8pm)	**bway**-nahs **no**-chess
Good-bye!	¡Adiós!/¡Hasta luego!	ah-dee-**ohss/ah** -stah **lwe**-go
Mr./Mrs.	Señor/Señora	sen-**yor**/ sen-**yohr**-ah
Miss	Señorita	sen-yo-**ree**-tah
Pleased to meet you	Mucho gusto	**moo**-cho **goose**-toh
How are you?	¿Que tal?	keh-tal

NUMBERS

one	un, uno	oon, **oo**-no
two	dos	dos
three	tres	tress
four	cuatro	**kwah**-tro
five	cinco	**sink**-oh
six	seis	saice
seven	siete	see-**et**-eh
eight	ocho	**o**-cho
nine	nueve	new-**eh**-vey
ten	diez	dee-**es**
eleven	once	**ohn**-seh
twelve	doce	**doh**-seh
thirteen	trece	**treh**-seh
fourteen	catorce	ka-**tohr**-seh
fifteen	quince	**keen**-seh
sixteen	dieciséis	dee-**es**-ee-**saice**
seventeen	diecisiete	dee-**es**-ee-see-**et**-eh
eighteen	dieciocho	dee-**es**-ee-**o**-cho
nineteen	diecinueve	dee-**es**-ee-new-**ev**-eh
twenty	veinte	**vain**-teh
twenty-one	veintiuno	**vain**-te-**oo**-noh
thirty	treinta	**train**-tah
forty	cuarenta	kwah-**ren**-tah
fifty	cincuenta	seen-**kwen**-tah
sixty	sesenta	sess-**en**-tah
seventy	setenta	set-**en**-tah
eighty	ochenta	oh-**chen**-tah
ninety	noventa	no-**ven**-tah
one hundred	cien	see-**en**

one thousand	mil	meel
one million	un millón	oon meel-**yohn**

COLORS

black	negro	**neh**-groh
blue	azul	ah-**sool**
brown	marrón	mah-**ron**
green	verde	**ver**-deh
orange	naranja	na-**rahn**-hah
red	rojo	**roh**-hoh
white	blanco	**blahn**-koh
yellow	amarillo	ah-mah-**ree**-yoh

DAYS OF THE WEEK

Sunday	domingo	doe-**meen**-goh
Monday	lunes	**loo**-ness
Tuesday	martes	**mahr**-tess
Wednesday	miércoles	me-**air**-koh-less
Thursday	jueves	hoo-**ev**-ess
Friday	viernes	vee-**air**-ness
Saturday	sábado	**sah**-bah-doh

MONTHS

January	enero	eh-**neh**-roh
February	febrero	feh-**breh**-roh
March	marzo	**mahr**-soh
April	abril	ah-**breel**
May	mayo	**my**-oh
June	junio	**hoo**-nee-oh
July	julio	**hoo**-lee-yoh
August	agosto	ah-**ghost**-toh
September	septiembre	sep-tee-**em**-breh
October	octubre	oak-**too**-breh
November	noviembre	no-vee-**em**-breh
December	diciembre	dee-see-**em**-breh

USEFUL WORDS AND PHRASES

Do you speak English?	¿Habla usted inglés?	ah-**blah** oos-**ted** in-**glehs**
I don't speak Spanish.	No hablo español	no **ah**-bloh es-pahn-**yol**
I don't understand.	No entiendo	no en-tee-**en**-doh
I understand.	Entiendo	en-tee-**en**-doh
I don't know.	No sé	no **seh**
I'm American.	Soy americano (americana)	soy ah-meh-ree-**kah**-no (ah-meh-ree-**kah**-nah)
What's your name?	¿Cómo se llama ?	koh-mo seh **yah**-mah
My name is . . .	Me llamo . . .	may **yah**-moh
What time is it?	¿Qué hora es?	keh **o**-rah es
How?	¿Cómo?	**koh**-mo
When?	¿Cuándo?	**kwahn**-doh
Yesterday	Ayer	ah-**yehr**
Today	hoy	oy
Tomorrow	mañana	mahn-**yah**-nah

English	Spanish	Pronunciation
Tonight	Esta noche	es-tah no-cheh
What?	¿Qué?	keh
What is it?	¿Qué es esto?	keh es es-toh
Why?	¿Por qué?	pore keh
Who?	¿Quién?	kee-yen
Where is ...	¿Dónde está ...	dohn-deh es-tah
... the train station?	la estación del tren?	la es-tah-see-on del trehn
... the subway station?	estación de metro	la es-ta-see-on del meh-tro
... the bus stop?	la parada del autobus?	la pah-rah-dah del ow-toh-boos
... the terminal? (airport)	el aeropuerto	el air-oh-pwar-toh
... the post office?	la oficina de correos?	la oh-fee-see- nah deh koh-rreh-os
... the bank?	el banco?	el bahn-koh
... the hotel?	el hotel?	el oh-tel
... the museum?	el museo?	el moo-seh-oh
... the hospital?	el hospital?	el ohss-pee-tal
... the elevator?	el ascensor?	el ah-sen-sohr
Where are the restrooms?	el baño?	el bahn-yoh
Here/there	Aquí/allí	ah-key/ah-yee
Open/closed	Abierto/cerrado	ah-bee-er-toh/ ser-ah-doh
Left/right	Izquierda/derecha	iss-key-eh-dah/ dare-eh-chah
Is it near?	¿Está cerca?	es-tah sehr-kah
Is it far?	¿Está lejos?	es-tah leh-hoss
I'd like ...	Quisiera ...	kee-see-ehr-ah
... a room	un cuarto/una habitación	oon kwahr-toh/oo-nah ah-bee-tah-see-on
... the key	la llave	lah yah-veh
... a newspaper	un periódico	oon pehr-ee-oh-dee-koh
... a stamp	un sello de correo	oon seh-yo deh korr-eh-oh
I'd like to buy ...	Quisiera comprar ...	kee-see-ehr-ah kohm-prahr
... soap	jabón	hah-bohn
... suntan lotion	crema solar	kreh-mah soh-lar
... envelopes	sobres	so-brehs
... writing paper	papel	pah-pel
... a postcard	una tarjeta postal	oon-ah tar-het-ah post-ahl
... a ticket	un billete (travel)	oon bee-yee-teh
	una entrada (concert etc.)	oona en-trah-dah
How much is it?	¿Cuánto cuesta?	kwahn-toh kwes-tah
It's expensive/ cheap	Es caro/barato	es kah-roh/ bah-rah-toh
A little/a lot	Un poquito/mucho	oon poh-kee-toh/ moo-choh
More/less	Más/menos	mahss/men-ohss
Enough/too (much)	Suficiente/	soo-fee-see-en-teh/

English	Spanish	Pronunciation
I am ill/sick	Estoy enfermo(a)	es-toy en-fehr-moh(mah)
Call a doctor	Llame a un medico	ya-meh ah oon med-ee-koh
Help!	Socorro	soh-koh-roh
Stop!	Pare	pah-reh
DINING OUT		
I'd like to reserve a table ...	Quisiera reservar una mesa ...	kee-syeh-rah rreh-sehr-bahr oo-nah meh-sah ...
... for two people.	para dos personas.	pah-rah dohs pehr-soh-nahs
... for this evening.	para esta noche.	pah-rah ehs-tah noh-cheh
... for 8 PM.	para las ocho de la noche.	pah-rah lahs oh-choh deh lah noh-cheh
A bottle of ...	Una botella de ...	oo-nah bo-teh-yah deh
A cup of ...	Una taza de ...	oo-nah tah-sah deh
A glass of ...	Un vaso (water, soda, etc.) de...	oon vah-so deh
	Una copa (wine, spirits, etc.) de...	oona coh-pah deh
Bill/check	La cuenta	lah kwen-tah
Bread	El pan	el pahn
Breakfast	El desayuno	el deh-sah-yoon-oh
Butter	La mantequilla	lah man-teh-kee-yah
Coffee	Café	kah-feh
Dinner	La cena	lah seh-nah
Fork	El tenedor	el ten-eh-dor
I don't eat meat	No como carne	noh koh-moh kahr-neh
I cannot eat ...	No puedo comer ...	noh pweh-doh koh-mehr
I'd like to order ...	Quiero pedir ...	kee-yehr-oh peh-deer
I'd like ...	Me gustaría ...	Meh goo-stah-ee-ah
I'm hungry/thirsty	Tengo hambre/sed	Tehn-goh hahm-breh/seth
Is service/the tip included?	¿Está incluida la propina?	es-tah in-cloo-ee-dah lah pro-pee-nah
Knife	El cuchillo	el koo-chee-yo
Lunch	La comida	lah koh-mee-dah
Menu	La carta, el menú	lah cart-ah, el meh-noo
Napkin	La servilleta	lah sehr-vee-yet-ah
Pepper	La pimienta	lah pee-mee-en-tah
Plate	plato	
Please give me ...	Por favor déme ...	pore fah-vor deh-meh
Salt	La sal	lah sahl
Spoon	Una cuchara	oo-nah koo-chah-rah
Sugar	El ázucar	el ah-su-kar

Contacts

Air

AIRPORT Granada Airport (GRX). ⊕ *granadaairport. com.* **Madrid–Barajas (MAD).** ☎ *902/404704* ⊕ *www.aeropuertoma- drid-barajas.com.* **Seville Airport (SVQ).** ⊕ *www. sevilla-airport.com/en.*

AIRLINES AENA. ☎ *902/404704* ⊕ *www. aena.es.* **Air Europa.** ☎ *911/401501* ⊕ *www. aireuropa.com.* **Iberia.** ☎ *901/111–500* ⊕ *www. iberia.com.* **Iberia Express.** ☎ *901/200424* ⊕ *www.ibe- riaexpress.com.* **Vueling.** ☎ *902/808005* ⊕ *www. vueling.com.* **Transportation Security Administration.** ⊕ *www.tsa.gov.*

Bike

CONTACTS BiciMAD. ⊕ *www.bicimad.com.*

Bus

CONTACTS ALSA. ☎ *902/422242* ⊕ *www. alsa.es.* **Eurolines Spain.** ⊕ *www.eurolines.es.*

Public Transportation

SUBWAY INFORMATION Metro Madrid. ☎ *90/244– 4403* ⊕ *www.metroma- drid.es.*

Taxi

TAXI SERVICES Radio Taxi Gremial. ☎ *91/447–3232, 91/447–5180* ⊕ *www. radiotaxigremial.com.* **Radioteléfono Taxi.** ☎ *91/547–8200* ⊕ *www. radiotelefono-taxi.com.* **Tele-Taxi.** ☎ *91/371–2131* ⊕ *www.tele-taxi.es.*

Train

CONTACTS Eurail. ⊕ *www. eurail.com.* **Rail Europe.** ⊕ *www.raileurope.com.* **RENFE.** ☎ *912/320320 for tickets and info* ⊕ *www. renfe.es.*

 Activities

BASKETBALL WiZink Center. ✉ *Avda Felipe II, Retiro* ⊕ *www.wizink- center.es* Ⓜ *Goya.*

PARKS AND PLAY- GROUNDS Casa de Campo. ✉ *Casa de Campo* Ⓜ *Casa de Campo.* **Madrid Río.** ✉ *Palacio.* **Parque del Buen Retiro. Parque del Oeste.** ✉ *Moncloa* Ⓜ *Moncloa.*

SKIING La Pinilla. ⊕ *www. lapinilla.es.* **Puerto de Navacerrada.** ⊕ *www. puertonavacerrada.com.* **Valdesquí.** ⊕ *www.valdes- qui.es.*

SOCCER Estadio Santiago Bernabeú. ✉ *Avda de Con- cha Espina 1, Chamartín* ⊕ *www.realmadrid.com/ en* Ⓜ *Santiago Bernabeú.* **Estadio Wanda Metro- politano.** ✉ *Avda Luis Aragonés 4* ⊕ *www. atleticodemadrid.com* Ⓜ *Estadio Metropolitano.*

TENNIS Caja Mágica. ✉ *Camino de Perales 23* ⊕ *www.madrid-open.com* Ⓜ *San Fermín.*

Tours

ART Atlas Travel Center/ Escorted Spain Tours. ☎ *888/942–3301* ⊕ *www. escortedspaintours.com.* **Heritage Tours.** ☎ *800/378– 4555, 212/206–8400* ⊕ *www.heritagetours. com.* **Olé Spain Tours.** ☎ *915/515294* ⊕ *www. olespaintours.com.*

BIKE BravoBike. ✉ *Calle Juan Álvarez Mendizábal 19, Calle Juan Álvarez Mendizábal 19, Moncloa* ☎ *91/758–2945, 60/744– 8440 for WhatsApp* ⊕ *www.bravobike.com.*

BIRD-WATCHING Discovering Doñana. ☎ *620/964369* ⊕ *www. discoveringdonana.com.*

BUS Madrid City Tours. ☎ *90/202–4758* ⊕ *www. madrid.city-tour.com.*

FOOD AND WINE Artisans of Leisure. ☎ *800/214– 8144, 212/243–3239* ⊕ *www.artisansoflei- sure.com.* **Cellar Tours.** ☎ *911/436553 in Spain, 310/496–8061 in U.S.* ⊕ *www.cellartours.com.*

HIKING Spain Adventures. ☎ *772/564–0330* ⊕ *www. spainadventures.com.*

LEARNING Go Abroad. ☎ *720/570–1702* ⊕ *www. goabroad.com.*

PERSONALIZED TOURS Madrid and Beyond. ☎ *91/758–0063 in Spain, 917/470–9460 in U.S.* ⊕ *www.madridandbe- yond.com.* **Toma Tours.** ☎ *650/733116* ⊕ *tomaand- coe.com.*

WALKING TOURS Asoci- ación Nacional de Guías de Turismo (APIT). ✉ *Calle Jacometrezo 4, 9° 13, Sol* ☎ *91/542–1214* ⊕ *www. apit.es.* **Carpetania Madrid.** ✉ *Calle Jesús del Valle 11, Malasaña* ☎ *91/531–1418* ⊕ *www.carpetaniama- drid.com.* **Devour Madrid.** ✉ *Calle de la Torrecilla del Leal 10, Cortes* ☎ *94/458– 1022* ⊕ *www.madridfood- tour.com.*

⚠ Emergencies

FOREIGN EMBASSIES AND CONSULATES U.S. Embassy. ✉ *Calle Serrano 75, Madrid* ☎ *91/587– 2200 for U.S.-citizen emer- gencies* ⊕ *es.usembassy. gov.*

🎭 Performing Arts

CONTACTS Auditorio Nacional de Música. ✉ *Calle del Príncipe de Vergara 146, Salamanca* ☎ *91/337–0140* ⊕ *www. auditorionacional.mcu.es* Ⓜ *Cruz del Rayo.* **Círculo de Bellas Artes.** ✉ *Calle del Marqués de Casa Riera 2, Sol* ☎ *90/242–2442* ⊕ *www.circulobellasartes. com* Ⓜ *Banco de España.* **Las Carboneras.** ✉ *Pl. del Conde de Miranda 1, La Latina* ☎ *91/542–8677* ⊕ *www.tablaolascarbon- eras.com* Ⓜ *La Latina, Ópera.* **Teatro Real.** ✉ *Pl. de Isabel II, Palacio* ☎ *91/516–0660* ⊕ *www. teatro-real.com* Ⓜ *Ópera.*

Great Itineraries

5 Days: Madrid Plus Granada or Seville and Side Trips

DAYS 1 AND 2: MADRID

Start the day with a visit to either the Prado, the Museo Thyssen-Bornemisza, or the Centro de Arte Reina Sofía. Then head to the elegant Plaza Mayor—a perfect jumping-off point for a tour of the Spanish capital. To the west, see the Plaza de la Villa, Palacio Real (the Royal Palace), Teatro Real (Royal Theater), and the royal convents; to the south, wander around the maze of streets of La Latina and El Rastro and try some local tapas.

On Day 2, visit the sprawling Barrio de las Letras, centered on the Plaza de Santa Ana. This was the favorite neighborhood of writers during the Spanish golden literary age in the 17th century (Cervantes lies buried under a convent nearby), and it's still crammed with theaters, cafés, and good tapas bars. For here, you can pop to the Paseo del Prado on the east and visit any of the art museums in the area. After lunch, take an afternoon stroll in the Parque del Buen Retiro or wander in Chueca or Malasaña, the two funky hipster neighborhoods favored by young locals. From here, walk to the Parque del Oeste and the Templo de Debod to marvel at the city's sunset.

GRANADA

Getting Here: Four daily flights connect Granada with Madrid and it's easy to get to the city from the airport by taxi, airport bus, or rental car. There are a couple of daily high-speed AVE trains from Madrid to Granada daily.

Day 3: After arriving in Granada, visit the Catholic Monarchs' tomb at the Capilla Real before exploring more Moorish monuments such as the Palacio Madraza (seminary) or El Bañuelo (bathhouse). Stroll around the Moorish Albayzín neighborhood for extraordinary views of Granada's highlight, the Alhambra, and the Sierra Nevada backdrop, extra special at sunset. Dine on the city's excellent tapas or take in a flamenco show.

Day 4: Granada's star of the show is, of course, La Alhambra, the most visited attraction in Spain. Its palace, fortress, patios, gardens, and museums alone merit the trip to Granada and need at least half a day to do them justice. Try to get an early-morning ticket to experience this wonder with less crowds. Note: reserve your ticket as far in advance as possible and show up at your ticketed time (preferably, before) or you will not be allowed entry. Lunch early before you pick up your hire car for a side trip excursion.

EVENING 4, DAY 5: SIDE TRIP OPTIONS

Option 1: Drive north to Priego de Córdoba (1¼ hours) to see one of the region's prettiest towns with a plethora of baroque churches, white facades decked with geraniums and stunning views. From here, drive to Córdoba and your hotel. Spend the next day exploring the Mezquita (mosque) and the Jewish Quarter and dine on the city's famous oxtail stew or *flamenquín* (pork fritter) washed down with local Montilla wine.

Option 2: Drive northeast to Baeza (1½ hours) and then to Úbeda, two jewels in Spain's Renaissance crown. Both are home to stunning architecture, seen in intricate facades on the many monuments; allow more time for Úbeda where you can visit the historic potter's quarter.

Option 3: Head south for the Sierra Nevada (1 hour drive) for a paradise of skiing in winter and trekking and climbing in summer. Or explore the Alpujarras, a unique mountain region dotted with picturesque Moorish villages set in stunning landscapes where time appears to have stopped still.

SEVILLE

Getting Here: Andalusia's second-largest airport, after Málaga, is in Seville and there are flights from Madrid every four hours or so. From Madrid, the best approach to Andalusia is via the high-speed AVE. In just 2½ hours, the spectacular ride winds through olive groves and rolling fields of Castile to Córdoba and on to Seville. From Seville's Santa Justa train station, get a cab (or rental car) to your hotel.

Day 3: Must-sees in the Andalusian capital include the cathedral with its La Giralda tower and the Reales Alcazares Moorish palace. Between visits, explore the nearby Barrio de Santa Cruz neighborhood with its typical architecture, orange blossom trees, and tiny squares. Dine early on delicious tapas at one of the traditional tavernas before an evening stroll along the banks of the Guadalquivir River.

Day 4: Start Day 4 with a visit to one of the city's great private houses—Palacio de las Dueñas, Casa de Pilatos, or Palacio de la Condesa de Lebrija—to see how the other half lived in the city. After lunch on tapas, admire the Plaza de Toros Real Maestranza (bullring) and stroll around the Parque de María Luisa before an aperitif in the bar at the Hotel Alfonso XIII. Then take in a flamenco show.

DAY 5: DAY TRIP OPTIONS

Seville is perfectly placed for several excellent side trips: taste the world-famous sherries of Jerez de la Frontera and admire the dancing horses before dining on Spain's freshest seafood at Puerto de Santa María or Sanlúcar de Barrameda; visit Spain's largest and one of its greatest Roman sites at Itálica, just outside Seville; drive to Ronda, one of Andalusia's most beautiful white towns, perched on a river gorge and the cradle of bullfighting; head for Europe's oldest city, the maritime Cádiz and soak up the history in its narrow streets and along the fortress walls; or go to Córdoba where the city's breathtaking Mezquita (mosque) and medieval Jewish Quarter await you. Don't miss the vibrant flower-packed patios while you're there.

Travel Smart GREAT ITINERARIES

Great Itineraries

10 Days: Madrid to the Alhambra

This trip takes in the best of vibrant Madrid and its world-class art museums and showcases some of Castile's historic gems before whisking you to the Moorish south where Córdoba's majestic mosque, Seville's fragrant orange blossoms, and Granada's "heaven on earth" await.

DAYS 1–3: MADRID

Start the day with a visit to either the **Prado,** the **Museo Thyssen-Bornemisza,** or the **Centro de Arte Reina Sofía.** Then head to the elegant **Plaza Mayor**—a perfect jumping-off point for a tour of the Spanish capital. To the west, see the **Plaza de la Villa, Palacio Real** (the Royal Palace), **Teatro Real** (Royal Theater), and the royal convents; to the south, wander around the maze of streets of **La Latina** and **El Rastro** and try some local tapas.

On Day 2, visit the sprawling **Barrio de las Letras,** centered on the Plaza de Santa Ana. This was the favorite neighborhood of writers during the Spanish golden literary age in the 17th century (Cervantes lies buried under a convent nearby), and it's still crammed with theaters, cafés, and good tapas bars. It borders the Paseo del Prado on the east, allowing you to comfortably walk to any of the art museums in the area. If the weather is pleasant, take an afternoon stroll in the **Parque del Buen Retiro.**

For your third day in the capital, wander in **Chueca** and **Malasaña,** the two funky hipster neighborhoods most favored by young Madrileños. Fuencarral, a landmark pedestrianized street that serves as the border between the two, is one of the city's trendiest shopping enclaves. From there you can walk to the **Parque del Oeste** and the **Templo de Debod**—the best spot from which to see the city's sunset. Among the lesser-known museums, consider visiting the captivating **Museo Sorolla,** Goya's frescoes and tomb at the **Ermita de San Antonio de la Florida,** or the **Real Academia de Bellas Artes de San Fernando** for classic painting. People-watch at any of the terrace bars in either Plaza de Chueca or Plaza 2 de Mayo in Malasaña.

Logistics: If you're traveling light, the subway (Metro Línea 8) or the bus (No. 203 during the day and N27 at night) will take you from the airport to the city for €5. The train costs €2.60 and a taxi is a fixed price of €30. Once in the center consider walking or taking the subway rather than cabbing it in gridlock traffic.

DAYS 4 AND 5: CASTILIAN CITIES

There are several excellent options for half- or full-day side trips from Madrid to occupy Days 4 and 5. **Toledo** and **Segovia** are two of the oldest Castilian cities— both have delightful old quarters dating back to the Romans. There's also **El Escorial,** which houses the massive monastery built by Felipe II. Two other nearby towns also worth visiting are **Aranjuez** and **Alcalá de Henares.**

Logistics: Toledo and Segovia are stops on the high-speed train line (AVE), so you can get to either of them in a half hour from Madrid. To reach the old quarters of both cities, take a bus or cab from the train station or take the bus from Madrid. Buses and trains both go to El Escorial. Reach Aranjuez and Alcalá de Henares via the intercity train system.

PORTUGAL

Segovia
El Escorial
CASTILIAN
CITIES
Cáceres
Trujillo Guadalupe
EXTREMADURA

Toledo

Alcalá de Henares
Madrid
Aranjuez

Córdoba
Seville
ANDALUSIA
Granada

Sanlúcar de Barrameda
Jerez de la Frontera

Gulf of Cadiz

Mediterranean Sea

DAY 6: CORDOBA OR EXTREMADURA

Córdoba, the capital of both Roman and Moorish Spain, was the center of Western art and culture between the 8th and 11th centuries. The city's breathtaking **Mezquita** (mosque), which is now a cathedral, and the medieval **Jewish Quarter** bear witness to the city's brilliant past. From Madrid you could also rent a car and visit the lesser-known cities in the north of **Extremadura,** such as **Guadalupe** and **Trujillo,** and overnight in **Cáceres,** a UNESCO World Heritage Site, then return to Madrid the next day.

Logistics: The AVE will take you to Córdoba from Madrid in less than two hours. One alternative is to stay in Toledo, also on the route heading south, and then head to Córdoba the next day, although you need to return to Madrid by train first. Once in Córdoba, take a taxi for a visit out to the summer palace at Medina Azahara.

DAYS 7 AND 8: SEVILLE

Seville's **cathedral,** with its tower La Giralda, **Plaza de Toros Real Maestranza,** and **Barrio de Santa Cruz** are visual feasts. Forty minutes south by train, you can sip the world-famous sherries of **Jerez de la Frontera,** then munch jumbo shrimp on the beach at **Sanlúcar de Barrameda.**

Logistics: From Seville's AVE station, take a taxi to your hotel. After that, walking and hailing the occasional taxi are the best ways to explore the city. A rental car is the best option to reach towns beyond Seville, except for Jerez de la Frontera, where the train station is an architectural gem in its own right.

DAYS 9 AND 10: GRANADA

The hilltop **Alhambra** palace, Spain's most visited attraction, was conceived by the Moorish caliphs as heaven on earth. Try any of the city's famous tapas bars and tea shops, and make sure to roam the magical, steep streets of the **Albayzín,** the ancient Moorish quarter.

Logistics: The Seville–Granada leg of this trip is best accomplished by renting a car; Antequera makes a good quick stop on the way. However, the Seville–Granada trains (4 daily, about 3½ hours, €30) are one alternative. Another idea is to head first from Madrid to Granada, and then from Granada to Seville via Córdoba.

Great Itineraries

Madrid Walking Tour

The Spanish have a term for their favorite pastime, *paseo,* which means a leisurely walk, and in Madrid it is a way of life. As clean, modern, and affordable as the Madrid metro is, walking really is the best way to get to know this vibrant city. Pack your practical shoes and make sure your paseo allows for impromptu stops for people-watching with cafés con leches and baskets of churros.

PLAZAS, PALACES, AND GARDENS

Start your tour at the Plaza Mayor, built in 1619 and one of the largest squares in Europe. Its almost 240 balconies have witnessed eclectic events from public executions, bullfights, and royal weddings, to today's famous Christmas market. Don't miss the Mercado de San Miguel for a foodie feast.

From here, walk west to Plaza de la Villa, one of the oldest parts of the city whose jewel is the Casa de la Villa, built in the classic Madrid architectural style. Continue west to the Catedral de la Almudena, one of Europe's most modern cathedrals although built in Madrid style and with a Gothic interior. Just next door is the imposing Palacio Real, an early-18th-century palace with 2,800 rooms and modeled on French royal residences. Catch your breath from all the opulence in the Plaza de Oriente square with pleasant fountains and statues of Spanish monarchs to the east or the Jardines de Sabatini, formal gardens to the north.

MADRID'S CHAMPS-ÉLYSÉES, SHOPPING, AND A MONASTERY

Head northwest to the Gran Vía, Madrid's answer to the Parisian Champs-Élysées and flanked by designer shops and theaters housed in fine buildings in Neo-classical and Art Deco styles. At Plaza de Callao, art lovers should make a side trip to the Monasterio de las Descalzas Reales, a monastery whose bare facade hides a treasure trove of European artwork by Titian, Zurbarán, Brueghel the Elder, and Rubens among others.

VIEWS, THE BIG THREE MUSEUMS, AND THE PARK

Continue on to Plaza del Sol, Madrid's bustling hub and km 0 for Spain's six national highways. Enjoy the street performers and don't miss the iconic clock tower whose 12 chimes bring in the Spanish New Year. From here, take the elegant Calle de Alcalá, flanked on both sides by fine architecture. At the Círculo de Bellas Artes, head for the seventh floor where you'll find some of the best views in Madrid.

Back on ground level, make your way to the Paseo del Prado, also known as the Paseo del Arte as three of Europe's top art museums are nearby. Take your pick from the **Museo Thyssen-Bornemisza,** Museo del Prado or the Centro de Arte Reina Sofía (your walk will be derailed if you try to see all three in the one afternoon). Enjoy some time-out from all the art and city bustle in the Parque del Buen Retiro with more than 300 acres of gardens and parkland plus boating lake. Horticultural fans may want to pop into the Jardín Botánico, home to an impressive range of botanical species.

Chapter 3

SOL

WITH PLAZA MAYOR

Updated by
Benjamin Kemper

👁 **Sights**
★★★★★

🍴 **Restaurants**
★★☆☆☆

🏨 **Hotels**
★★★★★

🛍 **Shopping**
★★★★★

🍸 **Nightlife**
★★★★★

NEIGHBORHOOD SNAPSHOT

TOP EXPERIENCES

- **Chocolatería San Ginés:** Sample Spain's most legendary churros.

- **La vida nocturna:** Kill the night Madrid-style at a bumping *discoteca*.

- **Rooftop-hopping:** Take in panoramic views from a ritzy roof decks.

- **Casa de Diego:** Snap up a hand-painted fan or umbrella.

- **Puerta del Sol:** Get caught up in the mayhem of Madrid's busiest square.

GETTING HERE

All roads—and bike lanes and train tracks—lead to Sol, Spain's kilómetro cero ("kilometer zero"), the point from which the distances of all of Spain's official roads are measured. The Sol metro station (Líneas 1, 2, 3) is one of the busiest in the country as it is also a main hub for the commuter rail (*cercanías*). BiciMAD bike-share has docks on most blocks in this area. Sol lies within a low-emission zone and therefore cannot be accessed by most rental cars.

PLANNING YOUR TIME

Puerta del Sol and its surrounding streets and plazas are Madrid's cultural nerve center. Like Times Square in New York or Las Ramblas in Barcelona, Sol is eternally thronged with crowds both local and foreign—this is a place to watch your wallet, especially after dark. If it's your first time in Madrid, begin your sightseeing here. After checking out the curiosities of the semicircular "square" at Puerta del Sol (the "Kilómetro Cero" plaque; the equestrian statue of Carlos III; the sculpted bear in the *madroño* tree, Madrid's emblem), make your way to Plaza Mayor, the city's historical main square; then, explore the cobblestone lanes east of the plaza in the direction of Plaza de Canalejas to wind up at Círculo de Bellas Artes, whose roof deck affords some of the city's most stunning views.

QUICK BITES

- **Bar La Campana.** Scarfing down a hot calamari-filled baguette (*bocadillo de calamares*) while strolling through the Plaza Mayor is a Madrid tradition, and this bar's rendition is a cut above the rest. ⊠ *Calle de Botoneras 6, Sol* Ⓜ *Sol*

- **Casa Labra.** The traditional tapa at this old-fashioned bar is battered bacalao (salt cod) fritters. ⊠ *Calle de Tetuán 12, Sol* ⊕ *www.casalabra.es* Ⓜ *Sol*

- **Mesón del Champiñón.** This bar opened in 1964 and has been feeding garlicky griddled mushrooms to the hungry masses ever since. ⊠ *Cava de San Miguel 17, Sol* Ⓜ *Sol*

This neighborhood, built in the 16th century around the Puerta del Sol, used to mark the city's geographic center, which today sits a tad to its east. Sol encompasses, among other sites, the monumental Plaza Mayor and popular pedestrian shopping area around Callao.

There's never a dull moment in Puerta del Sol, the bustling semicircular plaza where friends gather, buskers perform, and bar crawls begin. The Puerta ("gate") designation is a holdover from when this spot bore entry into the medieval city walls; Sol ("sun"), on the other hand, is a reference to a sun carving that adorned the gate. Let your gaze wander to the clocktower atop the Casa de Correos, the oldest building on the square. It ushers Madrid into the New Year each December as onlookers partake in the Spanish tradition of eating 12 grapes in the last 12 seconds of the year.

Sights

★ Plaza Mayor

PLAZA | A symbol of imperial Spain's might and grandeur, this public square is often surprisingly quiet, perhaps since most locals wrote it off long ago as too touristy. The plaza was finished in 1619 under Felipe III, whose equestrian statue stands in the center, and is one of the largest in Europe, clocking in at 360 feet by 300 feet. It's seen it all: *autos-da-fé* ("trials of faith," or public burnings of heretics); the canonization of saints; criminal executions; royal marriages, such as that of Princess María and the king of Hungary in 1629; bullfights (until

1847); and masked balls. Special events still take place here.

This space was once occupied by a city market, and many of the surrounding streets retain the charming names of the trades and foods once headquartered there. Nearby are Calle de Cuchilleros (Cutlers' Street), Calle de Lechuga (Lettuce Street), Calle de Fresa (Strawberry Street), and Calle de Botoneros (Button Makers' Street). The plaza's oldest building is the one with the brightly painted murals and gray spires, called Casa de la Panadería (Bakery House) in honor of the bread shop over which it was built; it is now the tourist office. Opposite is the Casa de la Carnicería (Butcher Shop), now a boutique hotel.

The plaza is closed to motorized traffic, making it a pleasant place for sidewalk sitting and coffee-sipping as alfresco artists and street musicians put on impromptu shows. Sunday morning brings a stamp and coin market. Around Christmas the plaza fills with stalls selling trees, ornaments, and Nativity scenes. ⌧ *Sol* Ⓜ *Sol.*

Puerta del Sol

PLAZA | Crowded with locals, tourists, hawkers, and street performers, the Puerta del Sol is the nerve center of Madrid. It is scheduled for a massive renovation beginning in June 2021, so

beware of possible closures. A brass plaque in the sidewalk on the south side of the plaza marks Kilometer Zero, the point from which all distances in Spain are measured. The restored 1756 French-Neoclassical building near the marker now houses the offices of the regional government, but during Franco's reign, it was the headquarters of his secret police and is still known colloquially as the Casa de los Gritos (House of Screams). Across the square are a bronze statue of Madrid's official symbol, a bear with a *madroño* (strawberry tree), and a statue of King and Mayor Carlos III on horseback. Puerta del Sol has been the nucleus of countless protests and political movements through the centuries. It was here, in 2011, that the 15-M movement started as sleep-in against government austerity measures and blossomed into an organized anticorporate revolution. The grassroots political party Podemos was created as a result. Pablo Iglesias, leader of Podemos and Spain's current vice president, was one of the movement's key figures. The 15-M demonstrations would go on to inspire Occupy Wall Street and other future prodemocracy and anticapitalist protests around the world. ⊠ *Sol* Ⓜ *Sol.*

Real Academia de Bellas Artes de San Fernando (*St. Ferdinand Royal Academy of Fine Arts*)

MUSEUM | Designed by José Benito de Churriguera in the waning baroque years of the early 18th century, this museum showcases 500 years of Spanish painting, from José Ribera and Bartolomé Esteban Murillo to Joaquín Sorolla and Ignacio Zuloaga. The tapestries along the stairways are stunning. The gallery displays paintings up to the 18th century, including some by Goya. Worthwhile guided tours are available on Tuesday, Thursday, and Friday at 11, except during August. The same building houses the **Instituto de Calcografía** (Prints Institute), which sells limited-edition prints from original plates engraved by Spanish artists. Check the website for classical concerts and literary events in the small upstairs hall. ⊠ *Calle de Alcalá 13, Sol* ☎ *91/524–0864* ⊕ *www.realacademia-bellasartessanfernando.com* ⊠ *€8 (free Wed.)* ⊙ *Closed Mon.* Ⓜ *Sol.*

🍴 Restaurants

La Casa del Abuelo

$$ | **TAPAS** | This rustic tapas hall is the oldest of three branches in a beloved local chain. It has barely changed since it was founded at the beginning of the 20th century. **Known for:** killer gambas al ajillo; bold proprietary Toro wines; traditional atmosphere. 💲 *Average main: €16* ⊠ *Calle de la Victoria 12, Sol* ☎ *91/521–2319* ⊕ *www.lacasadelabuelo.es* Ⓜ *Sol.*

La Hojaldrería

$$ | **CAFÉ** | A veritable temple of all things flaky and buttery (*hojaldre* is Spanish for "puff pastry"), this concept café by Javier Bonet (the brains behind the buzzy Sala de Despiece and Muta) is a sophisticated spot to enjoy a pastry and well-made cappuccino at breakfast or innovative bistro fare at lunch and dinner. **Known for:** exquisite viennoiserie; throwback rococo decor; gourmet sandwiches. 💲 *Average main: €16* ⊠ *Calle Virgen de los Peligros 8, Sol* ☎ *91/059–5193* ⊕ *www.hojaldreria. com* ⊙ *No dinner Sun.* Ⓜ *Sevilla.*

La Pulpería de Victoria

$$ | **SPANISH** | **FAMILY** | A modern, urban interpretation of a traditional Galician *pulpería* (octopus restaurant), this casual restaurant specializes in *polbo á feira*, boiled octopus cut into coins, drizzled with olive oil, and dusted with smoked paprika. Pair with an icy glass of Albariño and a heap of blistered *Padrón* peppers. **Known for:** Galician-style octopus; ocean-fresh shellfish; great variety of Galician wines. 💲 *Average main: €16* ⊠ *Calle de La Victoria 2, Sol* ☎ *91/080–4929* Ⓜ *Sol.*

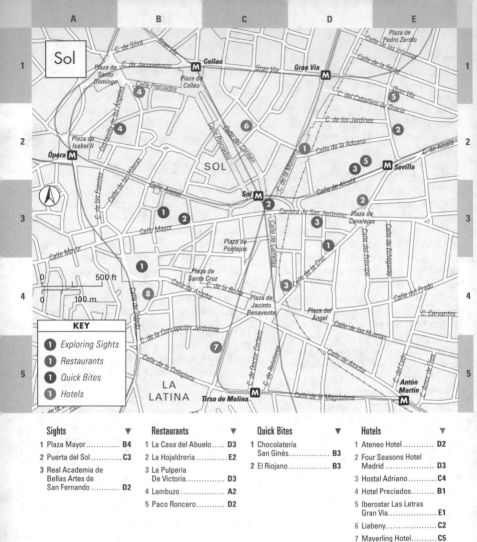

Sights ▼

1 Plaza Mayor............ **B4**
2 Puerta del Sol.......... **C3**
3 Real Academia de
  Bellas Artes de
  San Fernando.......... **D2**

Restaurants ▼

1 La Casa del Abuelo..... **D3**
2 La Hojaldrería........... **E2**
3 La Pulpería
  De Victoria............... **D3**
4 Lambuzo................. **A2**
5 Paco Roncero........... **D2**

Quick Bites ▼

1 Chocolatería
  San Ginés............... **B3**
2 El Riojano............... **B3**

Hotels ▼

1 Ateneo Hotel **D2**
2 Four Seasons Hotel
  Madrid **D3**
3 Hostal Adriano........... **C4**
4 Hotel Preciados......... **B1**
5 Iberostar Las Letras
  Gran Vía.................. **E1**
6 Liabeny.................. **C2**
7 Mayerling Hotel.......... **C5**
8 Pestana
  Plaza Mayor............. **B4**

Lambuzo

$$ | **SPANISH** | **FAMILY** | This laid-back Andalusian bar room, one of two locations (the other is in Retiro neighborhood), embodies the soul and joyful spirit of that sunny region. Let cheerful waiters guide you through the extensive menu, which includes fried seafood, unconventional *croquetas* (flecked with garlicky shrimp, for instance), and heftier dishes like cuttlefish meatballs and seared Barbate tuna loin. **Known for:** carefree Andalusian vibe; an ocean's-worth of seafood dishes; free marinated carrots with every drink. [$] *Average main: €16* ✉ *Calle de las Conchas 9, Sol* ☎ *91/143–4862* 🌐 *www.barlambuzo.com* 🕓 *Closed Mon. No dinner Sun.* [M] *Ópera.*

★ Paco Roncero

$$$$ | **ECLECTIC** | This award-winning restaurant, formerly called La Terraza del Casino, occupies an aerie above one of Madrid's oldest, most exclusive gentlemen's clubs. Local designer Jaime Hayón recently revamped the dining room and rooftop terrace, adding playful, almost circuslike touches such as bright blue pushcarts, checkered floors, and yellow velvet chairs. **Known for:** Instagrammable interiors; two Michelin stars; foams, jellies, and sensational flourishes. [$] *Average main: €40* ✉ *Calle Alcalá 15, Sol* ☎ *91/532–1275* 🌐 *www.pacoroncerorestaurante.com* 🕓 *Closed Sun. and Mon.* 👔 *Jacket required* [M] *Sol.*

☕ Coffee and Quick Bites

Chocolatería San Ginés

$ | **CAFÉ** | **FAMILY** | San Ginés is to Madrid what Café du Monde is to New Orleans. A national sensation, for generations this 19th-century café has been frying spirals of piping-hot churros and *porras* (a churro's larger cousin—try them) day and night. **Known for:** churros with chocolate; central location. [$] *Average main:* ✉ *Pasadizo de San Ginés, Sol* ✥ *Enter by Arenal 11* ☎ *91/365–6546* 🌐 *www.chocolateriasangines.com* [M] *Sol.*

🍴 Gourmet Experience Callao

On the rooftop of El Corte Inglés, Spain's largest department store, there's a gourmet food court with some of the best views in the city. Grab a couple of tapas and a glass of wine here after perusing the shops around Callao. The space features outposts of well-known Spanish restaurants like La Máquina (seafood) and Asador Imanol (pinchos) as well as international options (hamburgers, Mexican, and Chinese, for example). Take the second entrance to El Corte Inglés as you're walking down Callao on Calle Carmen and across from Fnac.

El Riojano

$ | **CAFÉ** | The opulent Confitería El Riojano was founded in 1855 by Dámaso Maza, the personal pastry chef (*personal pastry chef!*) of Queen Maria Christina of Austria. Maza was born in La Rioja, hence the name of the shop. **Known for:** ladyfingers dipped in melted chocolate; Art Deco interiors; lots of history and lore. [$] *Average main: €6* ✉ *Calle Mayor 10, Sol* ☎ *91/366–4482* 🌐 *www.confiteriaelriojano.com* [M] *Sol.*

🛏 Hotels

Ateneo Hotel

$$ | **HOTEL** | This clean and economical property is set in an 18th-century building that was once home to the Ateneo, a club founded in 1835 to promote freedom of thought. **Pros:** sizable rooms; triples and quadruples available; some rooms have skylights and balconies. **Cons:** safe yet slightly sketchy street; noisy area; dated decor. [$] *Rooms from: €169* ✉ *Calle de la Montera 22, Sol* ☎ *91/521–2012* 🌐 *www.hotel-ateneo.*

Enjoy tapas and a clara (half beer, half lemonade) at Mercado de San Miguel, one of the city's most popular covered food markets in the city center.

com ⤷ 44 rooms ⦿| Free breakfast Ⓜ Gran Vía, Sol.

Four Seasons Hotel Madrid

$$$$ | HOTEL | Madrid's most hotly antic-ipated hotel opening in recent memory is the Four Seasons Hotel Madrid, which occupies a stunning corner building on Plaza de Canalejas. **Pros:** above-and-beyond service touches; comfortable modern luxury; celebrity chef restaurant. **Cons:** no sense of place; conventional interiors; situated above chain restau-rants and boutiques. $ *Rooms from: €484* ✉ *Calle de Sevilla 3, Sol* ☎ *91/088–3333* ⊕ *www.fourseasons.com* ⤷ *200 rooms* ⦿| *No meals.*

Hostal Adriano

$ | HOTEL | On a street with dozens of bland competitors a couple of blocks from Sol, this budget hotel stands out for its price and quality. **Pros:** friendly service; good value; charming touches. **Cons:** shares the building with other hostals; reception desk not staffed 24 hours; street noise. $ *Rooms from: €75* ✉ *Calle de la Cruz 26, 4th fl., Sol* ☎ *91/521–1339*

⊕ *www.hostaladriano.com* ⤷ *22 rooms* ⦿| *No meals* Ⓜ *Sol.*

Hotel Preciados

$$ | HOTEL | In a 19th-century building on the quieter edge of one of Madrid's main shopping districts, Preciados is a charm-ing midrange hotel ideal for travelers who value space and comfort. **Pros:** conven-iently located; complimentary minibar (you read that correctly!); valet parking a steal at €20 per day. **Cons:** expensive breakfast; chaotic street; dated decor. $ *Rooms from: €160* ✉ *Calle Preciados 37, Sol* ☎ *91/454–4400* ⊕ *www.preciado-shotel.com* ⤷ *101 rooms* ⦿| *No meals* Ⓜ *Callao.*

★ Iberostar Las Letras Gran Vía

$$$ | HOTEL | A modern, clubby hotel on the stately avenue of Gran Vía, Iberostar Las Letras is a welcoming oasis from the area's constant hubbub of tourists and shoppers. **Pros:** state-of-the-art gym; many rooms have balconies; happening rooftop bar. **Cons:** finicky a/c; no spa; awk-ward bathroom design. $ *Rooms from: €207* ✉ *Gran Vía 11, Sol* ☎ *91/523–7980*

⊕ *www.iberostar.com/en/hotels/madrid/ iberostar-las-letras-gran-via* ↘ *110 rooms* � *No meals* Ⓜ *Banco de España.*

Liabeny

$$ | HOTEL | This classically decorated hotel situated between Gran Vía and Puerta del Sol has large, comfortable carpeted rooms with striped fabrics and big windows. **Pros:** spacious bathrooms; near Princesa shopping area; upscale Castilian restaurant. **Cons:** small rooms; crowded, noisy neighborhood; stairs to access public areas. Ⓢ *Rooms from: €146* ⊠ *Calle de la Salud 3, Sol* ☎ *91/531–9000* ⊕ *www. liabeny.es* ↘ *220 rooms* 101 *No meals* Ⓜ *Sol.*

Mayerling Hotel

$ | HOTEL | Sleek minimalism at just the right value can be found on this former textile wholesaler's premises, now a 22-room boutique hotel a few blocks off Plaza Mayor and Plaza Santa Ana. Serene (if slightly clinical) white rooms come in three sizes—standard, superior, and triple—and are decorated with colorful headboards, charcoal valances, and small open closets. **Pros:** triples available; 24-hour "help yourself" bar with coffee, snacks, and juices; prime location. **Cons:** rooms are smallish by U.S. standards; white walls show smudges; no restaurant or gym. Ⓢ *Rooms from: €120* ⊠ *Calle del Conde de Romanones 6, Sol* ☎ *91/420–1580* ⊕ *www.mayerlinghotel. com* ↘ *22 rooms* 101 *No meals* Ⓜ *Tirso de Molina.*

Pestana Plaza Mayor

$$$$ | HOTEL | Opened in May 2020 after an €11 million renovation, Pestana is the newest outpost from the Portuguese boutique hotel chain and Madrid's first hotel situated directly on the Plaza Mayor. **Pros:** upgraded rooms have balconies overlooking the plaza; sun-drenched breakfast area; cloud-soft beds and linens. **Cons:** newfangled interiors clash with the historical building; spa has no chaises; some service issues still being ironed out. Ⓢ *Rooms from: €230* ⊠ *Calle*

Mercado de San Miguel

Adjacent to the Plaza Mayor, this "gastronomic market" is a feast for the senses. Its bustling interior—a mixture of tapas spots and immaculately arranged grocery stalls—sits beneath a fin-de-siècle glass dome reinforced by elaborate wrought iron. Enjoy a glass of wine and a snack here, but save your appetite: the market has become overpriced and underwhelming in recent years. There are two diamonds in the rough: Amaiketako, with its Basque-style pintxos, and Daniel Sorlut, a posh oyster bar. ⊕ *www. mercadodesanmiguel.es*

Imperial 8, Sol ☎ *99/129–3113* ⊕ *www. pestanacollection.com* ↘ *89 rooms* 101 *No meals* Ⓜ *Sol.*

Nightlife

DANCE CLUBS
★ Cha Chá the Club

DANCE CLUBS | For trendy twentysomethings, there may be no buzzier place to be on Friday nights than this converted multifloor movie theater that erupts into epic DJ-fueled parties. Expect a mixed, LGBTQ-friendly crowd. Buy tickets online ahead of time. ⊠ *Calle de Alcalá 20, Sol* ⊕ *www.xceed.me/tickets-club/madrid/ cha-cha-the-club* Ⓜ *Sol.*

Cocó Madrid

DANCE CLUBS | This club, with its wild color palette, huge dance floor, and better-than-average cocktails, is best known for its Mondo Disko nights (Thursday and Saturday) that rage until dawn with house and electronic music often by international DJs. ⊠ *Calle Alcalá 20, Sol* ☎ *91/445–7938* ⊕ *www.web-mondo.com* ⊗ *Closed Mon.–Wed.* Ⓜ *Sevilla.*

El Sol

DANCE CLUBS | Madrid's oldest *discoteca* continues to win over its patrons with all-night dancing to live music (around midnight Thursday–Saturday) and DJ sets. ✉ *Calle Jardines 3, Sol* ☎ *91/532–6490* ⊕ *www.elsolmad.com* ⊗ *Closed Mon.* Ⓜ *Gran Vía.*

Joy Eslava

DANCE CLUBS | A downtown club in a converted theater, this is a long-established standby that attracts a varied, somewhat bourgeois crowd of locals and tourists. ✉ *Calle del Arenal 11, Sol* ☎ *91/366–3733* ⊕ *www.joy-eslava.com* Ⓜ *Sol.*

MUSIC CLUBS

Costello

MUSIC CLUBS | A multiuse space that combines a café and a lounge, this place caters to a relaxed, conversational crowd; the bottom floor is suited to partygoers, with the latest in live and club music. On weekdays, there are theater and stand-up comedy shows. Check the website for events and ticket prices. ✉ *Calle Caballero de Gracia 10, Sol* ☎ *91/522–1815* ⊕ *www.costelloclub.com* Ⓜ *Gran Vía.*

🎭 Performing Arts

Círculo de Bellas Artes

CONCERTS | Concerts, theater, dance performances, art exhibitions, and events are all part of the calendar here. There is also an extremely popular (and wildly overpriced) café and a rooftop restaurant-bar with great views of the city. ✉ *Calle del Marqués de Casa Riera 2, Sol* ☎ *90/242–2442* ⊕ *www.circulobellasartes.com* Ⓜ *Banco de España.*

🛍 Shopping

CLOTHING

Capas Seseña

CLOTHING | Seseña is the oldest cape tailor in the world. Since 1901, this family-run business, now in its fourth generation, has outfitted the likes of Picasso, Hemingway, and Michael Jackson in traditional merino wool and velvet capes, some lined with red satin. ✉ *Calle de la Cruz 23, Sol* ☎ *91/531–6840* ⊕ *www.sesena.com* ⊗ *Closed Sun.* Ⓜ *Sol.*

CRAFTS AND DESIGN

El Arco Artesanía

CRAFTS | El Arco sells contemporary, whimsical handicrafts from all over Spain, including modern ceramics, handblown glassware, jewelry, and leather items. ✉ *Pl. Mayor 9, Sol* ☎ *68/904–4374* ⊕ *www.artesaniaelarco.com* Ⓜ *Sol.*

Taller Puntera

SHOES/LUGGAGE/LEATHER GOODS | You can watch the artisans at work at this inviting atelier-boutique hybrid situated steps from the Plaza Mayor. Regardless of what catches your eye—a leather card holder, handbag, or perhaps a hand-bound notebook—you'll be pleasantly surprised by the affordable prices. ✉ *Pl. del Conde de Barajas 4, Sol* ☎ *91/364–2926* ⊕ *www.puntera.com* ⊗ *Closed Sun.* Ⓜ *Ópera, Tirso de Molina.*

Chapter 4

PALACIO AND MONCLOA

4

Updated by
Benjamin Kemper

 Sights
★★★★★

 Restaurants
★★★☆☆

 Hotels
★★★★★

 Shopping
★★★★☆

 Nightlife
★★★★★

NEIGHBORHOOD SNAPSHOT

TOP EXPERIENCES

■ **Faro de Moncloa:** Ride the elevator to the observation deck of this defunct transmission tower for sweeping mountain and city views.

■ **Parque del Oeste:** Spot Civil War–era bunkers and a transplanted Egyptian temple on a walk through this stately park.

■ **Casa de Campo:** Hike, bike, or run in this 4,260-acre park that feels a world away from the city bustle.

■ **Museo Cerralbo:** Discover the secret riches of a discerning marquis.

■ **Ermita San Antonio de la Florida:** Visit Goya's tomb and savor frescoes painted by the master himself.

■ **Teleférico:** Dangle above the city skyline on a retro cable car.

GETTING HERE

In Palacio, Ópera (Líneas 2, 5) is the closest metro stop to the Royal Palace, while Callao (Líneas 3, 5) is shopping and dining central. The metro stops at Moncloa (Líneas 3, 6) and Argüelles (Líneas 3, 4, 6) are a fine jumping-off point to explore the urban corners of Moncloa, such as Calle de la Princesa (shopping, dining) and the district's historical sites, while Príncipe Pío (Líneas 6, 10) and Lago (Línea 10) are where to alight for adventures in Casa de Campo, situated on the far side of the river but still a part of this district. Public bike-share service BiciMAD services all areas east of the Manzanares.

PLANNING YOUR TIME

Allot three hours for a brisk walk through the winding streets of these neighborhoods and Parque del Oeste, which contains the Templo de Debod, Civil War bunkers, and a rose garden; budget additional time for touring the Royal Palace. Urban areas are safe at all hours of the day and night, but it's best to avoid parks after sunset.

QUICK BITES

■ **Chocolatería Valor.** Dunk, crunch, repeat: some of Madrid's most heavenly churros are found here. ✉ *Calle del Postigo de San Martín 7, Palacio ⊕ www. valor.es* Ⓜ *Callao*

■ **Los Bocadillos.** Unhinge your jaw and devour a bocadillo de calamares, the classic Madrid sub overstuffed with fried calamari, at the most popular outpost of this local chain; ask for lemon and aioli to zhuzh it up. ✉ *Calle del Marqués de Urquijo 1, Moncloa* Ⓜ *Argüelles*

■ **Tutti Frutti.** Ice cream made on the premises with fresh fruit, top-quality chocolate, and all sorts of other add-ins make this corner *heladería* a neighborhood favorite come summer. ✉ *Cuesta de San Vicente 22, Moncloa ⊕ www. heladeriatuttifrutti.com* Ⓜ *Callao; Ópera*

On the western edge of the city center, Palacio and Moncloa are well-to-do districts packed with historical sites, palaces, parks, and restaurants suited to any budget. Palacio, named for the Royal Palace, is naturally a tourist magnet. Moncloa, developed centuries later, is more residential and expansive, taking in Casa de Campo and the Universidad Complutense campus.

Palacio is a must on any travel itinerary given that it's Madrid's oldest neighborhood and contains Spain's Royal Palace, Europe's largest in terms of surface area. This is where Muhammad I established the city's first military post in the 9th century, essentially founding the city. Situated just west of Plaza Mayor, the neighborhood is a labyrinthe of winding cobblestone streets lined with a mix of international chains and boutiques and time-worn Spanish holdouts.

Moncloa, by contrast, is the Wild West, diverse, unurbanized in certain pockets, and less touristy. There are high-society communities like Aravaca and Puerta de Hierro, livelier urban areas like Argüelles (where college kids commandeer entire sidewalk cafés), and green lungs like the manicured Parque del Oeste, sections of the Madrid Río esplanade, and the more rugged Dehesa de la Villa and Casa de Campo.

Palacio

 Sights

You can feel the history and grandeur of this noble district by simply tracing the palace's endless walls and wandering in and around Plaza de Oriente.

Arab Wall (*Muralla Árabe*)
ARCHAEOLOGICAL SITE | The remains of the Moorish military outpost that became the city of Madrid are visible on Calle Cuesta de la Vega. The sections of wall here protected a fortress built in the 9th century by Emir Muhammad I. In addition to being an excellent defensive position, the site had plentiful water and was called Mayrit, Arabic for "source of life" (this is the likely origin of the city's name). All that remains of the *medina*—the old Arab city within the walls of the fortress—is the neighborhood's chaotic web of streets and plazas, which probably follow the same layout they did more than 1,100 years ago. ✉ *Calle Cuesta de la Vega, Palacio* Ⓜ *Ópera.*

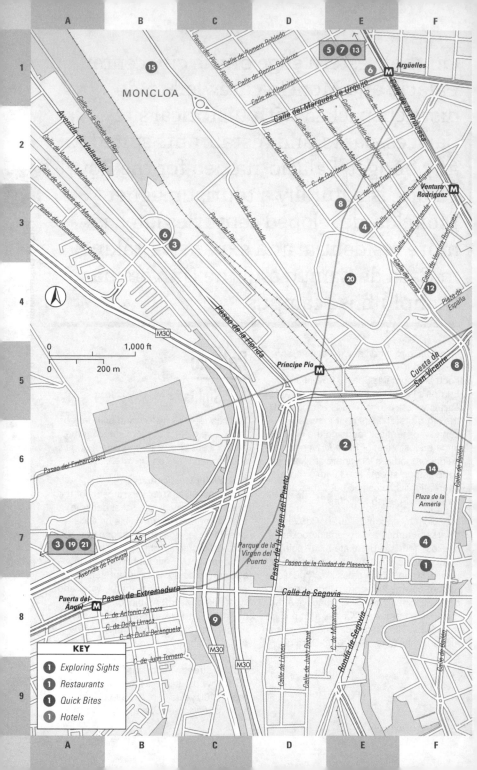

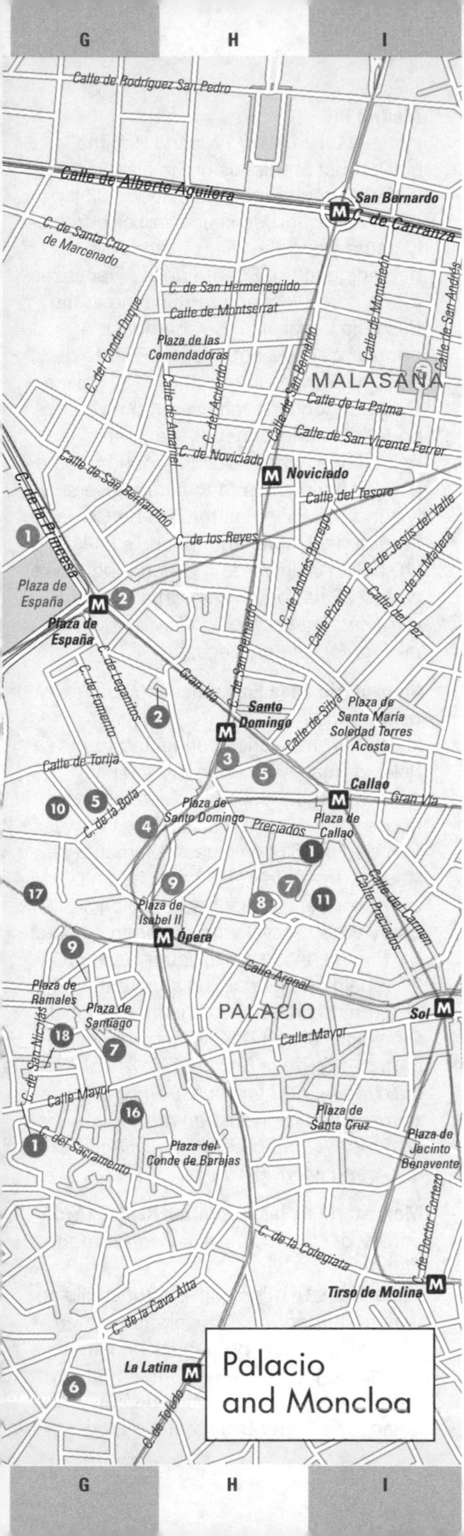

G
H
I
Calle de Rodríguez San Pedro
Calle de Alberto Aguilera
San Bernardo
C. de Carranza
C. de Santa Cruz de Marcenado
C. de San Hermenegildo
Calle de Montserrat
Plaza de las Comendadoras
C. del Conde Duque
Calle de Amaniel
C. del Acuerdo
Calle de San Bernardo
Calle de Monteleón
Calle de San Andrés
MALASAÑA
Calle de la Palma
Calle de San Vicente Ferrer
C. de Noviciado
Noviciado
Calle del Tesoro
Calle de San Bernardino
C. de la Princesa
C. de los Reyes
C. de Andrés Borrego
C. de Jesús del Valle
C. de la Madera
Calle del Pez
Calle Pizarro
Plaza de España
Plaza de España
C. de Leganitos
C. de Fomento
Gran Vía
C. de San Bernardo
Santo Domingo
Calle de Silva
Plaza de Santa María Soledad Torres Acosta
Calle de Torija
Callao
Gran Vía
C. de la Bola
Plaza de Santo Domingo
Preciados
Plaza de Callao
Calle del Carmen
Calle Preciados
Plaza de Isabel II
Ópera
Calle Arenal
Plaza de Ramales
Plaza de Santiago
PALACIO
Sol
Calle Mayor
C. de San Nicolás
Calle Mayor
Plaza de Santa Cruz
Plaza de Jacinto Benavente
C. del Sacramento
Plaza del Conde de Barajas
C. de la Colegiata
C. de Doctor Cortezo
Tirso de Molina
C. de la Cava Alta
La Latina
C. de Toledo
Palacio and Moncloa

Sights

1 Arab Wall F7
2 Campo del Moro E6
3 Casa de Campo A7
4 Catedral de la Almudena................. F7
5 Dehesa de la Villa........ E1
6 Ermita de San Antonio de la Florida B3
7 Faro de Moncloa......... E1
8 Jardines de Sabatini F5
9 Madrid Río................ C8
10 Monasterio de la Encarnación............. G5
11 Monasterio de las Descalzas Reales......... I6
12 Museo Cerralbo.......... F4
13 Museo del Traje.......... E1
14 Palacio Real.............. F6
15 Parque del Oeste B1
16 Plaza de la Villa G7
17 Plaza de Oriente G6
18 San Nicolás de los Servitas G7
19 Teleférico A7
20 Templo de Debod E4
21 Zoo Aquarium Madrid A7

Restaurants

1 Casa Ciriaco............. G7
2 Casa Lafu G5
3 Casa Mingo.............. B3
4 Cuenllas.................. E3
5 La Bola.................. G5
6 La Copita Asturiana G9
7 La Gastroteca de Santiago G7
8 La Montaña.............. E3
9 Le Bistroman Atelier ... G6

Quick Bites

1 Chocolatería Valor........ I6

Hotels

1 Barceló Torre de Madrid G4
2 Dear Hotel G4
3 Generator Madrid H5
4 Gran Meliá Palacio de Los Duques G5
5 Hotel Indigo Madrid - Gran Vía.................. H5
6 Hotel Indigo Madrid - Princesa E1
7 Hotel Intur Palacio San Martín............... H6
8 Room Mate Laura....... H6
9 Room Mate Mario H6

Campo del Moro

NATIONAL/STATE PARK | Essentially the Royal Palace's back yard, the Campo del Moro has enough shaded footpaths for a 45-minute stroll. The lone entrance is (rather inconveniently located) at the bottom of Cuesta de San Vicente on Paseo de la Virgen del Puerto. Enjoy the lush copses, narrow trails, and great lawn leading up to the palace. The park closes at 6 pm October–March and at 8 pm April–September. ⊠ *Paseo de la Virgen del Puerto, Palacio* Ⓜ *Príncipe Pío.*

Catedral de la Almudena

RELIGIOUS SITE | The first stone of the cathedral, which faces the Royal Palace, was laid in 1883 by King Alfonso XII, and the resulting edifice was consecrated by Pope John Paul II in 1993. Built on the site of the old church of Santa María de la Almudena (the city's main mosque during Arab rule), the cathedral has a wooden statue of Madrid's female patron saint, the Virgin of Almudena, reportedly discovered after the Christian Reconquest of Madrid. Legend has it that when the Berbers invaded Spain, the local Christian population hid the statue of the Virgin in a vault carved in the old Roman wall that encircled the city. When the Christians "reconquered" Madrid in 1083, they looked for it, and after nine days of intensive praying—others say it was after a procession honoring the Virgin—the wall opened up to show the statue framed by two lighted candles. The cathedral's name is derived from the place where the relic was found: the wall of the old citadel (in Arabic, *al-mudayna*). ⊠ *Calle Bailén 10, Palacio* 🕾 *91/542–2200* ⊕ *www.catedraldelaalmudena.es* 🎫 *Free; museum and cupola €6* Ⓜ *Ópera.*

Jardines de Sabatini (*Sabatini Gardens*)

GARDEN | The meticulously manicured gardens to the north of the Palacio Real, located to where the royal stables once were, are a pleasant place to rest or watch the sun set. ⊠ *Calle Bailén, Palacio* Ⓜ *Ópera.*

Madrid Río

PROMENADE | FAMILY | Madrid Río, the city's most ambitious urban planning initiative in recent history, added 32 km (20 miles) of green space and bike-friendly paths along the Manzanares River, beginning at the Puente de los Franceses in the northwest and terminating at the Pasarela Legazpi in the southeast. A popular place to enter is the Puente de Segovia, downhill from the Royal Palace. Outdoor concerts (check out the Veranos de la Villa series; lineups are posted online) and riverside dining round out the park's offerings. Note to nature lovers: Madrid Río connects to Casa de Campo, Parque del Oeste, and Madrid's 64-km (40-mile) Anillo Verde ("Green Ring") bike path. ⊠ *Palacio* ⊕ *www.esmadrid.com/ en/whats-on/veranos-de-la-villa* Ⓜ *Príncipe Pío, Pirámides, Legazpi.*

Monasterio de la Encarnación (*Monastery of the Incarnation*)

RELIGIOUS SITE | Once connected to the Palacio Real by an underground passageway, this Augustinian convent now houses fewer than a dozen nuns. It was founded in 1611 by Queen Margarita de Austria, the wife of Felipe III, and has several artistic treasures including a reliquary where a vial with the dried blood of St. Pantaleón is said to liquefy every July 27 (Spain and its colorful superstitions!). The ornate church has superb acoustics for medieval and Renaissance choral concerts. ⊠ *Pl. de la Encarnación 1, Palacio* 🕾 *91/454–8803 for tourist office* ⊕ *www. patrimonionacional.es/en/real-sitio/ real-monasterio-de-la-encarnacion* 🎫 *€6* 🕑 *Closed Mon.* Ⓜ *Ópera.*

Monasterio de las Descalzas Reales (*Monastery of the Royal Discalced/Barefoot Nuns*)

RELIGIOUS SITE | This 16th-century building was restricted for 200 years to women of royal blood. Its plain, brick-and-stone facade begets an opulent interior strewn with paintings by Francisco de Zurbarán, Titian, and Pieter Brueghel the Elder—all

With 3,748 rooms, Palacio Real is the largest palace in Western Europe.

part of the dowry that novices had to provide when they joined the monastery—as well as a hall of sumptuous tapestries crafted from drawings by Peter Paul Rubens. The convent was founded in 1559 by Juana of Austria, one of Felipe II's sisters, who ruled Spain while he was in England and the Netherlands. It houses 33 different chapels—the age of Christ when he died and the maximum number of nuns allowed to live at the monastery—and more than 100 sculptures of Jesus as a baby. About 30 nuns (not necessarily of royal blood) still live here and grow vegetables in the convent's garden. ■TIP→ **You must take a tour in order to visit the convent; tours in English don't follow a set schedule but usually run from 4 pm to close.** ☒ *Pl. de las Descalzas Reales 3, Palacio* ☎ *91/454–8800* ⊕ *www.patrimonionacional.es/en/real-sitio/monasterio-de-las-descalzas-reales* ☒ *From €6* ☽ *Closed Mon.* Ⓜ *Sol.*

★ **Palacio Real** (*Royal Palace*)
CASTLE/PALACE | The Palacio Real was built over first defensive fortress, established by Berbers in the 9th century. It overwhelms with its sheer immensity against the city's silhouetted background. The palace was commissioned in the early 18th century by the first of Spain's Bourbon rulers, Felipe V. Outside, classical French architecture adorns the **Patio de Armas**: Felipe was obviously inspired by his childhood days at Versailles with his grandfather Louis XIV. Look for the stone statues of Inca prince Atahualpa and Aztec king Montezuma, perhaps the only tributes in Spain to these pre-Columbian American rulers. Notice how the steep bluff drops west to the Manzanares River—on a clear day, this vantage point commands a view of the mountain passes leading into Madrid from Old Castile; it's easy to see why Madrid's Berber rulers picked this spot for a fortress.

Inside, 2,800 rooms compete with one another for over-the-top opulence. A two-hour guided tour in English winds a mile-long path through the palace. Highlights include the **Salón de Gasparini,** King Carlos III's private apartments, with swirling, inlaid floors and curlicued stucco wall and ceiling decoration, all glistening in the light of a 2-ton crystal chandelier; the **Salón del Trono,** a grand throne room with the royal seats of King Felipe VI and Queen Letizia; and the **banquet hall,** the palace's largest room, which seats up to 140 people for state dinners. Despite being the official seat of the throne, no monarch has lived here since 1931, when Alfonso XIII was deposed after a Republican electoral victory. The current king and queen live in the far simpler Zarzuela Palace on the outskirts of Madrid.

Also inside the palace are the **Museo de Música** (Music Museum), where five-stringed instruments by Antonio Stradivari form the world's largest such collection; the **Painting Gallery,** which displays works by Spanish, Flemish, and Italian artists from the 15th century on; the **Armería Real** (Royal Armory), with historic suits of armor and frightening medieval torture implements; the **Real Oficina de Farmacia** (Royal Pharmacy), with vials and flasks used to mix the king's medicines; and the **Real Cocina,** Europe's best-preserved royal kitchens, opened to the public for the first time in 2017 and whose framed hand-written menus, antediluvian wood-burning ovens, enormous copper cauldrons, wooden iceboxes, and nearly 3,000 antique kitchen utensils make it a must-stop for foodies. On Wednesday the Changing of the Guard takes place (every 30 minutes, 11–2) at the Puerta del Príncipe, across Plaza de Oriente, with a more solemn and lavish ceremony (with up to 100 guards and horses) the first Wednesday of each month at noon. ⊠ *Calle Bailén, Palacio* ☎ *91/454–8800* ⊕ *www.entradas.patrimonionacional.es* 🎫 *From €13* Ⓜ *Ópera.*

Plaza de la Villa
PLAZA | Madrid's town council met in this medieval-looking complex from the Middle Ages until 2009, when it moved to the Palacio de Cibeles. It now houses municipal offices. The oldest building on

the plaza is the **Casa de los Lujanes**, the one with the Mudejar tower. Built as a private home in the late 15th century, the house carries the Lujanes crest over the main doorway. Also on the plaza's east end is the brick-and-stone **Casa de la Villa,** built in 1629, a classic example of Dutch-influenced Madrid design, with clean lines and spire-topped corner towers. Connected by an overhead walkway, the **Casa de Cisneros** was commissioned in 1537 by the nephew of Cardinal Cisneros. It's one of Madrid's rare examples of the flamboyant plateresque style, which has been likened to splashed water. Sadly, none of these landmarks are open to the public. ⊠ *Palacio* Ⓜ *Sol, Ópera.*

Plaza de Oriente
PLAZA | This stately plaza, in front of the Palacio Real, is flanked by massive statues of Spanish monarchs. They were meant to be mounted on the railing on top of the palace, but Queen Isabel of Farnesio, one of the first royals to live in the palace, had them removed because she was afraid their enormous weight would bring the roof down. (At least that's the *official* reason; according to local lore, the queen wanted the statues removed because her own likeness wouldn't have been placed front and center.) A Velázquez drawing of King Felipe IV is the inspiration for the statue in the plaza's center. It's the first equestrian bronze ever cast with a rearing horse. The sculptor, Italian artist Pietro de Tacca, enlisted Galileo Galilei's help in configuring the statue's weight so it wouldn't tip over. ⊠ *Palacio* Ⓜ *Ópera.*

San Nicolás de los Servitas (*Church of St. Nicholas of the Servites*)
RELIGIOUS SITE | There's some debate over whether this church, perhaps the oldest in Madrid, once formed part of an Arab mosque. It was more likely built after the so-called Reconquest of Madrid in 1083, but the brickwork and horseshoe arches are evidence that it was crafted

by either Mudejars (workers of Islamic origin) or Christian Spaniards well versed in the style. Inside, exhibits detail the Islamic history of early Madrid. ⊠ *Pl. de San Nicolás, Palacio* ☎ *91/559–4064* ✉ *Suggested donation* Ⓜ *Ópera.*

🍽 Restaurants

Casa Ciriaco

$$$ | SPANISH | Casa Ciriaco will celebrate its 100th anniversary this decade, and its wine cellar is even older, dating to 1897. The Madrid institution is as famous for its *callos a la madrileña* (Madrid-style tripe) as it is for *gallina en pepitoria* , an old-school Spanish stew of wine-braised chicken thickened with hard-boiled yolks that's become increasingly hard to find. **Known for:** abuela-approved local comfort food; a neighborhood institution; fame in Spanish literature. 💲 *Average main: €23* ⊠ *Calle Mayor 84, Palacio* ☎ *91/548–0620* ⊕ *www.casaciriaco.es* ⊗ *No dinner Sun. or Mon.* Ⓜ *Ópera.*

Casa Lafu

$$ | CHINESE | FAMILY | Casa Lafu stands out for its expertly prepared repertoire of regional Chinese dishes, from Sichuan-style *má là* (spicy) plates to Shanghainese wine-cooked meats and Cantonese dim sum. Well-priced tasting menus round out the offerings. **Known for:** hot pot; white-tablecloth Chinese cuisine at affordable prices; rare regional specialties. 💲 *Average main: €17* ⊠ *Calle Flor Baja 1, Palacio* ☎ *91/548–7096* ⊕ *www. casalafu.com* Ⓜ *Santo Domingo.*

La Bola

$$ | SPANISH | La Bola is renowned for its cocido madrileño, a soul-satisfying chickpea and meat stew, and for its decor, which has hardly changed a lick since 1868, when the restaurant was founded. Originally, La Bola served three types of cocido: a simple rendition at noon for blue-collar workers and employees, a chicken-only version at 1 for students, and a multimeat extravaganza at 2 for

politicians and journalists; the third, still finished in *cazuelas* (earthenware pots) on a charcoal stove, is what's on the menu today. **Known for:** cocido madrileño; 19th-century decor; postcard-worthy facade. 💲 *Average main: €22* ⊠ *Calle La Bola 5, Palacio* ☎ *91/547–6930* ⊕ *www. labola.es* ⊗ *No dinner Sun.* Ⓜ *Ópera.*

★ La Copita Asturiana

$$ | SPANISH | In the heart of the tourist fray but blissfully under-the-radar, this eensy lunch-only restaurant (est. 1959) with an old tin bar serves all the Asturian favorites, from *fabada* (bean stew) to *cachopo* (ham-and-cheese-stuffed cutlets) to ultracreamy rice pudding. Asturian cider is the requisite beverage. **Known for:** northern Spanish comfort food; easy-on-the-wallet prices; kitsch decor. 💲 *Average main: €17* ⊠ *Calle de Tabernillas 13, Palacio* ☎ *91/365–1063* ⊕ *www.lacopitaasturiana.com* ⊗ *Closed Sat. No dinner* Ⓜ *Tirso de Molina.*

La Gastroteca de Santiago

$$ | MEDITERRANEAN | This modern dining spot has a short and creative menu (barely a dozen dishes) that changes monthly. Despite the chef's newfangled presentations and imaginative flavor pairings, the restaurant remains unpretentious and accessible. **Known for:** Spanish bistro fare; lovely setting; intimate dining. 💲 *Average main: €19* ⊠ *Pl. de Santiago 1, Palacio* ☎ *91/548–0707* ⊗ *Closed Mon. No dinner Sun.* Ⓜ *Ópera.*

Le Bistroman Atelier

$$$ | FRENCH | For a country that borders France, Spain has a surprising dearth of good French restaurants, which makes Le Bistroman all the more remarkable— not only is the food good by Spanish standards, it would be a hit in Paris with its homemade *everything*, from terrines to breads to pastries. Wild game (venison, squab) features prominently on the menu, and other highlights include an old-school cheese cart and throwback desserts like babas au rhum and vanilla bean soufflé. **Known for:** game meats;

Teatro Real was one of the world's first opera houses to return to the stage after lockdown with a production of Verdi's La Traviata, tweaked to reflect life in the time of Covid-19.

varied French wine list; elevated bistro cooking. $ *Average main: €28* ⊠ *Calle de la Amnistia 10, Palacio* ☎ *91/447–2713* ⊕ *www.lebistroman.es* ⊙ *Closed Mon. No dinner Sun.* Ⓜ *Ópera.*

Coffee and Quick Bites

Chocolatería Valor

$ | **CAFÉ** | **FAMILY** | Walk along the western side of the Monasterio de las Descalzas Reales until you reach Chocolatería Valor, an ideal spot to indulge in piping-hot churros dipped in thick hot chocolate. **Known for:** one of the best chocolaterías in town; family-friendly atmosphere; outdoor seating. $ *Average main: €6* ⊠ *Calle Postigo de San Martín 7, Palacio* ☎ *91/899–4062* ⊕ *www.valor.es* Ⓜ *Callao.*

🛏 Hotels

Generator Madrid

$ | **HOTEL** | Forget the grotty, dilapidated "youth hostels" from study-abroad days of yore—Generator Madrid (opened in 2018) might be a budget hotel with shared (up to eight-person) rooms, but it's as much a "hotel" as any of the major brands. **Pros:** bubbly staff and fellow guests; PlayStation in the lobby; USB sockets in rooms. **Cons:** towels (€5 rental) not included in the rate; storing luggage in lockers is exorbitant at €2 per hour; no laundry facilities or kitchen. $ *Rooms from: €44* ⊠ *Calle de San Bernardo 2, Palacio* ☎ *91/047–9801* ⊕ *www.staygenerator.com* 🛏 *129 rooms* ⊙ *No meals* Ⓜ *Callao.*

★ Gran Meliá Palacio de Los Duques

$$$$ | **HOTEL** | Spanish-art lovers will geek out at the new Gran Meliá Palacio de los Duques, a luxury hotel tucked behind Gran Vía where reproductions of famous Diego Velázquez paintings feature in every room. **Pros:** Dos Cielos, one of the city's best hotel restaurants; underfloor heating and deep-soak tubs; rooftop pool and bar. **Cons:** rooms are distinctly less attractive than public areas; rooftop often off-limits because of private events; no great views from rooms. $ *Rooms from: €301* ⊠ *Cuesta Santo Domingo 5, Palacio*

☎ 91/276–4747 ⊕ www.melia.com ⇨ 180 rooms ⦿ No meals Ⓜ Santo Domingo.

Hotel Indigo Madrid – Gran Vía

$$ | **HOTEL** | A hip, vibrant hotel off the bustling Gran Vía thoroughfare, Indigo is best known for its stunning rooftop lounge and outdoor infinity pool, rare features in Madrid. **Pros:** sceney rooftop infinity pool; restaurant that punches above its weight; surprisingly well-equipped gym. **Cons:** interior rooms get little natural light; loses much of its vitality in cold-weather months; decor might be gaudy to some. Ⓢ *Rooms from: €150* ✉ *Calle de Silva 6, Palacio* ☎ *91/200–8585* ⊕ *www.indigomadrid.com* ⇨ *85 rooms* ⦿ *No meals* Ⓜ *Santo Domingo.*

Hotel Intur Palacio San Martín

$$ | **HOTEL** | In an unbeatable location across from one of Madrid's most celebrated landmarks (Monasterio de las Descalzas Reales), this newly renovated hotel—once the U.S. embassy and later a luxurious residential building crowded with noblemen—has the architectural bones of a turn-of-the-century mansion with its hand-carved ceilings, marble foyers, and intricate iron balconies. **Pros:** good variety at breakfast; spacious rooms; lobby with glass-domed atrium. **Cons:** bland interiors; bare-bones gym; head-splitting church bells in the morning. Ⓢ *Rooms from: €164* ✉ *Pl. de San Martín 5, Palacio* ☎ *91/701–5000* ⊕ *www.intur.com* ⇨ *94 rooms, 8 suites* ⦿ *No meals* Ⓜ *Ópera, Callao.*

Room Mate Laura

$$ | **HOTEL** | A quirky, clubby hotel located overlooking Plaza de San Martín near the Royal Theater and Palace, Room Mate Laura feels like a time warp to an IKEA catalog of the early aughts—so thank god the service and amenities are so outstanding. **Pros:** free portable Wi-Fi gadgets; kitchenettes; clean and comfortable. **Cons:** only the best rooms have views of the convent; no restaurant; some bathrooms need to be revamped.

Ⓢ *Rooms from: €132* ✉ *Travesía de Trujillos 3, Palacio* ☎ *90/081–8320* ⊕ *www.room-matehotels.com* ⇨ *36 rooms* ⦿ *No meals* Ⓜ *Ópera.*

Room Mate Mario

$$ | **HOTEL** | In the city center, steps from the Royal Palace and Teatro Real, Mario is small with limited services but a welcome alternative to Madrid's traditional hotel options at a good price. **Pros:** centrally located; good breakfast served until noon; most affordable of the Room Mate chain in Madrid. **Cons:** no restaurant or in-room coffee-making facilities; cramped entry-level rooms; unremarkable views compared to other Room Mate hotels. Ⓢ *Rooms from: €150* ✉ *Calle Campomanes 4, Palacio* ☎ *91/548–8548* ⊕ *www.room-matehotels.com* ⇨ *57 rooms* ⦿ *Free breakfast* Ⓜ *Ópera.*

 Nightlife

DANCE CLUBS
Cool

DANCE CLUBS | This gritty, Berlin-style underground club hosts techno-driven dance parties on weekend nights for a young, primarily LGBT+ clientele. ✉ *Calle Isabel la Católica 6, Palacio* ☎ *63/459–6212* Ⓜ *Santo Domingo.*

Velvet

DANCE CLUBS | Trippy and chameleonlike, thanks to colorful LED lights and the undulating shapes of the columns and walls, this is the place to go if you want a late-night drink without the thunder of a full-blown DJ. The venue opens at 11 and closes at 5:30 am. ✉ *Calle Jacometrezo 6, Palacio* ☎ *63/341–4887* ⊕ *www.velvet-disco.es* Ⓜ *Callao.*

MUSIC CLUBS
★ **Café Berlín**

MUSIC CLUBS | For a space so small, Café Berlín packs quite the acoustic punch and draws an international, eclectic crowd. Before midnight, catch nightly live music acts in a panoply of styles (flamenco, swing, soul, and more); from around 1 am on, drop in for the disco-inflected DJ sets that ooze good vibes until 6 am. ⊠ *Costanilla de los Ángeles 20, Palacio* ☎ *91/559–7429* ⊕ *www.berlincafe.es* Ⓜ *Santo Domingo.*

El Amante

MUSIC CLUBS | Blocks from Plaza Mayor, this might be the closest thing you'll find in Madrid to a posh private New York club. There are two winding floors filled with nooks hosting the city's best-heeled crowds. Music is usually bass-heavy electronic or house. The door is tough, so be sure to dress to impress (no sneakers allowed, gents). Get here before 1:30 am or be ready to wait in line. ⊠ *Calle Santiago 3, Palacio* ☎ *91/755–4460* Ⓜ *Ópera.*

Marula

MUSIC CLUBS | Popular for its quiet summer terrace under the Puente de Segovia arches, its unbeatable electro-funk mixes, and for staying open into the wee hours, this is a cleverly designed narrow space with lots of illuminated wall art. There's a branch in Barcelona, too. Check the website for concert listings. Live music usually begins at 11 pm. ⊠ *Calle Caños Viejos 3, Palacio* ☎ *91/366–1596* ⊕ *www.marulacafe.com* Ⓜ *La Latina.*

🎭 Performing Arts

★ Teatro Real

OPERA | This resplendent Neoclassical theater is the city's premier venue for opera and dance performances. Built in 1850, it fell into disuse from 1925 to 1966 because of political upheaval. A major restoration project endowed it with golden balconies, plush seats, and state-of-the-art stage equipment. Opera buffs rave about the choir, said to be one of the best in the world. There's often flamenco on Friday evenings in the smaller auditorium; check the website for details. ⊠ *Pl. de Isabel II, Palacio* ☎ *91/516–0660* ⊕ *www.teatro-real.com* Ⓜ *Ópera.*

FLAMENCO

Café de Chinitas

DANCE | This touristy spot fills up fast. Make reservations because shows often sell out. The restaurant, which specializes in paella and rice dishes, opens at 8. Performances run Monday–Saturday at 8:15 and 10:30. ⊠ *Calle Torija 7, Palacio* ☎ *91/559–5135* ⊕ *www.chinitas.com* Ⓜ *Santo Domingo.*

Corral de la Morería

DANCE | A Michelin-starred dinner followed by a world-class flamenco performance in the same building sounds too good to be true, but at Corral de la Morería, the food (Basque with an Andalusian twist) is as invigorating as the twirling and stomping *bailaoras*. Opt for an elegant, market-driven prix-fixe menu to be enjoyed during the show, or splurge on an exclusive tasting experience at the four-table Gastronómico restaurant that earned the venue its coveted star. Wine pairings, which hinge on rare back-vintage sherries and other *vinos generosos* (fortified wines), are well worth the extra euros. ⊠ *Calle de la Morería 17, Palacio* ☎ *91/365–8446* ⊕ *www.corraldelamoreria.com* Ⓜ *La Latina.*

🛍 Shopping

CERAMICS

★ Antigua Casa Talavera

CERAMICS/GLASSWARE | This shop, opened in 1904, is the best of Madrid's many ceramics vendors. Despite the name, the finest wares sold here are from Manises, near Valencia, but the blue-and-yellow Talavera ceramics are also excellent. All pieces are hand-painted and bear traditional Spanish motifs that have been used for centuries. ⊠ *Calle de Isabel la Católica 2, Palacio* ☎ *91/547–3417* ⊕ *www.antiguacasatalavera.com* 🕙 *Closed Sun.* Ⓜ *Santo Domingo.*

The city's cable car, Teleférico, connects Parque del Oeste and Casa de Campo and offers views of the top attractions, including the Royal Palace.

SPECIALTY STORES

Alambique

SPECIALTY STORES | Amateur and professional cooks will love this terrific little shop (est. 1978) that sells everything from paella pans to earthenware cazuelas to olive-wood cheese boards. Cooking classes (in Spanish) are also available. ✉ *Pl. de la Encarnación 2, Palacio* ☎ *91/547–4220* ⊕ *www.alambique.com.*

Moncloa

Sights

★ Casa de Campo

CITY PARK | FAMILY | Over five times the size of New York's Central Park, Casa de Campo is Madrid's largest park and a nature-lover's paradise, complete with bike trails, picnic tables, pine forests, and a public outdoor pool (€5 entry). See if you can spot wildlife like hawks, foxes, hares, and red squirrels. The park's name ("country house") is a holdover from when the grounds were the royal family's hunting estate. It became pubic property in May 1931 with the arrival of the Spanish Second Republic, which dissolved royal landholdings; it's said that more than 300,000 Madrileños visited the park on opening day. ✉ *Moncloa* Ⓜ *Casa de Campo, Lago, Batán.*

Dehesa de la Villa

CITY PARK | FAMILY | Unlike Retiro and Parque del Oeste, this secluded 158-acre park is mostly forested and unlandscaped, making it ideal for disconnecting in nature. Its location in the Ciudad Universitaria neighborhood makes it a popular meeting place for university students in warm-weather months. You won't run into any tourists here. ✉ *Calle de Francos Rodríguez, Northeast entrance, Moncloa* Ⓜ *Valdezarza.*

Ermita de San Antonio de la Florida (*Goya's Tomb*)

RELIGIOUS SITE | Built between 1792 and 1798 by the Italian architect Francisco Fontana, this Neoclassical chapel was financed by King Carlos IV, who also commissioned Goya to paint the vaults

Yes, it's a little odd to find an ancient Egyptian temple in downtown Madrid, but rest (or, pose) easy; it was a gift from the Egyptian government.

and the main dome. It took him 120 days to fully depict events of the 13th century (St. Anthony of Padua resurrecting a dead man) as if they had happened five centuries later, with naturalistic images never used before to paint religious scenes. Opposite the image of the frightening dead man on the main dome, Goya painted himself as a man covered with a black cloak. Goya, who died in Bordeaux in 1828, is buried here (without his head, because it was stolen in France) under an unadorned gravestone. ⊠ *Glorieta de San Antonio de la Florida 5, Moncloa* 🕿 *91/542–0722* ⊕ *www.sanantoniodelaflorida.es* ⊠ *Free* 🕐 *Closed Mon.* Ⓜ *Príncipe Pío.*

Faro de Moncloa
VIEWPOINT | FAMILY | This UFO-like tower is 360 feet tall and an excellent viewpoint from which to gaze at some of the city's most outstanding buildings including the Palacio Real, Palacio de Cibeles (city hall), the four skyscrapers to the north, and up to 50 landmarks for which you'll find descriptions in English

and Spanish. ⊠ *Av. Arco de la Victoria 2, Moncloa* ⊕ *www.esmadrid.com/en* ⊠ *€3* Ⓜ *Moncloa.*

Museo Cerralbo
MUSEUM | One of Madrid's most captivating museums is also one of its least-known. This former palace, built in 1893 by the marquis of the same name, preserves the nobleman's art collection including works by El Greco, Tintoretto, Van Dyck, and Zurbarán. These hang in gilded and frescoed halls appointed with ornate period furniture. ⊠ *Calle de Ventura Rodríguez 17, Moncloa* 🕿 *91/547–3646* ⊕ *www.culturaydeporte.gob.es/mcerralbo/en/home.html* ⊠ *€3* 🕐 *Closed Mon. (free Thurs. 5–8 pm, Sat. 2–3 pm, Sun.)* Ⓜ *Ventura Rodríguez.*

Museo del Traje (*Costume Museum*)
MUSEUM | Trace the evolution of dress in Spain here, from rare old royal burial garments to French fashion pieces of Felipe V's reign and the haute couture creations of Balenciaga and Pertegaz. Explanatory notes are in English, and the museum has a superb modern Spanish

restaurant, Café de Oriente, overlooking the gardens. ✉ *Av. Juan de Herrera 2, Moncloa* ☎ *91/550-4700* ⊕ *www.cultur-aydeporte.gob.es/mtraje/inicio.html* ☒ *€3 (free Sat. after 2:30 and Sun.)* ⊘ *Closed Mon.* Ⓜ *Ciudad Universitaria.*

★ **Parque del Oeste**

CITY PARK | FAMILY | This is many Madrileños' favorite park for its pristine yet unmobbed paths and well-pruned lawns and flower beds. From dawn to dusk, expect to see dogs cavorting off leash, couples sprawled out beneath the trees, and groups of friends playing Frisbee and *fútbol.* From Paseo del Pintor Rosales, meander downhill toward Avenida de Valladolid, crossing the train tracks, and you'll hit Madrid Río; walk southwest and you'll find Templo de Debod (see separate entry). This park also contains the city's only cablecar (see "Teleférico") and, 100 yards beneath it, a rose garden (Rosaleda; free entry) containing some 20,000 specimens of more than 650 rose varieties that reach their peak in May. In the quieter northern section of the park (along Avenida Séneca), you'll happen upon Civil War–era bunkers interspersed among plane tree-lined promenades, a sobering reminder that Parque del Oeste was the western front of Madrid's resistance against Franco's armies. ✉ *Paseo del Pintor Rosales, Moncloa* Ⓜ *Argüelles, Moncloa, Ventura Rodríguez, Pl. de España.*

Teleférico

TRANSPORTATION SITE (AIRPORT/BUS/FERRY/ TRAIN) | FAMILY | Kids and adults alike appreciate the sweeping views from this retro cable car, which swoops you 2.5 km (1.6 miles) from the Rosaleda gardens (in the Parque del Oeste) to the center of Casa de Campo in about 10 minutes. If you're feeling active, take a (very) long hike to the top and ride back into the city, or pause in Casa de Campo for primo picnicking. ■ **TIP→ This is not the best way to get to the zoo and theme park, located approximately 2 km (1 mile) from**

the drop-off point in Casa de Campo. You're better off riding the Teléferico out and back, then taking the bus to the zoo. ✉ *Estación Terminal Teleférico, Paseo de Pintor Rosales, at Calle Marqués de Urquijo, Moncloa* ☎ *91/541-1118* ⊕ *teleferico.emt-madrid.es* ☒ *From €5* Ⓜ *Arguelles.*

Templo de Debod

RELIGIOUS SITE | It's not every day that you can marvel at a fully reconstructed ancient Egyptian temple from the 4th century BC, but thanks to the Egyptian government, which bequeathed the edifice to Spain in 1968 for its assistance with the construction of the Aswan Dam, it's free for the public to appreciate. The highlight is the chapel dedicated to Isis and Amun decorated with reliefs. Visit at sunset and watch as the day's last light radiates off the time- (and, sadly, tourist-) worn stones. As of 2020, the pool that used to surround the temple is currently devoid of water as the entire complex is being studied for renovation and/or enclosure. ✉ *Paseo del Pintor Rosales, Moncloa* ☎ *91/765-1008* ☒ *Free* ⊘ *Closed Mon.* Ⓜ *Pl. de España, Ventura Rodríguez.*

Zoo Aquarium Madrid

ZOO | FAMILY | Madrid's zoo-aquarium houses one of Europe's largest variety of animals (including rarities such as a white tiger that birthed triplets in 2020) grouped according to geographical origin. It also has a dolphinarium (currently worth skipping due to animal abuse allegations) and a wild bird sanctuary that holds entertaining exhibitions twice a day on weekdays and more often on weekends—check times on arrival and show up early to get a good seat. ■ **TIP→ Although the nearest metro stop is Casa de Campo, it's best reached via the Príncipe Pío stop, then Bus No. 33.** ✉ *Casa de Campo, Moncloa* ☎ *91/154-7479* ⊕ *www.zoomadrid.com* ☒ *€24* Ⓜ *Casa de Campo; Príncipe Pío, then Bus No. 33.*

🍴 Restaurants

Casa Mingo

$ | **SPANISH** | **FAMILY** | Madrid's oldest sidrería (cider house) is a grand, cathedral-like hall with barrel-lined walls, double-height ceilings, and creaky wooden chairs. The star menu item is roast chicken, hacked up unceremoniously and served swimming in a pool of cider jus—old-school bar food at its finest. **Known for:** Asturian cider; roast chicken; a Madrid institution. $ *Average main: €10* ✉ *Paseo de la Florida 34, Moncloa* ☎ *91/547–7918* ⊕ *www.casamingo.es* Ⓜ *Príncipe Pío.*

★ Cuenllas

$$$ | **SPANISH** | Epitomizing Old World luxury, Cuenllas ("kwen-yas") is Moncloa's most iconic dining establishment, in business since 1939. What began as a small *mantequería* (dairy shop) evolved to become Madrid's toniest wine and tapas bar, thanks to the influx of well-to-do Madrileños who reclaimed the area surrounding the Parque del Oeste after the Spanish Civil War. **Known for:** standout traditional wine list; French-inflected Spanish dining; charmingly old-fashioned waiters. $ *Average main: €23* ✉ *Calle Ferraz 5, Moncloa* ☎ *91/559–1705* ⊕ *www.cuenllas.es* ☽ *Closed Sun.* Ⓜ *Ventura Rodríguez.*

La Montaña

$$ | **SPANISH** | **FAMILY** | The average customer age in this time-warpy tavern is pushing 70, which is always a good sign—Madrid's abuelos and abuelas never settle for subpar Spanish cooking. In the snug, tile-walled dining room, tuck into disappearing classics like braised squid in ink sauce and stewed baby fava beans (verdinas) with prawns; then satisfy your sweet tooth with a custardy fried *torrija* (Spanish "French" toast). **Known for:** kitschy Spanish décor; locals-only clientele; dependable down-home cooking. $ *Average main: €16* ✉ *Calle del Rey Francisco 28, Moncloa* ☎ *91/547–3111* ☽ *No dinner Sun.* Ⓜ *Ventura Rodríguez.*

🛏 Hotels

★ Barceló Torre de Madrid

$$$ | **HOTEL** | A jewel box of glowing lights, harlequin furniture, and gilded mirrors, the soaring Barceló Torre de Madrid opened in 2017 and remains one of the trendiest hotels in town. **Pros:** cutting-edge design by local artists; sleek pool and spa area; excellent Somos restaurant. **Cons:** certain bathrooms offer questionable privacy; bathing cap required to use the pool; pool opens at 11 am. $ *Rooms from: €210* ✉ *Pl. de España 18, Moncloa* ☎ *91/524–2339* ⊕ *www.barcelo.com* ⤴ *256 rooms* ⦿ *No meals* Ⓜ *Pl. de España.*

Dear Hotel

$$ | **HOTEL** | Overlooking the tree-lined Plaza de España, Dear Hotel is a sleek urban property designed by Tarruella Trenchs Studio, the firm behind such lauded projects as H10 La Mimosa hotel in Barcelona and La Bien Aparecida restaurant in Madrid. **Pros:** all rooms face out; swanky rooftop bar with 360-degree views; Scandi-chic furnishings. **Cons:** tiny pool; no gym or spa; cramped lobby. $ *Rooms from: €147* ✉ *Gran Vía 80, Moncloa* ☎ *91/412–3200* ⊕ *www.dear-hotelmadrid.com* ⤴ *162 rooms* ⦿ *No meals* Ⓜ *Pl. de España.*

Hotel Indigo Madrid – Princesa

$ | **HOTEL** | This budget newcomer (opened in December 2019) is situated in the heart of residential Argüelles, steps from the busting shopping street Calle Princesa. **Pros:** five-minute walk from Parque del Oeste; cheery decor; rain showers. **Cons:** poor sound-proofing; still ironing out some kinks in service; bathrooms are basic. $ *Rooms from: €120* ✉ *Calle del Marqués de Urquijo 4, Moncloa* ☎ *91/548–1900* ⊕ *www.ihg.com* ⤴ *101 rooms* ⦿ *No meals* Ⓜ *Argüelles.*

Chapter 5

CHUECA AND MALASAÑA

Updated by
Benjamin Kemper

👁 **Sights**
★★☆☆☆

🍽 **Restaurants**
★★★★☆

🛏 **Hotels**
★★☆☆☆

🛍 **Shopping**
★★★★★

🍸 **Nightlife**
★★★★★

THE SECRETS OF THE LIRIA PALACE

If you wanted to visit the seat of the late Duchess of Alba, Liria Palace, before it opened to the public in September 2019 you made a formal request and waited—for approximately three years. Why the extreme exclusivity? And what lay beyond the palace walls that people would willingly wait so many years in advance to see?

The House of Alba owns the greatest private art collection in Spain, and the aristocratic family's highlight reel is on display in the halls of Liria Palace. Rooms loosely organized by artistic movement drip with paintings by Spanish greats like El Greco, Goya, Zurbarán, Zuloaga, and Velázquez, and there's a surprisingly deep assemblage of Italian Renaissance works as well, by Perugino, Sanzio, and Fra Bartolomeo, among others. In the library, you'll find Columbus's hand-written logbooks, Ferdinand II's original will, and a weathered first edition of Don Quixote. The opulently decorated rooms appointed with period furniture are art pieces in themselves.

DETAILS

✉ *Calle de la Princesa 20*

☎ *912/302200*

🌐 *www.palaciodeliria. com*

Tickets: 14€ (includes tour)

Group tours start every 30 minutes and last 65 minutes. Your ticket has an assigned tour time.

■ TIP➜ Visits are by tour only. Buy tickets in advance online. If tours are sold out for the date in question, try your luck as a walk-in 15 minutes before the tour is set to depart.

WHAT IS THE HOUSE OF ALBA?

Meet one of Spain's most powerful dukedoms—past, present, and (if history is any indication) future. Tracing its origins to 14th-century Castile, the family is worth an estimated $3.8 billion today and owns approximately 130 square miles of land across the Iberian Peninsula. Of the twentysome castles and palaces it presides over, most notable are the Palacio de Las Dueñas in Seville, Castillo de Coca in Segovia, and Palacio Monterrey in Salamanca.

The Salón Goya

THE LATE, GREAT DUCHESS

No one has made more of a splash in Liria Palace's 254-year history than Duchess of Alba Cayetana Fitz-James Stuart, who died in 2014. Bearing more officially recognized titles than any royal on earth, according to Guinness World Records, she was baptized in Madrid's Royal Palace and was related to Christopher Columbus, Winston Churchill, and the Queen of England. But a prim-and-proper aristocrat she was not—during Franco's reign, she hosted racy fashion shows (famously for Yves Saint-Laurent) and was known to break out spontaneously in gutsy flamenco dance.

A FRAUGHT LEGACY

For the better part of a century, members of the House of Alba have graced the front pages of tabloids—Cayetana for her outlandish remarks and scandalous relationships (she wedded a possibly closeted ex-Jesuit priest and later a suitor 30 years her junior) and her children for infighting and drugs and sex. On the other hand, the late duchess was a great defender of the Roma in Seville, and even built a church for them. The family has done an admirable job when it comes to preserving some of Spain's finest artistic treasures; indeed, Liria Palace was reconstructed virtually in its entirety after the Spanish Civil War. But the power that dynasties like the House of Alba continue to wield in Spain is unpalatable to many modern Spaniards.

OTHER PALACES WORTH VISITING IN MADRID

Cerralbo Palace, within walking distance of Liria, is a nobleman's 19th-century abode that is now a sumptuous art museum. In Parque del Buen Retiro you'll find the Palacio de Cristal, or "Glass Palace," a soaring turn-of-the-century greenhouse that now holds modern art exhibitions. The Royal Palace, the official residence of the Spanish monarchs, is nearly double the size of Versailles with 2,800 rooms.

The Salón Italiano

NEIGHBORHOOD SNAPSHOT

TOP EXPERIENCES

- **"La hora del vermú":** Happy hour is synonymous with vermouth and tapas in this part of Madrid.

- **Palacio de Liria:** Tour the newly opened abode of the late Duchess of Alba.

- **LGBT+ nightlife:** Party the night away in Madrid's "gayborhood."

- **Espadrille shopping:** Snap up colorful rope-soled sandals at a 158-year-old artisan shop.

- **Plaza-hopping:** Stroll among picturesque plazas: San Ildefonso, Dos de Mayo, Juan Pujol, Chueca, and Pedro Zerolo, to name a few.

GETTING HERE

Malasaña is serviced by metro stations around its perimeter; clockwise from the neighborhood's northwest corner, these are: Argüelles (Líneas 3, 4, 6), San Bernardo (Líneas 2, 4), Bilbao (Líneas 1, 4), Tribunal (Líneas 1, 10), Gran Vía (Líneas 1, 5), Callao (Líneas 3, 5), Ventura Rodríguez (Línea 3), and Plaza de España (Líneas 3, 10). Noviciado (Línea 2) is roughly in Malasaña's center.

Chueca is also serviced by metro stations on its periphery; clockwise from the neighborhood's northwest corner, these are: Bilbao, Alonso Martínez (Líneas 4, 5, 10), Banco de España (Línea 2), Gran Vía, and Tribunal. Chueca (Línea 5) is located in the heart of the neighborhood.

Malasaña and Chueca are also accessible via the new and completely free (launched in 2020) Línea 001 bus route, which connects Moncloa and Atocha stations via Gran Vía with periodic stops along the way. BiciMAD bike-share has docks throughout both neighborhoods.

PLANNING YOUR TIME

Allot a few hours to explore these neighborhoods on foot, or more if you plan on making pit stops to wine, dine, and people-watch. Tapas and cocktail bars are particularly mobbed on weekend nights.

QUICK BITES

- **Casa Camacho.** An essential Malasaña experience is gulping down a few ice-cold "yayos"—vermouth, gin, seltzer, lemon slice—at the tin bar alongside free tapas like olives and stewed chickpeas. ⊠ *Calle de San Andrés 4, Malasaña* Ⓜ *Tribunal*

- **Casa Julio.** Ooey-gooey oversize croquetas stuffed with hot béchamel and any range of fixings (start with the classic jamón) are the tapa to order at this snug neighborhood hangout. ⊠ *Calle de la Madera 37, Malasaña* Ⓜ *Tribunal*

- **La Carbonera.** Cheese geeks unite at this pocket *queso* bar with enough manchego, Idiazábal, Mahón, and other delectable national varieties to make you an armchair expert on Spanish cheeses. ⊠ *Calle de Bernardo López García 11, Malasaña* ⊕ *www.lacarboneramadrid.com* Ⓜ *Ventura Rodríguez*

Chueca and Malasaña were ground zero for Madrid's countercultural revolution called the Movida Madrileña, a political and artistic reawakening that followed Franco's death in 1975. The movement's motto *Madrid nunca duerme* (Madrid never sleeps) still rings true in Chueca, Spain's favorite "gayborhood," and in Malasaña, a bastion of nonconformist nightlife.

Chueca, a subsection of Justicia district, is named after the Plaza de Chueca, which is in turn named after Federico Chueca, author and composer of *zarzuelas* (short musical plays). Today the neighborhood is Spain's most iconic LGBT+ quarter, and it has held that unofficial title since the 1980s, when the first gay bars arrived on the scene. Nowadays most young LGBT+ Madrileños live and party elsewhere because of the barrio's soaring rents, tourist crowds, and increasingly older clientele, but for a fun, carefree, and rowdy night out, Chueca never disappoints regardless of your sexual orientation. The downside of Chueca's reputation as gay district is that its myriad other attractions—ranging from museums to pretty plazas to fantastic galleries and restaurants—are often overshadowed.

Malasaña has a youthful, off-beat pulse rivaled only, perhaps, by Lavapiés, its more multicultural counterpart. Formerly called Barrio de las Maravillas, the neighborhood is centered on Plaza de Dos de Mayo, which commemorates the May 2 uprising against French occupation in 1808. Manuela Malasaña, for whom the barrio is named, was a martyr in the conflict. At the end of the 20th century, Malasaña emerged as an emblem of the Movida Madrileña, its rough-and-ready streets featuring prominently in music and cinema thanks to emerging talents like Alaska, Mecano, Hombres G, and film director Pedro Almodóvar. These days the neighborhood is far cleaner and less rambunctious than it was in its cultural heyday, thanks to massive waves of gentrification in the early 2000s and 2010s, but its rebellious spirit lives on—head to Plaza de Dos de Mayo any weekend night, and you'll see crowds of locals flouting open container laws.

Chueca

 Sights

Museo de Historia de Madrid (*Madrid History Museum*)
MUSEUM | FAMILY | The intricate, over-the-top 18th-century doorway to this museum, formerly a hospice, is one of the

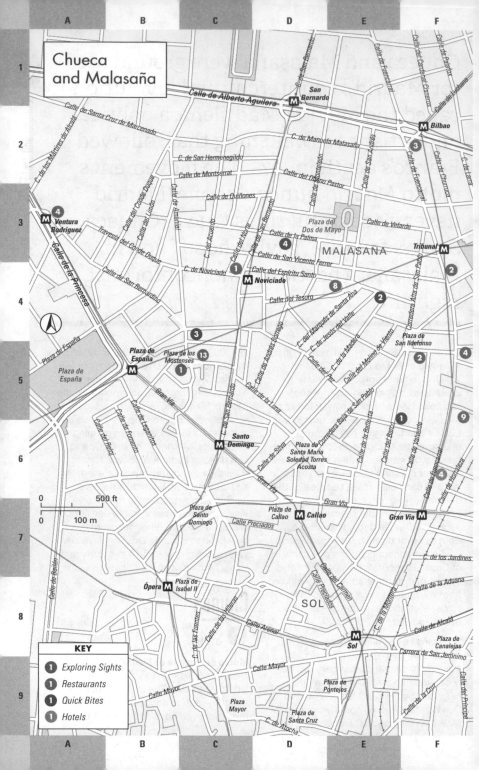

Chueca and Malasaña

KEY
- ❶ Exploring Sights
- ❶ Restaurants
- ❶ Quick Bites
- ❶ Hotels

Map labels:

Calle del Españoleto
Calle de Caracas
Calle de Santa Engracia
Calle de Zurbano
Calle de Manuel Silvela
Calle de Covarrubias
Calle de Nicasio Gallego
Calle de Zurbarán
Calle de Sagasta
Calle de Fernando El Santo
Calle de Almagro
Calle de Monte Esquinza
Calle de Serrano Anguita
Alonso Martínez
M
Calle de Génova
Calle de Zurbano
Calle de Fortuny
Jardines del Arquitecto Ribera
Calle de María de Molina
Calle de la Beneficencia
C. de San Mateo
Calle de Campoamor
Calle de Orellana
Calle del General Castaños
Colón
M
Plaza de la Villa de París
Calle de Hortaleza
Calle de General Arrando
Calle del Marqués de la Ensenada
C. de San Lucas
Calle de Doña Bárbara de Braganza
Chueca
M
Calle del Almirante
Calle de Prim
Calle de Pelayo
Calle de San Bartolomé
Calle del Barquillo
Paseo de Recoletos
Paseo de Recoletos
CHUECA
Plaza de Pedro Zerolo
Calle de Barbieri
Calle de la Libertad
C. de San Marcos
Calle del Barquillo
Calle de los Infantes
Gran Vía
Calle de la Reina
Banco de España
M
C. de Alcalá
Sevilla
M
Calle de Alcalá
Calle de los Madrazo
Calle de Montalbán
Calle de Zorrilla
Calle Juan de Mena
Carrera de San Jerónimo
Paseo del Prado
Calle de Echegaray
Calle del Prado
Calle de Felipe IV
Calle de Ruiz de Alarcón

Sights ▼

1 Mercado de Los Mostenses C5
2 Museo de Historia de Madrid.....F4
3 Museo del Romanticismo.........G3
4 Palacio de Liria A3

Restaurants ▼

1 Bar La Gloria C4
2 Bodega de la Ardosa..............F5
3 Café Comercial......................F2
4 Casa Hortensia
  Restaurante y Sidrería F5
5 Casa Salvador......................G6
6 Celso y Manolo H7
7 Dspeakeasy H4
8 La Colmada..........................E4
9 La Tita Rivera.......................F5
10 Lettera Trattoria Moderna G7
11 Mercado de la Reina..............G7
12 Roostiq..............................H6
13 Selva C5
14 Trattoria Pulcinella H4

Quick Bites ▼

1 Café de la Luz E6
2 Lolina Vintage Café.................E4
3 Misión Café..........................C4
4 Toma Café D3

Hotels ▼

1 Only YOU Boutique Hotel H6
2 The Principal Madrid..............H7
3 Room Mate Óscar G6
4 7 Islas Hotel F6
5 URSO Hotel and Spa G3

finest pieces of baroque civil architecture in Spain, so it's a wonder that what lies beyond it flies under the radar of most tourists. Painted fans, period clothing, gleaming china and porcelain, and an exhibit on the Dos de Mayo Uprising are the main attractions, and there are usually a few paintings on loan from the Prado Museum as well. ✉ *Calle de Fuencarral 78, Chueca* ☎ *91/701–1863* 🕒 *Closed Mon.* [M] *Tribunal.*

★ **Museo del Romanticismo** (*Museum of Romanticism*)

MUSEUM | To catch a glimpse of how the Spanish bourgeoisie lived in the early 19th century, step into the this former palace of a marquis. Each room sparkles with ornate period furniture, evocative portraits, and other historical artifacts culled from the height of Spanish Romanticism. It's worth spending a few minutes admiring the flamboyantly decorated fans and backlit lithophanes. Although the museum can be seen in an hour or two, don't rush out: the plant-filled interior patio is a gorgeous, tranquil place to enjoy tea and pastries. ✉ *Calle de San Mateo 13, Chueca* ☎ *91/448–1045* 🌐 *www.culturaydeporte.gob.es/mromanticismo/en/inicio.html* 🕒 *Closed Mon.* [M] *Tribunal.*

🍴 Restaurants

★ **Casa Hortensia Restaurante y Sidrería**

$$ | SPANISH | FAMILY | Approximate a vacation to the north of Spain by dining at this true-blue Asturian restaurant (or at the more casual *sidrería,* located in the bar area), where that region's unsung comfort-food dishes—such as *fabada* (pork-and-bean stew), Cabrales cheese, and *cachopo* (cheese-stuffed beef cutlets)—take center stage. The obligatory tipple is *sidra,* bone-dry Asturian cider that's aerated using a battery-powered gadget designed for this task. **Known for:** authentic fabada; cider bottles with fun DIY aerators; locals-only crowd. [$] *Average main: €19* ✉ *Calle Farmacia 2, 2nd and 3rd fl., Chueca* ✥ *Situated in what appears to be an apartment building* ☎ *91/539–0090* 🌐 *www.casahortensia.com* 🕒 *Closed Mon. No dinner Sun.* [M] *Chueca.*

★ **Casa Salvador**

$$ | SPANISH | Whether you approve of bullfighting or not, the culinary excellence of Casa Salvador—a checkered-tablecloth, taurine-theme restaurant that opened in 1941—isn't up for debate. Sit down to generous servings of feather-light fried hake, hearty oxtail stew, and other stodgy (in the best way) Spanish classics, all served by hale old-school waiters clad in white jackets. **Known for:** time-warpy decor; walls packed with bullfighting paraphernalia; cloud-light fried hake and stewed oxtail. [$] *Average main: €18* ✉ *Calle de Barbieri 12, Chueca* ☎ *91/521–4524* 🌐 *www.casasalvadormadrid.com* 🕒 *Closed Sun.* [M] *Chueca.*

Celso y Manolo

$ | TAPAS | Named after the brothers who founded the restaurant (though under new ownership), this place has around a dozen tables and an extensive, eclectic menu geared toward sharing that hinges on natural products—game meats, seafood, cheeses—from the mountainous northerly region of Cantabria. Natural and often organic wines sourced from around the country make for spot-on pairings. **Known for:** market-driven cuisine; Cantabrian specialties; extremely varied menu. [$] *Average main: €14* ✉ *Calle Libertad 1, Chueca* ☎ *91/531–8079* 🌐 *www.celsoymanolo.es* [M] *Chueca.*

Dspeakeasy

$$$ | SPANISH | Diego Guerrero, the punk rock chef of two-Michelin-star Dstage, opened this more casual outpost in 2019. The menu turns classic Spanish dishes—for example, monkfish in salsa verde, Canarian wrinkly potatoes, stewed *verdinas* (baby favas)—on their heads by adding unorthodox ingredients like seaweed, kimchi, whey, and liquid-nitrogen-frozen fruit, and the result is thrilling.

A quirky wine list heavy on natural and low-yield producers complements the cuisine nicely. Take the stairs one flight down to the cocktail bar for a preprandial personality drink or nightcap. **Known for:** experimental Spanish dining; big-name chef; buzzy subterranean cocktail bar. $ *Average main: €25* ✉ *Calle de Fernando VI 6, Chueca* ☎ *91/319–5435* ⊕ *www.dstageconcept.com* ☾ *Closed Mon. and Tues.* Ⓜ *Tribunal, Alonso Martínez.*

La Tita Rivera
$ | **TAPAS** | This budget-friendly place—specializing in hot stuffed bread rolls (called *casis*) and flavored hard cider—has an industrial vibe, thanks to exposed pipes, high ceilings, and a semiopen kitchen. But the bar's most exceptional asset is its under-the-radar interior patio. **Known for:** stuffed bread rolls; hidden interior patio; flavored draft ciders. $ *Average main: €11* ✉ *Calle Pérez Galdós 4, Chueca* ☎ *91/522–1890* ⊕ *www.latitarivera.com* Ⓜ *Chueca.*

Lettera Trattoria Moderna
$$ | **ITALIAN** | Sicilian chef Francesco Ingargiola re-creates the bold flavors of his childhood—with plenty of fine-dining flourishes—at this inviting ultramodern trattoria opened in 2019 one block from the Gran Vía thoroughfare. Start with an order of crisp arancini (rice fritters), flavored with real saffron and stuffed with pork and mozzarella, before moving on to homemade pastas like grouper tortelli or Madrid's best carbonara. Memorable mains, if a third course is in the cards, include stuffed baby squid and roast rabbit with tomato sauce. **Known for:** regional Italian cooking; unusual homemade pastas; new and trendy. $ *Average main: €18* ✉ *Calle de la Reina 20, Chueca* ☎ *91/805–3342* ⊕ *www.letteramadrid.com* Ⓜ *Gran Vía, Chueca.*

Mercado de la Reina
$$ | **TAPAS** | Perhaps the only worthwhile tapas restaurant on Gran Vía, Madrid's main commercial artery, Mercado de la Reina serves everything from croquetas to grilled vegetables to tossed salads. Enjoy them in the casual bar area, in the slightly more formal dining room, or on the outdoor patio. A downstairs lounge bar with an extensive gin menu accommodates those who want to keep the night rolling. **Known for:** inexpensive eats; the only decent spot on Gran Vía; lounge bar downstairs. $ *Average main: €20* ✉ *Calle Gran Vía 12, Chueca* ☎ *91/521–3198* ⊕ *www.grupomercadodelareina.com* Ⓜ *Banco de España, Gran Vía.*

Roostiq
$$ | **EUROPEAN** | Fire is the secret ingredient at Roostiq, where pizzas sizzle and puff in a wood-burning oven and meat, fish, and vegetables char until tender over white-hot embers. Even the cheesecake is of the Basque "burnt" variety, all brown and caramel-ly on the outside and gooey within. The open-hearth technology may be older than the hills, but the buffed concrete walls, zany ceramic plates, and sturdy wooden and marble tables are unmistakably 2021. **Known for:** open-hearth cooking; Neapolitan-style pizzas; trendy industrial digs. $ *Average main: €18* ✉ *Calle de Augusto Figueroa 47, Chueca* ☎ *91/853–2434* ⊕ *www.roostiqmadrid.com* ☾ *No dinner Sun.* Ⓜ *Chueca.*

Trattoria Pulcinella
$ | **ITALIAN** | **FAMILY** | When Enrico Bosco arrived in Madrid from Italy in the early '90s, he couldn't find a decent Italian restaurant, so he decided to open one. Always bustling and frequented by families and young couples, this trattoria seems like a direct transplant from Naples with its superb fresh pastas, pizzas, and focaccias. (La Cantina di Pulcinella, located across the street, is under the same ownership and serves the same food.) **Known for:** affordable down-home Italian fare; family-friendly vibe; excellent fresh pastas. $ *Average main: €14* ✉ *Calle de Regueros 7, Chueca* ☎ *91/319–7363* ⊕ *www.gruppopulcinella.com* Ⓜ *Chueca.*

The heart of Madrid's LGBTQ community is centered around a neighborhood named after Spanish composer and author Federico Chueca.

Hotels

★ Only YOU Boutique Hotel

$$$$ | HOTEL | The Ibizan owners of this hotel bring that island's mix of glamour, energy, and cutting-edge music and design to one of Madrid's most happening neighborhoods. **Pros:** location among trendy cafés and shops; double-paned glass blocks out street noise; late check-out. **Cons:** sleeping area is a bit cramped; rooms with views of Calle Barquillo are pricey; scant storage space for suitcases. [$] *Rooms from: €260* ✉ *Calle Barquillo 21, Chueca* ☎ *91/005–2222* 🌐 *www.onlyyouhotels.com* 🛏 *70 rooms* 🍴 *No meals* [M] *Chueca.*

The Principal Madrid

$$$$ | HOTEL | Dozens of hotels flank Gran Vía, Madrid's main artery, but only the Principal can claim five stars. **Pros:** hotel rooftop with best views in Madrid; Ramón Freixa–helmed restaurant; luxury feel with personal touches. **Cons:** rooms not properly soundproofed; rooftop pool is tiny; gym doesn't open until 10 am. [$] *Rooms from: €280* ✉ *Calle Marqués de Valdeiglesias 1, Chueca* ☎ *91/521–8743* 🌐 *www.theprincipalmadridhotel.com* 🛏 *76 rooms* 🍴 *No meals* [M] *Chueca.*

★ Room Mate Óscar

$$$ | HOTEL | Boasting one of the swankiest rooftop pools in the heart of Chueca, Madrid's "gayborhood," Room Mate Óscar caters to an artsy crowd. **Pros:** playful design accents; see-and-be-seen clientele; rooftop pool and lounge. **Cons:** noisy street and rooftop; might be too happening for some; pool only open in summer. [$] *Rooms from: €175* ✉ *Pl. Vázquez de Mella 12, Chueca* ☎ *91/701–1173* 🌐 *www.room-matehotels.com* 🛏 *69 rooms* 🍴 *Free breakfast* [M] *Chueca.*

URSO Hotel and Spa

$$$ | HOTEL | Housed in a regal turn-of-the-20th-century municipal building, this luxury hotel and spa boasts old-world luxury and avant-garde design to satisfy alternative types and jet-setters alike. **Pros:** stunning facade; Natura Bissé spa with 7-meter hydromassage pool; sanctuary-like rooms. **Cons:** bar closes at midnight; ground-level rooms are dark and cramped; smallish gym and chilly pool. $\mathbb{S}$ *Rooms from: €202* ✉ *Calle de Mejía Lequerica 8, Chueca* ☎ *91/444–4458* ⊕ *www.hotelurso.com* ⛵ *78 rooms* ⓧ *No meals* Ⓜ *Alonso Martinez.*

Nightlife

Most of Chueca's LGBT-oriented venues—and all of those listed below—are welcoming to customers of all genders and sexual orientations.

BARS

Bar Cock
BARS/PUBS | This classic—if hilariously named—bar (est. 1921) resembles a gentlemen's club with dark-wood interiors and cathedral-like ceilings. It serves a variety of cocktails to an older, business-y crowd. ✉ *Calle de la Reina 16, Chueca* ☎ *91/532–2826* ⊕ *www.barcock.com* Ⓜ *Gran Vía.*

Café Belén
CAFES—NIGHTLIFE | The handful of tables here are rarely empty on weekends, thanks to the candlelit, cozy atmosphere. Expect a young, mixed crowd. Weeknights are more mellow. ✉ *Calle Belén 5, Chueca* ☎ *91/308–2747* ⊕ *www.elcafebelen.com* Ⓜ *Chueca.*

Del Diego
BARS/PUBS | There are no fripperies of modern mixology to be found at Del Diego, and that's just how the dyed-in-the-wool regulars like it. This legendary bar has been pouring flawless classic cocktails like cosmos, dirty martinis, and white Russians since the late 1990s, and *amigos*, you better believe they're all that and a bag of chips. ✉ *Calle de la Reina 12, Chueca* ☎ *91/523–3106* ⊕ *www.deldiego.com* Ⓜ *Gran Vía.*

El Supremo Tribunal de Vinos
WINE BARS—NIGHTLIFE | The newly opened "Supreme Court of Wines" is located across from the highest court in the land and pours only natural and minimum-intervention wines from tiny Spanish producers. *Open weeknights only.* ✉ *Calle del Marqués de la Ensenada 6, Chueca* ☎ *60/068–9124* Ⓜ *Colón.*

La Kama
DANCE CLUBS | If you feel like dancing but don't want to commit to a full-fledged nightclub, pop into La Kama for a garishly garnished *gin-tónic* and endless singalong pop. ✉ *Calle de Gravina 4, Chueca* ☎ *91/522–3226* Ⓜ *Chueca.*

★ Macera Taller Bar
BARS/PUBS | The age-old technique of maceration rules at Macera, where bartenders treat spirits like blank canvases, imbuing them with surprising flavor combinations. Gin, for instance, is steeped with fresh cilantro, lime, and jalapeño until it achieves a grassy piquancy that shocks and pleases the palate all at once. Dark spirits more your speed? Choose a whiskey cocktail infused with almonds, fresh cherries, mint, or vanilla bean. ✉ *Calle San Mateo 21, Chueca* ☎ *91/011–5810* ⊕ *www.maceradrinks.com* Ⓜ *Alonso Martínez, Tribunal.*

Vinoteca Vides
WINE BARS—NIGHTLIFE | This dressed-down wine bar is a great spot to sample rare, boutique bottles at a terrific price. There's a particularly deep selection of grippy Monastrels from the blackhorse wine region of Yecla, in Murcia province. ✉ *Calle Libertad 12, Chueca* ☎ *91/531–8444* ⊕ *www.vinotecavides.es* Ⓜ *Chueca.*

DANCE CLUBS

DLRO Live
DANCE CLUBS | This unpretentious, unapologetically campy bar attracts a motley crew of LGBT+ (but primarily gay male) revelers of all ages and nationalities with its pop and reggaeton music. ✉ *Calle Pelayo 59, Chueca* ☎ *91/319–5302* ⊕ *www.deliriochueca.com* Ⓜ *Chueca.*

Fulanita de Tal

DANCE CLUBS | Chueca's favorite lesbian bar hosts popular concerts and dusk-to-3:30 am dance parties in an intimate, unpretentious space. The music varies night to night and mixes pop, oldies, reggaeton, and electro. ⊠ *Calle de Regueros 9, Chueca* ☎ *91/319–5069* Ⓜ *Alonso Martínez, Chueca.*

★ **Pavoneo**

BARS/PUBS | Tourists have yet to discover Chueca's buzziest new gay bar, which caters to well-dressed creatives, selfie-snapping influencers, and models on their nights off. Bartenders may not know what a Negroni is (even if they have all the requisite ingredients), but their sigh-worthy looks make them easy to forgive. ⊠ *Calle de Belén 9, Chueca* ☎ *64/679–6485* Ⓜ *Chueca.*

MUSIC CLUBS

Café Libertad 8

MUSIC CLUBS | Almost every classic Madrileño songwriter, musician, and poet has passed through this timeworn evenings-only hangout (it opens at 4 pm and entertainment starts at 9 pm). Acoustic guitar concerts are fantastic—and virtually tourist-free. ⊠ *Calle de la Libertad 8, Chueca* ☎ *91/532–1150* ⊕ *www.libertad-8cafe.com* Ⓜ *Chueca.*

Intruso Bar

MUSIC CLUBS | Easy to miss (it's tucked inside a building just a block off Fuencarral), this is one of Chueca's best lounge-bars. There are live DJs and funk and jazz bands almost every night from 9 pm playing for a mostly thirtysomething crowd. ⊠ *Calle Augusto Figueroa 3, Chueca* ⊕ *www.intrusobar.com* ۞ *Closed Mon.* Ⓜ *Chueca.*

Museo Chicote

MUSIC CLUBS | This landmark cocktail bar–lounge is said to have been one of Hemingway's haunts. Much of the interior can be traced back to the 1930s, but modern elements (like the in-house DJ and hordes of international visitors) keep this spot firmly in the present. ⊠ *Gran Vía 12, Chueca* ☎ *91/532–6737* ⊕ *www. grupomercadodelareina.com* ۞ *Closed Sun.* Ⓜ *Gran Vía.*

 Performing Arts

JAZZ CLUBS

El Junco

MUSIC CLUBS | Rising-star talents perform till late at this cozy jazz venue, which occasionally branches out into other music genres. Check the website for upcoming acts and to buy tickets in advance for shows, held nightly Tuesday to Saturday. ⊠ *Pl. de Santa Bárbara 10, Chueca* ☎ *91/734–5678* ⊕ *www.eljunco. com* Ⓜ *Alonso Martínez.*

🛍 **Shopping**

BOUTIQUES AND FASHION

Oteyza

CLOTHING | Every garment sold at master tailor Oteyza takes at least two months to make, and the classic craftsmanship shows in the immaculate suits, jackets, and shirts. Get fitted while you're in Madrid and pony up the euros for shipping—you won't regret it. ⊠ *Calle Conde de Xiquena 11, Chueca* ☎ *91/448–8623* ⊕ *www.deoteyza.com* ۞ *Closed Sun.* Ⓜ *Chueca.*

Nac

CLOTHING | You'll find a broad selection of European designer brands (e.g., Bergamot, Forte Forte, Pomandere, Babo) at Nac. The store on Calle Génova is the biggest of the six in Madrid. ⊠ *Calle de Génova 18, Chamberí* ☎ *91/310–6050* ⊕ *www.nac.es* Ⓜ *Colón, Alonso Martínez.*

Pez

CLOTHING | A favorite among local fashionistas, this store has two branches—one dedicated to high-end women's wear and another to furniture and decor—on the same street. ⊠ *Calle de Regueros 2 and*

15, Chueca ☎ *91/308–6677* ⊕ *www.pez-pez.es* Ⓜ *Chueca.*

Próxima Parada

CLOTHING | The bubbly owner of this womenswear store culls daring, colorful garments from Spanish designers for her devoted (mostly 40-and-above) clientele. ✉ *Calle Conde de Xiquena 9, Chueca* ☎ *91/523–1929* ⊗ *Closed Sun.* Ⓜ *Chueca.*

CERAMICS

Guille García-Hoz

CERAMICS/GLASSWARE | Take home one of this iconic ceramicist's painted plates or gleaming white urns decorated with animal motifs. ✉ *Calle Pelayo 43, Chueca* ☎ *91/308–3149* ⊕ *www.guillegarciahoz. com* ⊗ *Closed Sun.* Ⓜ *Chueca.*

FOOD AND WINE

Poncelet Punto Selecto Quesos

FOOD/CANDY | At this gourmet cheese bar and shop, you can find more than 120 different cheeses from all over Spain as well as some 300 others from France, Portugal, Italy, and the Netherlands. Marmalades, wines, and other assorted cheese accompaniments are available. ✉ *Calle de Argensola 27, Chueca* ☎ *91/308–0221* ⊕ *www.poncelet.es* Ⓜ *Alonso Martínez.*

Malasaña

◉ Sights

Mercado de Los Mostenses

MARKET | Forget the architectural fruit displays and polished tapas stalls of Mercado de San Miguel or Mercado de la Paz—this market's allure is its rough-and-ready atmosphere, neighborhood crowd, and rock-bottom prices. In the morning and late afternoon, you'll spot locals filling their shopping carts with always-fresh meat and produce; from 1:30 to 3 pm, all three floors teem with families and workers on their lunch break scoping out *menú del día* options—choose from Peruvian (Como en Perú), Thai (Wicked

Thai), and classic Madrileño (La Chelito) restaurants, among others. ✉ *Pl. de Los Mostenses, Malasaña* ☎ *91/542–5838* ⊕ *www.mercadolosmostenses.es* ⊗ *Closed Sun.* Ⓜ *Plaza de España, Noviciado.*

★ Palacio de Liria (*Liria Palace*)

HOUSE | In 2019, this working palace belonging to the House of Alba, one of Spain's most powerful noble families, formally opened to the public. Its sumptuous halls and creaky passages are hung with works selected from what many consider to be Spain's finest private art collection—you'll spot Titians, Rubens, Velázquezes, and other instantly recognizable paintings. In the library, Columbus's diaries from his voyage to the so-called New World are on display as well as the first Spanish-language bible and other priceless official documents. The Neoclassical palace was built in the 18th century but was bombed to smithereens during the Spanish Civil War (only the façade survived), its works thankfully safeguarded during the conflict. The Duchess of Alba oversaw the reconstruction of the palace to its precise original specifications. ■ **TIP→ Visits are by tour only, but if online tickets are sold out, try your luck as a walk-in.** ✉ *Calle de la Princesa 20, Malasaña* ☎ *91/230–2200* ⊕ *www.palaciodeliria.com* 🎟 *€14 (includes tour)* Ⓜ *Ventura Rodríguez.*

🍴 Restaurants

Bar La Gloria

$ | **SPANISH** | **FAMILY** | Your reward for overlooking the soulless Ikea furnishings of this family-run dinette is honest home-cooked food served at exceptionally reasonable prices for the neighborhood. Try Cordoban-style *flamenquines* (ham-and-cheese-stuffed pork paupiettes), salmon tartare, or, on Sunday, a downright rave-worthy paella Valenciana. **Known for:** budget weekday prix fixes; Sunday paella; local crowd. $ *Average main: €11* ✉ *Calle del Noviciado*

2, Malasaña ☎ 91/083–1401 🌐 www.barlagloria.es 🕒 Closed Mon. No dinner Sun. [M] Noviciado.

★ Bodega de la Ardosa

$ | **SPANISH** | A 19th-century bodega (wine vendor), with barrel tables and dusty gewgaws hanging from the walls, Bodega de la Ardosa is a welcome anachronism in modern Malasaña. The bar's claim to fame—and the dish Madrileños make special trips for—is its award-winning *tortilla española,* or Spanish omelet, always warm with a runny center. The fried *ortiguillas* (sea anemones) dunked in lemony aioli are the menu's sleeper hit. **Known for:** 100-plus years of history; award-winning tortilla española; draft vermú and unfiltered sherry "en rama". [$] *Average main: €13* ✉ *Calle Colón 13, Malasaña* ☎ *91/521–4979* 🌐 *www.laardosa.es* 💳 *No credit cards* [M] *Tribunal.*

Café Comercial

$$ | **SPANISH** | When this centenary café—one of the oldest in Madrid—shuttered in 2015, ostensibly for good, the public outcry was so great that it inspired Grupo El Escondite (of Lady Madonna, Barbara Ann, and El Escondite) to buy the property and give it a much-needed revamp in 2017. In a dining room that combines original elements (huge mirrors, carved wooden columns) with new high-design fixtures, feast on a menu that's a dance between Café Comercial *clásicos,* including ham croquetas and tuna-topped *ensaladilla rusa* (potato salad), and novel creations by chef Pepe Roch. **Known for:** one of Madrid's first literary cafés; modern menus by Pepe Roch; outstanding seafood rice. [$] *Average main: €18* ✉ *Glorieta de Bilbao 7, Malasaña* ☎ *91/088–2525* 🌐 *www.cafecomercialmadrid.com.*

La Colmada

$ | **TAPAS** | The first thing you'll notice about this teeny seafood-centric tapas bar is its bright blue walls, a nod to the sea. Sure, you could cobble together a full meal from the menu of delectable cheeses, cured sausages, hams, and *conservas* (canned seafood; seek out La Pureza and Ana María brands), but La Colmada is better suited to casual, booze-fueled snacking. Fallen in love with a certain *queso* or chorizo? The staff will happily sell you a goodie bag. **Known for:** top-quality canned food; affordable Spanish wines; jovial atmosphere. [$] *Average main: €10* ✉ *Calle del Espíritu Santo 19, Malasaña* ☎ *91/017–6579* 🌐 *www.lacolmada.com* [M] *Tribunal.*

Selva

$ | **SPANISH** | At this secret local hangout tucked behind Gran Vía and Mercado de los Mostenses, €11 gets you an appetizer, entrée, dessert, and drink—and a free cordial if the old-school waiters like your manners. The menu is a highlight reel of Spanish soul food including *cocido madrileño* (meat and garbanzo stew; served on Wednesdays when it's cold out), *salmorejo* (chilled tomato-garlic soup), kidneys *al Jerez,* Asturian *fabada* (white bean stew), and *huevos rotos* (lacy fried eggs and potatoes). **Known for:** affordable Spanish soul food; old-school atmosphere; hidden gem off Gran Vía. [$] *Average main: €11* ✉ *Pl. de los Mostenses 7, Malasaña* ☎ *91/542–5516* 🕒 *Closed Sun.* [M] *Noviciado, Plaza de España.*

☕ Coffee and Quick Bites

Café de la Luz

$ | **CAFÉ** | The grandmotherly upholstery, fringed lampshades, plush wingback chairs, and wooden bookshelves make Café de la Luz a cozy spot to curl up with a book, catch up with friends, or get some work done. Coffees cost less than €2 apiece, and if you're peckish, there's a good variety of sweets and open-faced sandwiches to sate your appetite. Come evening (closing time is 2 am most nights), the lights get dimmed and coffees turn into cocktails. **Known for:** cheap and cheerful coffees and sandwiches; homey digs; laptops allowed.

$ *Average main: €9* ✉ *Calle de la Puebla 8, Malasaña* ☎ *91/523–1199* Ⓜ *Gran Vía, Tribunal.*

Lolina Vintage Café
$ | CAFÉ | Diverging in spirit from the stuffier baroque-style cafés of the neighborhood, this romantic spot with mismatched vintage furniture attracts an artsy crowd with its free Wi-Fi and assortment of teas, booze, and baked goods. $ *Average main:* ✉ *Calle del Espíritu Santo 9, Malasaña* ☎ *91/523–5859* ⊕ *www. lolinacafe.com* Ⓜ *Tribunal.*

★ Misión Café
$ | CAFÉ | From the owners of Hola Coffee, Madrid's preeminent third-wave coffee shop, comes this uber-trendy, roomier outpost two blocks (yet a world away) from Gran Vía. Beyond the single-origin espressos, cappuccinos, and other classic coffee beverages made from roasted-in-house beans, there are gut-warming chai lattes plus shrubs and (seasonally) coldbrew. Misión quietly makes some of the best pastries in town—try the hand-rolled all-butter croissants, zippy lemon-poppyseed cake, or any other sweets in the ever-rotating dessert case. There are plenty of vegan-friendly options on the breakfast and lunch menu as well. **Known for:** complex brews made with roasted-in-Madrid beans; killer pastries; cool-kid hangout. $ *Average main: €10* ✉ *Calle de los Reyes 5, Malasaña* ☎ *91/064–0059* ⊕ *www.hola.coffee* Ⓜ *Noviciado, Plaza de España.*

★ Toma Café
$ | CAFÉ | The originator of Madrid's third-wave coffee revolution, Toma is a Malasaña institution and a favorite among expats and coffee-geek locals. After satisfying your cold brew, flat white, or pour-over cravings, indulge in any of the delicious open-face *tostas*. Toma opened a second outpost in 2017 off Plaza de Olavide (Chamberí) at Calle Santa Feliciana 5; it's less packed and more conducive to leisurely laptopping. **Known for:** excellent coffee selection; always busy;

local institution. $ *Average main:* ✉ *Calle de la Palma 49, Malasaña* ☎ *91/704–9344* ⊕ *www.tomacafe.es* Ⓜ *Noviciado.*

 Hotels

★ 7 Islas Hotel
$$ | HOTEL | Minimalist industrial design—think polished concrete floors, Edison bulbs, and workbench stools—mixes with eye-popping original art at this trendy, independently owned hotel one block north of Gran Vía. **Pros:** rooms fit for a design magazine photo shoot; cutting-edge bar with "healthy" cocktails; room service with eclectic dishes. **Cons:** no gym, pool, or sauna; bar closes at 11 pm; so-so soundproofing. $ *Rooms from: €142* ✉ *Calle de Valverde 14, Malasaña* ☎ *91/523–4688* ⊕ *www.7islashotel. com* ⟿ *79 rooms* ❍| *No meals* Ⓜ *Gran Vía.*

 Nightlife

BARS
Cazador
BARS/PUBS | You may as well be in Williamsburg or Kreuzberg at this popular and un-campy (mostly) gay bar where a bearded-and-bunned clientele sips cañas and dangerously cheap cocktails before heading out to the discoteca. ✉ *Calle Pozas 7, Malasaña* ☎ *63/997–0916* Ⓜ *Noviciado.*

De Vinos
WINE BARS—NIGHTLIFE | A snug, casual wine bar situated in the artsy Conde Duque area of Malasaña, De Vinos pours hard-to-find wines from regions like Bierzo, Somontano, and—*claro que sí*—Madrid. Cured sausages and Spanish cheeses make fine accompaniments. ✉ *Calle de la Palma 76, Malasaña* ☎ *91/182–3499* Ⓜ *Noviciado.*

1862 Dry Bar
BARS/PUBS | One of Madrid's swankiest and most skilled coctelerías, 1862 Dry Bar shakes and stirs meticulously

prepared cocktails that incorporate sherries and unconventional aromatics. The only snag? On busy nights, drinks take forever to arrive. ✉ *Calle Pez 27, Malasaña* ☎ *60/953–1151* ⊕ *www.1862drybar.com* Ⓜ *Noviciado.*

Fábrica Maravillas

BREWPUBS/BEER GARDENS | This is Madrid's only city-center brewpub; taste fun and funky beers that zany French brewmaster Thierry Hascoët ferments in the "beer lab" a few feet from your barstool. ✉ *Calle de Valverde 29, Malasaña* ☎ *91/521–8753* ⊕ *www.fmaravillas.com* Ⓜ *Gran Vía.*

Santamaría La Coctelería de Al Lado

BARS/PUBS | This cocktail bar mixes vintage design with artsy touches and caters to a laid-back, bohemian crowd. Choose from a variety of not-too-fussy cocktails including one bearing the club's name, made with mixed-berry juice and vodka or gin. ✉ *Calle de la Ballesta 6, Malasaña* ☎ *91/166–0511* Ⓜ *Gran Vía.*

V Manneken

BARS/PUBS | V Manneken is downright debonair. Cut-glass decanters filled with Scotch sit on the marble bar top; gold-framed oil paintings accent the walls; and yellowed, out-of-print books sit on tables for you to thumb through while sipping staunchly classic cocktails like Cream Fizzes, Last Words, and Tom Collinses. ✉ *Calle Marqués de Sta. Ana 30, Malasaña* ☎ *61/564–2480* Ⓜ *Tribunal.*

DANCE CLUBS

★ BarCo

DANCE CLUBS | One of Malasaña's most popular nightclubs, for both its live shows (funk, jazz, and more) and late-night DJ sets, BarCo is a guaranteed good time. Acoustics here are top-notch. ✉ *Calle del Barco 34, Malasaña* ☎ *91/531–7754* ⊕ *www.barcobar.com* Ⓜ *Tribunal.*

Ocho y Medio

DANCE CLUBS | Not for the faint of heart, the booze-fueled pop and techno parties here are frequented by college kids and peak at 4 am. Arrive before 1 am to avoid slow, snaking lines. ✉ *Calle Barceló 11, Malasaña* ☎ *91/541–3500* ⊕ *www.ochoymedioclub.com* ⊙ *Closed Mon.–Wed.* Ⓜ *Tribunal.*

MUSIC CLUBS

Café la Palma

MUSIC CLUBS | There are four different spaces in this divey local favorite: a bar in front, a music venue for intimate concerts (pop, rock, electronic, hip-hop), a chill-out room in the back, and a café in the center room. ✉ *Calle de La Palma 62, Malasaña* ☎ *91/522–5031* ⊕ *www.cafelapalma.com* Ⓜ *Noviciado.*

Tupper Ware

DANCE CLUBS | Throw on a T-shirt and a pair of ripped jeans and fist-pump the night away at this alternative rock and indie bar that blasts throwback cult classics 'til 3 am. ✉ *Corredera Alta de San Pablo 26, Malasaña* ☎ *91/446–4204* Ⓜ *Tribunal.*

 **Performing Arts**

Centro Cultural de Conde Duque

CONCERTS | This massive venue is best known for its summer live music concerts (flamenco, jazz, pop) and has free exhibitions, lectures, and theater performances. The quiet, well-lit library is a good place for studying or working. The wing at the southern end of the complex is dedicated to contemporary art. ✉ *Calle Conde Duque 11, Malasaña* ☎ *91/588–5834* ⊕ *www.condeduquemadrid.es* Ⓜ *Ventura Rodríguez.*

FLAMENCO

★ Teatro Flamenco

CONCERTS | **FAMILY** | Less traditional *tablao* and more modern performance venue, Teatro Flamenco hosts a variety of classical and modern interpretations of flamenco dance and song. Check the website for upcoming acts. ✉ *Calle del Pez 10, Malasaña* ☎ *91/159–2005* ⊕ *www.teatroflamencomadrid.com* Ⓜ *Noviciado.*

Shopping

ART AND DESIGN

Hijo de Epigmenio

CERAMICS/GLASSWARE | Owners Juanma and Rigas travel from village to village to source the stunning artisan ceramics, fabrics, glass, and more on display at this sunlight-filled boutique. Don't miss the Níjar ceramics with their cheery colorful splotches and the Caribbean-blue vases of hand-blown Mallorcan glass. ⊠ *Calle de la Puebla 13, Malasaña* ☎ *91/066–7019* Ⓜ *Gran Vía, Callao.*

La Fiambrera

ART GALLERIES | The polar opposite of your standard stuffy gallery, La Fiambrera sells colorful pop art at affordable prices. There's a small bookshop and café, should your feet need a rest. ⊠ *Calle del Pez 7, Malasaña* ☎ *91/704–6030* ⊕ *www. lafiambrera.net* Ⓜ *Noviciado, Santo Domingo.*

BOOKS

J&J Books and Coffee

BOOKS/STATIONERY | A block off San Bernardo, this is a charming café and bookstore with a good selection of used books in English. They sell bagels, too—a rarity in Madrid. ⊠ *Calle del Espíritu Santo 47, Malasaña* ☎ *91/521–8576* ⊕ *www. jandjbooksandcoffee.com* Ⓜ *Noviciado.*

BOUTIQUES AND FASHION

★ **Antigua Casa Crespo**

SHOES/LUGGAGE/LEATHER GOODS | Alpargatas, or espadrilles, grace the feet of chic beachgoers from Nantucket to Nevis, but Madrileños have been rocking these rope-soled sandals (in some form or another) for at least six centuries. Antigua Casa Crespo opened in 1863 on what was then the outskirts of town, and it remains the city's most legendary *alpargatería*, thanks to the breadth of styles, colors, and patterns on offer. Their wares are still made by hand from esparto grass in Spain. ⊠ *Calle del Divino*

Pastor 29, Malasaña ☎ *91/521–5654* ⊕ *www.antiguacasacrespo.com* ☽ *Closed Sun.* Ⓜ *San Bernardo.*

★ **Aramayo**

CLOTHING | A well-curated selection of vintage threads keeps this boutique packed with cool kids. There's a particularly wide selection of billowy patterned shirts and worn-in Levis. There's another location five minutes away at Calle de Hernán Cortés 14. ■TIP→ **As in all vintage stores, be sure to check garments for stains, tears, and missing buttons before buying.** ⊠ *Corredera Alta de San Pablo 2, Malasaña* ☎ *91/013–4753* Ⓜ *Tribunal.*

Magpie Vintage

CLOTHING | A fashion temple that screams "Movida Madrileña," the '80s countercultural movement that ushered Madrid into the modern era, this vintage store is decked out with wildly patterned skirts and dresses and fluorescent track jackets. ⊠ *Calle Velarde 3, Malasaña* ☎ *91/448–3104* ⊕ *www.magpie.es* Ⓜ *Bilbao.*

Muroexe

SHOES/LUGGAGE/LEATHER GOODS | Try on Muroexe's ultracomfy, streamlined lace-ups that toe the line between sneakers and dress shoes, and you'll likely walk out the door wearing them. The independently owned boutique also sells durable backpacks, slippers, and raincoats. ⊠ *Calle de Fuencarral 67, Malasaña* ☎ *91/046–8383* ⊕ *www.muroexe.com* Ⓜ *Muroexe.*

Natalia Lumbreras

JEWELRY/ACCESSORIES | Splurge on eye-popping hand-painted (and printed) silk scarves at this appointment-only boutique. Lumbreras's handiwork has been sold as far afield as Paris, Tokyo, and New York. ⊠ *Calle San Lorenzo 11, Malasaña* ☎ *63/087–5700* ⊕ *www.natalialumbreras. com* Ⓜ *Tribunal, Alonso Martínez.*

Peseta

JEWELRY/ACCESSORIES | Shop made-in-Spain handbags, backpacks, clutches, totes, and more at this boutique by Asturian seamstress and fashion designer Laura Martínez. Expect splashy, wild patterns in every hue. ✉ *Calle San Vicente Ferrer 8, Madrid* ☎ *91/052–5971* ⊕ *www.peseta.org* Ⓜ *Tribunal.*

Sportivo

CLOTHING | Time to bust out the big bucks—Sportivo is the best menswear boutique in the city with two floors of hand-picked garments by the buzziest designers out of Spain, France, Japan, and beyond. ✉ *Calle Conde Duque 20, Malasaña* ☎ *91/542–5661* ⊕ *www.sportivostore.com.*

FOOD

★ Quesería Cultivo

FOOD/CANDY | This sleek *quesería* with its own on-site "caves" for aging is a cheese lover's paradise. Seek out rare treasures like Torrejón, a raw ashed-rind sheep's cheese from Castile, and snap up a bottle of natural Spanish wine while you're at it. Cultivo is also the brains behind the popular Rocklette grilled cheese stand in Mercado de Vallehermoso (Chamberí). ✉ *Calle Conde Duque 15, Malasaña* ☎ *91/127–3126* ⊕ *www.queseriacultivo.com* Ⓜ *San Bernardo.*

Chapter 6

BARRIO DE LAS LETRAS

Updated by
Benjamin Kemper

👁 Sights	🍴 Restaurants	🛏 Hotels	🛍 Shopping	🍸 Nightlife
★★☆☆☆	★★★★★	★★★★★	★★★★☆	★★★★★

NEIGHBORHOOD SNAPSHOT

TOP EXPERIENCES

■ **Tapas:** Strike out on a tapas crawl in this buzzy, bar-lined neighborhood.

■ **Museo Thyssen-Bornemisza:** Time-travel to different eras of European art through some of the Continent's most prized works.

■ **Plaza de Santa Ana:** Claim a bench or outdoor table on this quintessentially Spanish square.

■ **Nightlife:** Dance until your legs are jelly at a trendy *discoteca*.

■ **Crafts:** Shop for one-of-a-kind artisan wares.

GETTING HERE

Letras is such a small neighborhood that no metro stop falls within its limits, but Sol (Líneas 1, 2, 3), Antón Martín (Línea 1), and Sevilla (Línea 2) are each less than a five-minute walk away. BiciMAD bike-share services the area with docks scattered throughout. Letras falls within the Madrid Central low-emission zone, so check with your car rental agency to see if your particular vehicle is allowed entry.

PLANNING YOUR TIME

Evenings are particularly magical in Letras: traffic-free streets teem with groups of well-dressed Madrileños out for tapas and drinks, outdoor terrazas overflow onto cobblestone plazas, and historical buildings are lit up to reveal dramatic facades. As the night wears on, restaurants close shop and cocktail bars and nightclubs become the center of the action. Dining and nightlife are Letras's main attractions, but don't let that dissuade you from wandering the area by day, when streets are comparatively tranquil, museums like the Thyssen-Bornemisza are open, and restaurants and cafés aren't short on tables.

QUICK BITES

■ **Casa Toni.** The tapas are offal-y good at this pocket-size tasca specializing in variety meats like pig ear (served crackly with spicy bravas sauce) and *zarajos* (lamb intestines wrapped around a stick and fried until crisp, an old-school Madrid snack). ⊠ *Calle de la Cruz 14, Las Letras* Ⓜ *Sol*

■ **Cervecería Alemana.** Fried calamari *a la romana*, made with fresh, ultra-tender squid as opposed to the standard frozen stuff, is the star tapa at this 117-year-old Hemingway hangout. ⊠ *Pl. de Santa Ana 6, Las Letras* ⊕ *www.cerveceriaalemana.com* Ⓜ *Sol*

■ **Chocolat.** Always crisp and never greasy—that's the mark of a well-made churro, and Chocolat's piping-hot baskets always hit the spot. ⊠ *Calle de Santa María 30, Las Letras* ⊕ *www.chocolatmadrid.com* Ⓜ *Antón Martín*

Barrio de las Letras (just "Letras" to locals) is known for its charming balconied buildings and electric restaurant and bar scene. It's named for the writers and playwrights of the Spanish Golden Age who lived here. Once a *castizo* (Madrid jargon for "authentic") part of town, Letras is now packed with well-to-do tourists and Madrid's nouveau riche. In short, it's a *scene.*

Letras is a historical (read: unofficial) neighborhood that technically belongs to the district of Cortes, but Madrileños use its colloquial, more descriptive name. At the heart of the barrio is Plaza de Santa Ana with its noble buildings, iconic theater, and crowded tapas bars, though you'll see more locals wining and dining on and around the pedestrianized Calle de Huertas. As you explore, remember to look down—sidewalks here bear quotes in bronze from the neighborhood's one-time denizens—Quevedo, Góngora, Lope de Vega, and Cervantes, to name a few.

 Sights

CaixaForum

MUSEUM | Swiss architects Jacques Herzog and Pierre de Meuron, who designed London's Tate Modern, converted an early-20th-century power station into a stunning arts complex that arguably turns Madrid's "Golden Triangle" of art museums into a quadrilateral. Belonging to one of the country's wealthiest foundations (La Caixa bank), the structure seems to float above the sloped public plaza, with a tall vertical garden designed by French botanist Patrick Blanc on its northern side contrasting with a geometric rust-color roof. Inside, the soaring exhibition halls display ancient as well as contemporary art including pieces from La Caixa's proprietary collection. The Vilaplana restaurant on the fourth floor has good views. Visits are by online appointment only. ⊠ *Paseo del Prado 36, Barrio de las Letras* ☎ *91/330–7300* ⊕ *www.caixaforum.es* ⊠ *€6* Ⓜ *Estación del Arte.*

Casa Museo Lope de Vega

HOUSE | A contemporary and adversary of Cervantes, Lope de Vega (1562–1635) wrote some 1,800 plays and enjoyed great success during his lifetime. His former home is now a museum with an intimate look into a bygone era: everything from the whale-oil lamps and candles to the well in the tiny garden and the pans used to warm the bedsheets brings you closer to the great dramatist. There is a 35-minute guided tour in English starting every half-hour (reservations required, either by phone or email) that runs through the playwright's professional and personal life—including his lurid love

Sights ▼

Restaurants ▼

Hotels ▼

life—and touches on 17th-century traditions. ✉ *Calle Cervantes 11, Barrio de las Letras* ☎ *91/429–9216* ⊕ *www.casam-useolopedevega.org* 🎫 *Free* ⊗ *Closed Mon.* ☞ *Advance booking by phone or email required* Ⓜ *Antón Martín, Sol.*

★ Museo Thyssen-Bornemisza
MUSEUM | The Thyssen, inaugurated in 1922, occupies the light-filled galleries of the late-18th-century Villahermosa Palace. Its collection of almost 1,000 paintings traces the history of Western art with examples from every important movement, from the 13th-century Italian Gothic through 20th-century American pop art. The works were gathered from the 1920s to the 1980s by Swiss industrialist Baron Hans Heinrich Thyssen-Bornemisza and his father. At the urging of his wife, the baron donated the entire collection to Spain in 1993, and a renovation in 2004 increased the number of paintings on display to include the baroness's personal collection (considered of lesser quality). Critics have described the museum's paintings as the minor works of major artists and the major works of minor artists, but the collection still traces the development of Western humanism as no other in the world.

One highlight is Hans Holbein's *Portrait of Henry VIII* (purchased from the late Princess Diana's grandfather, who used the money to buy a Bugatti sports car). American artists are also well-represented; look for the Gilbert Stuart portrait of George Washington's cook, and note how closely the composition and rendering resemble the artist's famous painting of the Founding Father. Two halls are devoted to the Impressionists and Postimpressionists including Camille Pissarro, Pierre-Auguste Renoir, Claude Monet, Edgar Degas, Vincent van Gogh, and Paul Cézanne. Track down Pissarro's *Saint-Honoré Street in the Afternoon, Effect of Rain* for a jolt of mortality, or Renoir's *Woman with a Parasol in a Garden* for a sense of bucolic beauty lost.

Within 20th-century art, the collection is strong on dynamic German Expressionism with works by Georgia O'Keeffe and Andrew Wyeth along with Edward Hoppers, Francis Bacons, Robert Rauschenbergs, and Roy Lichtensteins. The temporary exhibits can be fascinating and in summer are sometimes open until 11 pm. A rooftop restaurant serving tapas and drinks is open in the summer until past midnight. You can buy tickets to the museum in advance online. ✉ *Paseo del Prado 8, Barrio de las Letras* ☎ *91/369–0151* ⊕ *www.museothyssen.org* 🎫 *€13* Ⓜ *Banco de España.*

Plaza de Santa Ana
PLAZA | This plaza was the heart of the theater district in the 17th century—the Golden Age of Spanish literature—and is now one of Madrid's many thumping nightlife centers. A statue of 17th-century playwright Pedro Calderón de la Barca faces the **Teatro Español,** where other literary legends such as Lope de Vega, Tirso de Molina, Pedro Calderón de la Barca, and Ramón del Valle-Inclán released some of their plays. Opposite the theater, beside the ME by Meliá hotel, is the diminutive **Plaza del Ángel,** with one of Madrid's best jazz clubs, **Café Central. Cervecería Alemana,** a favorite haunt of Hemingway, is on the southeast corner and makes phenomenally tender fried calamari. ✉ *Barrio de las Letras* Ⓜ *Sol, Sevilla.*

🍴 Restaurants

Amano
$$ | **TAPAS** | "A mano" means "by hand" in Spanish, and lest this experimental white-walled tapas and wine bar (opened in 2019) come across as too pretentious, there's an entire section of the menu devoted to finger food. Whet your appetite with one-bite wonders like roasted endive topped with creamy La Peral cheese, horseradish, and a smoked sardine, and then settle in for heftier plates like onion soup garnished

with fresh thyme and translucent shards of jamón ibérico. **Known for:** innovative vegetable-driven tapas; varied wine list with French selections; stylish minimalist interiors. [$] *Average main: €18* ✉ *Pl. de Matute 4, Barrio de las Letras* ☎ *91/527–7970* 🌐 *www.amanomadrid.com* [M] *Antón Martín.*

Casa Alberto

$$ | TAPAS | Enter through the firetruck-red facade of this 194-year-old bar and restaurant and be transported to a typical Spanish tavern of yore. The banged-up tin wash basin, the baroque cash register, the wooden bar shelves and low tables with wooden stools—these details haven't changed in over a century. **Known for:** a living museum of how taverns used to be; traditional tapas; homemade vermouth. [$] *Average main: €18* ✉ *Calle Huertas 18, Barrio de las Letras* ☎ *91/429–9356* 🌐 *www.casaalberto.es* 🕒 *Closed Mon.* [M] *Antón Martín.*

★ Casa González

$ | SPANISH | This gourmet shop (est. 1931) contains a cozy bar where you can sample most of its fare including canned asparagus, charcuterie, anchovies, and a good, well-priced selection of Spanish cheeses and wines. It also serves good, inexpensive breakfasts. **Known for:** wines and cheeses; pickled olives; quaint setting. [$] *Average main:* ✉ *Calle León 12, Barrio de las Letras* ☎ *91/429–5618* 🌐 *www.casagonzalez.es* [M] *Antón Martín.*

Cervecería Cervantes

$ | TAPAS | Cervecería Cervantes is improbably down-to-earth for such a posh, tourist-oriented neighborhood—the kind of place where you throw your olive pits and napkins right onto the floor. Most patrons come for the ice-cold *cañas* (half pints), but if you're peckish, there's a fine menu of Spanish standbys including *pulpo a la gallega* (octopus with potatoes, olive oil, and paprika), *empanada* (tuna pie), and stuffed piquillo peppers. **Known for:** free tapa with beer; diamond in the touristy rough; generous portions of Galician-style octopus. [$] *Average main: €13* ✉ *Pl. de Jesús 7, Barrio de las Letras* ☎ *91/429–6093* 🕒 *No dinner Sun.* [M] *Antón Martín.*

El Barril de las Letras

$$$ | SEAFOOD | Seafood lovers shouldn't miss this modern, rustic-chic marisquería with original wrought-iron columns, white tablecloths, and ample alfresco seating. The sweet griddled prawns from Dénia are always a treat, as is the cloud-like roasted sole and any number of rice dishes. **Known for:** romantic ambience; impeccable seafood; outdoor dining. [$] *Average main: €25* ✉ *Calle de Cervantes 28, Barrio de las Letras* ☎ *91/186–3632* 🌐 *www.barrildelasletras.com* [M] *Antón Martín.*

Gofio

$$$ | FUSION | Savor a rare taste of Canary Island cuisine—with quite a few twists—at this envelope-pushing restaurant helmed by Canarian chef Safe Cruz that bagged a Michelin star in 2019. Dinner might start with olives marinated in green *mojo,* a garlicky cilantro-and-parsley sauce ground in a mortar, and continue with crispy goat tacos or Gomero cheese (smoked tableside) before finishing with *gofio* ice cream, made with the Canarian corn flour from which the restaurant takes its name. **Known for:** Canarian "fusion"; smoky volcanic wines; gorgeous, uncontrived plating. [$] *Average main: €23* ✉ *Calle Lope de Vega 9, Barrio de las Letras* ☎ *91/599–4404* 🌐 *www.gofiorestaurant.com* 🕒 *Closed Mon. and Tues.* [M] *Antón Martín.*

★ La Huerta de Tudela

$$ | SPANISH | Real talk: it can be hard to find a vegetable in Madrid, but in Navarra, the region this restaurant looks to for inspiration, there's never a shortage of asparagus, artichokes, cardoons, piquillo peppers, and other seasonal delicacies. Savor a vegetable-centric tasting menu that hinges on ingredients from the owners' family farm for €39, a steal in this increasingly overpriced neighborhood.

The vertical outdoor garden is a stunning element of the CaixaForum cultural center. The sculpture in front of the building is changed periodically.

Known for: vegetarian- and celiac-friendly cuisine; bottles of wine starting at €15; delectable crispy artichokes. $ *Average main: €22* ✉ *Calle del Prado 15, Barrio de las Letras* ☎ *91/420–4418* ⊕ *www.lahuertadetudela.com* ⊗ *No dinner Sun. or Mon.* Ⓜ *Antón Martín.*

Sua

$$$$ | STEAKHOUSE | Madrid's best modern steak house arrived in 2019 with the opening of Sua ("fire" in Basque), a restaurant dedicated to meats and wild-caught fish cooked over open flame. Occupying a stunning circular indoor courtyard, the restaurant has an ample list of Champagnes, cavas, and bold Spanish reds, fittingly luxurious sidekicks to, say, a 40-day dry-aged sirloin from Galicia or roasted scarlet shrimp plucked from Andalusia's Atlantic coast. **Known for:** flame-licked steaks and seafood; impressive cathedral-like dining room; attentive service. $ *Average main: €30* ✉ *Calle Moratín 22, Barrio de las Letras* ☎ *91/527–7165* ⊕ *eltriciclo.es/sua* ⊗ *Closed Mon. and Tues.* Ⓜ *Antón Martín.*

Taberna de la Dolores

$ | TAPAS | A lively corner bar (est. 1908) with a colorful *trencadís* tiled facade, this is a solid spot for a cold beer and a nosh after visiting the nearby museums. Try the *matrimonio* ("marriage") tapa, which weds a pickled and a cured anchovy on a slice of crusty baguette. **Known for:** affordable, no-nonsense tapas; refreshing cañas; mixed crowd of foreigners and locals. $ *Average main: €12* ✉ *Pl. de Jesús 4, Barrio de las Letras* ☎ *91/429–2243* Ⓜ *Antón Martín.*

★ Taberna La Elisa

$$ | TAPAS | The old-fashioned *azulejo* walls, painted red façade, and squat wooden barstools might fool you into thinking this newcomer is any old tavern, but behind the swinging door, cooks are busy plating novel takes on tapas that you didn't know needed improving. Take the crispy pig ear, doused in the usual spicy brava sauce—it gets an unorthodox hit of freshness from parsley-packed *mojo verde*. **Known for:** flavor-bomb tapas; Andalusian-style digs; trendy

While exploring the side streets that branch off Plaza de Santa Ana, keep an eye out for the various tapas restaurants, art galleries, bookstores, and boutiques that make this neighborhood so authentic.

crowd. $ *Average main: €16* ⊠ *Calle de Santa María 42, Barrio de las Letras* ☎ *91/421–6409* ⊕ *www.eltriciclo.es/la-elisa* ⏱ *Closed Mon.* Ⓜ *Antón Martín.*

Triciclo

$$$ | TAPAS | Triciclo serves inventive Spanish-style *bistronomie*—think baby Asturian favas with mushrooms and seaweed and spot prawn ravioli with saffron and borage. This may be the only restaurant in town that serves raciones in one-third portions as well as half and full ones—ideal for creating your own tasting menu whether at the bar or in the dining room. **Known for:** tapas with a modern twist; top-quality ingredients; excellent service. $ *Average main: €23* ⊠ *Calle Santa María 28, Barrio de las Letras* ☎ *91/024–4798* ⊕ *www.eltriciclo.es* ⏱ *Closed Sun.* Ⓜ *Antón Martín.*

★ Vinoteca Moratín

$$ | SPANISH | You'd be hard-pressed to find a more romantic restaurant than this snug wine bar with a rotating menu of 12-ish dishes and eclectic Spanish wines. Antique wooden tables are tucked among bookshelves and wine cabinets, and fresh flowers grace the entryway and wait stations. **Known for:** Spanish wine list with quirky small-production bottles; seasonal bistro fare; intimate digs. $ *Average main: €17* ⊠ *Calle de Moratín 36, Barrio de las Letras* ☎ *91/127–6085* ⊕ *www.vinotecamoratin.com* ⏱ *Closed Sun. and Mon.* Ⓜ *Antón Martín.*

Hotels

Catalonia Puerta del Sol

$$ | HOTEL | The regal cobblestone corridor leading to the reception desk, the atrium with walls made partly of original granite blocks, and the magnificent main wooden staircase (presided over by a lion statue) reveal this building's 18th-century origins. **Pros:** grand, quiet building; spacious rooms; room service. **Cons:** rather uncharming street; rooms and common areas lack character; smoking permitted in the courtyard. $ *Rooms from: €133* ⊠ *Calle de Atocha 23, Barrio de las Letras*

☎ 91/369–7171 ⊕ www.hoteles-catalo-nia.es ⇲ 63 rooms ⍟ No meals Ⓜ Tirso de Molina.

DoubleTree by Hilton Madrid-Prado
$$$ | HOTEL | Opened in 2017, this Dou-bleTree may appear corporate, but any stuffiness is mitigated by a warm staff eager to help with everything. **Pros:** relax-ing earth-tone accents; excellent in-room amenities; one of the city's best Japa-nese restaurants. **Cons:** no valet parking; dull bar; no sense of place. Ⓢ Rooms from: €224 ✉ Calle de San Agustín 3, Barrio de las Letras ☎ 91/360–0820 ⊕ www.hilton.com ⇲ 61 rooms ⍟ No meals Ⓜ Antón Martín.

Gran Hotel Inglés
$$$$ | HOTEL | This legendary hotel, inaugu-rated in 1853, is the oldest in Madrid—and after a long, painstaking renovation, it reopened in 2018 to great fanfare. **Pros:** one of the city's most iconic hotels; mag-azine-cover-worthy design; all rooms at least 280 square feet. **Cons:** pricey food and beverages; stairs to get to some rooms; occasional weekend street noise. Ⓢ Rooms from: €358 ✉ Calle Echegaray 8, Barrio de las Letras ☎ 91/360–0001 ⊕ www.granhotelingles.com ⇲ 48 rooms ⍟ No meals Ⓜ Sevilla.

Hotel Catalonia Las Cortes
$$$ | HOTEL | A late-18th-century palace formerly owned by the Duke of Noble-jas, this hotel, situated a few yards from Plaza Santa Ana, still bears traces of opulence and grandeur. **Pros:** tastefully decorated rooms; big walk-in showers; gorgeous architectural details. **Cons:** common areas are rather dull; no gym, pool, or spa; no bar. Ⓢ Rooms from: €200 ✉ Calle del Prado 6, Barrio de las Letras ☎ 91/389–6051 ⊕ www.cataloniahotels. com/en/hotel/catalonia-las-cortes ⇲ 74 rooms ⍟ No meals Ⓜ Sevilla, Antón Martín.

Hotel Urban
$$$$ | HOTEL | A five-minute walk from Puerta del Sol, Hotel Urban conveys Madrid's cosmopolitan spirit with its styl-ish mix of Papua New Guinean artifacts and rare designer wares. **Pros:** eclectic, internationally sourced art; rooftop swim-ming pool; award-winning restaurant. **Cons:** some rooms are small, and those near the elevator can be noisy; forgetta-ble gym; no coffee makers in entry-level rooms. Ⓢ Rooms from: €230 ✉ Carrera de San Jerónimo 34, Barrio de las Letras ☎ 91/787–7770 ⊕ www.derbyhotels.com ⇲ 103 rooms ⍟ No meals Ⓜ Sevilla.

★ ME Madrid Reina Victoria
$$$ | HOTEL | In an unbeatable location, this ultramodern hotel bears a few reminders of the era when bullfighters would convene here before setting off to Las Ventas—a few bulls' heads hang in the lounge and some abstract pictures of bullfighting are scattered around, but the old flair has been superseded by cutting-edge amenities. **Pros:** cool, clubby vibe; buzzy restaurant; rooftop bar boasts great views of city. **Cons:** some rooms are cramped; plaza-facing rooms can be noisy; key cards demagnetize easily. Ⓢ Rooms from: €214 ✉ Pl. Santa Ana 14, Barrio de las Letras ☎ 91/531–4500 ⊕ www.melia.com ⇲ 191 rooms ⍟ No meals Ⓜ Sol.

NH Collection Madrid Suecia
$$$ | HOTEL | The building the NH Collec-tion Madrid Suecia occupies was once home to Ernest Hemingway and Che Guevara; today's guests are decidedly tamer, but the retro aesthetic lives on in the hotel's brown velvet couches, towering tropical plants, and suave concierges. **Pros:** renovated rooms; rooftop bar with great views; nine-minute walk from Prado Museum. **Cons:** robes and slippers not provided in entry-level rooms; windowless gym; overpriced res-taurant. Ⓢ Rooms from: €217 ✉ Calle del Marqués de Casa Riera 4, Barrio de las Letras ☎ 91/200–0570 ⊕ www.nh-hotels. com ⇲ 123 rooms ⍟ No meals Ⓜ Banco de España.

NH Collection Paseo del Prado
$$$ | **HOTEL** | In a turn-of-the-20th-century palace overlooking Plaza de Neptuno, this hotel preserves the building's erstwhile grandeur with canopy beds, gold-framed mirrors, and wing chairs. **Pros:** within the Golden Triangle of museums; gym with panoramic views; "lazy Sunday check-out" at 3 pm. **Cons:** need to upgrade to get good views; inconsistent food at Estado Puro; dated decor. [$] *Rooms from: €185* ✉ *Pl. Cánovas del Castillo 4, Barrio de las Letras* ☎ *91/330–2400* 🌐 *www.nh-hoteles.es* 🛏 *115 rooms* 🍴 *No meals* [M] *Banco de España.*

★ **Only YOU Atocha**
$$$ | **HOTEL** | One of the trendiest, most youthful hotels in town, Only YOU Atocha has a swanky high-design lobby, rooftop restaurant, spacious gym, and industrial-chic accommodations. **Pros:** sceney rooftop brunch; interesting pop-ups in the lobby; cutting-edge design. **Cons:** exterior-facing rooms can be noisy; food quality could be better in both restaurants; ugly views of major intersection. [$] *Rooms from: €200* ✉ *Paseo de la Infanta Isabel 13, Barrio de las Letras* ☎ *91/409–7876* 🌐 *www.onlyyouhotels.com* 🛏 *205 rooms* 🍴 *No meals* [M] *Estación del Arte.*

Radisson Blu Hotel, Madrid Prado
$$$ | **HOTEL** | Surprisingly boutique-y for a Radisson, this hotel has a streamlined urban feel that suits its middle-of-it-all location. **Pros:** pool and spa; room service; breakfast from 6:30 am. **Cons:** some standard rooms are rather small; pricey breakfast; middling restaurant. [$] *Rooms from: €205* ✉ *Calle de Moratín 52, Barrio de las Letras* ☎ *91/524–2626* 🌐 *www.radissonblu.com* 🛏 *54 rooms* 🍴 *No meals* [M] *Estación del Arte.*

★ **Room Mate Alba**
$$ | **HOTEL** | The Room Mate chain's fifth and newest hotel in Madrid, opened in 2019, occupies a 17th-century nobleman's home on Letras's most popular pedestrianized street. **Pros:** modern, brand-new property; breakfast 'til a cool noon; perks like gym, bar, and free Wi-Fi portal. **Cons:** standard rooms are small; some street noise in exterior-facing rooms; clashing patterns might be jarring to some. [$] *Rooms from: €158* ✉ *Calle Huertas 16, Barrio de las Letras* ☎ *91/080–6471* 🌐 *www.room-matehotels.com* 🛏 *80 rooms* 🍴 *No meals* [M] *Antón Martín.*

Room Mate Alicia
$$ | **HOTEL** | Room Mate Alicia's all-white lobby with curving walls, backlit ceiling panels, and gilded columns feels a bit early-2000s, but its prime location and competitive rates make up for the questionable aesthetics. **Pros:** good value; brightly colored rooms; laid-back atmosphere. **Cons:** standard rooms are small; zero-privacy bathroom spaces; no restaurant or gym. [$] *Rooms from: €165* ✉ *Calle Prado 2, Barrio de las Letras* ☎ *91/389–6095* 🌐 *www.room-matehoteles.com* 🛏 *34 rooms* 🍴 *No meals* [M] *Sevilla.*

Suite Prado
$$ | **HOTEL** | Popular with Americans, this basic yet comfortable apart-hotel is situated steps from the Prado, the Thyssen-Bornemisza, and Plaza de Santa Ana. It has attractive attic studios on the fourth floor (with sloped, wood-beam ceilings) and larger suites downstairs; all apartments are brightly decorated and have marble bathrooms and basic kitchens. **Pros:** variety of room types; great for families and longer stays; complimentary room-service breakfasts. **Cons:** a bit noisy; dated décor; low ceilings on the top floor. [$] *Rooms from: €150* ✉ *Calle Manuel Fernández y González 10, Barrio de las Letras* ☎ *91/420–2318* 🌐 *www.suiteprado.com* 🛏 *18 apartments* 🍴 *Free breakfast* [M] *Sevilla.*

Urban Sea Atocha 113
$ | **HOTEL** | A metropolitan outpost of the Blue Sea resort chain, Urban Sea Atocha 113 is a basic 36-room hotel just

north of the eponymous railway station. **Pros:** equidistant between Barrio de las Letras and Lavapiés; rooftop terrace with gorgeous views; single rooms ideal for solo travelers. **Cons:** bare-bones services; in-room sinks; exterior rooms facing Calle Atocha are pricey. [$] *Rooms from: €100* ✉ *Calle Atocha 113, Barrio de las Letras* ☎ *91/369–2895* 🌐 *www.blueseahotels.com* 🛏 *36 rooms* 🍴 *No meals* [M] *Estación del Arte.*

Westin Palace

$$$$ | **HOTEL** | An iconic hotel situated inside the "Golden Triangle" (the district connecting the Prado, Reina Sofía, and Thyssen museums), the Westin Palace is known for its unbeatable location, stately facade, and classical decor. **Pros:** historic grand hotel; 24-hour gym with adjoining roof deck; renovated rooms have USB ports and antifog mirrors. **Cons:** standard rooms face a backstreet; daily turndown provided only on request; redesigned areas clash with those that haven't been updated. [$] *Rooms from: €312* ✉ *Pl. de las Cortés 7, Barrio de las Letras* ☎ *91/360–8000* 🌐 *www.palacemadrid.com* 🛏 *467 rooms* 🍴 *No meals* [M] *Banco de España, Sevilla.*

🍸 Nightlife

BARS

La Venencia

WINE BARS—NIGHTLIFE | This dusty sherry-only bar hasn't changed a lick since the Spanish Civil War, from its no-tipping policy to its salty waiters to its chalked bar tabs. The establishment is named for the tool used to extract sherry through the bunghole of a barrel. ⚠ **No photography allowed.** ✉ *Calle de Echegaray 7, Barrio de las Letras* ☎ *91/429–7313* [M] *Sol.*

Radio

CAFES—NIGHTLIFE | This bar in the ME Madrid Reina Victoria is split between a bottom-floor lounge, ideal for after-work martinis, and a more exclusive rooftop terrace with 360-degree views—a boon to chic summer revelers. The doorman planted outside means you shouldn't dress too casual. ✉ *ME Madrid Reina Victoria, Pl. de Santa Ana 14, Barrio de las Letras* ☎ *91/445–6886* 🌐 *www.melia.com* [M] *Antón Martín.*

★ Salmon Guru

BARS/PUBS | Regularly featured on best-of lists, Salmon Guru is Madrid's—and perhaps Spain's—most innovative *coctelería.* Come here to impress your boss or date or to geek out with mixology-loving friends over eye-popping concoctions like the Chipotle Chillón, made with mezcal, absinthe, and chipotle syrup. The nueva cocina tapas are almost as impressive as the drinks. ✉ *Calle de Echegaray 21, Barrio de las Letras* ☎ *91/000–6185* 🌐 *www.salmonguru.es* [M] *Antón Martín.*

Viva Madrid

BARS/PUBS | The Argentine celebrity mixologist behind Salmon Guru (see previous entry) has converted one of Madrid's oldest tabernas, built in 1856, into a see-and-be-seen cocktail hot spot. The building's architectural bones remain, from the carved-wood bar to the arched doorways to the tiled walls, but the rest, particularly the flamboyantly garnished drinks and sceney crowd they attract, feels distinctly current. ✉ *Calle Manuel Fernández y González 7, Barrio de las Letras* ☎ *91/605–9774* [M] *Sevilla, Antón Martín.*

DANCE CLUBS

Azúcar

DANCE CLUBS | Salsa has become a fixture of Madrid nightlife. Even if you don't have the guts to twirl and shake with the pros on the dance floor, you'll be almost as entertained sipping a mojito on the sidelines. Entry with two cocktail vouchers costs €12. ✉ *Calle de Atocha 107, Barrio de las Letras* ☎ *91/429–6208* 🕓 *Closed Sun.–Wed.* [M] *Estación del Arte.*

★ Teatro Kapital

DANCE CLUBS | Easily Madrid's most famous nightclub, Kapital has seven floors—each of which plays a different type of music (spun by top local and international DJs, of course)—plus a small movie theater and rooftop terrace. Dress to impress for this one: no sneakers, shorts, or tanks allowed. VIP tables overlooking the dance floor (approximately €170 for four people) are a worthwhile splurge if you can swing it. ⊠ *Calle Atocha 125, Barrio de las Letras* ☎ *91/420–2906* ⊕ *www.grupo-kapital. com* Ⓜ *Estación del Arte.*

MUSIC CLUBS

★ Café Central

MUSIC CLUBS | Madrid's best-known jazz venue is swanky, and the musicians are often internationally known. Performances are usually 9–11 nightly, and tickets can be bought at the door or online (the latter is advisable if traveling around holiday time). ⊠ *Pl. de Ángel 10, Barrio de las Letras* ☎ *91/369–4143* ⊕ *www.cafecentralmadrid.com* Ⓜ *Antón Martín.*

 # Performing Arts

FLAMENCO

Casa Patas

DANCE | Along with tapas and Andalusian-inflected entrées, this well-known space offers good, authentic flamenco. Prices are more reasonable than elsewhere. Shows are at 10:30 pm Monday to Thursday and at 9 pm and midnight Friday and Saturday. ⊠ *Calle Cañizares 10, Barrio de las Letras* ☎ *91/369–0496* ⊕ *www.casapatas.com* Ⓜ *Antón Martín.*

🛍 Shopping

BOUTIQUES AND FASHION

★ Andrés Gallardo

JEWELRY/ACCESSORIES | Madrid's porcelain whisperer, Gallardo fashions second-hand shards and custom-made porcelain elements into runway-ready jewelry and accessories. ⊠ *Calle Moratín 17, Barrio de las Letras* ☎ *91/053–5352* ⊕ *www.andresgallardo.com* ⦿ *Closed Sun.* Ⓜ *Antón Martín.*

The Concrete

CLOTHING | Fashion designer Fernando García de la Calera is redefining what it means to be a tailor by custom-making garments out of materials usually associated with streetwear such as denim and canvas. His creations are surprisingly affordable for being artisan made. ⊠ *Calle de San Pedro 10, Barrio de las Letras* ☎ *91/242–1803* ⊕ *www.concretemadrid. com* ⦿ *Closed Sun. and Mon.* Ⓜ *Antón Martín.*

Elisa & Eduardo Rivera

CLOTHING | A block off Plaza de Santa Ana, this is the flagship store of two young Spanish designers with clothes and accessories for both men and women. All garments are made by hand in an atelier 40 minutes north of Madrid. Other stores can be found on Calle Sagasta 4 and Calle Clavel 4. ⊠ *Pl. del Ángel 4, Barrio de las Letras* ☎ *91/843–5852* ⊕ *www. eduardorivera.es* Ⓜ *Sol.*

Santacana

JEWELRY/ACCESSORIES | Keep your hands warm—and stylish—during Madrid's chilly winters with a pair of custom handmade gloves by Santacana, a family-run business that's been open since 1896. ⊠ *Calle Huertas 1, Barrio de las Letras* ☎ *91/704–9670* ⊕ *www.santacana.es* Ⓜ *Antón Martín.*

Chapter 7

RETIRO AND SALAMANCA

7

Updated by
Benjamin Kemper

◉ Sights	🍴 Restaurants	🛏 Hotels	🛍 Shopping	🍸 Nightlife
★★★★☆	★★★★☆	★★★★★	★★★★★	★★★☆☆

NEIGHBORHOOD SNAPSHOT

TOP EXPERIENCES

■ **Parque del Buen Retiro:** Walk, jog, or rent a rowboat and bob around the carp-filled *estanque* (pool).

■ **Museo del Prado:** Feast your eyes on some of the world's most iconic and recognizable paintings.

■ **Tapas:** Hop around the bar-lined streets of Ibiza neighborhood and feast on rave-worthy upmarket tapas.

■ **Calle de Serrano:** Swipe your way down this high-end shopping street brimming with boutiques.

■ **Palacio de Cibeles:** Take the elevator to the observation deck for breathtaking views at sunset.

GETTING HERE

The Retiro district takes in such disparate neighborhoods as the noble Paseo del Arte (metro: Banco de España, Línea 2), containing the Prado Museum and Royal Botanical Garden; the well-to-do Ibiza (metro: Ibiza, Línea 9), popular for its tapas bars; the blue-collar Pacífico (metro: Pacífico, Líneas 1, 6), home to the royal tapestry factory; and humbler barrios like Estrella and Adelfas.

Directly above Retiro Park lies Salamanca, a famously posh district whose restaurants and boutiques are concentrated around the following metro stops: Retiro (Línea 2), Serrano (Línea 4), and Velázquez (Línea 4).

PLANNING YOUR TIME

Take the better part of a day to explore, starting at the Prado Museum (allot at least 2 hours) and continuing on to Retiro Park, where a two-hour stroll is enough time to both see the main attractions—the central pond, Palacio de Cristal, and manicured gardens near the Felipe IV Gate—and unwind on a bench. Cross to the park's eastern edge, and you're in the Ibiza neighborhood, an ideal spot for tapas; head north to Calle de Alcalá, and you're in Salamanca, where clothing and jewelry shops intermingle with restaurants both classic and modern.

QUICK BITES

■ **Confitería Rialto.** Rialto's famous *moscovitas*, slightly salty almond-toffee wafers coated in chocolate, are one of Madrid's most delectable—and addictive—confections. ⊠ *Calle de Núñez de Balboa 86, Salamanca* ⊕ *www.moscovitas. com* Ⓜ *Núñez de Balboa*

■ **Oriol Balaguer.** Catalan chef Oriol Balaguer takes chocolates and croissants to new heights at this ritzy *bombonería*, whose attractive treats make phenomenal gifts—or afternoon pick-me-ups. ⊠ *Calle de José Ortega y Gasset 44, Salamanca www.oriolbalaguer. com* Ⓜ *Lista*

■ **Platea Madrid.** This fancy tapas hall, with a variety of grab-and-go stalls and a handful of sit-down concepts by big-name chefs like Ramón Freixa and Ricard Camarena, spans multiple floors and nearly 65,000 square feet. ⊠ *Calle de Goya 5, Salamanca* ⊕ *www.plateamadrid.com* Ⓜ *Colón*

Straighten your tie and zhuzh your hair—you've arrived in the Madrid equivalent of New York's Upper East Side or London's Kensington: a charming, tree-lined playground for the rich complete with luxury apartments, Michelin-starred restaurants, and one of Europe's most scenic parks, Parque del Buen Retiro.

But get off the main shopping streets, and you'll see that these districts are not all glitz and glam. East and south of the park, in Retiro, you'll find upper-middle-class neighborhoods like Ibiza and Pacífico with their fair share of modest apartments and mom-and-pop bars and restaurants. In addition to the eponymously named park, the Retiro district holds the prestigious Museo del Prado, an essential stop on any Madrid itinerary. The sliver of Retiro real estate called Paseo del Arte, sandwiched between the western side of the park and the Paseo del Prado, is where you'll find some of the city's most exclusive and expensive homes.

Salamanca was part of the 19th-century city expansion program called the *Ensanche,* which removed the city walls and created new, gridded neighborhoods. The area was originally intended to provide shelter for the working class, but because of its desirable parkside location, it swiftly became a hot spot for the well-to-do, a legacy that remains as the district contains the most expensive homes per square foot in the country.

Retiro

 Sights

Cuesta de Moyano

PEDESTRIAN MALL | Home to Madrid's permanent book fair since 1925, this famous pedestrian avenue has around 30 wooden stalls filled with new and second-hand books. In addition to being a pleasant street to stroll—it connects the Paseo del Prado avenue near Atocha station with Madrid's Buen Retiro park—this is also a good place to find books which are hard to come by in traditional libraries, such as first editions. ⊠ *Calle Claudio de Moyano, Retiro.*

Estación de Atocha

TRANSPORTATION SITE (AIRPORT/BUS/FERRY/ TRAIN) | Madrid's main train station is a steel-and-glass hangar built in the late 19th century by Alberto Palacio Elissague, who became famous for his work with Ricardo Velázquez in the creation of the Palacio de Cristal (Glass Palace) in Madrid's Parque del Buen Retiro. Today, following renovations by architect Rafael Moneo, the station's main hall resembles

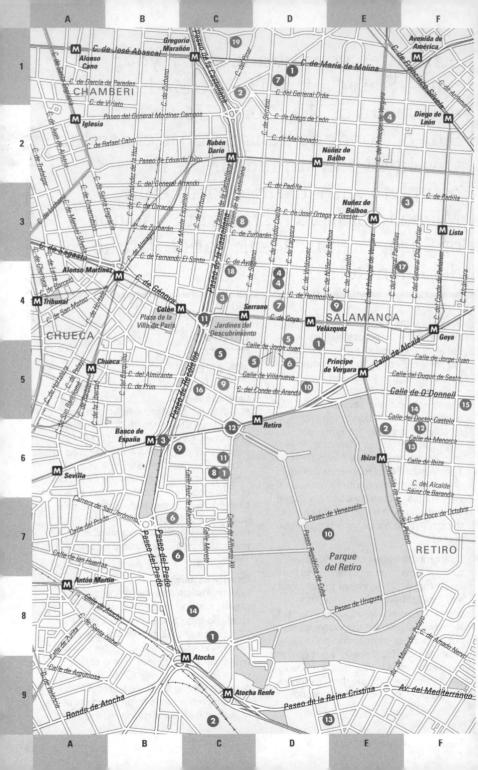

Retiro and Salamanca

Sights ▼

1 Cuesta de Moyano **C8**
2 Estación de Atocha...... **C9**
3 Fuente de Cibeles....... **B6**
4 Mercado de la Paz **D4**
5 Museo Arqueológico Nacional **C5**
6 Museo del Prado **B7**
7 Museo Lázaro Galdiano **D1**
8 Museo Nacional de Artes Decorativas **C6**
9 Palacio de Cibeles...... **B6**
10 Parque del Buen Retiro.............. **D7**
11 Plaza de Colón **C4**
12 Puerta de Alcalá **C6**
13 Real Fábrica de Tapices................... **D9**
14 Real Jardín Botánico....**C8**

Restaurants ▼

1 Álbora................... **D5**
2 Bar Martín................ **E6**
3 Casa Carola **F3**
4 Casa Dani................ **D4**
5 Cinco Jotas Jorge Juan **D5**
6 El Paraguas.............. **D5**
7 El Pescador.............. **G3**
8 El Rincón de Jaén **G3**
9 Estay **E4**
10 Goizeko Wellington..... **D5**
11 Horcher................... **C6**
12 La Castela **F6**
13 La Catapa **F6**
14 La Raquetista............. **F5**
15 La Tasquería............. **F5**
16 Noi........................ **C5**
17 Punto MX................. **E4**
18 Ten Con Ten **C4**
19 Zalacaín.................. **C1**

Quick Bites ▼

1 Religion Specialty Coffee **D1**

Hotels ▼

1 AC Palacio del Retiro....**C6**
2 Barceló Emperatriz......**C1**
3 Gran Meliá Fénix.........**C4**
4 Heritage Madrid Hotel....................... **E2**
5 ICON Wipton by Petit Palace **D5**
6 Mandarin Oriental Ritz Madrid **B7**
7 Tótem Madrid **D4**
8 Villa Magna............... **C3**
9 VP Jardín de Recoletos................. **C5**

KEY

● Sights
● Restaurants
● Quick Bites
● Hotels

Estación de Atocha's covered tropical garden contains 7,000 plants from more than 260 species.

a greenhouse; it's filled with tropical trees and contains a busy turtle pool, a magnet for kids. ⊠ *Paseo de Atocha, Retiro* ☎ *91/243–2323* Ⓜ *Estación del Arte, Atocha RENFE.*

Fuente de Cibeles (*Cybele Fountain*)
FOUNTAIN | The Plaza de Cibeles, where three of Madrid's most affluent districts (Centro, Retiro, and Salamanca) intersect, is both an epicenter of municipal grandeur and a crash course in Spanish architecture. Two palaces, Buenavista and Linares (baroque and baroque revival, respectively), sit on the northerly corners of the plaza and are dwarfed by the ornate Palacio de Cibeles. In the center of the plaza sits one of Madrid's most defining symbols, the Cybele Fountain, a depiction of the Roman goddess of the Earth driving a lion-drawn chariot. During the civil war, patriotic Madrileños risked life and limb to sandbag it as Nationalist aircraft bombed the city. ⊠ *Retiro* Ⓜ *Banco de España.*

★ **Museo del Prado** (*Prado Museum*)
MUSEUM | When the Prado was commissioned by King/Mayor Carlos III, in 1785, it was as a natural science museum. By the time the building was completed in 1819, its purpose had changed to exhibiting the art gathered by Spanish royalty since the time of Ferdinand and Isabella. The Prado's jewels are its works by the nation's three great masters: Goya, Velázquez, and El Greco. The museum also holds masterpieces by Flemish, Dutch, German, French, and Italian artists, collected when their lands were part of the Spanish Empire. The most famous canvas of all, Velázquez's *Las Meninas* (*The Maids of Honor*), combines a self-portrait of the artist with a mirror reflection of the king and queen. Among Goya's early masterpieces are portraits of the family of King Carlos IV; later works include his famous Black Paintings. Other highlights include the *Garden of Earthly Delights* by Hieronymus Bosch and two of El Greco's greatest works, *The Resurrection* and *The Adoration of the Shepherds.* ⊠ *Paseo del Prado, Retiro*

☎ 91/330–2800 ⊕ www.museodelprado. es ✉ €15 (permanent collection free Mon.–Sat. 6–8 pm, Sun. 5–7 pm) Ⓜ Banco de España, Estación del Arte.

Museo Nacional de Artes Decorativas

MUSEUM | This palatial building showcases 70,000 items including textiles, furniture, jewelry, ceramics, glass, crystal, and metalwork. The collection, displayed in chronological order, starts with medieval and Renaissance items on the first floor and ends with 18th- and 19th-century pieces on the top floor. The ground floor, currently holding a tapestry woven by women from 46 countries as a statement against femicide, rotates temporary exhibitions and some avant-garde works. This museum can be seen as part of the Abono Cinco Palacios, a €12 pass that grants access to five mansion-museums. ✉ Montalbán 12, Retiro ☎ 91/532–6499 ⊕ mnartesdecorativas.mcu.es ✉ €3 (free Thurs. after 5, Sun. all day) ⊙ Closed Mon. Ⓜ Retiro.

Palacio de Cibeles (Cybele Palace)

VIEWPOINT | This ornate building on the southeast side of Plaza de la Cibeles, built at the start of the 20th century and formerly called Palacio de Comunicaciones, is a massive stone compound of French, Viennese, and traditional Spanish influences. It first served as the city's main post office and, after renovations, is now an administrative building housing the mayor's office, a cultural center called CentroCentro (a pleasant place to study or work), several exhibition halls, dining options (on the second and sixth floors), and a rooftop lookout. ✉ Pl. de Cibeles, Retiro ☎ 91/480–0008 ⊕ www.centrocentro.org ✉ Free, Mirador Madrid €3 ⊙ Closed Mon. Ⓜ Banco de España.

★ Parque del Buen Retiro (El Retiro)

NATIONAL/STATE PARK | FAMILY | Once the private playground of royalty, Madrid's crowning park is a vast expanse of green encompassing formal gardens, fountains, lakes, exhibition halls, children's play areas, outdoor cafés, and a puppet theater

(shows on Saturday at 1 and on Sunday at 1, 6, and 7). The park, especially lively on weekends, also holds a book fair in May and occasional flamenco concerts in summer. From the entrance at the Puerta de Alcalá, head straight toward the center to find the Estanque (lake), presided over by a grandiose equestrian statue of King Alfonso XII. The 19th-century Palacio de Cristal (Glass Palace) was built to house exotic plants—and, horrifically, actual tribesmen displayed as a "human zoo"—from the Philippines. The Rosaleda (Rose Garden) is bursting with color and heady with floral scents for most of the summer. Madrileños claim that a statue called the Ángel Caído (Fallen Angel) is the only one in the world depicting the Prince of Darkness before his fall from grace. ✉ Puerta de Alcalá, Retiro ✉ Free Ⓜ Retiro.

Puerta de Alcalá

BUILDING | This triumphal arch, today a popular backdrop for photos, was built by Carlos III in 1778 to mark the site of one of the ancient city gates. You can still see numerous bullet and cannonball holes on its exterior, left intentionally as a reminder of Madrid's tumultuous past. ✉ Calle de Alcalá, Retiro Ⓜ Retiro.

Real Fábrica de Tapices

FACTORY | Tired of previous monarchs' dependency on Belgian and Flemish thread mills and craftsmen, King Felipe V decided to establish the Royal Tapestry Factory in Madrid in 1721. It was originally housed near Alonso Martínez and moved to its current location in 1889. Some of Europe's best artists collaborated on the factory's tapestry designs, the most famous of whom was Goya, who produced a number of works on display at the Prado. The factory, the most renowned of its kind in Europe, is still in operation—you can tour the workshop floor and watch weavers at work. They apply traditional weaving techniques from the 18th- and 19th centuries to

Continued on page 117

7

Retiro and Salamanca **RETIRO**

EL PRADO:
MADRID'S BRUSH WITH GREATNESS

One of the world's top museums, the Prado is to Madrid what the Louvre is to Paris, or the Uffizi to Florence: a majestic city landmark and premiere art institution that merits the attention of every traveler who visits the city.

The Prado celebrated its 200th anniversary in 2019, and its unparalleled collection of Spanish paintings (from the Romanesque period to the 19th century—don't expect to find Picassos here) makes it one of the most visited museums in the world. Foreign artists are also well represented—the collection includes masterpieces of European painting such as Hieronymus Bosch's *Garden of Earthly Delights*, *The Annunciation by Fra Angelico*, *Christ Washing the Disciples' Feet* by Tintoretto, and *The Three Graces* by Rubens—but the Prado is best known as home to more paintings by Diego Velázquez and Francisco de Goya than anywhere else.

Originally meant by King Charles III to become a museum of natural history, the Prado nevertheless opened, in 1819, as a sculpture and painting museum under the patronage of his grandchild, King Philip VII. For the first bewildered *madrileños* who crossed the museum's entrance back then, there were only about 300 paintings on display. Today there are more than 3 million visitors a year and 2,000-plus paintings are on display (the whole collection is estimated at about 8,000 canvases, plus 1,000 sculptures).

WHEN TO GO
The best time to visit the Prado is during lunch time, from 1-3, to beat the rush.

HUNGRY?
If your stomach rumbles during your visit, check out the café/restaurant in the foyer of the new building.

CONTACT INFORMATION
✉ Paseo del Prado s/n, 28014 Madrid
☎ (+34) 91 330 2800.
🌐 www.museodelprado.es
Ⓜ Banco de España, Estacíon del Arte

HOURS OF OPERATION
🕐 Mon.–Sat. 10 AM–8 PM, Sun. 10 AM–7 PM, Closed New Year's Day, Fiesta del Trabajo (May 1), and Christmas.

ADMISSION
💶 €15. Free Mon. to Sat. 6 PM–8 PM, Sun. 5 PM-7 PM. To avoid lines, buy tickets in advance online.

The Trinity by El Greco, 1577. Oil on canvas.

THREE GREAT MASTERS

FRANCISCO DE GOYA 1746–1828
Goya's work spans a staggering range of tone, from bucolic to horrific, his idyllic paintings of Spaniards at play and portraits of the family of King Carlos IV contrasting with his dark, disturbing "black paintings." Goya's attraction to the macabre assured him a place in posterity, an ironic statement at the end of a long career in which he served as the official court painter to a succession of Spanish kings, bringing the art of royal portraiture to unknown heights.

Francisco de Goya

Goya found fame in his day as a portraitist, but he is admired by modern audiences for his depictions of the bizarre and the morbid. Beginning as a painter of decorative Rococo figures, he evolved into an artist of great depth in the employ of King Charles IV. The push-pull between Goya's love for his country and his disdain for the enemies of Spain yielded such masterpieces as *Third of May 1808*, painted after the French occupation ended. In the early 19th century, Goya's scandalous *The Naked Maja* brought him before the Spanish Inquisition, whose judgment was to end his tenure as a court painter.

DIEGO VELÁZQUEZ 1599–1660
A native of Seville, Velázquez gained fame at age 24 as court painter to King Philip IV. He developed a lifelike approach to religious art in which both saints and sinners were specific people rather than generic types. The supple brushwork of his ambitious history paintings and portraits was unsurpassed. Several visits to Rome, and his friendship with Rubens, made him the quintessential baroque painter with an international purview.

Diego Velázquez

DOMENIKOS THEOTOKOPOULOS (AKA "EL GRECO") 1541–1614
El Greco's art was one of rapture and devotion, but beyond that his style is almost impossible to categorize. "The Greek" found his way from his native Crete to Spain through Venice; he spent most of his life in Toledo. His twisted, elongated figures imbue both his religious subjects and portraits with a sense of otherworldliness. While his palette and brushstrokes were inspired by Italian Mannerism, his approach to painting was uniquely his own. His inimitable style left few followers.

Domenikos Theotokopoulos

SIX PAINTINGS TO SEE

SATURN DEVOURING ONE OF HIS SONS (1819)
FRANCISCO DE GOYA Y LUCIENTES
In one of fourteen nightmarish "black paintings" executed by Goya to decorate the walls of his home in the later years of his life, the mythological God Kronos, or Saturn, cannibalizes one of his children in order to derail a prophecy that one of them would take over his throne. *Mural transferred to canvas.*

Saturn Devouring One of His Sons

THE GARDEN OF DELIGHTS OR LA PINTURA DEL MADROÑO (1500)
HIËRONYMUS BOSCH
Very little about the small-town environment of the Low Countries where the Roman Catholic Bosch lived in the late Middle Ages can explain his thought-provoking, and downright bizarre, paintings. His depictions of mankind's sins and virtues, and the heavenly rewards or demonic punishments that await us all, have fascinated many generations of viewers. The devout painter has been called a "heretic," and compared to Salvador Dalí for his disturbingly twisted renderings. In this three-panel painting, Adam and Eve are created, mankind celebrates its humanity, and hell awaits the wicked, all within a journey of 152 inches! *Wooden Triptych.*

The Garden of Delights

LAS MENINAS (THE MAIDS OF HONOR) (1656-57)
DIEGO VELÁZQUEZ DE SILVA
Velázquez's masterpiece of spatial perspective occupies pride-of-place in the center of the Spanish baroque galleries. In this complex visual game, *you* are the king and queen of Spain, reflected in a distant hazy mirror as the court painter (Velázquez) pauses in front of his easel to observe your features. The actual subject is the Princess Margarita, heir to the throne in 1656. *Oil on canvas.*

Las Meninas

STILL LIFE (17th Century; no date)
FRANCISCO DE ZURBARÁN
Best known as a painter of contemplative saints, Zurbarán, a native of Extremadura who found success working with Velázquez in Seville, was a peerless observer of beauty in the everyday. His rendering of the surfaces of these homely objects elevates them to the stature of holy relics, urging the viewer to touch them. But the overriding mood is one of serenity and order. *Oil on canvas.*

Still Life

DAVID VICTORIOUS OVER GOLIATH (1599)
MICHELANGELO MERISI (CARAVAGGIO)

Caravaggio used intense contrasts between his dark and light passages (called *chiaroscuro* in Italian) to create drama in his bold baroque paintings. Here, a surprisingly childlike David calmly ties up the severed head of the giant Philistine Goliath, gruesomely featured in the foreground plane of the picture. The astonishing realism of the Italian painter, who was as well known for his tempestuous personal life as for his deftness with a paint brush, had a profound influence on 17th century Spanish art. *Oil on canvas.*

David Victorious over Goliath

THE TRINITY (1577)
DOMENIKOS THEOTOKOPOULOS (EL GRECO)

Soon after arriving in Spain, Domenikos Theotokopoulos created this view of Christ ascending into heaven supported by angels, God the Father, and the Holy Spirit. It was commissioned for the altar of a convent in Toledo. The acid colors recall the Mannerist paintings of Venice, where El Greco was trained, and the distortions of the upward-floating bodies show more gracefulness than the anatomical contortions that characterize his later works. *Oil on canvas.*

The Trinity

PICASSO AND THE PRADO

The Prado contains no modern art, but one of the greatest artists of the 20th century had an important history with the museum. **Pablo Picasso** (1891–1973) served as the director of the Prado during the Spanish civil war, from 1936 to 1939. The Prado was a "phantom museum" in that period, Picasso once noted, since it was closed for most of the war and its collections hidden elsewhere for safety.

Picasso with his wife
Jacqueline Roque

Later that century, the abstract artist's enormous *Guernica* hung briefly on the Prado's walls, returning to Spain from the Museum of Modern Art in 1981. Picasso had stipulated that MoMA give up his anti-war masterpiece after the death of fascist dictator Francisco Franco, and it was displayed at the Prado and the Casón del Buen Retiro until the nearby Reina Sofia was built to house it in 1992.

Picasso in his atelier

modern and classic designs—including Goya's. Prebooking online is required, and all visitors get a tour (English tours at 12:30 pm weekdays). ✉ *Calle de Fuenterrabía 2, Retiro* ☎ *91/434–0550* 🌐 *www.realfabricadetapices.com* 🎟 *€5* 🕒 *Closed weekends and Aug.* [M] *Menéndez Pelayo, Estación del Arte.*

Real Jardín Botánico (*Royal Botanical Garden*)
GARDEN | You don't have to be a horticulturalist to appreciate the breadth of the exotic plant collection here. Opened in 1781 and emblematic of the Age of Enlightenment, this lush Eden of bonsais, orchids, cacti, and more houses more than 5,000 species of living plants and trees in just 20 acres. Its dried specimens number over a million, and many were brought back from exploratory voyages to the New World. ✉ *Pl. de Murillo 2, Retiro* ☎ *91/420–3017* 🌐 *www.rjb.csic.es* 🎟 *€6* [M] *Estación del Arte.*

¡A correr!

Explore Madrid on your morning run but be prepared for hills. The best running spots are the Parque del Buen Retiro—where the main path circles the park (approximately 2½ miles) and others weave under trees and through gardens—and the Parque del Oeste, which has more uneven terrain and fewer people. Casa de Campo is crisscrossed by hilly trails and ideal for distance runners (bring your phone so you don't get lost); same goes for the Madrid Río esplanade and much longer Anillo Verde ("Green Ring"), which you can access by crossing a bridge at the northwest corner of Parque del Oeste.

🍴 Restaurants

Bar Martín
$ | **SPANISH** | This hole-in-the-wall opened in 1940 serves no-frills Castilian classics like *patatas revolconas* (mashed potatoes with paprika and pork rinds), ham croquettes, and meatballs so good they're often gone before the dinner rush. Don't expect to find a seat unless you go at off hours. **Known for:** affordable Spanish bar food; crowds on weekends; outdoor parkside dining. [$] *Average main: €11* ✉ *Av. de Menéndez Pelayo 17, Retiro* ☎ *91/573–1167* [M] *Ibiza.*

Horcher
$$$$ | **GERMAN** | A beacon of old-world Spanish hospitality, Horcher is a Madrid classic with German influences. Wild game—boar, venison, partridge, and duck—is the centerpiece of the menu, which also includes comfort-food classics like ox Stroganoff with a Pommery mustard sauce and pork chops with sauerkraut. **Known for:** wild game dishes; German-inflected wine list; to-die-for baumkuchen (a German-style spit cake). [$] *Average main: €37* ✉ *Calle de Alfonso XII 6, Retiro* ☎ *91/522–0731* 🌐 *www.restaurantehorcher.com* 🕒 *Closed Sun. No lunch Sat.* 👔 *Jacket and tie* [M] *Retiro.*

La Castela
$$ | **TAPAS** | Traditional taverns with tin-top bars, vermouth on tap, and no-nonsense waiters are a dying breed in Madrid, but this one, just a couple of blocks from the Parque del Buen Retiro, has stood the test of time. It's always busy with locals clamoring over plates of sautéed wild mushrooms, anchovies served with a *pipirrana* (chopped cucumber and tomato salad), and clams in white wine. **Known for:** attractively plated tapas; friendly staff; neighborhood crowd. [$] *Average main: €18* ✉ *Calle Doctor Castelo 22, Retiro* ☎ *91/574–0015* 🌐 *restaurantelacastela.com* 🕒 *No dinner Sun.* [M] *Ibiza.*

★ **La Catapa**
$$ | **SPANISH** | La Catapa's tapas are classic but never old hat, inventive but never pretentious. The burst-in-your mouth

The grand Palacio de Cibeles was opened to the public in 2011, so you can now enjoy drinks or dinner with a view on the eighth floor terrace or just chill in the Centro Cultural on the ground floor.

croquetas and garlicky razor clams may lure the crowds, but the hidden gems are in the vegetable section: it's hard to decide between the artichoke *menestra* with crisped jamón, ultracreamy salmorejo (gazpacho's richer, more garlicky sibling), and umami-packed seared mushrooms. **Known for:** elevated tapas; decadent cream-filled pastry "cigars"; a Retiro institution. $ *Average main: €18* ⊠ *Calle Menorca 14, Retiro* ☎ *68/614–3823* ⊘ *Closed Sun. and Mon.* Ⓜ *Ibiza.*

La Raquetista

$$ | FUSION | A relative newcomer on Retiro's traditional tapas scene, La Raquetista has been turning heads with its *nueva cocina* dishes since opening in 2015. Book a seat in the snug five-table dining room or post up at the bar, and get ready to be wowed by palate-bending plates like tuna "pastrami," Segovian suckling pig tacos, and stewed chickpeas with foie and botifarra sausage. **Known for:** eye-popping fusion tapas; to-die-for torreznos (fried pork rinds); unusual Spanish wines. $ *Average main: €21* ⊠ *Calle del Dr. Castelo 19, Retiro* ☎ *91/831–1842* ⊕ *www.laraquetista.com* ⊘ *No dinner Sun.* Ⓜ *Ibiza.*

Hotels

AC Palacio del Retiro

$$$$ | HOTEL | A palatial early-20th-century building, once owned by a noble family with extravagant habits (the elevator carried their horses up and down from the rooftop exercise ring), this spectacular hotel shows that mixing classical and modern décor can work when done right. **Pros:** spacious, stylish rooms; within walking distance of the Prado; bathrooms stocked with all sorts of complimentary products. **Cons:** pricey breakfast; lower rooms facing the park can get noisy; cumbersome room keys. $ *Rooms from: €300* ⊠ *Calle de Alfonso XII 14, Retiro* ☎ *91/523–7460* ⊕ *www.ac-hotels.com* ⊅ *58 rooms* ⦵ *No meals* Ⓜ *Retiro.*

Performing Arts Tickets

As Madrid's reputation as a vibrant, contemporary arts center has grown, artists and performers have been arriving in droves. Consult the online listings and Friday city-guide supplements in any of the leading newspapers—*El País, El Mundo,* or *ABC*—all of which are fairly easy to understand, even if you don't read much Spanish. Websites such as 🌐 *www.guiadelocio.com* and 🌐 *www.timeout.es* are also useful.

El Corte Inglés You can buy tickets for major concerts online. ☎ *90/240–0222* 🌐 *www.elcorteingles.es/entradas.*

Entradas.com This website sells tickets for musicals and big-name concerts. ☎ *90/222–1622* 🌐 *www.entradas.com.*

Ticketea ☎ *90/204–4226* 🌐 *www.ticketea.com.*

Mandarin Oriental Ritz Madrid
$$$$ | **HOTEL** | A €99-million renovation by Mandarin Oriental, completed in 2020, brought new life to an aging historical hotel overlooking the Prado Museum, replacing heavy Victorian drapes, wingback chairs, and red carpets with muted whites and beiges with gold accents and minimalist contemporary art. **Pros:** celebrity chef restaurant; newly renovated; Prado- and Retiro-side location. **Cons:** new interiors lack Spanish art and antiques; steep prices year round; chain hotel blandness. [$] *Rooms from: €300* ✉ *Pl. de la Lealtad 5, Retiro* ☎ *91/701–6767* 🌐 *www.mandarinoriental.com* 🛏 *153 rooms* 🍴 *No meals* [M] *Banco de España.*

🍸 Nightlife

BARS

Florida Retiro
BARS/PUBS | Retiro Park became a nightlife destination in 2016 with the opening of Florida Retiro, a see-and-be-seen leisure complex with six separate spaces: El Pabellón, a white-tablecloth restaurant; La Galería, an informal tapas bar; La Terraza, a chic rooftop terrace; Los Kioscos, an indoor-outdoor bar with live music; La Cúpula, a cocktail bar open late; and La Sala, a tony nightclub that heats up on weekends. ✉ *Parque del Buen Retiro, Paseo de la República Dominicana 1, Retiro* ☎ *91/827–5275* 🌐 *www.floridaretiro.com* [M] *Ibiza.*

🛍 Shopping

Qava de Quesos por Martín Afinador
FOOD/CANDY | Finally Ibiza has a cheese shop of the same caliber as its cult tapas bars. Featuring exclusively Spanish cheeses from small producers, Qava (est. 2018) doesn't just source and sell killer *quesos* that make great gifts—it also ages each wheel to perfection in on-site "caves." Sample them in an eight-table tasting area alongside carefully selected wines. The 11 pm closing time means you can work Qava into a tapas crawl or—if you're feeling European—make it a final dessert stop. ✉ *Calle del Dr. Castelo 34, Retiro* ☎ *91/853–2853* 🌐 *www.qavadequesos.com* [M] *Ibiza, O'Donnell.*

Salamanca

Sights

Mercado de la Paz

MARKET | Salamanca's gleaming high-end market is a hangar-like food emporium hawking everything from wild game to Calanda peaches to sashimi-grade tuna to the finest *jamón* and canned seafood money can buy. There are a number of standout restaurants here including Casa Dani (for Spanish omelet), La Despensa (for Venezuelan arepas), and Matteo Cucina Italiana (for homemade pastas and risotto). ✉ *Calle Ayala 28, Salamanca* ☎ *91/435–0743* 🌐 *www.mercadodelapaz.com* 🕓 *Closed Sun., Sat. after 4 pm* [M] *Serrano.*

Museo Arqueológico Nacional (*Museum of Archaeology*)

MUSEUM | This museum boasts three large floors filled with Spanish relics, artifacts, and treasures ranging from ancient history to the 19th century. Among the highlights are *La Dama de Elche* , the bust of a wealthy 5th-century-BC Iberian woman (notice that her headgear vaguely resembles the mantillas and hair combs still associated with traditional Spanish dress); the ancient Visigothic votive crowns discovered in 1859 near Toledo, believed to date back to the 7th century; and the medieval ivory crucifix of Ferdinand and Sancha. There is also a replica of the early cave paintings in Altamira (access to the real thing, in Cantabria Province, is highly restricted). ■ **TIP→ Consider getting the multimedia guide offering select itineraries to make your visit more manageable.** ✉ *Calle de Serrano 13, Salamanca* ☎ *91/577–7912* 🌐 *www.man.es* 🎫 *€3 (free Sat. after 2 and Sun. before 2)* 🕓 *Closed Mon.* [M] *Colón, Serrano.*

Museo Lázaro Galdiano

MUSEUM | This stately mansion of writer and editor José Lázaro Galdiano (1862–1947) is a 10-minute walk across the Castellana from Museo Sorolla. Its remarkable collection spans five centuries of Spanish, Flemish, English, and Italian art. Bosch's *St. John the Baptist* and a number of Goyas are highlights with El Greco's *San Francisco de Assisi* and Zurbarán's *San Diego de Alcalá* close behind. This museum can be seen as part of the Abono Cinco Palacios, a €12 pass that grants access to five local mansion-museums. ✉ *Calle de Serrano 122, Salamanca* ☎ *91/561–6084* 🌐 *www.flg.es* 🎫 *€7 (free last hr)* 🕓 *Closed Mon.* [M] *Gregorio Marañón.*

Plaza de Colón

PLAZA | Named for Christopher Columbus, this plaza surrounds a statue of the explorer (identical to the one in Barcelona's port) looking west from a high tower. Beyond Plaza de Colón is **Calle de Serrano,** the city's premier shopping street (think Gucci, Prada, and Loewe). Stroll in either direction on Serrano for some window-shopping. ✉ *Salamanca* [M] *Colón.*

Restaurants

Álbora

$$$ | **TAPAS** | The owners of this award-winning restaurant also produce cured hams and top-notch canned foods, and these ingredients feature prominently on a menu that manages to be both traditional and creative—unlike the decor, which feels stuck in the early 2000s. There's a tony tapas bar on the street level, ideal for cocktails and quick bites (don't miss the plump Ibérico pork-filled ravioli swimming in *jamón* jus), and a refined tasting-menu restaurant on the second floor. **Known for:** top-quality charcutería; experimental Spanish cuisine; well-heeled clientele. [$] *Average main: €25* ✉ *Calle de Jorge Juan 33, Salamanca* ☎ *91/781–6197* 🌐 *www.*

The Puerta de Alcalá (Door of Alcalá) was once one of the five doors used to enter the walled city of Madrid when travelers visited from France, Aragón, and Catalonia.

restaurantealbora.com ⊙ *No dinner Sun.* Ⓜ *Velázquez.*

Casa Carola

$$$$ | SPANISH | *Cocido madrileño,* Madrid's quintessential boiled dinner of rich consommé, butter-soft chickpeas, and some half-dozen cuts of meat, is the must-order item at this Salamanca institution, especially in the winter, when temperatures plummet. The wooden straight-back chairs, kitschy cotton bibs, and walls hung with black-and-white photos belie the fact that the lunch-only restaurant opened just two decades ago, but one taste of its famous cocido, and you might as well be at an abuela's kitchen table. **Known for:** cocido madrileño served in three courses; old-timey interiors; warm service. Ⓢ *Average main:* €29 ✉ *Calle de Padilla 54, Salamanca* ☎ *91/401–9408* ⊕ *www.casacarola.com* ⊙ *No dinner* Ⓜ *Lista.*

★ Casa Dani

$ | SPANISH | Casa Dani is a legendary no-frills bar in Mercado de la Paz, the neighborhood's famed traditional market. What's all the fuss about? *Tortilla de patata, amigos*—easily the best in town, and perhaps the country, if first place in the "National Spanish Omelet Championship" of 2019 is any indication. **Known for:** world's best tortilla española; value prix-fixe lunch; long lines that are worth the wait. Ⓢ *Average main: €12* ✉ *Calle de Ayala 28, Salamanca* ☎ *91/575–5925* ⊕ *www.casadanimadrid.blogspot.com* ⊙ *Closed Sun. No dinner* Ⓜ *Serrano.*

Cinco Jotas Jorge Juan

$$$ | TAPAS | Cinco Jotas Ibérico ham is a sight to behold, translucent and shimmering like shards of red-stained glass, a shade darker than prosciutto and twice as fragrant. That's because this famous producer uses only 100% purebred, acorn-fed Iberian hogs. **Known for:** the Rolls Royce of jamón; ritzy white-tablecloth patio; Ibérico pork dishes. Ⓢ *Average main: €26* ✉ *Calle Puigcerdà, Local 2, Salamanca* ☎ *91/575–4125* ⊕ *www. cincojotas.es* Ⓜ *Serrano.*

★ El Paraguas

$$$$ | SPANISH | Step into a low-ceiling dining room appointed with plush armchairs, starched white tablecloths, and colorful bouquets, and feast on refined Asturian dishes like sea urchin gratin, morels stuffed with truffles and foie gras, pheasant with braised green beans, and suckling lamb confit. Weather permitting, request a patio table to watch Madrid's one percent parade down Calle Jorge Juan. **Known for:** haute Asturian cuisine; romantic dining room and terrace; fantastic seafood. $ *Average main: €30* ✉ *Calle Jorge Juan 16, Salamanca* ☎ *91/431–5950* ⊕ *www.elparaguas.com* ☾ *No dinner Sun.* Ⓜ *Serrano.*

El Pescador

$$$ | SEAFOOD | Owned by the proprietors of one of the best fish markets in town, Pescaderías Coruñesas, this seafood restaurant with a warm, modern interior welcomes guests with an impressive window display of fresh seafood—red and white prawns, Kumamoto oysters, goose barnacles, and the renowned Galician Carril clams are just some of what you might see. Fish (including turbot, sole, grouper, and sea bass) is cooked to each customer's liking in the oven, on the grill, in a pan with garlic, or battered and fried. **Known for:** extravagant seafood displays; dayboat fish; crisp Albariño. $ *Average main: €25* ✉ *Calle de José Ortega y Gasset 75, Salamanca* ☎ *91/402–1290* ⊕ *www.marisqueri-aelpescador.net* ☾ *Closed Sun.* Ⓜ *Lista, Núñez de Balboa.*

El Rincón de Jaén

$$ | SPANISH | FAMILY | An Andalusian-style taberna, El Rincón de Jaén evokes the raucous energy and down-home cuisine of that sunny region. Start with the *pescaíto frito,* a mix of seafood that's lightly fried and served with lemon halves, before moving on to more substantial dishes like the peeled tomato salad topped with oil-cured tuna belly (easily one of the best salads in town) and whole roasted fish and braised meats. **Known for:** Andalusian joie de vivre; tomato and tuna salad; complimentary tapas with drinks. $ *Average main: €22* ✉ *Calle Don Ramón de la Cruz 88, Salamanca* ☎ *91/401–6334* ⊕ *www.elrincondejaen. es* Ⓜ *Lista.*

Estay

$$ | SPANISH | This is a quintessential Salamanca bar-restaurant: a spacious, tranquil establishment presided over by white-jacketed waitstaff that makes fine breakfasts (choose from *pan con tomate,* toast with jam, or a griddled all-butter croissant plus coffee) for €3 and filling prix-fixe lunches on weekdays. The interiors got a makeover in 2016, but the unassuming elegance of Estay was retained. **Known for:** runny tortilla española; weekday prix fixe; preppy Salamanca atmosphere. $ *Average main: €20* ✉ *Calle de Hermosilla 46, Salamanca* ☎ *91/578–0470* ⊕ *www.estayrestau-rante.com* ☾ *Closed Sun.* Ⓜ *Velázquez.*

Goizeko Wellington

$$$ | SPANISH | Aware of the sophisticated palate of Spain's new generation of diners, the owners of Goizeko Kabi (a terrific restaurant in its own right) opened this more modern outpost, which shares the virtues of its kin but none of its stuffiness—think neutral tones, bright wood paneling, and personable service. Stars of the menu include Basque staples like *bacalao al pil pil* (cod in an oil and garlic sauce) and Bilbao-style baked spider crab. **Known for:** elevated Basque cuisine; simply perfect seafood; elegant atmosphere. $ *Average main: €27* ✉ *Hotel Wellington, Calle de Villanueva 34, Salamanca* ☎ *91/577–6026* ⊕ *www. goizekogaztelupe.com* ☾ *Closed Sun.* Ⓜ *Retiro, Príncipe de Vergara.*

La Tasquería

$$ | TAPAS | Ever since La Tasquería opened in 2015, its exposed-brick dining room has been drawing restaurant industry pros and food writers with its bold menu revolving around off cuts like liver, kidneys, tripe, and tongue—one-time staples of the Spanish diet that fell out of favor but are now getting a modern makeover. Even the squeamish shouldn't think twice about ordering objectively delectable dishes like lamb necks with corn and huitlacoche and brain-and-potato omelet. **Known for:** offal everything; good-value €55 tasting menu; craft beers and sherries. $ *Average main: €16* ⊠ *Calle Duque de Sesto 48, Salamanca* ☎ *91/451–1000* ⊕ *www.latasqueria.com* Ⓜ *Príncipe de Vergara.*

Noi

$$$ | **MODERN ITALIAN** | Hand-rolled pastas, craveable vegetable dishes, and reimagined Italian classics keep Salamanca prepsters pouring into this newcomer night after night since opening in 2019. Wow your date, boss—or simply your hungry self—with dishes like leeks and cockles swimming in saffron cream, tagliatelle tossed in arugula ragù, and crunchy broccoli and beef lasagna. **Known for:** inventive Italian cooking; Salamanca hot spot; colorful Instagram-ready interiors. $ *Average main: €23* ⊠ *Calle de Recoletos 6, Salamanca* ☎ *91/069–4007* ⊕ *www.restaurantenoi.com* Ⓜ *Banco de España, Retiro.*

Punto MX

$$$$ | **MEXICAN** | The first Mexican restaurant in Europe to land a Michelin star, and certainly the premier Mexican restaurant in Spain, Roberto Ruiz's Punto MX draws on Spanish ingredients and international techniques to redefine Mexican food with dishes like nopal "ceviche," Ibérico pork tacos, and squab mole. If you can't snag a reservation in the dining room, book a more casual experience in the Mezcal Lab bar area. **Known for:** award-winning Mexican restaurant; real-deal Oaxacan moles; Spanish twists on Mexican classics. $ *Average main: €38* ⊠ *Calle de General Pardiñas 40, Salamanca* ☎ *91/402–2226* ⊙ *Closed Sun. and Mon.* Ⓜ *Lista.*

★ Ten Con Ten

$$$ | **SPANISH** | This is one of the "gin bars" that started the Spanish gin-tónic craze of the late aughts, and though perhaps not as avant-garde as it once was, the quality of food and drinks at Ten Con Ten is consistently excellent. Grab a cocktail at one of the wooden high-tops in the bar area, or sit down for a soup-to-nuts dinner in the classy dining room at the back—just remember to book a table weeks, if not months, in advance. **Known for:** expertly made gin-tónics; memorable gastro-bar fare; hand-cut jamón ibérico. $ *Average main: €24* ⊠ *Calle de Ayala 6, Salamanca* ☎ *91/575–9254* ⊕ *www.restauranteenconten.com* Ⓜ *Serrano.*

Zalacaín

$$$$ | **BASQUE** | This newly renovated restaurant, which in its heyday held three Michelin stars, introduced nouvelle Basque cuisine to Spain in the 1970s and has long been a Madrid classic. It's particularly known for its signature steak tartare with *pommes soufflés* (puffed potatoes) prepared tableside as well as other meticulously prepared, French-inflected dishes *de la vieja escuela. ¡Ojo!* Zalacaín is back with a vengeance and ready for its close-up. **Known for:** old-guard Spanish fine dining; revamped interiors and menus; unbeatable "materia prima". $ *Average main: €40* ⊠ *Calle Álvarez de Baena 4, Salamanca* ☎ *91/561–4840* ⊕ *www.restaurantezalacain.com* ⊙ *Closed Sun., Easter wk, and Aug. No lunch Sat.* 🔒 *Jacket and tie* Ⓜ *Gregorio Marañón.*

☕ Coffee and Quick Bites

Religion Specialty Coffee

$ | **CAFÉ** | After browsing the art collection at Museo Lázaro Galdiano, walk north a block to reach this charming café ideally suited to working and leisurely schmoozing, On the menu there are sandwiches, chia bowls, smoothies, and pastries in addition to teas and the usual coffee

Barrio de Salamanca is Madrid's most stylish district, with gorgeous buildings housing the usual designer suspects like Chanel and Hermes as well as High Street standbys like Muji and Zara.

drinks. The handful of wooden tables fill up fast at brunch on weekends. **Known for:** affordable brunch; well-made coffees and teas; laptop-friendly. [$] *Average main: €9* ✉ *Calle de María de Molina 24, Salamanca* ☎ *91/069–8221* 🌐 *www.religioncoffee.es* [M] *Gregorio Marañón.*

Hotels

Barceló Emperatriz

$$$ | **HOTEL** | Worthy of an empress as its name implies, this sumptuous property on a tree-shaded block opened in 2016 and offers knowledgeable concierge services, healthy breakfast options (tahini toast! spirulina omelets!), an updated gym, and an extensive pillow menu. **Pros:** private terraces; king-size beds and in-room hot tubs; portable Wi-Fi hot spot. **Cons:** cramped lobby; 10-minute taxi from center of town; small pool and gym. [$] *Rooms from: €181* ✉ *Calle de López de Hoyos 4, Salamanca* ☎ *91/342–2490* 🌐 *www.barcelo.com* 🛏 *146 rooms* 🍴 *No meals* [M] *Núñez de Balboa.*

Gran Meliá Fénix

$$$$ | **HOTEL** | A Madrid institution that has played host to the likes of the Beatles, Cary Grant, and Rita Hayworth, this hotel is a mere hop from the posh shops of Calle Serrano. **Pros:** close to shopping; great breakfast buffet; opulent, spacious rooms. **Cons:** small bathrooms; below-average restaurant; elitist VIP policy that excludes standard-room guests from certain areas. [$] *Rooms from: €230* ✉ *Calle de Hermosilla 2, Salamanca* ☎ *91/431–6700* 🌐 *www.melia.com* 🛏 *225 rooms* 🍴 *No meals* [M] *Colón.*

Heritage Madrid Hotel

$$$$ | **HOTEL** | Hotel Orfila's new stylish sibling, the Relais & Château Heritage lies north of Salamanca's commercial hubbub in a stately residential area. **Pros:** standout old-meets-new furnishings; secret rooftop bar and terrace; Mario Sandoval-run restaurant. **Cons:** far from most sights; no gym, pool, or sauna; not the most family-friendly. [$] *Rooms from: €320* ✉ *Calle de Diego de León 43, Salamanca* ☎ *91/088–7070*

www.heritagemadridhotel.com 🗗 46 rooms ❙⊙❙ No meals Ⓜ Avenida de América.

ICON Wipton by Petit Palace

$$$ | HOTEL | Whites, grays, and dark woods define this boutique newcomer (opened in 2018) situated on Salamanca's most opulent street, Jorge Juan. **Pros:** calming atmosphere; location on main dining and nightlife street; standout breakfasts. **Cons:** entry-level rooms are a tight fit; noise travels from ground-floor bar; small desks in guest rooms. Ⓢ Rooms from: €195 ⊠ Calle de Jorge Juan 17, Salamanca 🕿 91/435–5411 ⊕ www.iconwipton.com 🗗 61 rooms ❙⊙❙ No meals Ⓜ Serrano, Velázquez.

★ Tótem Madrid

$$$ | HOTEL | A welcome ultramodern addition to the Madrid hotel scene, particularly in this notoriously stuffy part of town, Tótem checks all the boxes: genial service, state-of-the-art design, sought-after location, terrific food and cocktails—you name it, they've got it. **Pros:** charming tree-lined block; excellent cocktail bar and restaurant; stylish and contemporary. **Cons:** many attractions not within walking distance; slightly stodgy neighborhood; interior rooms not as pleasant. Ⓢ Rooms from: €200 ⊠ Calle Hermosilla 23, Salamanca 🕿 91/426–0035 ⊕ www.totem-madrid.com 🗗 64 rooms ❙⊙❙ No meals Ⓜ Serrano.

★ Villa Magna

$$$$ | HOTEL | If the Mandarin Oriental Ritz caters to old-money Madrid, then Villa Magna, located on the shady Castellana mall, is its low-profile, new-money counterpart, frequented by celebrities, foreign financiers, and other high-society types. **Pros:** exceptional service; arguably the best breakfast in Madrid; sleek new spa unveiled in 2019. **Cons:** expensive room service; the exterior is a little dull; overlooks traffic-packed thoroughfare. Ⓢ Rooms from: €415 ⊠ Paseo de la Castellana 22, Salamanca 🕿 91/587–1234

www.hotelvillamagna.es 🗗 150 rooms ❙⊙❙ No meals Ⓜ Rubén Darío.

VP Jardín de Recoletos

$$$ | HOTEL | FAMILY | This boutique apart-hotel offers great value on a quiet street just a couple of blocks from Retiro Park, the Prado, and Madrid's main shopping area. **Pros:** spacious rooms with kitchens; good restaurant; periodic deals on the hotel's website. **Cons:** the garden closes at midnight and can be noisy; could use a redesign; breakfast not served in the garden. Ⓢ Rooms from: €185 ⊠ Calle Gil de Santivañes 6, Salamanca 🕿 91/781–1640 ⊕ www. recoletos-hotel.com 🗗 43 rooms ❙⊙❙ No meals Ⓜ Colón.

🍸 Nightlife

DANCE CLUBS
Bling Bling

DANCE CLUBS | This glitzy nightclub (opened in 2018 by the owners of equally exclusive Opium Madrid) attracts a well-heeled local crowd. Dress to impress: this isn't an easy door. ⊠ Calle Génova 28, Salamanca 🕿 91/064–4479 ⊕ www. blingblingmadrid.com Ⓜ Colón.

🎭 Performing Arts

Auditorio Nacional de Música

CONCERTS | This is Madrid's main concert hall, with spaces for both symphonic and chamber music. ⊠ Calle del Príncipe de Vergara 146, Salamanca 🕿 91/337–0140 ⊕ www.auditorionacional.mcu.es Ⓜ Cruz del Rayo.

Cafetín La Quimera

CABARET | FAMILY | The noncentral location of this old-fashioned flamenco *tablao* keeps the touristy crowds at bay. Choose between a full dinner package (prices vary) or a €20 performance-only ticket and prepare for a soulful, invigorating show. Start times are 8 and 10 pm nightly, and there are often after-hours jam sessions on Friday and Saturday night. ⊠ *Callede Sancho Dávila 34, Salamanca* ☎ *91/356–9361* ⊕ *www.tablaolaquimera. com* Ⓜ *Ventas, Manuel Becerra.*

 # Shopping

BOUTIQUES AND FASHION
Adolfo Domínguez
CLOTHING | This popular Galician designer creates simple, sober, and elegant lines for both men and women. Of the numerous locations around the city, the flagship at Calle Serrano 5 is the most varied. There's also a large store at Madrid–Barajas Airport. ⊠ *Calle de Serrano 5, Salamanca* ☎ *91/436–2600* ⊕ *www. adolfodominguez.com* Ⓜ *Serrano.*

Loewe
CLOTHING | This sumptuous store carries high-quality designer purses, accessories, and clothing made of butter-soft leather in gorgeous jewel tones. The store at Serrano 26 displays the women's collection; men's items are a block away at Serrano 34. The Gran Vía location opened a small fashion museum (free entry) in 2019 chronicling the history of the iconic Spanish brand with pieces dating back to the 19th century. ⊠ *Calle de Serrano 26 and 34, Salamanca* ☎ *91/577–6056* ⊕ *www.loewe.com* Ⓜ *Serrano.*

FOOD AND WINE
★ Lavinia
WINE/SPIRITS | Welcome to one of the largest wine stores in Europe. Beyond the encyclopedic selection of bottles, find books, glasses, and bar accessories here as well as a restaurant, Enomatic tasting bar, and newly opened outdoor patio. ⊠ *Calle de José Ortega y Gasset 16, Salamanca* ☎ *91/426–0604* ⊕ *www. lavinia.es* Ⓜ *Núñez de Balboa.*

Mantequerías Bravo
FOOD/CANDY | Stock up on Spanish wines, olive oils, cheeses, and hams at this old-timer (est. 1931) situated in the heart of Salamanca's shopping area. ⊠ *Calle de Ayala 24, Salamanca* ☎ *91/576–7641* ⊕ *www.mantequeriasbravo.com* Ⓜ *Serrano.*

TEXTILES
★ Ábbatte
TEXTILES/SEWING | Every blanket, tablecloth, throw, and rug sold at this contemporary textile shop is woven by hand using the finest natural fibers in the Cistercian abbey of Santa María de la Sierra in Segovia. ⊠ *Calle Villanueva 27, Salamanca* ☎ *91/622–5530* ⊕ *www. abbatte.com* ⊘ *Closed Sun.*

Chapter 8

LA LATINA, LAVAPIÉS, AND ARGANZUELA

8

Updated by
Benjamin Kemper

⊙ Sights	🍴 Restaurants	🛏 Hotels	⊖ Shopping	🍸 Nightlife
★★★★☆	★★★★★	★★☆☆☆	★★★★☆	★★★★★

NEIGHBORHOOD SNAPSHOT

TOP EXPERIENCES

■ **El Rastro:** Snap up eclectic antiques, clothes, and tchotchkes at this epic Sunday flea market.

■ **Traditional markets:** Rub shoulders with a local crowd while grazing on tapas, charcuterie, and natural wine.

■ **Street art:** Take an eye-popping tour.

■ **International food:** When jamón fatigue sets in, branch out in Lavapiés with dishes from Senegal, Cuba, Italy, and beyond.

■ **Matadero:** There's always a cutting-edge exhibit on in this converted abattoir.

■ **Reina Sofía:** Ponder Picasso's *Guernica* here.

GETTING HERE

Explore Lavapiés and La Latina from their eponymous metro stops (Línea 3 and Línea 5, respectively), or get off at Embajadores (Líneas 3, 5) or Estación de Arte (Línea 1) and weave up Lavapiés to end in La Latina.

Arganzuela is serviced by three stops on Línea 3. Finding parking is tricky in Lavapiés and La Latina, especially on weekends. BiciMAD bike-share services all three neighborhoods.

PLANNING YOUR TIME

Spend most of your time in the endlessly intriguing neighborhoods of Lavapiés and La Latina, and skip the less-colorful Arganzuela district unless you enjoy alternative art, in which case the Matadero cultural center is a must-see. Expect crowds and chaos in La Latina on Sundays as the area turns into flea market central. La Latina and Lavapiés are rather deserted during the day on weekdays (there aren't many offices in the area) but come to life evenings and weekends, when their many—many—bars and restaurants fling open their doors. The high concentration of family-run establishments here means restaurants and shops often shut for the afternoon siesta, usually 2–5 pm (restaurants 4–8 pm).

QUICK BITES

■ **Bar el Boquerón.** Step back in time in this hole-in-the-wall seafood restaurant specializing in *boquerones en vinagre* (marinated anchovies), freshly shucked oysters, and prawns *a la plancha.* ⊠ *Calle de Valencia 14, Lavapiés* Ⓜ *Lavapiés*

■ **Dakar Restaurante Senegalés.** Shell out just €6 for a heaping plate of *thieboudienne,* a spicy Senegalese fish stew ladeled over *al dente* fonio. ⊠ *Calle del Amparo 61, Lavapiés* Ⓜ *Lavapiés*

■ **La Taberna Sanlúcar.** This cozy tiled bar will teleport you to the coastal Andalusian city of the same name with briny olives, bone-dry manzanilla sherries, and shatteringly crisp *tortillitas de camarón* (shrimp fritters). ⊠ *Calle de San Isidro Labrador 14, La Latina* Ⓜ *La Latina*

■ **Pum Pum Café.** Get your brunch fix here with killer homemade pastries, eggs Benedict, and single-origin coffees. ⊠ *Calle de Tribulete 6, Lavapiés* ⊕ *www.pumpumcafe.com* Ⓜ *Lavapiés*

One of Madrid's most eccentric, fashionable, and fast-changing areas, the combined neighborhoods of La Latina, Lavapiés, and Arganzuela offer dining, sightseeing, and art to keep you busy for days. Snag a patio table on a neighborhood plaza and settle in for some primo people-watching: You might see teenagers kicking around a soccer ball, *abuelos* playing dominoes in the shade, or expats catching up over sudsy *cañas* at an outdoor café.

La Latina is perhaps Madrid's most *castizo* (loosely, "authentic") neighborhood with its deep-rooted history and hardscrabble spirit. Its layout has changed little since medieval times, with sinuous cobblestone streets emptying onto wide plazas, but its demographic makeup has in the last decade due to soaring rents and the arrival of Airbnb. Though its mom-and-pop businesses preserve the old-world aesthetic of La Latina of yore, the neighborhood has all but lost its original inhabitants and, with them, its pleasingly gritty edge. But that doesn't keep Madrileños from flocking here every chance they get, especially around August 15, when the neighborhood's famous Verbena de la Paloma street fair unfolds to the oompah of the *chotis*. When exploring, architecture buffs should keep an eye out for La Latina's *casas a la malicia*, illegally constructed apartments from the 16th to 18th century recognizable for their asymmetrical, randomly placed windows.

Their confusing floor plan was intended to dupe the municipal authorities into believing they contained fewer dwellings (allowing landlords to evade property taxes), one of many examples of this neighborhood's unruly character.

Cross Calle de Toledo, La Latina's eastern border, and you're in **Lavapiés,** another swiftly gentrifying barrio with steeper, narrower streets. First constructed as a poor settlement outside the city walls, today it's one of Madrid's most diverse and sought-after neighborhoods for expats and artsy types, a patchwork quilt of old-timey Spanish establishments intermingled with Chinese convenience stores, Indian restaurants, and North and West African jewelry shops. It's partly due to this cosmopolitan pulse that Lavapiés has overtaken Malasaña and La Latina as Madrid's trendiest district. The buzz is a double-edged sword as chain hotels go up and immigrants and longtime denizens are priced out of

A Good Walk: Old Madrid

Wander around Puerta del Sol for a look at Madrid's oldest buildings, bustling taverns, and cobblestone alleys. Allow about two hours, more if you visit the Palacio Real or Monasterio de la Encarnación.

Begin at **Puerta del Sol**, the center of Madrid and a major social and transportation hub, then take Calle Mayor to **Plaza Mayor**. Inaugurated in 1620 on the site of a thriving street market, this is Madrid's historical main square, where you'll find the Casa de la Panadería (Bakery House)—an imposing building with mythological figures painted on its facade, home of the main tourist office.

Exit Plaza Mayor through the "Cutler's Arch" (Arco de Cuchilleros) and go down the stairs: To the right is Calle Cava de San Miguel—an ancient-looking stretch of colorful taverns that inches uphill to the posh Mercado de San Miguel and Calle Mayor; to the left is Calle de Cuchilleros ("Cutlers' Street"), which leads to the Plaza de Puerta Cerrada, or "Closed Gate," named for the city gate that once stood here. The mural up to your right reads *Fui sobre agua edificada; mis muros de fuego son* ("I was built on water; my walls are made of fire"), a reference to the city's origins as a fortress with abundant springs and flint ramparts. Cross the street to **Calle Cava Baja**, packed with taverns and restaurants. At Plaza del Humilladero, walk past Plaza de San Andrés and take Costanilla de San Andrés from Plaza Puerta de Moros, down to **Plaza de la Paja**. The **Capilla del Obispo** (Bishop's Chapel), on the south edge of the plaza, completed in 1535, houses one of Spain's most magnificent Renaissance altarpieces. Look right on narrow Calle Príncipe Anglona—at its end you'll see a tall redbrick Mudejar tower, the only original element belonging to San Pedro el Real (St. Peter the Royal), one of Madrid's oldest churches.

Cross Calle Segovia to Plaza de la Cruz Verde, take the stairs (Calle del Rollo) to your right, go straight to Calle Cordón, then turn left. Walk up the stairs and cross the Plaza del Cordón and Calle Sacramento to get to **Plaza de la Villa**; noteworthy buildings here are (west) the former city hall main office, finished in 1692; (east) the Casa and Torre de los Lujanes, the oldest civil building in Madrid, dating to the mid-15th century; and (south) the Casa Cisneros, from the 16th century. Turn left on Calle Mayor and walk to Calle San Nicolás; on the corner is the Palacio del Duque de Uceda, a residential building from the 17th century now used as military headquarters. Turn right onto Calle San Nicolás (San Nicolás de los Servitas is Madrid's oldest standing church, with a Mudejar tower dating to the 17th century) and walk to Plaza de Ramales, where you'll find a display of a ruined section of the foundation of the medieval Iglesia de San Juan, demolished in the 19th century. Take Calle San Nicolas until it becomes Calle de Lepanto, which leads to the **Plaza de Oriente**. The equestrian statue of Felipe IV was sculpted from a drawing by Velázquez, who worked and died in what is now a residential building on the east side of the plaza. Take a breather in the plaza, then visit the **Palacio Real**, the adjacent **Jardines de Sabatini**, or nearby **Monasterio de la Encarnación**.

their apartments. Relics of the barrio's storied past are never far away: Like La Latina, Lavapiés has its own architecture hallmark, the *corrala*, a shared-living residence with communal bathrooms and a central patio that became popular in the 17th century as the neighborhood expanded.

Stretching south and west of La Latina and Lavapiés all the way to the banks of the Manzanares, **Arganzuela** is a working-class district with relatively few historical sights and places of import to the average traveler. Its prime attraction is Matadero Madrid, an arts and culture center occupying a defunct slaughter-house, and long swaths of the Madrid Río esplanade.

La Latina

Officially part of the Palacio neighborhood, this bustling area surrounding the eponymous metro stop is bordered by Calle de Segovia to the north, Calle Toledo to the east, Puerta de Toledo to the south, and Calle Bailén, with its imposing Basílica de San Francisco, to the west. It houses some of the city's oldest buildings, plenty of sloping streets, and an array of unmissable tapas spots—especially on Cava Baja and Cava Alta, and in the area around Plaza de la Paja.

◉ Sights

Basílica de San Francisco el Grande
RELIGIOUS SITE | In 1760 Carlos III built this basilica on the site of a Franciscan convent, allegedly founded by St. Francis of Assisi in 1217. The dome, 108 feet in diameter, is the largest in Spain, even larger than that of St. Paul's in London. The seven main doors, of American walnut, were carved by Casa Juan Guas. Three chapels adjoin the circular church, the most famous being that of **San Bernardino de Siena** containing a Goya masterpiece depicting a preaching San Bernardino. The figure standing on the right, not looking up, is a self-portrait of Goya. The 16th-century Gothic choir stalls came from La Cartuja del Paular, in rural Segovia Province. ✉ *Pl. de San Francisco, La Latina* ☎ *91/365–3800* 💶 *€5 guided tour (in Spanish)* 🕙 *Closed Mon. and some Sat.* Ⓜ *Puerta de Toledo, La Latina.*

Cava Baja
NEIGHBORHOOD | Madrid's most popular tapas street is crowded with excellent (if overpriced) tapas bars and traditional *tabernas.* Its lively, and rather touristy, atmosphere spills over onto nearby streets and squares including Almendro, Cava Alta, Plaza del Humilladero, and Plaza de la Paja. Expect full houses and long wait times on weekend nights. ✉ *La Latina* Ⓜ *La Latina.*

Jardín del Príncipe de Anglona (*Garden of the Prince of Anglona*)
CITY PARK | Enter this romantic 18th-century garden through a swinging wrought-iron gate at the north end of Plaza de la Paja. Hiding in plain sight, it is a little-known oasis with a burbling fountain, *mampuesto* stone paths, low-cut boxwood hedges, and a small arbor. Shaded benches around the perimeter feel a world away from the bustling plaza mere steps from where you sit. ✉ *Pl. de la Paja 6, La Latina* Ⓜ *La Latina.*

Mercado de la Cebada
MARKET | Unrenovated digs and budget-friendly tapas and groceries make this market a local favorite for both shopping and snacking. The mercado occupies a soaring hangar-like space and is at its busiest on Saturday from noon to 3 pm, when seafood stalls transform into make-shift fish and shellfish restaurants, frying, steaming, and boiling their freshest wares and serving them on plastic plates alongside jugs of unlabeled table wine—quite the party. Once buzzed and sated, pop into La Pecera, a chic stall dedicated to prints, paintings, and photography by

8

La Latina, Lavapiés, and Arganzuela LA LATINA

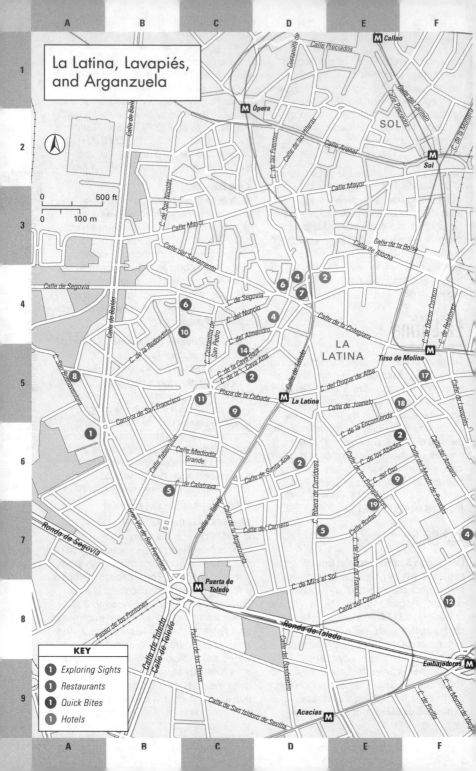

Sights ▼

Restaurants ▼

Quick Bites ▼

Hotels ▼

local artists. ✉ *Pl. de la Cebada, La Latina* ☎ *91/366–6966* 🌐 *www.mercadodelacebada.com* 🕓 *Closed Sun.* [M] *La Latina.*

Plaza de la Paja

PLAZA | At the top of a hill, on Costanilla San Andrés, sits the most important square of medieval Madrid. It predates the Plaza Mayor by at least two centuries. The sloped plaza's jewel is the **Capilla del Obispo** (Bishop's Chapel), built between 1520 and 1530, where peasants deposited their tithes, called *diezmas*—one-tenth of their crop. Architecturally the chapel traces the transition from the blocky Gothic period, which gave the structure its basic shape, to the Renaissance, the source of its decorations. It houses an intricately carved polychrome altarpiece by Francisco Giralta with scenes from the life of Christ. To visit the chapel (*Tuesday 9:30–12:30, Thursday 4–5:30*) reserve in advance (*91/559–2874* or *reservascapilladelobispo@archimadrid.es*). The chapel is part of the complex of the domed church of San Andrés, one of Madrid's oldest. ✉ *La Latina* [M] *La Latina.*

🍴 Restaurants

Casa Botín

$$$$ | **SPANISH** | According to *Guinness World Records*, Madrid is home to the world's oldest restaurant, Botín, established in 1725 and a favorite of Ernest Hemingway. The final scene of *The Sun Also Rises* is set in this very place. **Known for:** world's oldest restaurant; roast lamb and suckling pig; live music ensembles. [$] *Average main: €25* ✉ *Calle Cuchilleros 17, La Latina* ☎ *91/366–4217* 🌐 *www.botin.es* [M] *Tirso de Molina.*

★ **Casa Gerardo**

$ | **TAPAS** | Huge *tinajas*, clay vessels once filled to the brim with bulk wine (yet now defunct), sit behind the bar at this raucous no-frills bodega specializing in Spanish cheese and charcuterie. Ask the waiters what they've been drinking and eating lately, and order precisely that. **Known for:** unforgettable old-world atmosphere; wide selection of wines and charcuterie; frazzled yet friendly staff. [$] *Average main: €10* ✉ *Calle Calatrava 21, La Latina* ☎ *91/221–9660* [M] *La Latina, Puerta de Toledo.*

Casa Paco

$$$$ | **STEAKHOUSE** | **FAMILY** | Packed with Madrileños downing Valdepeñas wine, this Castilian tavern, with its zinc-top bar and tiled walls, wouldn't have looked out of place a century ago; indeed, it opened in 1933. Warm up with the city's best rendition of *sopa de ajo*, garlic soup crowned with a poached egg; then feast on thick slabs of Spanish beef *chuletones*, served medium rare and sizzling. **Known for:** ornate zinc-topped bar; rustic Valdepeñas wine; city's best garlic soup. [$] *Average main: €23* ✉ *Pl. Puerta Cerrada 11, La Latina* ☎ *91/366–3166* 🌐 *www.casapaco.com* 🕓 *Closed Mon. No dinner Sun.* [M] *Tirso de Molina.*

★ **Casa Revuelta**

$ | **SPANISH** | There's a cod—yes, cod—war in Madrid between Casa Lavra and Casa Revulta: both claim to make the city's best *pincho de bacalao*, or battered salt cod. As locals will tell you, Revuelta's rendition is far and away the superior choice—provided you're successful at elbowing your way to the 1930s-era bar. **Known for:** battered salt cod canapés; midmorning vermú (vermouth) rush; time-warp decor. [$] *Average main: €5* ✉ *Calle Latoneros 3, La Latina* ☎ *91/366–3332* 🕓 *Closed Mon. No dinner Sun.* 💳 *No credit cards* [M] *La Latina.*

El Landó

$$$$ | **SPANISH** | This *castizo* ("rootsy") restaurant, with dark wood-paneled walls lined with bottles of wine, serves classic Spanish food like *huevos estrellados* (fried eggs with potatoes and sausage), grilled meats, a good selection of fish (sea bass, haddock, grouper) with many different sauces, and steak tartare. Check out the pictures of famous celebrities who've eaten at this typically noisy

You can't leave Madrid without tasting the famous huevos estrellados (eggs with ham and fries) of Casa Lucio on Madrid's most famous tapas street, Cava Baja.

landmark; they line the staircase that leads to the main dining area. **Known for:** castizo ambience; huevos estrellados; impeccably cooked seafood. $ *Average main: €26* ⊠ *Pl. Gabriel Miró 8, La Latina* 🕾 *91/366–7681* 🕙 *No dinner Sun.* Ⓜ *La Latina.*

Juana la Loca
$$$ | TAPAS | This tony tapas bar serves newfangled tapas that can are as pricey as they are delightful. Spring for the *fideuà con butifarra de calamar* (a vermicelli "paella" with calamari sausage), *huevo confitado trufado* (poached egg with truffle), or any other tapa *del día*, but don't miss the famous *tortilla de patata* (Spanish omelet), so irresistible with its molten core and handfuls of caramelized onions that you might not notice the sorry service. **Known for:** nueva cocina tapas done right; earth-shatteringly good tortilla de patata; cheek-by-jowl crowds. $ *Average main: €21* ⊠ *Pl. Puerta de Moros 4, La Latina* 🕾 *91/366–5500* ⊕ *www.juanalaloca.es* 🕙 *No lunch Mon.* Ⓜ *La Latina.*

Los Huevos de Lucio
$$ | SPANISH | Don't let the crowds dissuade you from entering this Cava Baja stalwart (Casa Lucio's more casual sibling)—tables and spots at the bar open up fast. The non-negotiable dish to try here is *huevos estrellados*, "bashed" fried eggs tucked between olive-oil-fried potatoes and topped with optional add-ons like jamón, *txistorra* sausage, and *pisto* (Spanish ratatouille). **Known for:** fried egg nirvana; great salads and vegetable dishes; uproarious atmosphere. $ *Average main: €16* ⊠ *Calle Cava Baja 30, La Latina* 🕾 *91/366–2984* ⊕ *www. loshuevosdelucio.com* 🕙 *Closed Tues.* Ⓜ *La Latina.*

Hotels

★ The Hat
$ | HOTEL | The Hat epitomizes the fast-growing category of "designer hostels," affordable properties geared toward the millennial set with sleek multiperson (and private) rooms, bumping weekend events, and generous

Summer Terraces

Madrid is blazing hot in the late spring and summer, but locals have a relentless yearning for nightlife. As a result, the city boasts some 2,000 bars and restaurants with outdoor spaces (some fashioned with mist systems) for enjoying the cool nighttime air.

For formal summer dining, we recommend hotel restaurants with gardens or rooftop patios such as La Biblioteca del Santo Mauro (at Hotel Santo Mauro), El Jardín de Orfila (at Hotel Orfila), El Paraguas, and Paco Roncero.

Two midrange restaurants with good terraces are Sacha and Cinco Jotas Jorge Juan, run by the famous *jamón* company.

If you just want a glass of wine and a tapa or two, drop by La Latina neighborhood, especially Plaza de la Paja or Plaza de San Andrés, or the terraces at Plaza de Olavide in Chamberí. Calle Argumosa in Lavapiés is another famous street for *terraceo*

(terrace-hopping), but don't expect anything too gastronomical.

Among the younger, alternative set, go-to plazas include Plaza de Chueca, in the eponymous barrio (and the nearby Plaza de Vázquez de Mella), Plaza de Nelson Mandela, Plaza del Dos de Mayo, and Plaza de las Comendadoras, whose top hangout is Federal Café.

There's wonderful if slightly stuffy nightlife along the terraces on Paseo de la Castellana, at the popular Casamérica at—you guessed it—Casa de América, the Mercado de San Antón in Chueca, the rooftop at the Círculo de Bellas Artes, and at a variety of hotel rooftops that have become hot spots in the last few years: Hotel Urban, ME Madrid, The Principal, Iberostar Las Letras, Gran Meliá Palacio de los Duques, Heritage Madrid, and Room Mate Óscar, to name a few.

breakfasts. **Pros:** rooftop bar; steps from Plaza Mayor; bountiful breakfasts. **Cons:** hotel guests not prioritized on rooftop, which fills up fast; some rooms are dark; location means tourists are everywhere. $ *Rooms from: €45* ✉ *Calle Imperial 9, La Latina* ☎ *91/772–8572* ⊕ *www.thehatmadrid.com* ⇗ *42 rooms* ⧖ *Free breakfast* Ⓜ *Tirso de Molina.*

Posada del León de Oro

$$$ | HOTEL | More like a luxurious village inn than a metropolitan hotel, this refurbished late-19th-century property was built atop the remains of a stone wall that encircled the city in the 12th century, which you can see through glass floor panels at the hotel entrance and in the casual restaurant. **Pros:** unbeatable location; restaurant with more than

300 Spanish wines; high ceilings with exposed wood beams. **Cons:** interior-facing rooms are small; late-night noise; cramped entry-level rooms. $ *Rooms from: €146* ✉ *Calle Cava Baja 12, La Latina* ☎ *91/119–1494* ⊕ *www.posadadelleondeoro.com* ⇗ *27 rooms* ⧖ *No meals* Ⓜ *La Latina.*

Nightlife

BARS
Delic

CAFES—NIGHTLIFE | This warm, inviting café-bar is an all-hours hangout. Homesick travelers will find comfort in Delic's carrot cake, brownies, and pumpkin pie (seasonal), while low-key revelers will appreciate the bar's coziness and late hours (open until 2:30 on weekends).

⌧ *Pl. de la Paja, Costanilla de San Andrés 14, La Latina* ☎ *91/364–5450* ⊕ *www. delic.es* ⊗ *Closed Mon.* Ⓜ *La Latina.*

El Viajero
BARS/PUBS | You can find fine modern *raciones* here (the ultracreamy burrata stands out), but this place is better known among madrileños for its middle-floor bar, which fills up with a cocktail-drinking after-work crowd, and rooftop terrace decorated with potted plants. Beware of the 10% surcharge that comes with outdoor dining, and expect middling service. ⌧ *Pl. de la Cebada 11, La Latina* ☎ *91/366–9064* ⊕ *www. elviajeromadrid.com* ⊗ *Closed Sun. night and Mon.* Ⓜ *La Latina.*

★ Sala Equis
BARS/PUBS | This uber-trendy cinema-bar hybrid occupies a former adult film theater. The first floor is a high-ceilinged bar with bleacher seating, deckchairs, cushy sofas, and an ivy-covered wall. Head up the stairs, and there's a quieter lounge with velvet walls and warm neon lights; continue to the top floor and you've reached the main attraction, a 55-seat cinema with cocktail service that plays art-house films (buy tickets online in advance). ⌧ *Calle del Duque de Alba 4, La Latina* ☎ *91/429–6686* ⊕ *www. salaequis.es* Ⓜ *Tirso de Molina.*

 Performing Arts

FLAMENCO
Las Carboneras
DANCE | A prime flamenco showcase, this venue offers consistency and good value in an informal restaurant setting. Performers here run the gamut from young, less commercial artists to more established stars on tour. Showtimes are 8:30 and 10:30 Monday–Thursday and at 8:30 and 11 Friday and Saturday. ⌧ *Pl. del Conde de Miranda 1, La Latina* ☎ *91/542–8677* ⊕ *www.tablaolascarboneras.com* ⊗ *Closed Sun* Ⓜ *La Latina, Ópera.*

Tacones Manoli
CABARET | "A clandestine gastronomical flamenco experience" is how this new (since 2019), enigmatic performance venue bills itself, but don't expect the usual *bulerías* and paella—Tacones Manoli is an immersive, culturally charged show that's Spain's answer to *Sleep No More.* There's dark humor, allusions to works by Federico García Lorca, gender-bending attire, and foot-stomping scores performed by top-notch artists, plus inventive bites to keep you sated but not overstuffed. A high level of Spanish is a must to be in on the jokes. ⌧ *Calle de la Bolsa 12, La Latina* ☎ *91/521–6911* ⊕ *www.taconesmanoli.com* Ⓜ *Tirso de Molina.*

Shopping

CRAFTS AND DESIGN
★ Cocol
CRAFTS | There's no better shop in Madrid for top-quality Spanish artisan wares. The shelves in this tiny independently owned boutique off Plaza de la Paja are lined with everything from exquisite Andalusian pottery to hand-sewn blankets, antique esparto baskets, and leather soccer balls. ⌧ *Costanilla de San Andrés 18, La Latina* ☎ *91/919–6770* ⊕ *www. cocolmadrid.es* Ⓜ *La Latina.*

FOOD
Madrid & Darracott
WINE/SPIRITS | More than just a neighborhood wine shop with a well-curated cellar, Madrid & Darracott, opened in 2019, hosts themed wine tastings Thursday–Sunday evenings in English. Wondering about the difference between Rioja and Ribera del Duero or what makes cava sparkle? Reserve your spot online and show up sober—the pours are generous. ⌧ *Calle del Duque de Rivas 8, La Latina* ☎ *91/219–1975* ⊕ *www.madriddarracott. com* Ⓜ *Tirso de Molina.*

Lavapiés

Lavapiés, technically inside the Embajadores neighborhood, spokes out
from Plaza de Lavapiés. Its perimeter
is roughly delineated by the following
metro stops: La Latina, Tirso de Molina,
and Antón Martín to the north; Estación
de Arte (formerly Atocha) to the east; and
Embajadores to the south. Calle Argumosa has one of Spain's highest concentration of bars, and its sidewalks teem with
outdoor diners come summer. Calle del
Dr. Fourquet is lined with art galleries and
studios. Plaza de Nelson Mandela, Plaza
de Agustín Lara, and Plaza de Lavapiés
are the neighborhood's main social hubs.

Sights

★ Centro de Arte Reina Sofía
MUSEUM | Madrid's premier museum of
modern art, housed in a historic hospital
building, features more than 1,000 works
on four floors. Painting is the focus here,
but photography and cinema are also
represented. The new collection contex-
tualizes the works of the great modern
masters—Picasso, Miró, and Salvador
Dalí—and of other famed artists, such as
Juan Gris, Jorge Oteiza, Pablo Gargallo,
Julio Gonzalez, Eduardo Chillida, and
Antoni Tàpies, into broader narratives that
attempt to better explain the evolution
of modern art. This means, for instance,
that the Dalís are not all displayed together in a single area, but scattered around
the 38 rooms. The museum's showpiece
is Picasso's *Guernica*, in Room No. 206
on the second floor. The huge black-and-
white canvas depicts the horror of the
Nazi Condor Legion's ruthless bombing
of innocent civilians in the Basque town
of Gernika in 1937 during the Spanish
Civil War. Check out the rooftop area for
scenic city views. ⊠ *Calle de Santa Isabel
52, Lavapiés* 🕾 *91/467–5062* ⊕ *www.
museoreinasofia.es* 🕾 *From €10 (free
Mon. and Wed.–Sat. after 7 pm, Sun.
1:30–7)* ⊘ *Closed Tues.* Ⓜ *Atocha.*

Corrala de Sombrerete (*House of
Sombrerete*)
BUILDING | This historical 19th-century
residence overlooking Plaza de Agustín
Lara is one of Madrid's few remaining
corralas, tenement houses distinguished
by timber frames and a central patio. It
is closed to the public but still worth a
walk-by. There's a plaque here to remind
you that the setting of the famous
19th-century *zarzuela* (light opera) *La
Revoltosa* was a corrala like this one.
The abandoned brick building across the
street was the **Escolapíos de San Fernando,**
one of several churches and parochi-
al schools razed due to anti-Catholic
sentiments during the Spanish Civil War.
It is one of Madrid's only unrepaired Civil
War ruins. Though partially refurbished by
the Universidad Nacional de Educación
a Distancia (UNED), the entire building is
closed for renovations. ⊠ *Calle Sombrerete 13, Lavapiés* Ⓜ *Lavapiés.*

★ El Rastro
MARKET | Named for the *arrastre*
(dragging) of animals in and out of the
slaughterhouse that once stood here
and the *rastro* (blood trail) left behind,
this site explodes into a rollicking flea
market every Sunday 9–3 with scores of
street vendors with bizarre bric-a-brac
ranging from costume earrings to mailed
postcards and thrown-out love letters.
There are also plenty of traditional shops,
where it's easy to turn up treasures such
as old iron grillwork, a marble tabletop,
or a gilt picture frame. The shops (not
the vendors) are open during the week,
allowing for quieter and more serious
bargaining. Even so, people-watching at
the Sunday market is an essential Madrid
experience. ⊠ *Calle de la Ribera de los
Curtidores, Embajadores* Ⓜ *La Latina,
Puerta de Toledo.*

★ Mercado de Antón Martín
MARKET | Go on an international tapas
crawl here—nibbling on tacos (at
Cutzamala), sushi (at Yokaloka), homemade croissants (at Cafés Tornasol), and

The bustling Rastro flea market takes place every Sunday 10–2; you never know what kind of treasures you might find.

more—without so much as stepping outside. Olives from Variantes Juanjo and cheeses from La Quesería make excellent portable picnic snacks. ✉ *Calle de Santa Isabel 5, Lavapiés* ☎ *91/369–0620* 🌐 *www.mercadoantonmartin.com* 🕒 *Closed Sun.* [M] *Antón Martín.*

Plaza de Lavapiés
PLAZA | This oblong plaza is Lavapiés's nerve center. To the east is Calle de la Fe (Street of Faith), named for the church of **San Lorenzo**. ✉ *Lavapiés* [M] *Lavapiés.*

Tabacalera (*Tabacalera Art Promotion*)
MUSEUM | This cultural center, which occupies a dilapidated 18th-century cigarette factory, is divided in two parts: on the building's northwest corner, there's the city-funded exhibition and event space (called Espacio Promoción del Arte), a hub of contemporary art, while at its southwest corner is an entrance to the city's most famous art squat. Both venues are worth visiting, but the latter (with no official opening schedule) is truly unique with its political, in-your-face graffiti and sculptural art. ✉ *Calle de Embajadores 51, Lavapiés* ☎ *91/701–7045* 🌐 *www.facebook.com/tabacaleradelavapies* 🎟 *Free* 🕒 *Closed Mon.* [M] *Lavapiés.*

🍴 Restaurants

Bar Burlona
$$ | **TAPAS** | Indulge in some self-pampering, or impress a special someone at this sunlight-flooded gastro-tavern with minimalist decor that serves creatively plated dishes that taste as good as they look. Squash blossoms come stuffed with garlicky revolcona potatoes, oysters on the half-shell arrive swimming in homemade Bloody Mary mix, and gazpacho is gussied up with *ají amarillo* and succulent chunks of seared Almadraba tuna. **Known for:** eye-popping modern tapas; more than 30 small-production wines by the bottle; secret bar below. [$] *Average main: €17* ✉ *Calle de Santa Isabel 40, Lavapiés* ☎ *91/018–0018* 🕒 *Closed Mon.* [M] *Lavapiés.*

Bar Santurce

$ | **TAPAS** | This take-no-prisoners *abuelo* bar near the top of the Rastro is famous for griddled sardines, served hot and greasy in an odiferous heap with nothing but a flick of crunchy salt. Beware, supersmellers: *eau de sardine* is potent perfume. **Known for:** sardine mecca; inexpensive and unfussy; busy on Sunday. [$] *Average main: €10* ✉ *Pl. General Vara del Rey 14, Lavapiés* ☎ *64/623–8303* 🌐 *www.sites.google.com/barsanturce.com/barsanturce-en* 💳 *No credit cards* [M] *La Latina.*

El Rincón de Marco

$ | **CUBAN** | Step straight into Havana at this hidden Cuban bar and restaurant where *rumbas* and *sones* flow from the speakers and regulars burst into impromptu dance parties. Whatever you end up eating—a €6 *ropa vieja* (cumin-scented beef stew), or perhaps the heftier €10 *picapollo* (fried chicken)—be sure to nab an order or two of fried plaintains for the table. **Known for:** home-cooked Cuban food; kitschy decor; music that makes you want to dance. [$] *Average main: €8* ✉ *Calle Cabestreros 8, Lavapiés* ☎ *91/210–7500* 🕓 *Closed Mon.* [M] *Lavapiés.*

La Oveja Negra

$$ | **VEGETARIAN** | Traveling as a vegan in Madrid is becoming easier and easier, thanks to affordable, inviting restaurants with palate-popping food like Oveja Negra. Try vegan takes on Spanish classics: *sidre*-braised soy chorizo, leek-and-squash croquetas, and meatless pâtés, to name a few dishes. **Known for:** tasty vegan cuisine; pet-friendly; punk atmosphere. [$] *Average main: €13* ✉ *Calle Buenavista 42, Lavapiés* ☎ *65/533–6474* 🌐 *www.laoveja.net* 🕓 *Closed Mon.* [M] *Lavapiés.*

★ Los Chuchis

$$ | **BRITISH** | For groups larger than two, reservations are a must at this cozy neighborhood bar decorated with books, colorful knickknacks, and fresh flowers. You can count on British chef Scott Preston to provide craveable pub food like craggy-crispy potato skins and oozy baked feta, plus healthier, more Mediterranean options like curried vegetable couscous and flake-apart hake with clams and salsa verde. **Known for:** British pub food; romantic u-shape bar; down-home coziness. [$] *Average main: €13* ✉ *Calle del Amparo 82, Lavapiés* ☎ *91/127–6606* 🌐 *www.facebook.com/LosChuchisBar* 🕓 *Closed Mon.* [M] *Embajadores.*

Melo's

$ | **SPANISH** | This old-timey Galician bar serves eight simple dishes, and they're infallible. Come for the ultracreamy croquetas, blistered Padrón peppers, and football-size *zapatilla* sandwiches; stay for the dressed-down conviviality and the *cuncos* (ceramic bowls) overflowing with slatey Albariño. **Known for:** old-school Galician bar food; oversize ham croquetas; cheap, good Albariño. [$] *Average main: €8* ✉ *Calle del Ave María 44, Lavapiés* ☎ *91/527–5054* 🕓 *Closed Sun. and Mon.* 💳 *No credit cards* [M] *Lavapiés.*

★ Restaurante Badila

$$ | **SPANISH** | **FAMILY** | This mom-and-pop neighborhood staple resembles a blue-collar Italian trattoria with its paper tablecloths, walls hung with ceramic plates, and chalked food menu. The ever-rotating *menú del día* (prix-fixe) is the move here—for €13 (or €15 on Friday and Saturday evening), choose from, say, rustic bean stew, a honking T-bone steak, or a wild mushroom scramble followed by homemade chocolate cake. **Known for:** great-value prix-fixe; lovingly made modern Spanish food; bubbly staff. [$] *Average main: €13* ✉ *Calle de San Pedro Martir 6, Lavapiés* ☎ *91/429–7651* 🕓 *No dinner weekdays* [M] *Tirso de Molina.*

Taberna de Antonio Sánchez

$$ | **SPANISH** | A Lavapiés landmark opened in 1786, this taberna's regulars have included realist painter Ignacio Zuloaga, countless champion bullfighters, and King Alfonso XIII. Sip on a sudsy caña,

or half pint, in the creaky bar area, and nibble on house specialties like *cazón en adobo* (fried shark bites with cumin) and *torrijas* (custardy fried bread dusted with cinnamon). **Known for:** centuries-old decor; museum-grade bullfighting paraphernalia; cazón (fried shark). $ *Average main: €16* ✉ *Calle del Mesón de Paredes, Lavapiés* ☎ *91/539–7826* ⊕ *www.tabernaantoniosanchez.com* ☾ *No dinner Sun.* Ⓜ *Lavapiés.*

Tasca Barea

$$ | TAPAS | Floor-to-ceiling windows, an intimate corner bar, and throwback tapas keep this "tasca moderna" packed with neighborhood dwellers night after night. Particularly addictive are the gildas (anchovy skewers) and *marinera murciana*, loopy crackers filled with potato salad and draped with an anchovy. **Known for:** fun, breezy ambience; pet-friendly; traditional tapas in danger of disappearing. $ *Average main: €13* ✉ *Calle de Rodas 2, Lavapiés* ☾ *Closed Tues. No dinner Sun.* Ⓜ *Lavapiés.*

☕ Coffee and Quick Bites

★ Hola Coffee

$ | CAFÉ | Spaniards love their morning cafés con leche and afternoon *cortados* (espresso with steamed milk), but it's never been easy to find a truly great cup of joe in Madrid—until Hola Coffee came along with its multilayered third-wave espressos and cold brews made with beans the company roasts itself. Made-from-scratch baked goods and open-faced sandwiches will make you want to stay awhile. **Known for:** third-wave coffees made with house-roasted beans; expat staff and clientele; alternative music and atmosphere. $ *Average main: €5* ✉ *Calle del Dr. Fourquet 33, Lavapiés* ☎ *91/056–8263* ⊕ *www.hola.coffee* Ⓜ *Lavapiés.*

Plántate Café

$ | CAFÉ | Welcome to the jungle. This plant-filled coffee shop with exposed-brick walls is a verdant oasis worth

seeking out for its single-origin brews and delectable open-faced sandwiches and breakfast bowls. **Known for:** plants everywhere!; expertly pulled espressos; popular with expats. $ *Average main: €8* ✉ *Calle del Mesón de Paredes 28, Lavapiés* ☎ *91/023–0291* ⊕ *www.facebook.com/plantatecafe* Ⓜ *Lavapiés.*

Hotels

Artrip

$$$ | HOTEL | A stone's throw from Madrid's "Golden Triangle" of museums, Artrip is a gem of a budget hotel ideally suited to art-loving travelers. **Pros:** free portable Wi-Fi; independently owned; youthful design touches. **Cons:** street noise; small showers; no parking. $ *Rooms from: €170* ✉ *Calle de Valencia 11, Lavapiés* ☎ *91/539–3282* ⊕ *www.artriphotel.com* ➥ *17 rooms* ⦿ *No meals* Ⓜ *Embajadores.*

Hotel Freedom

$$$ | HOTEL | FAMILY | Rooms in this cheap and cheerful hotel overlooking Plaza de Antón Martín have turquoise walls, crimson sofas, and multicolor headboards. **Pros:** independently owned; trendy location; immaculately clean. **Cons:** lobby-adjacent room is noisy; no restaurant, bar, gym, or room service; no breakfast. $ *Rooms from: €130* ✉ *Calle de Santa Isabel 4, Lavapiés* ☎ *91/073–6271* ⊕ *www.hotel-freedom.hoteles-madrid.net* ➥ *21 rooms* ⦿ *No meals* Ⓜ *Antón Martín.*

▶ Nightlife

BARS
★ Bendito Vinos y Vinilos

WINE BARS—NIGHTLIFE | This unassuming stall inside Mercado de San Fernando is a wine-industry hangout—one of the city's top spots for sampling hard-to-find natural and biodynamic wines from Spain and beyond. Pair whatever wine the owner, José, is drinking lately with Bendito's hand-selected cheeses and charcuterie sourced from independent producers. ✉ *Mercado de San Fernando, Calle de Embajadores 41, Lavapiés* ☎ *66/175–0061* ⊕ *www.benditovino.com* Ⓜ *Lavapiés.*

La Caníbal

WINE BARS—NIGHTLIFE | Welcome to Madrid's newest hot spot for wine geeks. Pull up a stool in the warehouse-like bar area, with massive concrete pillars and long wooden tables, and choose from dozens of boutique bottles or some 15 small-production Spanish wines on tap. ✉ *Calle de Argumosa 28, Lavapiés* ☎ *91/539–6057* ⊕ *www.lacanibal.com* Ⓜ *Estación del Arte.*

La Fisna

WINE BARS—NIGHTLIFE | An ideal date spot, this understated yet elegant *vinoteca* pours more than 50 wines by the glass and serves a delectable if overpriced menu of market-driven tapas. You'd be hard pressed to find a more impressive roster of French wines anywhere in the city. ✉ *Calle Amparo 91, Lavapiés* ☎ *91/539–5615* ⊕ *www.lafisna.com.*

Savas

BARS/PUBS | It's about time Lavapiés upped its cocktail game. Enter Savas, opened in 2019, a pocket-size bar that has quickly become a cult hangout for mixology geeks and neighborhood scenesters with its expertly made classic cocktails—think white Russians and Tom Collinses at some €8 apiece—and local craft beers by La Virgen. ✉ *Calle de la Sombrerería 3, Lavapiés* Ⓜ *Lavapiés.*

MUSIC AND DANCE CLUBS
Club 33

DANCE CLUBS | This intimate nightclub caters to a local, alternative crowd and is a favorite stop on the lesbian party circuit, though revelers of all orientations are welcome. ✉ *Calle de la Cabeza 33, Lavapiés* ☎ *91/369–3302* ⊕ *www.club-33madrid.es* Ⓜ *Lavapiés.*

Medias Puri

DANCE CLUBS | A decades-old, exclusive underground party made public in 2017, Medias Puri is the brainchild of Puri, an ageless Madrid socialite who rolled with Ava Gardner and Lola Flores back in the day. Expect acrobatic entertainment, pulsing electronic music, anything-goes dancing, and colorful flashing lights. ✉ *Pl. Tirso de Molina 1, Lavapiés* ☎ *91/521–6911* ⊕ *www.mediaspuri.com* Ⓜ *Tirso de Molina.*

⚜ Performing Arts

FILM
Cine Doré (*Filmoteca*)

FILM | A rare example of Art Nouveau architecture in Madrid, the alternative Cine Doré shows movies from the Spanish National Film Archives and eclectic foreign films often at budget rates (you frequently get a short film or two in addition to a feature). The pink, neon-trimmed lobby has a sleek café-bar and a bookshop. ✉ *Calle de Santa Isabel 3, Lavapiés* ☎ *91/369–1125* ⊕ *www.culturaydeporte.gob.es/cultura/areas/cine/mc/fe/cine-dore* Ⓜ *Antón Martín.*

La Casa Encendida

CONCERTS | Film festivals, alternative art shows, dance performances, and weekend events for children are held here. In summer, check the website for outdoor concerts on the rooftop. ✉ *Ronda de Valencia 2, Lavapiés* ☎ *91/506–3875* ⊕ *www.lacasaencendida.es* Ⓜ *Embajadores, Lavapiés.*

FLAMENCO
★ **Sala Juglar**

DANCE | Sala Juglar is proof that nontouristy, affordable, and skillful flamenco still exists in Madrid (check the website for weekly performance times). Tropical-inflected dance parties, often held on the weekends, are another draw. ✉ *Calle de Lavapiés 37, Lavapiés* ☎ *91/528–4381* ⊕ *www.salajuglar.com* Ⓜ *Lavapiés.*

🛍 Shopping

ART

Swinton & Grant

ART GALLERIES | Equal parts gallery, book shop, and café, this art space sells works by contemporary names both Spanish and international including Augustine Kofie, Olga de Dios, and David de la Mano. Less pricey purchases can be made in the bookshop, which sells curious zines and hard-to-find art anthologies. ⊠ *Calle de Miguel Servet 21, Lavapiés* ☎ *91/449–6128* ⊕ *www.swintongallery.com* ⊗ *Closed Sun. and Mon.* Ⓜ *Embajadores.*

CRAFTS

★ Yolanda Andrés

CRAFTS | These are not your grandma's embroideries: in Yolanda Andrés's thought-provoking pieces, which she describes as "paintings with thread," she interprets the centuries-old technique through a modern-day lens—with stunning results. Beyond the framed artwork (don't miss the technicolor "Artichoke" line), there are embroidered pillow cases, totes, and more. ⊠ *Calle Encomienda 15, Lavapiés* ☎ *91/026–0742* ⊕ *www.yolandaandres.com* ⊗ *Closed Tues. and Sun.*

FLEA MARKETS

★ El Rastro

OUTDOOR/FLEA/GREEN MARKETS | **FAMILY** | On Sunday morning, Calle de Ribera de Curtidores is closed to traffic and jammed with outdoor booths selling everything under the sun—this is its weekly transformation into the Rastro flea market. Find everything from antique furniture to rare vinyls of flamenco music and keychains emblazoned with "CNT," Spain's old anarchist trade union. Practice your Spanish by bargaining with vendors over paintings, heraldic iron gates, new and used clothes, and even hashish pipes. Plaza General Vara del Rey has some of El Rastro's best antiques, and the streets beyond—Calles Mira el Río Alta and Mira el Río Baja—boast all sorts of miscellany and bric-a-brac. The market shuts down shortly after 2 pm, in time for a street party to start in the area known as La Latina, centered on the bar El Viajero in Plaza Humilladero. ■ **TIP→ Off the Ribera are two galerías, courtyards with higher-quality, higher-price antiques shops.** ⊠ *Calle de Ribera de Curtidores, Barrio de las Letras* ⊗ *Closed Mon.–Sat.* Ⓜ *La Latina.*

MUSIC

Percusión Campos

MUSIC STORES | This percussion shop and workshop—where Canarian Pedro Navarro crafts his own *cajones flamencos,* or flamenco box drums—is hard to find, but his pieces are greatly appreciated among professionals. Prices run €90–€220 and vary according to the quality of woods used. ⊠ *Calle Olivar 36, Lavapiés* ☎ *91/539–2178* ⊕ *www.percusioncampos.com* Ⓜ *Lavapiés.*

Arganzuela

Arganzuela is such a huge district that a born-and-bred Madrileño would never say, "let's meet in Arganzuela." Locals instead speak in terms of the neighborhood's many subdistricts: Imperial, Legazpi, Las Delicias, Palos de Moguer, La Chopera, Las Acacias, and Atocha. Arganzuela is bordered by Palacio and Retiro in the north and northeast, Puente de Vallecas in the southwest, Usera in the south, and Carabanchel and Latina in the west. The lack of historical sights—with the notable exception of Matadero Madrid—keeps this blue-collar area largely off tourists' radar.

👁 Sights

★ Matadero Madrid

FACTORY | What was once Madrid's largest slaughterhouse is now one of its most vibrant arts and cultural centers. Built in the early 1900s on a then-undeveloped swath of land on the outskirts of town,

8

La Latina, Lavapiés, and Arganzuela   ARGANZUELA

the "Matadero Municipal de Legazpi" was in operation from 1925 to 1996. At its peak, it comprised 64 buildings and processed over 500 cattle and 5,000 sheep per day. The complex is a stunning example of Spanish fin-de-siècle civil architecture, all stone-and-redbrick facades punctuated by wide doorways and arched windows. Today its bays are thronged with families, tourists, and plenty of pierced-and-tattooed artists and creative types. Check the website for events ranging from film screenings to poetry slams to art exhibits and design fairs. After moseying from building to building, rest your legs at La Cantina del Matadero, a casual restaurant inside the complex where artists and spectators break bread in the form of tapas and fresh-out-of-the-oven pizzas. ⊠ *Plaza de Legazpi 8, Arganzuela* ☎ *91/318–4670* ⊕ *www.mataderomadrid.org* Ⓜ *Legazpi.*

 ## Restaurants

Bar Toboggan

$ | INTERNATIONAL | It's thanks to independently owned gems like Toboggan that La Chopera neighborhood is beginning to attract a younger, cooler crowd. This corner bar with outdoor seating serves mouthwatering international tapas ranging from tacos to tortilla to homemade hummus in a sunlit space decorated with plants and metal barstools. **Known for:** local La Virgen beer; excellent tapas and desserts; good-vibes-only atmosphere. Ⓢ *Average main: €8* ⊠ *Plaza de Rutilio Gacis 2, Local 1, Arganzuela* ☎ *91/245–6432* ⊕ *www.bartoboggan. com* ☺ *Closed Mon. and Tues.* Ⓜ *Legazpi.*

Habesha

$ | ETHIOPIAN | Chili fiends are often disappointed that Spanish food is seldom spicy, but this mom-and-pop Ethiopian restaurant satisfies all capsaicin cravings with its fiery stews and sauces. Vegans and vegetarians flock here for fresh, crunchy slaws, lentil *sambusas*, and slow-cooked greens, while omnivores

return time and again for the doro wat (spiced chicken). **Known for:** home-cooked Ethiopian cuisine steps from the Reina Sofía; bountiful vegetarian and vegan options; terrific service. Ⓢ *Average main: €10* ⊠ *Paseo de Santa María de la Cabeza 16, Arganzuela* ☎ *63/256–0112* ☺ *Closed Mon.* Ⓜ *Estación de Arte.*

Piantao

$$$$ | ARGENTINE | Piantao, opened in 2019 across the street from Matadero Madrid, hits all the high notes of an upmarket Argentine asador (steak house) with its daintily crimped empanadas, rustic wooden tables, gutsy South American wines, and—*por supuesto*—flame-licked steaks airlifted in from La Pampa with just the right amount of char. **Known for:** industrial yet refined digs; ultrajuicy steaks of Argentine beef; inhalable empanadas. Ⓢ *Average main: €23* ⊠ *Paseo de la Chopera 69, Arganzuela* ☎ *91/467–5402* ⊕ *www.piantao.es* ☺ *Closed Mon.* Ⓜ *Legazpi.*

 ## Nightlife

La Riviera

MUSIC CLUBS | One of Madrid's largest nightlife venues, with nine bars and an outdoor terrace, La Riviera hosts big-name DJs, local and international bands, and sundown-to-sunup raves. It's a key party spot on the Madrid Pride week (early July) circuit. Check the website for up-to-date performance schedules. ⊠ *Paseo Bajo de la Virgen del Puerto, Arganzuela* ☎ *91/365–2415* ⊕ *www. salariviera.com* Ⓜ *Puerta del Ángel.*

Sala Caracol

MUSIC CLUBS | Live techno, jazz, funk, and rock shows with reasonably priced tickets keep music-loving Madrileños returning to this underground nightclub just south of Lavapiés. ⊠ *Calle de Bernardino Obregón 18, Arganzuela* ☎ *91/527–3594* ⊕ *www.salacaracol.com* Ⓜ *Embajadores.*

Chapter 9

CHAMBERÍ

Updated by
Benjamin Kemper

◉ Sights   🍴 Restaurants   🛏 Hotels   🛍 Shopping   🍸 Nightlife
★★★☆☆   ★★★★★   ★★★☆☆   ★★☆☆☆   ★★★☆☆

NEIGHBORHOOD SNAPSHOT

TOP EXPERIENCES

■ **Tapas on Calle Ponzano:** Go on a new-school tapas crawl through Madrid's hottest culinary corridor.

■ **Museo Sorolla:** Wander the halls of the surrealist painter's mansion-museum and see some of his boldest works.

■ **Plaza de Olavide:** Claim an outdoor table in the sun, order a round of drinks, and lose track of time on this stately circular plaza.

■ **Mercado de Vallehermoso:** Take a pulse on local food trends at this buzzy yet unpretentious gastro-market.

■ **Parque de Santander:** Jog a few laps around the track or let your kids loose on the playground at this secret inner-city oasis.

■ **Jazz at Sala Clamores:** Groove to airtight, foot-tapping jazz numbers at this intimate music club.

GETTING HERE

Covering nearly 2 square miles, Chamberí lies north of Malasaña and Chueca, south of Chamartín, east of Moncloa, and west of Salamanca. Its subdistricts Trafalgar and Almagro are where most of the action is, and they're serviced by the following metro stops: San Bernardo (Líneas 2, 4), Quevedo (Línea 2), Iglesia (Línea 1), Canal (Líneas 2, 7), Alonso Cano (Línea 7), Gregorio Marañón (Líneas 7, 10), Rubén Darío (Línea 5), and Alonso Martínez (Líneas 4, 5, 10).

PLANNING YOUR TIME

A fine itinerary would start with impressionist art at Museo Sorolla followed by tapas and gourmet shopping at Mercado de Vallehermoso; then, you might meander east to Plaza de Olavide for *al fresco* lounging and people-watching, or make a beeline to Calle Ponzano, where you can cobble together lunch or dinner by hopping from bar to bar.

QUICK BITES

■ **Charnela.** Welcome to mussel mecca—this instant hit, opened in 2019, spotlights the oft-overlooked mollusc in dishes like curried moules frites; fried, bechamel-stuffed *tigres*; and zippy ceviches and escabeches. ⌧ *Calle de Ponzano 8 (next door to Fide), Chamberí* ⊕ *www.charnela-madrid.com* Ⓜ *Alonso Cano, Iglesia*

■ **Fide.** Crack open a can of pristine Spanish seafood—elvers, scallops, cockles, and more—at this veteran bar on Ponzano, and you'll never think about tinned food the same way again. ⌧ *Calle de Ponzano 8, Chamberí* Ⓜ *Alonso Cano, Iglesia*

■ **Mazál Bagels & Café.** Hand-rolled New York–style bagels made fresh daily hit the spot when continental breakfast fatigue sets in. ⌧ *Calle Alonso Cano 30, Chamberí* ⊕ *www.mazal-madrid.com* Ⓜ *Alonso Cano, Ríos Rosas*

Until recently, Chamberí was largely dismissed as a staid and sleepy residential neighborhood with little to offer tourists, but in the last five years, it has established itself as the city's gastronomic nerve center with innovative tapas bars and fusion fine-dining restaurants springing up left and right.

Until the 19th century, Chamberí was a backwater, a desolate hodgepodge of orchards, dehesas, wheat fields, and royal forests. But as Madrid industrialized, the subdistrict of Almagro (aka the "Golden Triangle" for its shape) became the preferred residence of the aristocracy—a legacy that you can see today in opulent constructions like the Palacio de los Marqueses de Bermejilla del Rey on Paseo Eduardo Dato, now an administrative building, and the Beti Jai fronton on Calle Marqués de Riscal, restored and reopened to the public in 2019. Chamberí remains an affluent and conservative district, but a bumper crop of new and experimental tapas bars is attracting a younger crowd and changing the neighborhood's DNA.

 Sights

Andén Cero (*Platform Zero*)
TRANSPORTATION SITE (AIRPORT/BUS/FERRY/TRAIN) | The so-called ghost station of Chamberí is now a locomotive museum managed by Metro Madrid. It occupies the grand old Chamberí station, built in 1919 and defunct since 1966. There are vintage advertisements, old maps,

and other memorabilia. Tours (free) and placards are in Spanish only. ■TIP➔ Don't wait for staff to come fetch you after watching the introductory film—just head down to the platform. ✉ Pl. de Chamberí, Chamberí ☎ 90/244–4403 ⊕ www.metromadrid.es/en/who-we-are/anden-cero ♾ Closed Mon.–Wed. Ⓜ Iglesia, Bilbao.

Calle Ponzano
NEIGHBORHOOD | Locals will tell you that this street boasts more bars per square foot (nearly 100 in total) than anywhere else on earth. Alternative facts aside, there's a bar for every taste here, from tile-walled tabernas to louche cocktail lounges to newfangled fusion spots. Start with a caña (half pint) or glass of *vermú* at a time-worn standby like El Doble (No. 58) or Fide (No. 8) before sampling traditional tapas at Taberna Alipio Ramos (No. 30) or La Máquina (No. 39). More eclectic, refined bites can be found at the tuna-centric DeAtún (No. 59), cheffy Sala de Despiece (No. 11), and modern Basque Arima (No. 51). ✉ Calle Ponzano, Chamberí ⊕ www.ponzaning.es Ⓜ Iglesia, Alonso Cano.

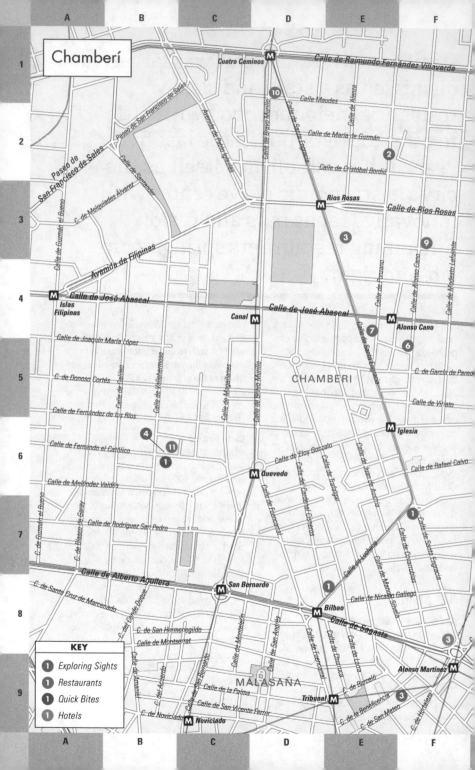

One of Madrid's most charming small museums was once home to Spain's most famous impressionist painter, Joaquin Sorolla.

Frontón Beti-Jai

SPORTS—SIGHT | Architecture and sports buffs alike are swooning over this meticulously restored Neo-Mudejar jai alai court that was built in 1896 and reopened in 2019 following a €5 million renovation—exactly 100 years after it closed to the public. The three-story stands, built to house 4,000 spectators, curve along one side to evoke a jai alai basket, and the fine elements of its construction—wrought-iron banisters, wooden beams, hand-laid brick—make the venue one of a kind. Over the years, the building was used as a parking lot, a jail, and a Citroën automotive repair center. While the local government mulls over possible uses of the building (cultural events, sports matches, etc.), visitors can tour the site via advance online booking. ✉ *Calle del Marqués de Riscal 7, Chamberí* ⊕ *www. betijaimadrid.es* ⊗ *Closed July and Aug.* Ⓜ *Ruben Darío.*

★ Mercado de Vallehermoso

MARKET | Choose from made-to-order *pinsas* (ancient Roman pizzas with a cloudlike crust) at Di Buono, flaky Argentine empanadas at Graciana, chifa tasting menus at Tripea, and high-octane Thai curries at Kitchen 154, among other flavor-packed options at this city-block-size market in the heart of Chamberí. ✉ *Calle de Vallehermoso 36, Chamberí* ☏ *91/138-9995* ⊕ *www.mercadovallehermoso.es* ⊗ *No dinner Sun.* Ⓜ *Quevedo.*

★ Museo Sorolla

MUSEUM | See the world through the once-in-a-generation eye of Spain's most famous impressionist painter, Joaquín Sorolla (1863–1923), who lived and worked most of his life at this home and garden that he designed and decorated. Every corner is filled with exquisite artwork—including plenty of original Sorollas—and impeccably selected furnishings, which pop against brightly colored walls that evoke the Mediterranean coast, where the painter was born.

The museum can be seen as part of the Abono Cinco Palacios, a €12 pass that grants access to five mansion-museums. ✉ *Paseo del General Martínez Campos 37, Chamberí* ☎ *91/310–1584* ⊕ *museoso-rolla.mcu.es* ✎ *€3 (free Sat. after 2 and all day Sun.)* ⊗ *Closed Mon.* Ⓜ *Rubén Darío, Gregorio Marañón.*

🍴 Restaurants

Apartaco
$$ | SOUTH AMERICAN | Venezuela's most craveable comfort foods draw the crowds to this bar-restaurant with cheery wait-staff and a soundtrack of Latin jazz. Start with a variety platter of appetizers includ-ing *tequeños* (gooey cheese sticks), *cachapas* (cheese-stuffed corn cakes), and *tostones* (green plantain fritters); then dive into a caveman-size portion of *pabellón criollo* (spiced shredded beef, black beans, and rice), the house special-ty. **Known for:** Venezuelan comfort food; tropical joie de vivre; fresh-squeezed juices. Ⓢ *Average main: €16* ✉ *Calle de Luchana 7, Chamberí* ☎ *68/697–4916* ⊕ *www.apartaco.es* Ⓜ *Bilbao.*

Kappo
$$$$ | SUSHI | Kappo delivers a classic, ultrarefined omakase experience free of fusion fripperies—a reminder that when the quality of fish is this good, there's no need for showy garnishes and tableside pyrotechnics. On a given night, chef Mario Payán might grace your chopsticks with grouper, yellowtail, horse mackerel, or scallop anointed with, say, a drop of ponzu or a scraggle of pickled daikon. **Known for:** multihour omakase experience; impeccably fresh fish; exclusive atmosphere. Ⓢ *Average main: €58* ✉ *Calle de Bretón de los Herreros 54, Chamberí* ☎ *91/042–0066* ⊕ *www.restaurantekappo.com* ⊗ *Closed Sun. and Mon.* Ⓜ *Gregorio Marañón.*

Lakasa
$$$ | SPANISH | Basque chef César Martín has a devoted local following for his hyperseasonal menus that show a sincere dedication to food sustainability. Lakasa may have moved into a big-ger, more modern space, but Martín's specialties haven't wavered: be sure to indulge in the Idiazabal fritters, crisp orbs redolent of smoky sheep's cheese. *Open weekdays only.* **Known for:** experimental Basque cuisine; Idiazabal fritters; pristine seafood. Ⓢ *Average main: €24* ✉ *Pl. del Descubridor Diego de Ordás 1, Chamberí* ☎ *91/533–8715* ⊕ *www.lakasa.es* ⊗ *Closed weekends* Ⓜ *Cuatro Caminos.*

Las Tortillas de Gabino
$$ | TAPAS | At this lively restaurant you'll find crowds of Spaniards gobbling up one of the city's finest, most upscale renditions of the tortilla española with unconventional add-ins like octopus, potato chips, and truffles. The menu also includes plenty of equally succulent non-egg choices (the rice dishes in particular stand out). **Known for:** fancy tortillas; date-night ambience; carefully selected wines. Ⓢ *Average main: €16* ✉ *Calle Rafael Cal-vo 20, Chamberí* ☎ *91/319–7505* ⊕ *www.lastortillasdegabino.com* ⊗ *Closed Sun.* Ⓜ *Rubén Darío.*

Perretxico Chamberí
$$ | BASQUE | The new Madrid outpost of a legendary Vitoria-Gasteiz (Basque Country) pintxo bar, Perretxico went viral in 2019 when it put a "cocido donut" on the menu—cocido being Spain's famous boiled dinner of chickpeas, various meats, and sausages. These are blended into a paste, stuffed inside a doughnut, and served alongside a demitasse of umami-packed bone broth for dunking, a wink to the classic doughnut-coffee combo. **Known for:** viral cocido doughnut; inventive Basque pintxos; new Chamberí hot spot. Ⓢ *Average main: €17* ✉ *Calle Rafael Calvo 29, Chamberí* ☎ *91/192–0069* ⊕ *www.perretxico.es* ⊗ *No dinner Sun.* Ⓜ *Rubén Darío.*

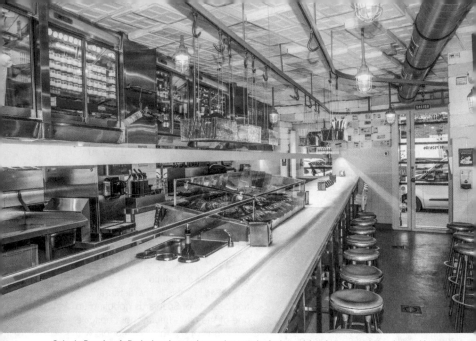

Sala de Despiece's flashy interiors and occasion-worthy fusion cuisine draw a trendy local crowd intent on sampling chef Javier Bonet's latest creations.

Restaurante Barrera

$$$ | SPANISH | Duck into this cozy hole-in-the-wall and be treated like family—Ana, the owner, recites the nightly menu to each table and flits around with a smile until the last guest saunters out. Barrera's famous *patatas revolconas*, paprika-spiced mashed potatoes topped with crispy pork belly, are always on offer; they might be followed by roast suckling lamb, wine-braised meatballs, or seared dayboat fish depending on the night. **Known for:** homey, romantic atmosphere; terrific patatas revolconas and ensaladilla rusa; unhurried all-night dining. Ⓢ *Average main: €25* ✉ *Calle de Alonso Cano 25, Chamberí* ☎ *91/594–1757* 🕙 *Closed Mon. No dinner Sun.* Ⓜ *Alonso Cano.*

Sala de Despiece

$$ | SPANISH | The opening of this ultratrendy butcher-shop-theme restaurant spurred the revival of Calle Ponzano as Madrid's most exciting tapas street. Feast on eye-catching, impeccably prepared dishes like carpaccio-truffle roll-ups and grilled octopus slathered in chimichurri. **Known for:** local celebrity chef; playful industrial decor; see-and-be-seen crowd. Ⓢ *Average main: €19* ✉ *Calle de Ponzano 11, Chamberí* ☎ *91/752–6106* ⊕ *www.saladedespiece.com* Ⓜ *Iglesia, Alonso Cano.*

Santceloni

$$$$ | MEDITERRANEAN | Chef Óscar Velasco delivers exquisite combinations of Mediterranean ingredients accompanied by a comprehensive and unusual wine list. Go with an appetite and lots of time (a minimum of three hours), because a meal here is ceremonious. **Known for:** varied cocktail and wine menu; impeccable service; sky's-the-limit luxury. Ⓢ *Average main: €50* ✉ *Hotel Hesperia, Paseo de la Castellana 57, Chamberí* ☎ *91/210–8840* ⊕ *www.restaurantesantceloni.com* 🕙 *Closed Sun. No lunch Sat.* Ⓜ *Gregorio Marañón.*

★ Sylkar

$$ | SPANISH | Budget time for a siesta after dining at this phenomenal down-home restaurant that hasn't changed a lick since opening a half-century

ago. Whether you're in the boisterous downstairs bar or cozy upstairs dining room with cloth napkins and popcorn walls, you'll be blown away by Sylkar's lovingly prepared specialties including creamy ham *croquetas*, braised squid in ink sauce, battered hake, and—drum roll, please—the best tortilla española in Madrid for those in the runnier-the-better camp. **Known for:** legendary tortilla española; irreverent banter with the waitstaff; free tapa with every drink. [$] *Average main: €19* ✉ *Calle de Espronceda 17, Chamberí* ☎ *91/554–5703* ⏲ *Closed Sun. No dinner Sat.* [M] *Alonso Cano.*

Taberna San Mamés

$$$ | **SPANISH** | What's that firetruck-red stew on every table in this tiny neighborhood tavern? *Callos a la madrileña*, Madrid-style tripe flavored with industrial quantities of garlic and smoky Extremaduran paprika. Other San Mamés standbys include fried bacalao (salt cod), truffled eggs and potatoes, and steak tartare. Book ahead or show up early (9 pm latest) to snag a table. **Known for:** abuela-approved tripe stew; cozy, traditional digs; neighborhood crowd. [$] *Average main: €27* ✉ *Calle de Bravo Murillo 88, Chamberí* ☎ *91/534–5065* 🌐 *www.tabernasanmames.es* ⏲ *Closed Sun. No dinner Mon.* [M] *Cuatro Caminos.*

★ Tripea

$$$$ | **FUSION** | Young-gun chef Roberto Martínez Foronda continues to turn food critics' heads with his Spanish-fusion restaurant hidden inside the Mercado de Vallehermoso, Chamberí's traditional market. Martínez's ever-changing tasting menu—a steal at €35—takes cues from *chifa* (Peruvian-Chinese) and *nikkei* (Peruvian-Japanese) culinary canons and incorporates fresh ingredients from the market. **Known for:** experimental tasting menus; Spanish-fusion cuisine; foodie buzz. [$] *Average main: €35* ✉ *Calle de Vallehermoso 36, Chamberí* ☎ *91/828–6947* 🌐 *www.tripea.es* ⏲ *Closed Sun. and Mon.* [M] *Quevedo.*

☕ Coffee and Quick Bites

Ciento Treinta Grados

$ | **CAFÉ** | These carb geeks cut no corners—breads here are leavened with sourdough and made with organic stone-ground flours, and the beans for their complex coffees are roasted in house. Drop into the postage-stamp dinette for breakfast or an afternoon pick-me-up, and savor airy all-butter croissants and any range of sweet and savory pastries and breads. **Known for:** sourdough breads and pastries; coffee made from house-roasted beans; location across from Mercado de Vallehermoso. [$] *Average main: €5* ✉ *Calle de Fernando el Católico 17, Chamberí* ☎ *91/006–7076* 🌐 *www.cientotreintagrados.com* [M] *Quevedo.*

🛏 Hotels

Hotel Orfila

$$$$ | **HOTEL** | On a leafy residential street not far from Plaza Colón and the gallery-lined Chueca district, this elegant 1886 town house bearing the Relais & Château fleur-de-lis boasts every comfort of larger five-star Madrid hotels—sans the stuffy corporate vibes. **Pros:** quiet street; Mario Sandoval restaurant; attentive service. **Cons:** bathrooms could use refurbishing; no on-site gym; love-it-or-hate-it Victorian decor. [$] *Rooms from: €370* ✉ *Calle Orfila 6, Chamberí* ☎ *91/702–7770* 🌐 *www.hotelorfila.com* 🛏 *32 rooms* 🍴 *No meals* [M] *Alonso Martínez.*

Hotel Santo Mauro, Autograph Collection

$$$$ | **HOTEL** | This fin-de-siècle palace, first a duke's residence and later the Canadian embassy, is now an intimate luxury hotel (managed by Marriott), an oasis of calm removed from the city center. **Pros:** a world away from the city's hustle and bustle; cloudlike beds; sophisticated restaurant. **Cons:** pricey breakfast; not in the historic center; some rooms are on the smaller side. [$] *Rooms from: €400* ✉ *Calle Zurbano 36, Chamberí*

☎ *91/319–6900* 🌐 *www.acsantomauro.com* 🛏 *51 rooms* 🍴 *No meals* [M] *Alonso Martínez, Rubén Darío.*

Hotel Sardinero

$$ | **HOTEL** | Steps from the trendy Malasaña and gay-friendly Chueca districts, and slightly off the tourist track, Hotel Sardinero occupies a turn-of-the-century palace directly above the Alonso Martínez metro stop. **Pros:** mellow earth-tone interiors; two rooftop terraces; gorgeous neoclassical facade. **Cons:** some guests report plumbing issues; no restaurant; kettles and coffeemakers only available on request. [$] *Rooms from: €140* ✉ *Pl. Alonso Martínez 3, Chamberí* ☎ *91/206–2160* 🌐 *www.hotelsardineromadrid.com* 🛏 *63 rooms* 🍴 *No meals* [M] *Alonso Martínez.*

Intercontinental Madrid

$$$$ | **HOTEL** | Chauffeur-driven town cars snake around the block day and night at the Intercontinental Madrid, a classically decorated hotel frequented by dignitaries, diplomats, and other international bigwigs. **Pros:** dependable if starchy elegance; newly refurbished 24-hour gym; excellent business facilities. **Cons:** cookie-cutter business hotel decor; removed from the center; street-facing rooms can be noisy. [$] *Rooms from: €239* ✉ *Paseo de la Castellana 49, Chamberí* ☎ *91/700–7300* 🌐 *www.ihg.com* 🛏 *302 rooms* 🍴 *No meals* [M] *Gregorio Marañón.*

★ The Pavilions Madrid

$$ | **HOTEL** | Hitting the sweet spot between high-end luxury and state-of-the-art design, The Pavilions is a new boutique hotel that stands out for its original art and sculpture by top Spanish artists, much of it available for purchase. **Pros:** high design on a budget; breakfast in solarium; upgraded rooms have outdoor terraces. **Cons:** small gym; unexciting environs; drab facade. [$] *Rooms from: €150* ✉ *Calle Amador de los Ríos 3, Chamberí* ☎ *91/310–7500* 🌐 *www.pavilionshotels.com/madrid* 🛏 *29 rooms* 🍴 *No meals* [M] *Colón.*

🍸 Nightlife

MUSIC CLUBS

★ Clamores

MUSIC CLUBS | Jive to live jazz concerts and world music until 5:30 am on weekdays and 6 am on weekends. Check the website for performance listings and to buy tickets, which rarely creep above €15. ✉ *Calle de Albuquerque 14, Chamberí* ☎ *91/445–5480* 🌐 *www.salaclamores.es* 🕒 *Closes at 11 pm Sun.* [M] *Bilbao.*

DANCE CLUBS

Opium

DANCE CLUBS | Sure, you can have a fancy Spanish fusion dinner in this upscale, modern nightclub, but most patrons come late, when the dance floor heats up with bumping electronic and reggaeton music. ✉ *Calle de José Abascal 56, Chamberí* ☎ *91/752–5322* 🌐 *www.opiummadrid.com* [M] *Gregorio Marañón.*

🛍 Shopping

FOOD

Casa Ruiz

FOOD/CANDY | For cooks on the hunt for hard-to-find Spanish ingredients, Casa Ruiz is an obligatory stop. The bulk purveyor specializes in dry ingredients, from beans to pulses to spices to chocolate, and they carry only the best. Seek out Manchegan saffron, *judiones* de La Granja (extra-large white runner beans), and Asturian *fabes* to make real-deal fabada (bean stew) in your home kitchen. ✉ *Calle de Andrés Mellado 46, Chamberí* ☎ *91/861–6128* 🌐 *www.casaruizgranel.com* 🕒 *Closed Sun.* [M] *Moncloa.*

CHAMARTÍN AND TETUÁN

Updated by
Benjamin Kemper

Sights	Restaurants	Hotels	Shopping	Nightlife
★★☆☆☆	★★★☆☆	★★★☆☆	★☆☆☆☆	★★☆☆☆

NEIGHBORHOOD SNAPSHOT

TOP EXPERIENCES

■ **Real Madrid's home turf:** Take a pilgrimage to Spanish *fútbol* mecca, Santiago Bernabéu stadium.

■ **DiverXO:** Settle in for a punk rock tasting menu unlike any other at Madrid's futuristic three-Michelin-star restaurant.

GETTING HERE

Chamartín and Tetuán sit directly above Salamanca and Chamberí, respectively, and clock in at a whopping 15 square km (nearly 6 square miles) in total. Chances are, if you must venture this far north, it's for a business meeting in Madrid's main financial corridor, (the northern reaches of Paseo de la Castellana) or for a soccer match at Santiago Bernabéu stadium (metro Santiago Bernabeu, Línea 10). BiciMAD, Madrid's bike-share service, has docks scattered throughout both neighborhoods. As Chamartín and Tetuán lie outside the Madrid Central low-emission zone, all rental cars are allowed entry. Parking is generally readily available except for around Santiago Bernabéu stadium on game nights.

PLANNING YOUR TIME

Chamartín and Tetuán are residential and business-oriented areas, so you'll want to make a beeline to your final destination and—unless you love wandering for the sake of wandering—move right along. The wide, stately boulevards of Chamartín are well-suited to jogging and strolling but aren't particularly intriguing otherwise. Steer clear of the dodgy Bellas Vistas neighborhood of Tetuán (particularly Calle Topete), and keep your wits about you in the area around Nuevos Ministerios station, where unsavory characters are wont to loiter.

QUICK BITES

■ **Casa Sotero.** We dare you to find better *torreznos* (hot, salty pork cracklings) in Madrid. ⌗ *Calle de Bravo Murillo 337, Tetuán* Ⓜ *Valdeacederas*

■ **El Enfriador.** Choose from a long list of well-priced tapas—shout out to the to-die-for empanadas—at this spacious bar and restaurant less than a block from Santiago Bernabéu stadium. ⌗ *Paseo de la Castellana 89, Tetuán* Ⓜ *Santiago Bernabéu*

■ **La Pampa.** Step back in time in this corner bar, one of the neighborhood's few surviving prewar buildings, and be sure to order a slice of homemade tortilla española. ⌗ *Calle de Francos Rodríguez 40, Tetuán* Ⓜ *Estrecho*

Tetuán and Chamartín sprawl north of the city center, and if you have tickets to a Real Madrid match (or a business meeting on Paseo de la Castellana), you'll end up here. But don't rush out—make the most of your visit by exploring the hidden-gem food and nightlife scenes.

The historical town of **Chamartín** wasn't formally annexed to Madrid until 1948. During the following decades, and due to the construction of new sites such as the Chamartín Train Station and the National Auditorium of Music, it gained popularity among Madrileños as a convenient and tranquil place to live. The famous leaning "Gate of Europe" towers are situated here, as are many office buildings, convention centers, business hotels, and the seat of Real Madrid, Santiago de Bernabéu stadium. **Tetuán** is decidedly working class. The main street through the neighborhood is Bravo Murillo, and on it you'll find plenty of old-school bars, kebab restaurants, pawn shops, and off-brand clothing stores. You won't find many tourists or hipster boutiques, but you will find locals enjoying an affordable and interesting food scene.

Chamartín

🍴 Restaurants

★ Casa Benigna

$$$ | SPANISH | Owner Norberto Jorge, a quirky, jolly gent, offers a produce-centric menu with painstakingly selected wines to match at this snug, book-lined restaurant. Rice dishes are the house specialty, and they're cooked in extra-flat paella pans specially manufactured for the restaurant. **Known for:** fantastic paella; larger-than-life owner; homey atmosphere. *[$] Average main: €26 ✉ Calle de Benigno Soto 9, Chamartín ☎ 91/416–9357 🌐 www.casabenigna.com 🕘 No dinner Sun. [M] Concha Espina, Prosperidad.*

★ DiverXO

$$$$ | ECLECTIC | When you ask a Madrileño about a remarkable food experience—something that stirs the senses beyond feeding one's appetite—David Muñoz's bombastic restaurant is often the first name you'll hear. Nothing is offered à la carte; it serves one take-no-prisoners tasting menu (called a "canvas") that runs €250. **Known for:** punk rock fine dining; courses that use the whole table as a canvas; Madrid's only Michelin three-star. *[$] Average main: €250 ✉ NH Hotel Eurobuilding, Calle Padre Damian 23, Chamartín ☎ 91/570–0766 🌐 www.diverxo.com 🕘 Closed Sun. and Mon. [M] Cuzco.*

Sacha

$$$$ | SPANISH | Settle into a unhurried feast at Sacha, a cozy bistro with soul-satisfying food and hand-selected wines, and you might never want to leave—especially if you strike up a conversation with Sacha himself, who's quite the character. The cuisine is regional Spanish—think *butifarra* sausages with

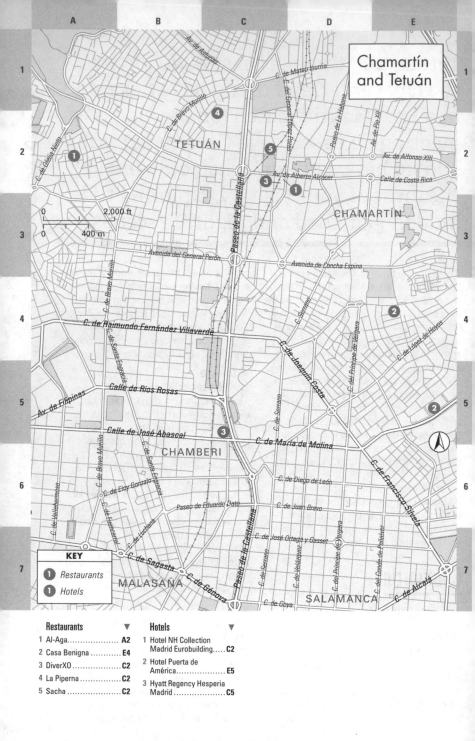

Chamartín and Tetuán

	A	B	C	D	E

TETUÁN

CHAMARTÍN

CHAMBERI

MALASAÑA

SALAMANCA

0 ——— 2,000 ft
0 ——— 400 m

C. de Mateo murria
C. del General López Poza
Paseo de la Habana
Av. de Pío XII
Av. de Alfonso XIII
Calle de Costa Rica
Av. de Alberto Alcocer
Avenida del General Perón
Avenida de Concha Espina
C. Serrano
C. de López de Hoyos
C. de Raimundo Fernández Villaverde
C. de Joaquín Costa
C. del Príncipe de Vergara
Calle de Ríos Rosas
Calle de José Abascal
C. de María de Molina
C. de Francisco Silvela
C. de Diego de León
C. de Juan Bravo
Paseo de Eduardo Dato
C. de José Ortega y Gasset
C. de Sagasta
C. de Génova
C. de Goya
C. de Alcalá
Av. de Filipinas
C. de Bravo Murillo
C. de Santa Engracia
C. de Eloy Gonzalo
C. de Luchana
C. de Valdehermoso
C. de Fuencarral
Av. de Diego Niño
Av. de Asturias
C. de Bravo Murillo
Paseo de la Castellana
Paseo de la Castellana
C. de Serrano
C. del Príncipe de Vergara
C. de Valázquez
C. del Conde de Peñalver

KEY
1 Restaurants
1 Hotels

Restaurants ▼
1 Al-Aga.................... **A2**
2 Casa Benigna **E4**
3 DiverXO **C2**
4 La Piperna **C2**
5 Sacha **C2**

Hotels ▼
1 Hotel NH Collection
   Madrid Eurobuilding..... **C2**
2 Hotel Puerta de
   América................... **E5**
3 Hyatt Regency Hesperia
   Madrid **C5**

sautéed mushrooms or razor clams with black garlic emulsion—with just enough imagination to make you wonder why the restaurant isn't better known. **Known for:** Spanish bistro fare; impeccable steak tartare; hard-to-find wines. [$] *Average main: €30* ✉ *Calle Juan Hurtado de Mendoza 11, Chamartín* ☎ *91/345–5952* ⏲ *Closed Sun.* [M] *Cuzco.*

Hotels

★ Hotel NH Collection Madrid Eurobuilding

$$ | **HOTEL** | The towering NH Collection Madrid Eurobuilding, located blocks from Real Madrid's home stadium, is a state-of-the-art luxury property with large, airy rooms, and an enormous pool and gym complex. **Pros:** 180-degree views from some rooms; excellent gym and spa; one of Madrid's top restaurants. **Cons:** inconsistent service; hotel can't secure bookings at DiverXO; area dies at night. [$] *Rooms from: €145* ✉ *Calle de Padre Damián 23, Chamartín* ☎ *91/353–7300* 🌐 *www.nh-hotels.com* 🛏 *440 rooms* 🍴 *No meals* [M] *Cuzco.*

Hotel Puerta de América

$$ | **HOTEL** | Inspired by Paul Eluard's *La Liberté*, whose verses are written across the facade, the owners of this hotel granted an unlimited budget to 19 of the world's top architects and designers. **Pros:** 12 hotels in one – an architect's dream; top-notch restaurant and bars; candlelit pool and steam room area. **Cons:** miles from the center; interiors don't always get the required maintenance; design impractical in places. [$] *Rooms from: €130* ✉ *Av. de América 41, Chamartín* ☎ *91/744–5400* 🌐 *www.hotelpuertamerica.com* 🛏 *315 rooms* 🍴 *No meals* [M] *Avenida de América.*

Hyatt Regency Hesperia Madrid

$$$ | **HOTEL** | The legendary Hesperia hotel was bought and renovated by Hyatt Regency and reopened in 2019 following a much-needed renovation. **Pros:** newly renovated; award-winning restaurant; 24-hour room service. **Cons:** interior rooms can be dark; stuffy, corporate feel; miles from the center. [$] *Rooms from: €185* ✉ *Paseo de la Castellana 57, Chamartín* ☎ *91/210–8800* 🌐 *www.hesperia.com* 🛏 *169 rooms* 🍴 *No meals* [M] *Gregorio Marañón.*

Nightlife

BARS

Domo Lounge and Terrace

BARS/PUBS | The NH hotel chain is building a top-notch food-and-drink stronghold north of the city around its Eurobuilding property. Besides DiverXO and Domo restaurants there's now a cocktail bar with an enclosed terrace, run by Diego Cabrera, the city's top mixologist. Choose from classic cocktails and original creations. ✉ *Calle de Padre Damián 23, Chamartín* ☎ *91/353–7300* 🌐 *www.nh-hotels.com* [M] *Cuzco.*

Tetuán

As Madrid grew dramatically in the second half of the 19th century, rough-and-tumble barrios like Tetuán got a face-lift. Today, it's main artery, Bravo Murillo, divides the more developed, business-oriented eastern section from the more residential and multicultural western area of the neighborhood.

Restaurants

★ Al-Aga

$ | **MIDDLE EASTERN** | **FAMILY** | Madrileños love kebabs, and the smoky, juicy version served at Al-Aga is far and away the city's best. Opened by a family of refugees fleeing Syria's civil war, Al-Aga draws on recipes handed down to the chef and owner, Labib, who cooks with care and attention to detail: meat is ground by hand for each order, and all the sauces are homemade. **Known for:** flame-grilled kebabs; grab-and-go style; Syrian specialties. [$] *Average*

¡GOOOOOLL!

Fútbol (or soccer) is Spain's number-one sport, and Madrid has four teams: Real Madrid, Atlético Madrid, Rayo Vallecano, and Getafe. The two major teams are Real Madrid and Atlético Madrid. For tickets, book online or call a week in advance to reserve and pick them up at the stadium—or, if the match isn't sold out, stand in line at the stadium of your choice. Ticket prices vary according to several factors: the importance of the rival, the seat location, the day of the week the match takes place, whether the match is aired on free TV or not, and the competition (Liga, Copa del Rey, Champions League or Europa League). Final dates and match times are often confirmed only a few days before so it can be hard to reserve in advance. That said, Real Madrid and Atlético Madrid never play at home the same week, so there is a football match every single week in the city.

Stadiums

Campo de Fútbol de Vallecas To enjoy a spirited match without the long lines and inflated price tag, step up to Rayo Vallecano's box office. The team's second-tier status doesn't make the games any less thrilling (think college ball vs. NBA), especially when you catch them on their home turf in Vallecas, which seats 14,708.

You can feel good about your ticket purchase, too, since Rayo is known for its community activism. During the Covid-19 crisis, the team's charitable foundation sewed and distributed 12,000 masks for undersupplied hospitals. ✉ *Calle del Payaso Fofó 0, Madrid* ☎ *91/478–4329* ⊕ *www.rayovallecano.es* Ⓜ *Portazgo.*

Santiago Bernabéu Stadium Home to Real Madrid, this stadium seats 85,400 and offers daytime tours of the facilities. A controversial $590 million renovation was approved by the city council in May 2019 and will take approximately 3½ years to complete; tour and game schedules may be affected, so check the website for updates. During the Covid-19 outbreak, the stadium was used as a storage facility for medical supplies. ✉ *Paseo de la Castellana 140, Chamartín* ☎ *91/398–4300* ⊕ *www.realmadrid.es* Ⓜ *Santiago Bernabeu.*

Wanda Metropolitano Since 2017, Atlético Madrid has called this stadium in the San Blas–Canillejas district home. ✉ *Av. de Luis Aragones 4, Madrid* ☎ *90/226–0403* ⊕ *en.atleticodemadrid.com/atm/new-stadium-atletico-de-madrid* Ⓜ *Estadio Metropolitano.*

∎ TIP➔ **On the ticket, "Puerta" is the door number that you enter, "Fila" is the row, and "Número" or "🚪" is the seat number.**

main: *€9* ✉ *Calle Villaamil 52, Tetuán* ☎ *91/070–3115* Ⓜ *Tetuán.*

★ La Piperna

$$ | ITALIAN | FAMILY | Tetuán is the unlikely location of this outstanding (and extremely well-priced) Italian restaurant run by a Naples native. Homemade pastas are the star of the show—try the ricotta-stuffed tortellini *alla nerano* topped with fresh basil and Parmiggiano or the

paccheri al ragut swimming in a 10-hour meat sauce—but the veal Milanese and desserts like panna cotta dolloped with raspberry sauce are equally divine. **Known for:** homemade regional pastas; expat Italian crowd; terrific eggplant parm. 💲 *Average main: €16* ✉ *Calle de la Infanta Mercedes 98, Tetuán* ☎ *91/169–4950* ⊕ *www.restaurantelapiperna.com* ⊗ *No dinner Sun.* Ⓜ *Valdeacederas.*

Chapter 11

CARABANCHEL, USERA, AND LATINA

Updated by
Benjamin Kemper

◉ Sights	🍴 Restaurants	🛏 Hotels	💼 Shopping	🍸 Nightlife
★☆☆☆☆	★★★★☆	★☆☆☆☆	★★☆☆☆	★★★☆☆

NEIGHBORHOOD SNAPSHOT

TOP EXPERIENCES

■ **Tapas:** Feast on affordable no-frills bar food and drinks.

■ **Alternative Madrid:** Get a pulse on Madrid's indie art scene and bang your head at an underground rock show.

■ **Chinatown:** Devour dumplings, dim sum, and more in unsung Usera.

■ **Puente de Toledo:** Traverse the city's most beautiful bridge.

■ **Mercado de Tirso de Molina:** Pick up culinary souvenirs and graze on budget tapas along the way.

GETTING HERE

Carabanchel, Usera, and Latina are serviced by metro lines 3, 5, 6, 10, and 11. Usera station (Línea 6) is a good jumping-off point for exporing Usera, while Oporto (Línea 5) is near Carabanchel's art studios and many restaurants and nightlife venues. Alternatively, access Usera by alighting at Legazpi (Línea 4); take a pleasant stroll through Madrid Río park to cross the river (15-minute walk). BiciMAD, Madrid's bikeshare service, does not service these neighborhoods. These neighborhoods lie outside the low-emission zone called Madrid Central, so all rental cars are free to enter and park.

PLANNING YOUR TIME

Carabanchel, Usera, and Latina are sprawling working-class barrios that are worth visiting for a handful of specific restaurants, bars, and sights, but given the area's enormous footprint and generally drab architecture, it's less suited to aimless wandering. So, pinpoint a down-home Chinese restaurant in Usera, an art gallery in Carabanchel, or a locals-only tapas bar in Latina, and make a beeline. Pay special attention to your surroundings and mind your belongings, especially at night, as certain pockets of these neighborhoods can be a bit dodgy.

QUICK BITES

■ **Casa de los Minutejos.** Griddled pig-ear sandwiches, which come crustless and bathed in spicy *brava* sauce, are the specialty here. ✉ *Calle de Antonio de Leyva, 17, Carabanchel* Ⓜ *Marqués de Vadillo*

■ **Chacón.** This greasy-spoon Galician spot serves up textbook-perfect braised octopus topped with copious olive oil, crunchy salt, and pimentón. ✉ *Calle Saavedra Fajardo, 16, Latina* Ⓜ *Puerta del Ángel*

■ **Jin Yun Shao Bing.** For the paltry price of €2, sink your teeth into a satisfying Northern Chinese shao bing (flatbread) stuffed with any combination of veggies and braised meats. ✉ *Calle de Nicolás Sánchez, 59, Usera* Ⓜ *Usera, Almendrales*

As rents soar in the city center—up more than 50% in the last five years alone—Madrid's cash-strapped youth are migrating south of the Manzanares to multicultural neighborhoods like Carabanchel, Usera, and Latina. But don't expect third-wave cafés and Brooklyn-esque trendster glamour—yet. Far from being fully gentrified, Madrid's "left bank" combines sleepy residential areas with grittier industrial ones. As these neighborhoods are relatively new, only urbanized in the second half of the 20th century, there are few historical sights and museums, which keeps tourists at bay.

Carabanchel is one of Madrid's most populous neighborhoods as well as one of its most diverse, as evidenced by streets lined with everything from arepa bars to West African groceries to rootsy Spanish taverns. For most of the year, Carabanchel sees little foot traffic beyond locals going about their business. Two festivals draw the crowds: Art Banchel and Fiestas de San Isidro Labrador (both held mid-May). The former is an alternative art event spotlighting the work of local artists, more than 300 of whom have studios in the neighborhood. The latter, centered on San Isidro Park, is one of Madrid's most popular *verbenas* (outdoor summer festivals), complete with traditional dance, booze-fueled partying, and bountiful *rosquillas* (anise-scented donuts), the classic fairground snack.

Usera, just east of Carabanchel, is—improbably—one of Europe's best, and newest, Chinatowns. Step off the metro and you're surrounded by Mandarin-lettered signs for markets and restaurants of countless regions styles such as Sichuan, Shanghainese, and Cantonese. Most shop owners are first-generation Chinese immigrants thanks to a diversity visa program that began some 20 years ago. (In 1980 there were barely 1,000 Chinese people in Spain; today there are over 11,000 in Usera alone.) If you happen to be in town for the Chinese New Year, Usera is a must for its colorful parade and late-night DJ sets.

Latina, not to be confused with La Latina neighborhood in the city center, is Carabanchel's western bookend. Cross Segovia Bridge, south of the Royal Palace, and you've arrived. Like its neighbors, Latina offers a lively mix of time-worn Spanish spots and immigrant-run restaurants and stores. The subdistrict Puerta del Ángel has been newly dubbed the "Brooklyn of Madrid," thanks to an influx of photographers, graffiti artists, and the like. The rest of the neighborhood is largely in decline, however, with more than 200 shops closing in the last five years and homelessness on the rise. Keep an eye on this barrio in flux.

 Sights

Ermita de Santa María la Antigua

RELIGIOUS SITE | Most Madrileños have no idea that the city's (and greater region's) oldest Mudejar church, erected in the 13th century, is located in Carabanchel. Though currently under renovation and closed to the public, it remains exceptionally well-preserved. The hermitage has a rectangular floorplan and a six-story brick-and-stone belfry with two bells (these were added in the 20th century). Note the intricate, Moorish-influenced arches above the doorways and windows fashioned out of brick. If by some stroke of luck you gain entry to the church—it purportedly opens occasionally on Saturday at 11 am—you'll find colorful medieval frescoes and a well within. ✉ *Calle de Monseñor Oscar Romero 92, Carabanchel* Ⓜ *Eugenia de Montijo.*

★ Mercado de Tirso de Molina

MARKET | Built in 1932 by Luis Bellido, the architect behind Matadero Madrid, this soaring brick market isn't found on the city-center plaza that shares its name but rather in the up-and-coming Puerta del Ángel neighborhood. After stocking up on Spanish charcuterie and pantry items (the best souvenirs!), nibble on Chinese-style tripe stew at El Bar de Paula, vegan huaraches at El Vegicano, and pristine conservas (canned seafood) at La Lattina. Take note, weekenders: this is one of Madrid's only traditional markets that stays open on Sunday. ✉ *Calle de Doña Urraca 15, Latina* ☎ *91/464–5235 for general information.* ⊕ *www.mercadotirsodemolina.es* Ⓜ *Puerta del Ángel.*

Parque de San Isidro

CITY PARK | FAMILY | Spring and fall are the best times to jog, stroll, or picnic in this tranquil park with none of the tourist hustle and bustle of Retiro. Come mid-May, Parque de San Isidro becomes party central with the arrival of the eponymous *fiestas*; bring family and friends and enjoy the fireworks, concerts, street food, and rides. ✉ *Carabanchel* ⊙ *www.esmadrid. com/agenda/sanisidro-madrid.*

Puente de Toledo (*Bridge of Toledo*)

BRIDGE/TUNNEL | A masterwork in Churrigueresque (Spanish baroque) architecture, this impressive granite bridge over the Manzanares connects Arganzuela and Carabanchel. Felipe IV commissioned its construction in order to shorten the route from Madrid to Toledo in the mid-17th century (hence the bridge's name), but floods destroyed the initial structure. The bridge you can walk across today (it is pedestrian-access-only) was completed in 1732 by architect Pedro de Ribera and contains nine arches buttressed by rounded columns. At night, these are uplit and look particularly magical from below on the Madrid Río esplanade. Midway across the bridge, don't miss the niches adorned with richly carved limestone statues of Madrid's patron saints, San Isidro Labrador and Santa María de la Cabeza. ✉ *Carabanchel* Ⓜ *Pirámides.*

Usera is one of Europe's best Chinatowns and while it doesn't have an archway at the entrance it does have an established Chinese community and lively Chinese New Year celebrations.

🍴 Restaurants

To discover Madrid's most soulful, unvarnished, and untouristed restaurants, you have to head south of the river. This is an intrepid foodie's paradise—uncharted even by local standards. The first thing you'll notice? A plunge in menu prices—working-class Madrid will fork over no extra euros for dainty portions or *nueva cocina* fripperies. Carabanchel and Latina are awash with old-timey bars hawking three-course €10 *menús del día* (prix-fixes) and greasy-spoon tapas late into the evening, while Usera contains a vibrant mix of decades-old neighborhood institutions and regional Chinese restaurants.

★ Aynaelda

$$ | SPANISH | FAMILY | Textbook-perfect paella in... Latina? Madrid is a notoriously disappointing city when it comes to the rice dishes popular on the Mediterranean coast, but Aynaelda slam-dunks with its sizzling paellas flavored with heady aromatics and concentrated stock. Be sure to scrape up the *socarrat*, that swoon-worthy layer of crisp rice that sticks to the bottom of the pan. Avoid Sunday lunch as there's usually a waitlist. **Known for:** rice dishes up to Valencian standards; bright, airy dining room; excellent croquettes. $ *Average main: €22* ⊠ *Calle los Yébenes 38, Latina* ☎ *91/710–1051* ⊕ *www.aynaelda.com* ⊘ *No dinner Sun.* Ⓜ *Laguna.*

Café Astral

$ | SPANISH | Salt cod croquettes, fresh tomato salad, roast suckling pig—these are some of the comfort-food classics you'll find on the menu at this neighborhood haunt whose diner-y decor (steel bar, beige awnings, paper place mats) hasn't changed in decades. If you can snag a patio table in the summer, you've hit pay dirt. **Known for:** affordable suckling pig; generous breakfasts from 6 am; hyperlocal crowd. $ *Average main: €11* ⊠ *Camino Viejo de Leganés 82, Carabanchel* ☎ *91/560–0818* ⊘ *Closed Sun.* Ⓜ *Oporto.*

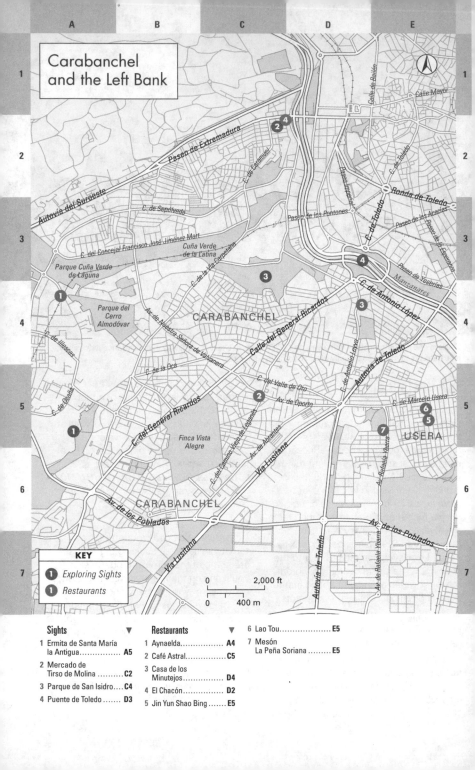

Carabanchel and the Left Bank

★ Casa de los Minutejos

$ | TAPAS | FAMILY | Stop into this no-frills bar for distressingly inhalable griddled sandwiches ("minutejos") of crispy pig ear doused in fiery *brava* sauce. Tamer fillings are available for the squeamish. To drink? An ice-cold Mahou, *por supuesto*. **Known for:** crustless "minutejo" sandwiches; ample space to spread out; no-nonsense service. [$] *Average main: €7* ✉ *Calle de Antonio de Leyva 17, Carabanchel* ☎ *91/560–6726* [M] *Vista Alegre, Oporto.*

★ El Chacón

$ | SPANISH | FAMILY | All the Galician greatest hits are on the menu at this Latina stalwart with an old tile floor and wooden benches. Paprika-dusted octopus, smoky *lacón* (cooked ham), and weighty slabs of *empanada gallega* (tuna pie) go down a bit too easily when accompanied by gallons of the house Albariño. **Known for:** Galician peasant food; devoted local crowd; hefty free tapa with every drink. [$] *Average main: €13* ✉ *Calle Saavedra Fajardo 16, Latina* ☎ *91/463–1044* ⏲ *Closed Wed.* [M] *Puerta del Ángel.*

Jin Yun Shao Bing

$ | NORTHERN CHINESE | FAMILY | Hot griddled flatbreads (shao bing) filled with soy-scented beef will set you back just €1.80 a pop at this hole-in-the-wall specializing in the northern Chinese delicacy. Noodle and wonton soups (average price: €4) hit the spot when it's cold out. **Known for:** addictive meat-filled flatbreads; made-to-order dumplings; shockingly affordable prices. [$] *Average main: €4* ✉ *Calle Nicolás Sánchez 59, Usera* ☎ *91/125–3620* [M] *Usera.*

Lao Tou

$ | CHINESE | FAMILY | Find primal pleasure here picking the meat off a hake head served in a cauldron of gingery broth or slurping your weight of wok-charred noodles tossed with chicken and seafood. Stir-fried okra, sweet-and-sour pork ribs, and shrimp soup are other perennial favorites among the mostly Chinese clientele. **Known for:** hake head soup on every table; non-Europeanized Chinese cuisine; feasting on a budget. [$] *Average main: €12* ✉ *Calle Nicolás Sánchez 35, Usera* ☎ *65/112–1287* ⏲ *Closed Thurs.* [M] *Usera.*

★ Mesón La Peña Soriana

$ | TAPAS | Madrileños pour in from far and wide for Esther's famous patatas bravas, fried potato wedges cloaked in vinegary paprika-laced chili sauce. A menu brimming with snails, fried lamb intestines, pork rinds, and Castilian blood sausage confirms that you're in *el Madrid profundo*. Breakfast is also served. **Known for:** killer patatas bravas; throwback interiors; Madrid-style offal dishes. [$] *Average main: €9* ✉ *Calle Fornillos 58, Usera* ☎ *64/562–6548* 🌐 *www.mesonlapenasoriana.wordpress.com* ⏲ *Closed Tues. and Wed.*

Nightlife

Gruta 77

MUSIC CLUBS | This snug nightclub is all about fist-pumping rock 'n roll. There are live concerts most nights, and the cover rarely exceeds €10. DJs make frequent appearances as well, especially late in the evening. Beers are cheap, the music is loud, and close quarters mean you'll probably make an amigo or two. ✉ *Calle Cuclillo 6, Carabanchel* ☎ *91/471–2370* 🌐 *www.gruta77.com* [M] *Oporto.*

Sala Live

MUSIC CLUBS | The most legendary nightlife venue in the south of Madrid, Live has been hosting—you guessed it—live music shows for over two decades. Check the website to see who's currently blasting over the 8,000-watt Nexo sound system. Past performances have run the gamut from flamenco artist José Mercé to rockers Danko Jones and undiscovered local punk bands. ✉ *Av. de Nuestra Señora de Fátima 42, Carabanchel* ☎ *91/525–5444* 🌐 *www.lasala.biz* [M] *Eugenia de Montijo*

Shopping

FOOD

Productos Zabala

FOOD/CANDY | Generously stuffed empanadas—double-crusted Galician pies stuffed with any range of meats and seafood—make terrific picnic fare, and Zabala (est. 1967) makes consistently sublime ones. Take a few slabs to go and savor them under the cherry trees in the nearby Cuña Verde de Latina park. ✉ *Paseo Perales 4, Latina* ☎ *91/463–3791* ⊕ *www.productoszabala.com* ⊗ *Closed Sun.* Ⓜ *Lucero.*

GALLERIES

Sabrina Amrani Gallery

ART GALLERIES | Sabrina Amrani, the Algerian-French gallerist behind this hangarlike art showroom, is also the president of Arte_Madrid, the city's top art gallery association. She put Carabanchel on the contemporary art map when she opened the blindingly white space in 2011. Expect an array of experimental, conceptual pieces from Europe, Asia, the Middle East, and beyond. ✉ *Calle Sallaberry 52, Carabanchel* ☎ *91/621–7859* ⊕ *www.sabrinaamrani.com* ⊗ *Closed Sun. and Mon.* Ⓜ *Oporto, Vista Alegre.*

Chapter 12

DAY TRIPS FROM MADRID

Updated by
Benjamin Kemper

👁 **Sights**
★★★★★

🍴 **Restaurants**
★★★★☆

🛏 **Hotels**
★★★★☆

🛍 **Shopping**
★★★★☆

🍸 **Nightlife**
★★☆☆☆

WELCOME TO DAY TRIPS FROM MADRID

TOP REASONS TO GO

★ **Fairy-tale castles and palaces:** Scurry up ancient towers and time-travel to Golden Age Spain.

★ **Castilian comfort food:** Plunge your fork into crackly roast meats and hearty game dishes.

★ **Unspoiled nature:** Embark on a scenic hike with gorgeous mountain views and birds swooping overhead.

★ **Gasp-worthy religious sights:** Ponder Spain's multicultural legacy in splendid cathedrals, synagogues, and mosques.

★ **History galore:** Uncover the secrets of Spain's rich past in towns and cities that predate Madrid.

1 Toledo. Discover a treasure trove of medieval art and in the pre-Madrid capital of Castile.

2 San Lorenzo de El Escorial. Travel less than an hour outside Madrid to see Felipe II's over-the-top abode.

3 Segovia. Marvel at a soaring Roman aqueduct and explore the fortress said to have inspired the Disney castle.

4 Ávila. Walk along the ramparts of the best-preserved city walls in Europe, and snack on sweet treats baked by nuns.

5 Sepúlveda. Descend into a medieval dungeon and in a town some call the most beautiful in Spain.

6 Sigüenza. Tour one of Spain's best-preserved Gothic cathedrals.

7 Cuenca. Marvel at the Hanging Houses, then explore the Ciudad Encantada ("Enchanted City") with its alien rock formations.

8 Almagro. Slow things down in this quintessential Manchegan town with a vibrant evening *tapeo* (tapas scene).

9 Salamanca. See if you can spot the frog on the plateresque facade of Spain's oldest university for good luck.

10 Burgos. Come for the stunning Gothic cathedral; stay for the nationally famous *morcilla* sausages.

Madrid, in the center of Spain, is an excellent jumping-off point for exploring, and the high-speed train—plus bountiful bus and rideshare options—puts dozens of destinations within easy reach, even without a rental car. You'll be surprised at how few tourists you'll encounter in many of these locales, particularly in the off season (winter and summer), when dramatic temperature swings drive most travelers elsewhere. Their loss—having a sleepy medieval town virtually to yourself is a greater luxury than any five-star hotel can provide. The Castiles, which bracket Madrid to the north and south, and Extremadura, bordering Portugal, are filled with compelling destinations steeped in tradition.

With so many options at your fingertips, deciding where to visit outside Madrid can be daunting. Toledo and Segovia are the no-brainer picks for travelers with a day or two to spare. The former, situated an hour south of Madrid, is the seat of Old Castile, once a bustling multicultural metropolis where Jews, Muslims, and Christians cohabitated before the Inquisition. Toledo's old town is essentially an open-air museum with its warren of streets lined with ancient mosques, monasteries, and old-timey shops. Ninety-four kilometers (58 miles) north of Madrid lies Segovia, which is smaller, more provincial, and easier to digest than Toledo—you can hit the main sights (the Roman aqueduct, Gothic cathedral, and soaring "Disney" castle) in the morning and still have time for a dozy lunch of *cochinillo asado* (suckling pig), a *Segoviano* specialty.

Travelers who have already hit Toledo and Segovia—and those who relish secluded, time-warpy small towns—should consider stealing away to Almagro, Sepúlveda, El Escorial, Cuenca, or Sigüenza, each with stunning architecture and boundless country hospitality. Salamanca, Burgos, and Ávila are larger, more historic cities that flourished in the Middle Ages and contain enough captivating monuments and intriguing restaurants to keep you occupied for a weekend. Over the centuries, poets and others have characterized Castile as austere and melancholy. Gaunt mountain ranges frame the horizons; gorges and rocky outcrops break up flat expanses; and the fields around Ávila and Segovia are littered with giant boulders. Castilian villages are built predominantly of granite, and their severe, formidable look contrasts markedly with the whitewashed walls of most of southern Spain.

Wherever you land in Madrid province, Castile and León, or Castile-La Mancha, it's worth dropping by the local tourist office to grab a map and inquire about the surrounding nature. In this part of Spain, you're never far from mountains, bird-watching hotspots, vineyards, and bike trails.

MAJOR REGIONS

Castile–La Mancha. Here is the land of Don Quixote, Miguel de Cervantes's chivalrous hero. Some of Spain's oldest and noblest cities are found here, steeped in culture and legend, though many have fallen into neglect. **Toledo,** the pre-Madrid capital of Spain, is the main attraction, though travelers willing to venture farther afield can explore **Cuenca,** with its Hanging Houses, and **Almagro,** with its green-and-white plaza and splendid parador.

Castile and León. This is Spain's windswept interior, stretching from the dry plains of Castile–La Mancha to the hilly vineyards of Ribera del Duero, and up to the foot of several mountain ranges: the Sierra de Gredos, Sierra de Francia, and northward toward the towering Picos de Europa. The area combines two of Spain's old kingdoms, Léon and Old Castile, each with its many treasures of palaces, castles, and cathedrals. The region's crown jewel is **Segovia** with its Roman aqueduct and 12th-century alcázar (fortress), though medieval **Ávila** gives it a run for its money. Farther north lies **Salamanca,** dominated by luminescent sandstone buildings, and the ancient capital of **Burgos,** an early outpost of Christianity with a jaw-dropping Gothic cathedral.

Planning

When to Go

July and August can be brutally hot, and November through February can get bitterly cold, especially in the mountains. Shoulder season, May and October, when the weather is sunny but relatively cool, are the two best months to visit—so if you plan on visiting then, be sure to book ahead.

Getting Here and Around

CAR TRAVEL

Major highways—the A1 through A6—spoke out from Madrid, putting most destinations in central Spain within an hour or two of the city. If possible, avoid returning to Madrid on major highways at the end of a weekend or a holiday. The beginning and end of August are notorious for traffic jams, as is Semana Santa (Holy Week), which starts on Palm Sunday and ends on Easter Sunday. National (toll-free) highways and back roads are slower but provide one of the great pleasures of driving around the Castilian countryside: surprise encounters with historical monuments and spectacular vistas.

12

Day Trips from Madrid PLANNING

Mileage from Madrid

- Madrid to Burgos is 243 km (151 miles).

- Madrid to Sepúlveda is 127 km (79 miles).

- Madrid to Cuenca is 168 km (104 miles).

- Madrid to Almagro is 204 km (127 miles).

- Madrid to Sigüenza is 131 km (81 miles).

- Madrid to Salamanca is 212 km (132 miles).

- Madrid to San Lorenzo de El Escorial is 60 km (37 miles).

- Madrid to Segovia is 91 km (57 miles).

- Madrid to Toledo is 88 km (55 miles).

- Madrid to Ávila is 114 km (71 miles).

Hotels

Many of the country's best-reviewed paradores (⊕ *www.paradores.es*) can be found in quiet towns such as Almagro, Ávila, Cuenca, and Sigüenza. Those in Toledo, Segovia, and Salamanca are modern buildings with magnificent views and, in the case of Segovia, have wonderful indoor and outdoor swimming pools. There are plenty of pleasant alternatives to paradores such as Segovia's Hotel Infanta Isabel, Salamanca's Hotel Rector, and Cuenca's Posada de San José, housed in a 16th-century convent.

Hotel reviews have been shortened. For full information, visit Fodors.com.

What It Costs in Euros			
$	$$	$$$	$$$$
FOR TWO PEOPLE			
under €90	€90–€125	€126–€180	over €180

Restaurants

This is Spain's rugged heartland, bereft of touristy hamburger joints and filled instead with the country's most traditional *tabernas,* which attract Spanish foodies from across the country. Some of the most renowned restaurants in this region are small and family run, while a few new avant-garde spots in urban areas serve up modern architecture as well as experimental fusion dishes.

Restaurant reviews have been shortened. For full information, visit Fodors. com.

What It Costs in Euros			
$	$$	$$$	$$$$
AT DINNER			
under €12	€12–€17	€18–€22	over €22

Tours

In summer the tourist offices of Segovia, Toledo, and Sigüenza organize Trenes Turísticos (miniature tourist trains) that glide past all the major sights; contact local tourist offices for schedules.

Equiberia

GUIDED TOURS | FAMILY | Horseback tours, ranging 1–10 days, offer a unique way to experience the gorges, fields, and forests of the Sierra de Guadarrama, Segovia, Ávila, and beyond. ✉ *Navarredonda de Gredos, Ávila* ☎ *68/934–3974* ⊕ *www. equiberia.com* ✈ *From €150.*

Toledo

88 km (55 miles) southwest of Madrid.

The spiritual capital of Castile, Toledo sits atop a rocky mount surrounded on three sides by the Río Tajo (Tagus River). When the Romans arrived here in 192 BC, they built their fortress (the Alcázar) on the highest point of the rock. Later, the Visigoths remodeled the stronghold.

In the 8th century, the Moors arrived and strengthened Toledo's reputation as a center of religion and learning. Today, the Moorish legacy is evident in Toledo's strong crafts tradition, the mazelike streets, and the predominance of brick construction (rather than the stone of many of Spain's historical cities). For the Moors—an imprecise catch-all term for Islam-practicing North African settlers of the Iberian Peninsula—beauty was to be savored from within rather than displayed on the surface. Even Toledo's cathedral—one of the most richly endowed in Spain—is hard to see from the outside, largely obscured by the warren of houses around it.

Under Toledo's long line of cardinals—most notably Mendoza, Tavera, and Cisneros—Renaissance Toledo was a center of the humanities. Economically and politically, however, the city began to decline at the end of the 15th century. The expulsion of the Jews from Spain in 1492, as part of the Spanish Inquisition,

eroded Toledo's economic and intellectual prowess. Then, when Madrid became the permanent center of the Spanish court in 1561, Toledo lost its political importance too, and the expulsion from Spain of the converted Arabs (Moriscos) in 1601 meant the departure of most of the city's artisans. The years the painter El Greco spent in Toledo—from 1572 to his death in 1614—were those of the city's decline, which is greatly reflected in his works. In the late 19th century, after hundreds of years of neglect, the works of El Greco came to be widely appreciated, and Toledo was transformed into a major tourist destination. Today, Toledo is conservative, prosperous, and proud—and a bit provincial (don't expect cosmopolitan luxury here). Its winding streets and steep hills can be tough to navigate, especially when you're searching for a specific sight, so take a full day (or three) to absorb the town's medieval trappings—and relish in getting lost from time to time.

GETTING HERE AND AROUND

The best way to get to Toledo from Madrid is the high-speed AVE train, which leaves from Madrid at least nine times daily from Atocha station and gets you there in 30 minutes. From the ornate Neo-Mudejar train station, take a taxi, bus (L61 or L62), or walk the 1½ km (1 mile) to the city center.

ALSA buses leave Madrid every half hour from Plaza Elíptica and take 1¼ hours.

TOURS

Cuéntame Toledo

GUIDED TOURS | The name means "Tell me about Toledo," and that's what they do. The company offers free tours (in English and Spanish; donation encouraged) of Toledo's historic center at 5 pm daily, plus a range of other paid tours of the city's monuments, best-kept secrets, underground passageways, and urban legends. There are also El Greco–theme tours, nighttime ghost tours, and other routes

Did You Know?

The alcázar of Toledo has dominated the city since at least the 3rd century. It is the setting for an important scene of Franquist lore: During the Spanish Civil War, the Nationalist colonel Moscardó was defending the building against overwhelming Republican forces. The Republicans held his son hostage, demanding the alcázar be surrendered. To his son's entreaties to "surrender or they will shoot me," the father replied, "Then commend your soul to God and die like a hero."

that include visits to ancient Arab baths. ⊠ *Corral de Don Diego 5* ☎ *92/521–0767, 60/893–5856* ⊕ *www.cuentametoledo. com* 🌐 *Historic center tour free, other tours from €12.*

★ Toledo de la Mano

GUIDED TOURS | Toledophile Adolfo Ferrero, author of a 200-page guidebook on the town, delves far deeper on his private tours than those run by competitors, touching on the city's history of multiculturalism and its significance in medieval Europe. Groups of up to 55 people can be accommodated. ⊠ *Calle Nuncio Viejo 10* ☎ *62/917–7810* ⊕ *www.toledodelamano.com* 🌐 *From €140.*

★ Toledo Tours

GUIDED TOURS | Self-guided tour packages cater to those interested in the city's gastronomy, art, history, and other aspects, with various mix-and-match "Toledopass" deals including admission to various museums and landmarks. Pick the itinerary that best suits your interests and cut the lines. ⊠ *Toledo* ☎ *92/582–6616* ⊕ *www.toledoturismo.org* 🌐 *From €19.*

Toledo Train Vision

TRAIN TOURS | FAMILY | This unabashedly touristy "train" chugs past many of Toledo's main sights, departing from the Plaza de Zocodover every hour on the hour during the week, and every 30 minutes on weekends. The tour takes 45–50 minutes and has recorded information in 16 languages (including English, Spanish, and French) plus children's versions in those three languages, too. Buy tickets at the kiosk in Plaza de Zocodover. ⊠ *Pl. de Zocodover* ☎ *62/530–1890* 🌐 *€7.*

VISITOR INFORMATION Toledo Tourist Office. ⊠ *Pl. de Zocodover 8* ☎ *92/526–7666, 68/785–4965, 92/523–9121* ⊕ *www.turismo.toledo.es.*

Sights

Alcázar

MILITARY SITE | Originally a Moorish citadel (*al-qasr* is Arabic for "fortress") and occupied from the 10th century until the Reconquest, Toledo's alcázar is on a hill just outside the walled city, dominating the horizon. The south facade—the building's most severe—is the work of Juan de Herrera, of Escorial fame, while the east facade incorporates a large section of battlements. The finest facade is the northern, one of many Toledan works by Miguel Covarrubias, who did more than any other architect to introduce the Renaissance style here. The building's architectural highlight is his Italianate courtyard, which, like most other parts of the building, was largely rebuilt after the Spanish Civil War, when the alcázar was besieged by the Republicans. Though the Nationalists' ranks were depleted, they held on to the building. Dictator Francisco Franco later turned the alcázar into a monument to Nationalist bravery. The alcázar now houses the **Museo del Ejército** (Military Museum), which was formerly in Madrid. ■ **TIP→ Hang onto your ticket—it's needed when you exit the museum.** ⊠ *Cuesta de los Capuchinos* ☎ *92/523–8800* ⊕ *www.museo.ejercito. es* 🌐 *From €5 (free Sun. 10–3).*

Calle del Comercio

NEIGHBORHOOD | Near Plaza de Zocodover, this is the town's narrow and busy pedestrian thoroughfare. It's lined with bars and shops and shaded in summer by awnings. ⊠ *Toledo.*

★ Cathedral

RELIGIOUS SITE | One of the most impressive structures in all of Spain, this is a must-see on any visit to the city. The elaborate structure owes its impressive Mozarabic chapel, with an elongated dome crowning the west facade, to Jorge Manuel Theotokópoulos. The rest of the facade is mainly early 15th century. Immediately to your right is a

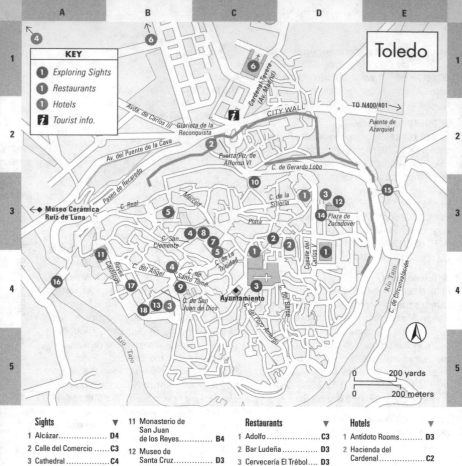

Toledo

KEY
- ① Exploring Sights
- ① Restaurants
- ① Hotels
- ⓘ Tourist info.

Sights ▼

1. Alcázar **D4**
2. Calle del Comercio **C3**
3. Cathedral **C4**
4. Convento de
   San Clemente **C3**
5. Convento de Santo
   Domingo el Antiguo **B3**
6. Hospital de Tavera **C1**
7. Iglesia de
   San Ildefonso **C3**
8. Iglesia de San Román ... **C3**
9. Iglesia de
   Santo Tomé **B4**
10. Mezquita del
    Cristo de la Luz **C3**
11. Monasterio de
    San Juan
    de los Reyes **B4**
12. Museo de
    Santa Cruz **D3**
13. Museo del Greco **B4**
14. Plaza de Zocodover **D3**
15. Puente de Alcántara **E3**
16. Puente de
    San Martín **A4**
17. Sinagoga de Santa
    María La Blanca **B4**
18. Sinagoga del
    Tránsito **B4**

Restaurants ▼

1. Adolfo **C3**
2. Bar Ludeña **D3**
3. Cervecería El Trébol **D3**
4. Churrería
   Santo Tomé **B4**
5. La Flor de la Esquina ... **C4**
6. Restaurante
   Iván Cerdeño **B1**

Hotels ▼

1. Antídoto Rooms **D3**
2. Hacienda del
   Cardenal **C2**
3. Hotel Pintor El Greco
   Sercotel **B4**
4. Miluna **A1**

beautifully carved Plateresque doorway by Covarrubias, marking the entrance to the Treasury, which houses a small crucifixion scene by the Italian painter Cimabue and an extraordinarily intricate late-15th-century monstrance by Juan del Arfe. The ceiling is an excellent example of Mudejar (11th- to 16th-century Moorish-influenced) workmanship. From here, walk around to the ambulatory. In addition to Italianate frescoes by Juan de Borgoña and an exemplary Baroque illusionism by Narciso Tomé known as the Transparente, you'll find several El Grecos, including one version of *El Espolio* (*Christ Being Stripped of His Raiment*), the first recorded instance of the painter in Spain. ✉ *Calle Cardenal Cisneros 1* ☎ *92/522–2241* 🌐 *www.catedralprimada.es* 🎫 *From €10.*

★ Convento de San Clemente

RELIGIOUS SITE | Founded in 1131, this is Toledo's oldest convent—and it's still in use. The handful of nuns who live here produce sweet wine and marzipan. The impressive complex, a bit outside the city center, includes ruins of a mosque on which a chapel was built in the Middle Ages, those of an Islamic house and courtyard (with an ancient well and Arab baths), and those of a Jewish house from the same period. Free tours, offered twice daily (though not dependably—be forewarned), might include a visit to the kitchen where the Mother Superior will let you sample some sweets if she's in a good mood. Skip the touristy marzipan shops and buy the real stuff here. There's also an adjacent cultural center with rotating history exhibits. ✉ *Calle San Clemente* ☎ *92/525–3080* 🎫 *Free* 🕒 *Closed sporadically (call before visiting).*

Convento de Santo Domingo el Antiguo (*Convento de Santo Domingo de Silos; Santo Domingo Convent*)

RELIGIOUS SITE | This 16th-century Cistercian convent houses the earliest of El Greco's Toledo paintings as well as the crypt where the artist is believed to be buried. The friendly nuns at the convent will show you around its odd little museum, which includes decaying bone relics of little-known saints and a life-size model of John the Baptist's decapitated head. ✉ *Pl. Santo Domingo el Antiguo* ☎ *92/522–2930* 🎫 *€3.*

Hospital de Tavera (*Hospital de San Juan Bautista*)

HOSPITAL—SIGHT | Architect Alonso de Covarrubias's last work, this hospital lies outside the city walls, beyond Toledo's main northern gate. A fine example of Spanish Renaissance architecture, the building also houses the **Museo de Duque de Lema** in its southern wing. The most important work in the museum's miscellaneous collection is a painting by the 17th-century artist José Ribera. The hospital's monumental chapel holds El Greco's *Baptism of Christ* and the exquisitely carved marble tomb of Cardinal Tavera, the last work of Alonso de Berruguete. Descend into the crypt to experience some bizarre acoustical effects. A full ticket includes the hospital, museum, old pharmacy, and Renaissance patios; a partial ticket includes everything except the museum. Guided tours are available at 45-minute intervals. ✉ *Calle Duque de Lerma 2 (aka Calle Cardenal Tavera)* ☎ *92/522–0451* 🌐 *www.fundacionmedinaceli.org/monumentos/hospital/* 🎫 *€6.*

★ Iglesia de San Ildefonso (*San Ildefonso Church, The Jesuits*)

RELIGIOUS SITE | Sometimes simply called "Jesuitas," for the religious order that founded it, the Iglesia de San Ildefonso is named for Toledo's patron saint, a local bishop in the 7th century. It was finally consecrated in 1718, after taking 150 years to build the baroque stone facade with twin Corinthian columns. Its semispherical dome is one of the icons of Toledo's skyline. This impressive building deserves a visit, and a climb up its tower (€3) affords some of the best views over Toledo. ✉ *Pl. Juan de Mariana 1* ☎ *92/525–1507* 🎫 *€3.*

Iglesia de San Román

RELIGIOUS SITE | Hidden in a virtually unspoiled part of Toledo, this early-13th-century Mudejar church (built on the site of an earlier Visigoth one) is now the **Museo de los Concilios y de la Cultura Visigoda** (Visigoth Museum) with exhibits of statuary, manuscript illustrations, jewelry, and an extensive collection of frescoes. The church tower is adjacent to the ruins of Roman baths. ⊠ *Calle San Román* ☎ *92/522–7872* 🎟 *€6 (free Fri. and Sat. 4:30–6:30 and Sun. 10–2:30).*

★ Iglesia de Santo Tomé (*Santo Tomé Church*)

RELIGIOUS SITE | Not to be confused with the marzipan shop bearing the same name, this chapel topped with a Mudejar tower was built specially to house El Greco's most masterful painting, *The Burial of Count Orgaz.* Using vivid colors and splashes of light, he portrays the benefactor of the church being buried with the posthumous assistance of St. Augustine and St. Stephen, who have appeared at the funeral to thank the count for his donations to religious institutions named after the two saints. Though the count's burial took place in the 14th century, El Greco painted the onlookers in contemporary 16th-century costumes and included people he knew; the boy in the foreground is one of El Greco's sons, and the sixth figure on the left is said to be the artist himself. Santo Tomé is Toledo's most visited church besides the cathedral, so to avoid crowds, plan to visit as soon as the building opens. ⊠ *Pl. del Conde 4, Calle Santo Tomé* ☎ *92/525–6098* ⊕ *www.santotome.org* 🎟 *€3.*

Mezquita del Cristo de la Luz (*Mosque of Christ of the Light*)

RELIGIOUS SITE | Originally a tiny Visigothic church, the mosque-chapel was transformed into a mosque during the Moorish occupation. The Islamic arches and vaulting survived, making this the most important relic of Moorish Toledo, even if a glaringly out-of-place sculpture of Jesus on the cross is the centerpiece of the building today. Legend has it that the chapel got its name when Alfonso VI's horse, striding triumphantly into Toledo in 1085, fell to its knees out front (a white stone marks the spot). It was then "discovered" that a candle had burned continuously behind the masonry the whole time the Muslims had been in power. Allegedly, the first Mass of the Reconquest was held here, and later a Mudejar apse was added. There are remnants of a Roman house in the yard nearby. ⊠ *Cuesta de Carmelitas Descalzos 10* ☎ *92/525–4191* 🎟 *€3.*

★ Monasterio de San Juan de los Reyes

RELIGIOUS SITE | This convent church in western Toledo was erected by Ferdinand and Isabella to commemorate their victory at the Battle of Toro in 1476. (It was also intended to be their burial place, but their wish changed after Granada was recaptured from the Moors in 1492, and their actual tomb is in that city's Capilla Real.) The breathtakingly intricate building is largely the work of architect Juan Guas, who considered it his masterpiece and asked to be buried there himself. In true Plateresque fashion, the white interior is covered with inscriptions and heraldic motifs. ⊠ *Calle San Juan de los Reyes 2* ☎ *92/522–3802* ⊕ *www.sanjuan-delosreyes.org* 🎟 *€3.*

Museo del Greco (*El Greco Museum*)

MUSEUM | This house that once belonged to Peter the Cruel's treasurer, Samuel Levi, is said to have later been El Greco's home, though historians now believe he actually lived across the street in a small house that's since been razed. Nevertheless, the interior of the museum has been decorated to resemble a typical house of the artist's time. There are also exhibition halls with El Greco paintings including a panorama of Toledo with the Hospital of Tavera in the foreground, plus works by several of El Greco's students (including his son) and other 16th- and 17th-century artists. Round out your visit with a stroll through the garden and medieval caves. ⊠ *Paseo del Tránsito* ☏ *92/522–3665* ⌕ *€3 (free Sat. after 2).*

Museo de Santa Cruz

MUSEUM | In a 16th-century Renaissance hospital with a stunning Classical-Plateresque facade, this museum is open all day without a break (unlike many of Toledo's other sights). Works of art have replaced the hospital beds, and among the displays is El Greco's *Assumption* of 1613, the artist's last known work. A small **Museo de Arqueología** (Museum of Archaeology) is in and around the hospital's delightful cloister. ⊠ *Calle Cervantes 3* ☏ *92/522–1036* ⌕ *Free, art exhibit €4* ⊗ *Closed Sun. after 2:30.*

Plaza de Zocodover

PLAZA | Toledo's main square was built in the early 17th century as part of an unsuccessful attempt to impose a rigid geometry on the chaotic Moorish streets. Over the centuries, this tiny plaza has hosted bullfights, executions (autos-da-fé) of heretics during the Spanish Inquisition, and countless street fairs. Today it's home to the largest and oldest marzipan store in town, Santo Tomé. You can catch intracity buses here, and the tourist office is on the south side of the plaza. ⊠ *Toledo.*

Puente de Alcántara

BRIDGE/TUNNEL | Roman in origin, this is the city's oldest bridge. Next to it is a heavily restored castle built after the Christian capture of 1085 and, above this, a vast and severe military academy, an eyesore of Franquist architecture. From the other side of the Río Tajo, the bridge offers fine views of Toledo's historic center and the Alcázar. ⊠ *Calle Gerardo Lobo.*

Puente de San Martín

BRIDGE/TUNNEL | This pedestrian bridge on the western edge of Toledo dates to 1203 and has splendid horseshoe arches. ⊠ *Toledo.*

Off the Beaten Path ◉

Museo Cerámica Ruiz de Luna. Most of the region's pottery is made in Talavera de la Reina, 76 km (47 miles) west of Toledo. At this museum you can watch artisans throw local clay, then trace the development of Talavera's world-famous ceramics, chronicled through some 1,500 tiles, bowls, vases, and plates dating back to the 15th century. ⊠ *Place de San Augustín, Calle San Agustín el Viejo 13, Talavera de la Reina* ☏ *92/580–0149* ⌕ *Free* ⊗ *Closed Mon.*

★ **Sinagoga de Santa María La Blanca**
RELIGIOUS SITE | Founded in 1203, Toledo's second synagogue—situated in the heart of the Jewish Quarter—is nearly two centuries older than the more elaborate Tránsito, just down the street. Santa María's white interior has a forest of columns supporting capitals with fine filigree work. ⊠ *Calle de los Reyes Católicos 4* ☏ *92/522–7257* ⌕ *€3.*

★ **Sinagoga del Tránsito** (*Museo Sefardí, Sephardic Museum*)
RELIGIOUS SITE | This 14th-century synagogue's plain exterior belies sumptuous interior walls embellished with colorful Mudejar decoration. There are inscriptions in Hebrew and Arabic glorifying God, Peter the Cruel, and Samuel Levi (the original patron). It's a rare example of architecture reflecting Arabic as the lingua franca of medieval Spanish Jews. It's said that Levi imported cedars from Lebanon for the building's construction, echoing Solomon when he built the First Temple in Jerusalem. This is one of only three synagogues still fully standing in Spain (two in Toledo, one in Córdoba), from an era when there were hundreds—though more are in the process

Toledo's Santa María la Blanca synagogue is a fascinating symbol of cultural cooperation: built by Islamic architects, in a Christian land, for Jewish use.

of being excavated. Adjoining the main hall is the **Museo Sefardí,** a small but informative museum of Jewish culture in Spain. ✉ *Calle Samuel Levi 2* ☎ *92/522–3665* 🌐 *www.mecd.gob.es/msefardi/home.html* 🎟 *€3 (free Sat. afternoon and Sun.).*

🍴 Restaurants

Adolfo

$$$$ | SPANISH | Visit this white-tablecloth restaurant, situated steps from the cathedral, for traditional Toledan recipes with fine-dining twists, complemented by a 2,800-bottle-deep wine list. Don't pass up the hearty partridge stew, deemed the best in Spain by the former Spanish king Juan Carlos I; it sings alongside a glass of Adolfo's proprietary red wine. **Known for:** chef's menu; historic building; game dishes. [$] *Average main: €50* ✉ *Calle del Hombre de Palo 7* ☎ *92/522–7321* 🌐 *www.grupoadolfo.com* 🕒 *No dinner Sun.*

Bar Ludeña

$$ | SPANISH | Locals and visitors come together at this old-timey tapas bar for steaming cauldrons of *carcamusas toledanas,* a local meat stew studded with peas and chorizo. (Give the rest of the menu a pass.) **Known for:** hearty carcamusa stew; free tapa with every drink; rustic ambience. [$] *Average main: €12* ✉ *Pl. de la Magdalena 10* ☎ *92/522–3384* 🕒 *Closed Wed.*

★ Cervecería El Trébol

$$ | SPANISH | You can't leave Toledo without indulging in one of El Trébol's famous *bombas,* fried fist-size spheres of mashed potato stuffed with spiced meat and anointed with aioli. They're best enjoyed on the twinkly outdoor patio with a locally brewed beer in hand. **Known for:** to-die-for bombas; most pleasant patio in town; local craft beers. [$] *Average main: €15* ✉ *Calle de Santa Fe 1* ☎ *92/528–1297* 🌐 *www.cerveceriatrebol.com.*

★ Churrería Santo Tomé

$ | SPANISH | FAMILY | Recharge at this adorable four-table *churrería,* established over a century ago, with hot homemade churros dipped in ultrathick melted chocolate. This churrería opens at 6 am so look like a local and come have light-but-crispy churros for breakfast. **Known for:** churros made on-site; churros for breakfast; local institution. $ *Average main: €5* ✉ *Calle Santo Tomé 27* ☎ *92/521–6324* ▤ *No credit cards.*

La Flor de la Esquina

$$$ | SPANISH | The most coveted seats at this charming restaurant are the patio tables on the Plaza del Padre, which boast views of Toledo's cathedral spires. Three-course lunch menus are a great value at €11 (don't expect anything too fancy), and there are tapas menus and charcuterie boards for those looking to sample a bit of everything. ⚠ **Service can be slow at peak hours. Known for:** steal prix-fixe menu; cathedral views; top-quality cured meats. $ *Average main: €20* ✉ *Pl. del Padre Juan de Mariana 2* ☎ *62/794–5020.*

★ Restaurante Iván Cerdeño

$$$$ | SPANISH | The buzziest opening in Toledo in recent memory, chef Iván Cerdeño's namesake restaurant, inaugurated in 2019, is a beacon of Castilian *alta gastronomía*—think architectural dishes composed of foams, spherified sauces, and edible flowers served in a modern white-tablecloth dining room. The ever-rotating tasting menus (€70–€130) almost always feature a course or two of local wild game such as partridge or roe deer. **Known for:** Castilian fine dining; hot new opening; secluded location across the Tagus. $ *Average main: €70* ✉ *Cigarral del Ángel, Ctra. de la Puebla* ☎ *92/522–3674* ⊕ *www.ivancerdeno.com* ⊗ *Closed Mon. and Tues.*

Tea Break

Teteria Dar Al-Chai. Rest your legs at this Arabian tea house–bar, appointed with plush couches, low tables, and colorful tapestries. Sample specially blended teas incorporating flowers, dried fruit, and spices. **Known for:** specially blended teas; delicious crepes and cakes; peaceful spot. ✉ *Pl. Barrio Nuevo 5* ☎ *92/522–5625.*

🛏 Hotels

★ Antídoto Rooms

$$ | HOTEL | Antídoto is a breath of fresh air in Toledo's mostly staid hotel scene: expect turquoise beamed ceilings, poured-concrete floors, and designer light fixtures. **Pros:** highly Instagrammable rooms; in the heart of the old town; friendly staff. **Cons:** awkward room layout; in-room bathrooms with no curtains and transparent doors; sheets could be softer. $ *Rooms from: €120* ✉ *Calle Recoletos 2* ☎ *92/522–8851* ⊕ *www.antidotorooms.com* ⇱ *10 rooms* ❧❉ *No meals.*

Hacienda del Cardenal

$$ | HOTEL | Once a summer palace for Cardinal Lorenzana, who lived in the 1700s, this serene three-star hotel on the outskirts of the old town hits the sweet spot between rustic and refined. **Pros:** lovely courtyard; convenient dining; spacious rooms. **Cons:** restaurant often full; parking is pricey; stairs inconvenient for those with heavy luggage. $ *Rooms from: €100* ✉ *Paseo de Recaredo 24* ☎ *92/522–4900* ⊕ *www.elhostaldelcardenal.com* ⇱ *27 rooms* ❧❉ *No meals.*

Hotel Pintor El Greco Sercotel

$$$ | HOTEL | Next door to the painter's house, this former 17th-century bakery is now a chic, contemporary hotel managed by the Sorcotel chain. **Pros:** parking

garage adjacent; cozy decor; complimentary wine and olives. **Cons:** street noise in most rooms; elevator goes to the second floor only; bar area sometimes closed for private events. $ *Rooms from: €130* ✉ *Alamillos del Tránsito 13* ☎ *92/528–5191* ⊕ *www.hotelpintorelgreco.com* ⤳ *60 rooms* �‖ *No meals.*

★ Miluna

$$$$ | **HOTEL** | Taking a page from the playbook of Aire de Bardenas, Navarra's avant-garde bubble hotel, Miluna opened in September 2018 on the outskirts of Toledo. **Pros:** a bubble hotel that won't break the budget; telescopes in every room; the ideal place to unplug. **Cons:** so popular it's difficult to get a reservation; outdoor temperatures can be extreme in winter and summer; no alternate dining options in vicinity. $ *Rooms from: €189* ✉ *C. Valdecarretas, Parcela 364* ☎ *92/567–9229* ⊕ *www.miluna.es* ⤳ *4 rooms* �‖ *Free breakfast.*

🛍 Shopping

The Moors established silverwork, damascene (metalwork inlaid with gold or silver), pottery, embroidery, and marzipan traditions here. A turn-of-the-20th-century art school next to the Monasterio de San Juan de los Reyes keeps some of these crafts alive. For inexpensive pottery, stop at the large stores on the outskirts of town, on the main road to Madrid. Many shops are closed on Sunday.

La Encina de Ortega

FOOD/CANDY | This is a one-stop-shop for local wines, olive oil, manchego cheese, and—most notably—*ibérico* pork products (ham, chorizo, dry-cured sausages) made from pigs raised on the family farm. ✉ *Calle La Plata 22* ☎ *92/510–2072* ⊕ *www.laencinadeortega.com.*

Santo Tomé Marzipan

FOOD/CANDY | Since 1856, Santo Tomé has been Spain's most famous maker of marzipan, a Spanish confection made from sugar, honey, and almond paste. Visit the main shop on the Plaza de Zocodover, or take a tour of the old convent-turned-factory where it's actually made at Calle Santo Tomé 3 (advance booking required). ✉ *Pl. de Zocodover 7* ☎ *92/522–1168, 92/522–3763* ⊕ *www.mazapan.com.*

San Lorenzo de El Escorial

50 km (31 miles) northwest of Madrid.

An hour from Madrid, San Lorenzo del Escorial makes for a leisurely day trip away from the hustle and bustle of the Spanish capital. The medieval town's main attraction is the Real Sitio de San Lorenzo de El Escorial, the Royal Site of San Lorenzo of El Escorial. A dozen or so trains leave daily from the Madrid Sol train station, or you can take the C3 regional line from Atocha, Chamartín, Nuevos Ministerios, or Recoletos. The journey takes about an hour, and the entrance to El Escorial is about a 15-minute walk from the train station.

👁 Sights

★ El Escorial

CASTLE/PALACE | A UNESCO World Heritage Site and one of Spain's most visited landmarks, the imposing Monastery and Real Sitio de San Lorenzo de El Escorial (or just El Escorial) was commissioned by Felipe II after the death of his father in the 1500s and remains the most complete and impressive monument of the later Renaissance in Spain. The monastery was built as an eternal memorial for his relatives and the crypt here is the resting place of the majority of Spain's kings, from Charles V to Alfonso XIII. A fantasy land of gilded halls, hand-painted chambers, and manicured French gardens, the gargantuan royal residence also houses an important collection of paintings by Renaissance and baroque

El Escorial's library, founded by Philip II, houses a rare collection of more than 4,700 manuscripts, many of them illuminated, and 40,000 printed books.

artists donated by the crown. It's worth paying the €12 entry fee to see the library alone, whose vibrant frescoes and leather-bound tomes spur the imagination. ⊠ *Pl. de España 1, San Lorenzo de El Escorial* ☎ *91/890–5903* ⊕ *www.sanlorenzoturismo.es* ⊡ *€12* ⊙ *Closed Mon.* Ⓜ *El Escorial.*

Segovia

91 km (57 miles) north of Madrid.

Medieval Segovia rises on a steep ridge that juts above a stark, undulating plain. It's defined by its ancient monuments, excellent cuisine, embroideries and textiles, and old-fashioned charm. An important military town in Roman times, Segovia was later established by the Moors as a major textile center. Captured by the Christians in 1085, it was enriched by a royal residence, and in 1474 the half sister of Henry IV, Isabella the Catholic (married to Ferdinand of Aragón), was crowned queen of Castile here. By that time Segovia was a bustling city of about 60,000 (its population hovers around 52,000 today), but its importance soon diminished as a result of its taking the losing side of the Comuneros in the popular revolt against Emperor Carlos V. Though the construction of a royal palace in nearby La Granja in the 18th century somewhat revived Segovia's fortunes, it never recovered its former vitality. Early in the 20th century, Segovia's sleepy charm came to be appreciated by artists and writers, among them painter Ignacio Zuloaga and poet Antonio Machado. Today the streets swarm with day-trippers from Madrid—if you can, visit sometime other than in summer, and spend the night to have much of the city to yourself.

You'll want to hit the triumvirate of basic sights: the aqueduct, alcázar, and cathedral. Come evening, don't miss the bustling food and nightlife scene around the Plaza Mayor.

GETTING HERE AND AROUND

High-speed AVE trains from Madrid's Chamartín station—the fastest and costliest option—take 30 minutes and drop you at the Guiomar station, about 7 km (4 miles) outside Segovia's center. Buses 11 and 12 are timed to coincide with arriving trains. Bus 11 will take you to the foot of the aqueduct after about a 15-minute ride, and Bus 12 drops you near the bus station.

La Sepulvedana buses depart Madrid (Moncloa station) for Segovia some 28 times a day. Direct routes take 55 minutes and cost €8 each way. There are also plentiful Blablacar options. (Check ⊕ *www.blablacar.com* or the app for details.)

Urbanos de Segovia operates the 13 inner-city bus lines and one tourist line, which are better options for getting around than struggling through the narrow streets (and problematic parking) with a car. Segovia's central bus station is a five-minute walk from the aqueduct along the car-free Paseo de Ezequiel González.

BUS CONTACTS Bus Station. ⊠ *Paseo de Ezequiel González* ☎ *92/142–7705.* **La Sepulvedana.** ⊠ *Pl. la Estación de Auto-buses* ☎ *90/211–9699* ⊕ *www.lasepulve-dana.es.* **Urbanos de Segovia.** ☎ *90/233–0080* ⊕ *segovia.avanzagrupo.com.*

VISITOR INFORMATION Segovia Tourist Office. ⊠ *Azoguejo 1* ☎ *92/146–6720, 92/146–6721* ⊕ *www.turismodesegovia. com.*

Sights

★ Alcázar

CASTLE/PALACE | FAMILY | It's widely believed that the Walt Disney logo is modeled after the silhouette of this castle, whose crenellated towers appear to have been carved out of icing. Possibly dating to Roman times, this castle was considerably expanded in the 14th century, remodeled in the 15th, altered again toward the end of the 16th, and completely reconstructed after being gutted by a fire in 1862, when it was used as an artillery school. The exterior, especially when seen below from the Ruta Panorámica, is awe-inspiring, as are the superb views from the ramparts. Inside, you can enter the throne room, chapel, and bedroom used by Ferdinand and Isabella as well as a claustropho-bia-inducing winding tower. The intricate woodwork on the ceiling is marvelous, and the first room you enter, lined with knights in shining armor, is a crowd pleaser, particularly for kids. There's also a small armory museum, included in the ticket price. ⊠ *Pl. de la Reina Victoria* ☎ *92/146–0759, 92/146–0452* ⊕ *www. alcazardesegovia.com* ⊠ *From €3.*

★ Aqueduct of Segovia

ARCHAEOLOGICAL SITE | Segovia's Roman aqueduct is one of the greatest surviving examples of Roman engineering and the city's main sight. Stretching from the walls of the old town to the lower slopes of the Sierra de Guadarrama, it's about 2,952 feet long and rises in two tiers to a height of 115 feet. The raised section of stonework in the center originally carried an inscription, of which only the holes for the bronze letters remain. Neither mortar nor clamps hold the massive granite blocks together, but miraculously, the aqueduct has stood since the end of the 1st century AD. ⊠ *Pl. del Azoguejo.*

★ Catedral de Segovia

RELIGIOUS SITE | Segovia's 16th-century cathedral was built to replace an earlier one destroyed during the revolt of the Comuneros against Carlos V. It's one of the country's last great examples of the Gothic style. The designs were drawn up by the leading late-Gothicist Juan Gil de Hontañón and executed by his son Rodrigo, in whose work you can see a transition from the Gothic to the Renaissance style. The interior, illuminat-ed by 16th-century Flemish windows, is

Segovia

KEY

- 1 Sights
- 1 Restaurants
- 1 Hotels
- i Tourist Information

0 ⊢———⊣ 200 yards
0 ⊢———⊣ 200 meters

Sights ▶
1 Alcázar.....................B2
2 Aqueduct of Segovia......H2
3 Catedral de Segovia.......E2
4 Iglesia de la Vera Cruz...D1
5 Iglesia de San Millán.....G3
6 Plaza Mayor...............E2

Restaurants ▶
1 Casa Duque................G3
2 El Fogón Sefardí..........E2
3 Mesón de Cándido..........G2
4 Mesón de José María...E2

Hotels ▶
1 Hotel Spa
   La Casa Mudéjar........E2
2 Infanta Isabel Hotel......E2
3 Parador de Segovia.....H1

12

Day Trips from Madrid SEGOVIA

Segovia's Roman aqueduct, built more than 2,000 years ago, is remarkably well preserved.

light and uncluttered (save the wooden neoclassical choir). Across from the entrance, on the southern transept, is a door opening into the late-Gothic cloister, the work of architect Juan Guas. Off the cloister, a small museum of religious art, installed partly in the first-floor chapter house, has a white-and-gold 17th-century ceiling, a late example of Mudejar *artesonado* (a type of intricately joined wooden ceiling) work. ⊠ *Pl. Mayor* ☎ *92/146–2205* ⊕ *www.catedralsegovia.es* 🖼 *From €3 (free Sun. Mass).*

Iglesia de la Vera Cruz

RELIGIOUS SITE | This isolated Romanesque church on the outskirts of town was built in 1208 for the Knights Templar. Like other buildings associated with the order, it has 12 sides, inspired by the Church of the Holy Sepulchre in Jerusalem. It's about a 45-minute walk from town (you can see this church on a cliffside from the castle windows), but the trek pays off in full when you climb the bell tower and see the Segovia skyline silhouetted against the Sierra de Guadarrama.

⚠ **Change is not given for bills larger than €20.** ⊠ *Ctra. de Zamarramia* ☎ *92/143–1475* 🖼 *€2 (free Tues. 4–6 pm).*

Iglesia de San Millán

RELIGIOUS SITE | Built in the 12th century and a perfect example of the Segovian Romanesque style, this church, a five-minute walk outside the town walls, may be the finest in town, aside from the cathedral. The exterior is notable for its arcaded porch, where church meetings were once held. The virtually untouched interior is dominated by massive columns, whose capitals carry such carved scenes as the Flight into Egypt and the Adoration of the Magi. The vaulting on the crossing shows the Moorish influence on Spanish medieval architecture. It's open for Mass only. ⊠ *Av. Fernández Ladreda 26* ⊕ *www.parroquiasanmillansegovia.com.*

Plaza Mayor

PLAZA | In front of the cathedral, this historic square comes alive every night and especially on weekends, when visiting Madrileños and locals gather at casual

Off the Beaten Path

Palacio Real de La Granja (*Royal Palace of La Granja).* If you have a car, don't miss the Palacio Real de La Granja (Royal Palace of La Granja) in the town of La Granja de San Ildefonso, on the northern slopes of the Sierra de Guadarrama. The palace site was once occupied by a hunting lodge and a shrine to San Ildefonso, administered by Hieronymite monks from the Segovian monastery of El Parral. Commissioned by the Bourbon king Felipe V in 1719, the palace has been described as the first great building of the Spanish Bourbon dynasty. The Italian architects Juvarra and Sachetti, who finished it in 1739, were responsible for the imposing garden facade, a late-baroque masterpiece anchored throughout its length by a giant order of columns. The interior was badly gutted by fire, but the collection of 15th- to 18th-century tapestries warrants a visit. Even if you don't go into the palace, walk through the magnificent gardens: terraces, ornamental ponds, lakes, classical statuary, woods, and baroque fountains dot the mountainside. On Wednesday, Saturday, and Sunday evenings in the summer (April–August, 5:30–7 pm), the illuminated fountains are turned on, one by one, creating an effect to rival that of Versailles. The starting time has been known to change on a whim, so call ahead. ✉ *Pl. de España 15, San Ildefonso* ✥ *About 11 km (7 miles) southeast of Segovia on N601* ☎ *92/147–0019, 92/147–0020* 🌐 *www.patrimonionacional.es* 🎫 *From €4.*

cafés that line the perimeter. There's a gazebo in the middle that occasionally hosts live music. (Otherwise it's occupied by children playing while their parents dine nearby.) ✉ *Segovia.*

🍴 Restaurants

Casa Duque

$$$$ | **SPANISH** | Segovia's oldest restaurant, founded in 1895 and still run by the same family, has a rustic interior with wood beams and bric-a-brac hanging on the walls. The decor suits the unfussy (if overpriced) cuisine, which features roast meats and stewed broad beans. **Known for:** ultratender cochinillo asado (roast suckling pig); tourist-friendly menus and service; historic setting. [$] *Average main: €30* ✉ *Calle Cervantes 12* ☎ *92/146–2487, 92/146–2486* 🌐 *www.restauranteduque.es.*

★ **El Fogón Sefardí**

$$$ | **SPANISH** | This tavern in Segovia's historic Jewish quarter is owned by La Casa Mudejar Hospedería hotel and wins awards year after year for the region's best tapas. The extensive menu highlights Segovian specialties like cochinillo as well as traditional Sephardic Jewish cuisine (though it's not a kosher kitchen), plus a variety of well-executed *raciones* (tapas). **Known for:** Sephardic-influenced cuisine; cochinillo; generous salads. [$] *Average main: €20* ✉ *Calle Judería Vieja 17* ☎ *92/146–6250* 🌐 *www.lacasamudejar.com* 💳 *No credit cards.*

Mesón de Cándido

$$$$ | **SPANISH** | Amid the dark-wood beams and Castilian knickknacks of this restaurant beneath the aqueduct hang photos of celebrities who have dined here, among them Ernest Hemingway and Princess Grace. The suckling pig (cochinillo) is the star; partridge stew

and roast lamb are also memorable, especially on cold afternoons. **Known for:** wood-fired-oven-roasted cochinillo; historic building; famous former patrons like Ernest Hemingway. $ *Average main: €30* ✉ *Pl. de Azoguejo 5* ☎ *92/142–5911* ⊕ *www.mesondecandido.es.*

★ Mesón de José María

$$$$ | SPANISH | According to foodies, this old-timey *mesón* (traditional tavern-restaurant) serves the most delectable cochinillo asado in town, but there are plenty of lighter, fresher dishes to choose from as well. Expect a boisterous mix of locals and tourists. **Known for:** best cochinillo in town; beamed dining room; local crowd (a rarity in this touristy town). $ *Average main: €35* ✉ *Calle Cronista Lecea 11, off Pl. Mayor* ☎ *92/146–1111, 92/146–6017* ⊕ *www.restaurantejosemaria.com.*

Hotels

Infanta Isabel Hotel

$$ | HOTEL | On the corner of the Plaza Mayor, this classically appointed hotel boasts cathedral views in a bustling shopping area. **Pros:** lived-in, cozy ambience; central location; some rooms have balconies overlooking the plaza. **Cons:** some rooms are cramped and oddly shaped; rooms facing the plaza can be noisy on weekends; decidedly unhip decor. $ *Rooms from: €120* ✉ *Pl. Mayor 12* ☎ *92/146–1300* ⊕ *www.hotelinfantaisabel.com* ➠ *37 rooms* ⦿ *No meals.*

Hotel Spa La Casa Mudejar

$$ | HOTEL | Built in the 15th century as a Mudejar palace, this historical property has spacious rooms and a well-priced spa (€30 per person) that's extremely popular, even with nonguests. **Pros:** terrific restaurant serving rare Sephardic dishes; historic building with Roman ruins; affordable spa. **Cons:** forgettable interiors; no nearby parking; beds nothing special. $ *Rooms from: €100* ✉ *Calle Isabel la Católica 8*

☎ *92/146–6250* ⊕ *www.lacasamudejar.com* ➠ *40 rooms* ⦿ *No meals.*

Parador de Segovia

$$ | HOTEL | From the large windows of this modern-style parador, 3 km (2 miles) from the old town, you can take in spectacular views of the cathedral and aqueduct. **Pros:** beautiful views of the city; sunny, picturesque pool area; spacious rooms. **Cons:** need a car (or €7 taxi) to get here; uncozy, passé decor; lacks antique touches of more historic paradores. $ *Rooms from: €120* ✉ *Ctra. de Valladolid* ☎ *92/144–3737* ⊕ *www.parador.es* ➠ *113 rooms* ⦿ *No meals.*

Shopping

After Toledo, the province of Segovia is Castile's most important area for traditional artisanry. Glass and crystal are specialties of La Granja, and ironwork, lace, basketry, and embroidery are famous in Segovia. You can buy good lace from the Romani vendors in Segovia's Plaza del Alcázar, but be prepared for some strenuous bargaining, and never offer more than half the opening price. The area around Plaza San Martín is a good place to buy crafts.

Calle Daoíz

CERAMICS/GLASSWARE | Leading to the Alcázar, this street overflows with locally made (if tourist-oriented) ceramics, textiles, and gift shops. ✉ *Segovia.*

Salchichería Briz

FOOD/CANDY | The city's best artisanal sausages—from chorizo to *morcilla* (blood sausage) and *lomo* (cured pork loin)—can be found at this 40-year-old butcher shop. The cured, vacuum-sealed meats travel well and can be kept for months at a cool room temperature. ✉ *Calle Fernández Ladreda 20* ☎ *92/146–1755* ⊕ *www.salchicheriabriz.es.*

Castillo de Coca

Perhaps the most famous medieval sight near Segovia—worth the 52 km (32-mile) detour northwest of the city en route to Ávila or Valladolid—is the Castillo de Coca. Built in the 15th century for Archbishop Alonso de Fonseca I, the salmon-hue castle is a turreted Mudejar structure of plaster and red brick surrounded by a deep moat. Highly Instagrammable, it looks like a stage set for a fairy tale, and, indeed, it was intended not as a fortress but as a place for the notoriously pleasure-loving archbishop to hold riotous parties. The interior, now occupied by a forestry school, has been modernized, with only fragments of the original decoration preserved. ⊕ www.castillodecoca.com

Sepúlveda

58 km (36 miles) northeast of Segovia.

A walled village with a commanding position, Sepúlveda has a charming main square, but the main reasons to visit are its 11th-century Romanesque church and striking gorge with a scenic hiking trail.

GETTING HERE AND AROUND
Sepúlveda is about an hour north of Madrid on the A1. There are also several buses (and Blablacar rideshares) a day from both Segovia and Madrid. The city is perched atop a hill overlooking a ravine, so you'll likely want transportation to the top. Don't park or get off the bus too soon.

VISITOR INFORMATION Sepúlveda Tourist Office. ⊠ Pl. del Trigo 6 ☏ 92/154–0237 ⊕ www.sepulveda.es.

Sights

★ Ermita de San Frutos
RELIGIOUS SITE | This 11th-century hermitage is in ruins, but its location, on a peninsula jutting out into a bend 100 meters above the Duratón River, is extraordinary. You'll need a car to get there, about 15 minutes' drive west of Sepúlveda. Stay on the marked paths—the surrounding area is a natural park and a protected nesting ground for rare vultures—and try to go at sunset, when the light enhances spectacular views of the sandstone monastery and river below. Inside the monastery, there's a small chapel and plaque describing the life of San Frutos, the patron saint of Segovia. An ancient pilgrimage route stretches 77 km (48 miles) from the monastery to Segovia's cathedral, and pilgrims still walk it each year. As an add-on to the trip, you can rent kayaks from **NaturalTur** (☏ 92/152–1727 ⊕ www.naturaltur.com) to paddle the river. ⊠ Carrascal del Río, Burgomillodo ☒ Free.

Iglesia de San Salvador
RELIGIOUS SITE | This 11th-century church is the oldest Romanesque church in Segovia Province. The carvings on its capitals, probably by a Moorish convert, are quite outlandish. ⊠ Calle Subida a El Salvador 10.

🍴 Restaurants

★ Restaurante Fogón del Azogue
$$$ | SPANISH | FAMILY | The menu at this white-tablecloth aerie, which overlooks rolling farmland, hinges on local delicacies like fried blood sausage, creamy ham croquettes, and—naturally, since we're in Segovia province—crackly roast milk-fed lamb and suckling pig. The spacious venue is well-suited to hosting

large groups. **Known for:** refined Castilian cuisine; wraparound windows with gorgeous views; brick-oven-roasted pork and lamb. $ *Average main: €22* ✉ *Calle de San Millán 6* ☎ *69/020–2772* ⊘ *Closed Mon.–Thurs. No dinner Sun.*

Ávila

114 km (71 miles) northwest of Madrid.

On a windy plateau littered with giant boulders, with the Sierra de Gredos in the background, Ávila is a walled fairy-tale town that wouldn't look out of place in *Game of Thrones*. After it was wrested from the Moors in 1090, soaring crenelated walls were erected around its perimeter—by some 1,900 builders, who allegedly finished the task in just nine years. The walls have nine gates and 88 cylindrical towers bunched together, making them unique to Spain in form—they're quite unlike the Moorish defense architecture that the Christians adapted elsewhere. They're most striking when seen from afar; for the best views (and photos), cross the Adaja River, turn right on the Carretera de Salamanca, and walk uphill about 250 yards to a monument of pilasters surrounding a cross known as the "Four Posts."

Ávila's fame is largely due to St. Teresa. Born here in 1515 to a noble family of Jewish origin, Teresa spent much of her life in Ávila, leaving a legacy of convents and the ubiquitous *yemas* (candied egg yolks), originally distributed free to the poor and now sold for high prices to tourists. The town comes to life during the Fiestas de la Santa Teresa in October, a weeklong celebration that includes lighted decorations, parades, singing in the streets, and religious observances.

GETTING HERE AND AROUND

Jiménez Dorado (⊕ *www.jimenezdorado. com*) and Avilabus (⊕ *www.avilabus.com*) serve Ávila and its surrounding villages.

Twenty-three trains depart for Ávila each day from Chamartín station, and there are usually plentiful Blablacar rideshares available. The city itself is easily managed on foot.

VISITOR INFORMATION Ávila Tourist Office. ✉ *Pl. de la Catedral, Av. de Madrid 39* ☎ *92/021–1387* ⊕ *www.turismoavila. com.*

 Sights

Basílica de San Vicente (*Basilica of St. Vincent*)
RELIGIOUS SITE | Where this Romanesque basilica stands, it's said that St. Vincent was martyred in 303 AD with his sisters, Sts. Sabina and Cristeta. Construction began in 1130 and continued through the 12th century, and the massive church complex was restored in the late 19th and early 20th centuries. The west front, shielded by a vestibule, displays damaged but expressive carvings depicting the death of Lazarus and the parable of the rich man's table. The sarcophagus of St. Vincent forms the centerpiece of the interior. The extraordinary, Eastern-influenced canopy above the sarcophagus is a 15th-century addition. Combined, these elements form one of Spain's most prized examples of Romanesque architecture. ✉ *Pl. de San Vicente 1* ☎ *92/022–5969* ⊕ *www.basilicasanvicente.es* 🎫 *€3 (free Sun.).*

Casa de los Deanes (*Deans' Mansion*)
MUSEUM | This 15th-century building houses the cheerful **Museo Provincial de Ávila,** full of local archaeology and folklore. Part of the museum's collection is housed in the adjacent Romanesque temple of San Tomé el Viejo, a few minutes' walk east of the cathedral apse. ✉ *Pl. de Nalvillos 3* ☎ *92/021–1003* 🎫 *€2 (free weekends)* ⊘ *Closed Mon.*

★ Catedral de Ávila
RELIGIOUS SITE | The battlement apse of Ávila's cathedral forms the most

Ávila's city walls, which still encircle the old city, have a perimeter of about 2½ km (1½ miles).

impressive part of the city's walls. Entering the town gate to the right of the apse, you can reach the sculpted north portal by turning left and walking a few steps. The west portal, flanked by 18th-century towers, is notable for the crude carvings of hairy male figures on each side. Known as "wild men," these figures appear in many Castilian palaces of this period. The Transitional Gothic structure, with its granite nave, is considered to be the first Gothic cathedral in Spain. Look for the early-16th-century marble sepulchre of Bishop Alonso de Madrigal. Known as El Tostado (the Toasted One) for his swarthy complexion, the bishop was a tiny man of enormous intellect. When on one occasion Pope Eugenius IV ordered him to stand—mistakenly thinking him to still be on his knees—the bishop pointed to the space between his eyebrows and hairline, and retorted, "A man's stature is to be measured from here to here!" ⊠ *Pl. de la Catedral s/n* ☎ *92/021–1641* ⊕ *catedrala-vila.es* 🎫 *€6.*

Centro de Interpretación del Misticismo
(*Mysticism Interpretation Center*)
MUSEUM | The only such museum of its kind in Europe, this center is devoted to mysticism, the practice of religious ecstasy made famous by Ávila's native daughter, St. Teresa—one of Christianity's first female mystics. Exhibits explain the role of mysticism in Judaism, Christianity, and a number of Eastern religions. The exterior of the building, a medieval house, is original, but the giant prism ceiling that reflects light throughout the interior is obviously a new addition. ⊠ *Paseo del Rastro* ☎ *92/021–2154* ⊕ *www. avilamistica.es* 🎫 *€2* ⌚ *Closed Mon.*

Convento de Santa Teresa
RELIGIOUS SITE | This Carmelite convent was founded in the 17th century on the site of the St. Teresa's birthplace. Teresa's account of an ecstatic vision, in which an angel pierced her heart, inspired many baroque artists, most famously the Italian sculptor Giovanni Bernini. The convent has a small museum with creepy relics including one of Teresa's fingers. You also

can see the small and rather gloomy garden where she played as a child. ✉ *Pl. de la Santa 2* ☎ *92/021–1030* 🌐 *www.santateresadejesus.com* 🎟 *Church and reliquary free, museum €2.*

Real Monasterio de Santo Tomás

RELIGIOUS SITE | In an unlikely location—among apartment blocks a good 10-minute walk from the walls—is one of the most important religious institutions in Castile. The monastery was founded by Ferdinand and Isabella with the backing of the Inquisitor-General Tomás de Torquemada, largely responsible for the expulsion of the Jews per the Alhambra Decree, who is buried in the sacristy. Further funds were provided by the confiscated property of converted Jews who were dispossessed during the Inquisition. Three decorated cloisters lead to the church; inside, a masterful high altar (circa 1506) by Pedro Berruguete overlooks a serene marble tomb by the Italian artist Domenico Fancelli. One of the earliest examples of the Italian Renaissance style in Spain, this work was built for Prince Juan, the only son of Ferdinand and Isabella, who died at 19. After Juan's burial here, his heartbroken parents found themselves unable to return. There are free guided tours at 6 pm on weekends and holidays. ✉ *Pl. de Granada 1* ☎ *92/022–0400* 🌐 *www.monasteriosantotomas.com* 🎟 *€4.*

🍴 Restaurants

Las Cancelas

$$$ | **SPANISH** | Locals flock to this little tavern for the tapas and fat, juicy steaks served in the boisterous barroom or white-tablecloth dining area, set in a covered arcaded courtyard. There are 14 hotel rooms available, too—simple, slightly ramshackle arrangements at moderate prices. **Known for:** chuletón de Ávila (gargantuan local steaks); quaint, romantic dining room; good value. [$] *Average main: €20* ✉ *Calle de la Cruz Vieja 6* ☎ *92/021–2249* 🌐 *www.lascancelas.com* 🕒 *Closed early Jan.–early Feb. No dinner Sun.*

Restaurante El Molino de la Losa

$$$$ | **SPANISH** | **FAMILY** | Sitting at the edge of the serene Adaja River, El Molino, housed in a 15th-century mill, enjoys one of the best views of the town walls. Lamb, the restaurant's specialty, is roasted in a medieval wood oven, and the beans from nearby El Barco de Ávila (*judías de El Barco*) are famous. **Known for:** succulent roast lamb; views of the river and city walls; refined cuisine. [$] *Average main: €30* ✉ *Calle Bajada de la Losa 12* ☎ *92/021–1101, 92/021–1102* 🌐 *www.elmolinodelalosa.com* 🕒 *No dinner Sun.*

🛏 Hotels

★ Palacio de los Velada

$$$ | **HOTEL** | Ávila's top four-star hotel occupies a beautifully restored 16th-century palace in the heart of the city next to the cathedral, an ideal spot if you like to relax between sightseeing. **Pros:** gorgeous glass-covered patio; amiable service; bountiful breakfast buffet. **Cons:** some rooms don't have views because the windows are so high; expensive off-site parking; lack of power outlets. [$] *Rooms from: €150* ✉ *Pl. de la Catedral 10* ☎ *92/025–5100* 🌐 *www.veladahoteles.com* 🛏 *145 rooms* 🍴 *No meals.*

Parador de Ávila

$$$ | **HOTEL** | **FAMILY** | This largely rebuilt 16th-century medieval castle is attached to the massive town walls, and a standout feature is its lush garden containing archaeological ruins. **Pros:** gorgeous garden and views; good restaurant; family-friendly rooms and services. **Cons:** long walk into town; interiors need a refresh; underwhelming breakfast. [$] *Rooms from: €130* ✉ *Marqués de Canales de Chozas 2* ☎ *92/021–1340* 🌐 *www.parador.es* 🛏 *61 rooms* 🍴 *No meals.*

Sigüenza

132 km (82 miles) northeast of Madrid.

The ancient university town of Sigüenza dates back to Roman, Visigothic, and Moorish times and still has splendid architecture and one of the most impressive Gothic cathedrals in Castile. It's one of the rare Spanish towns that has not surrendered to modern development and sprawl. If you're coming from Madrid via the A2, the approach, through craggy hills and ravines, is dramatic. Sigüenza is an ideal base for exploring the countryside on foot or by bike, thanks to the Ruta de Don Quixote, a network of paths named for Cervantes's literary hero that passes through the town center and nearby villages.

GETTING HERE AND AROUND

There are five train departures daily to Sigüenza from Madrid's Chamartín station, and the journey takes about 1½ hours. Sigüenza's train station is an easy walk from the historic walled center. Buses depart from Madrid's Avenida de América station once a day and take two hours. If you arrive by car, park near the train station to avoid the narrow cobblestone streets of the city center. Rideshares, such as Blablacar, are another option, provided there are trips that align with your schedule.

BICYCLE RENTAL
Neumáticos del Olmo
This company rents mountain bikes for €10 per day or €17 for two. Call ahead to reserve on busy holiday weekends. Note to parents: they don't have trailers or child seats. ⊠ *Ctra. de Moratilla, Nave 1* ☎ *94/939–0754, 60/578–7650.*

VISITOR INFORMATION Sigüenza Tourist Office. ⊠ *Calle Serrano Sanz 9* ☎ *94/934–7007* ⊕ *www.siguenza.es.*

◉ Sights

Castillo de Sigüenza
CASTLE/PALACE | FAMILY | This enchanting castle overlooking wild, hilly countryside from above Sigüenza is now a parador. Nonguests can visit the dining room and common areas. The structure was founded by the Romans and rebuilt at various later periods. Most of the current structure was erected in the 14th century, when it became a residence for the queen of Castile, Doña Blanca de Borbón, who was banished here by her husband, Pedro the Cruel. During the Spanish Civil War (1936–39), the castle was the scene of fierce battles, and much of the structure was destroyed. The parador's lobby has an exhibit on the subsequent restoration with photographs of the bomb damage. If you have a half hour to spare, there's a lovely walking path around the hilltop castle with a 360-degree view of the city and countryside below. ⊠ *Pl. de Castillo* ☎ *949/390100.*

Catedral de Sigüenza
RELIGIOUS SITE | Begun around 1150 and completed in the 16th century, Sigüenza's cathedral combines architecture from the Romanesque period to the Renaissance. Ask the sacristan (the officer in charge of the care of the sacristy, which holds sacred vestments) for a peek at the cathedral's wealth of ornamental and artistic masterpieces. From there, take a guided tour from the late-Gothic cloister to a room lined with 17th-century Flemish tapestries and onto the north transept, where the 15th-century plateresque sepulchre of Dom Fadrique of Portugal is housed. The Chapel of the Doncel (to the right of the sanctuary) contains Don Martín Vázquez de Arca's tomb, commissioned by Queen Isabella, to whom Don Martín served as *doncel* (page) before dying young (at 25) at the gates of Granada in 1486. ⊠ *Calle*

Serrano Sanz 2 ☎ *61/936–2715* ⊕ *www. lacatedraldesiguenza.com* 🎫 *Free, €6 for tour of chapel, cloister, and tower.*

Museo Diocesano de Sigüenza (*Diocesan Museum of Sacred Art*)
MUSEUM | FAMILY | In a refurbished early-19th-century house next to the cathedral's west facade, the small Diocesan Museum has a prehistoric section and mostly religious art from the 12th to 18th century. It also runs the tours of the burial chambers (catacombs) under the cathedral—a spooky favorite for kids. ✉ *Pl. Obispo Don Bernardo* ☎ *94/939–1023* ⊕ *www.lacatedraldesiguenza.com* 🎫 *From €1 (free on 3rd Wed. of month).*

Plaza Mayor
PLAZA | The south side of the cathedral overlooks this harmonious, arcaded Renaissance square, which hosts a medieval market on weekends. Legend has it, a group of American tycoons found the plaza so charming that they offered to buy it in order to reconstruct it, piece by piece, stateside. ✉ *Sigüenza.*

Tren Medieval
SCENIC DRIVE | FAMILY | Leaving from Madrid's Chamartín station, this delightful medieval-theme train service runs to Sigüenza mid-April through mid-November. The (otherwise thoroughly modern) train comes populated with minstrels, jugglers, and other entertainers, and it's a great activity for Spanish-speaking children. The ticket price includes round-trip fare, a guided visit to Sigüenza, entry to the main monuments and museums, and discounts at area restaurants. ✉ *Sigüenza* ☎ *90/232–0320* ⊕ *www.renfe.com/ trenesturisticos/otros-trenes-renfe.html* 🎫 *€35* ⊘ *Closed mid-Nov.–mid-Apr.*

 **Restaurants**

★ **Bar Alameda**
$$ | TAPAS | FAMILY | This family-run bar and restaurant punches above its weight with market-driven tapas that reflect a sense of place. Spring for the stuffed foraged mushrooms or seared Sigüenza-style blood sausage. **Known for:** thoughtfully prepared tapas; local wines by the glass; family-friendly atmosphere. $ *Average main: €15* ✉ *Calle de la Alameda 2* ☎ *94/939–0553* ⊘ *Closed Thurs.*

 Hotels

★ **Parador de Sigüenza**
$$$$ | HOTEL | FAMILY | This fairy-tale 12th-century castle has hosted royalty for centuries, from Ferdinand and Isabella right up to Spain's present king, Felipe VI. **Pros:** excellent food; sense of history and place; plenty of parking. **Cons:** much of castle is a neo-medieval replica; bland, modern furniture that doesn't jibe with the space; occasionally surly service. $ *Rooms from: €185* ✉ *Pl. del Castillo* ☎ *94/939–0100* ⊕ *www.parador.es* ⬅ *81 rooms* ⦿ *Free breakfast.*

Cuenca

168 km (105 miles) southeast of Madrid, 150 km (93 miles) northwest of Valencia.

Cuenca is one of the most surreal looking towns in Spain, built on a sloping escarpment whose with precipitous sides plunge down to the Huécar and Júcar rivers. When real estate grew scarce a few centuries back, local builders constructed gravity-defying homes that dangle over the abyss. These Casas Colgadas ("Hanging Houses") are a unique architectural attraction. The old town's dramatic setting grants spectacular views of the surrounding countryside, and its cobblestone streets, cathedral, churches, and taverns contrast starkly with the modern town, which sprawls beyond the river gorges. Though somewhat isolated, Cuenca makes a good overnight stop if you're traveling between Madrid and Valencia, or even a worthwhile detour between Madrid and Barcelona.

GETTING HERE AND AROUND

From Madrid, buses leave for Cuenca about every two hours from Conde de Casal. From Valencia, four buses leave every four to six hours, starting at 8:30 am. A high-speed AVE train leaves Madrid approximately every hour and stops in Cuenca (after about 55 minutes) on its way to Valencia. Slower, cheaper trains also run several times daily between Cuenca and Valencia, Madrid, Albacete, and Alicante, on the coast. Rideshares (such as Blablacar) to and from the city are plentiful.

VISITOR INFORMATION Cuenca. ⊠ *Av. Cruz Roja 1* ☎ *96/924–1051* ⊕ *turismo. cuenca.es.*

◉ Sights

Cuenca has more than a dozen churches and two cathedrals, but visitors are allowed inside only about half of them. The best views of the city are from the square in front of a small palace at the very top of Cuenca, where the town tapers out to the narrowest of ledges. Here, gorges flank the precipice, and old houses sweep down toward a distant plateau. The lower half of the old town is a maze of tiny streets, any of which will take you up to the Plaza del Carmen. From here the town narrows and a single street, Calle Alfonso VIII, continues the ascent to the Plaza Mayor, which passes under the arch of the town hall.

★ **Casas Colgadas** (*Hanging Houses*)
BUILDING | As if Cuenca's famous Casas Colgadas, suspended impossibly over the cliffs below, were not eye-popping enough, they also house one of Spain's finest and most curious museums, the **Museo de Arte Abstracto Español** (Museum of Spanish Abstract Art)—not to be confused with the adjacent Museo Municipal de Arte Moderno. Projecting over the town's eastern precipice, these houses originally formed a 15th-century palace, which later served as a town hall before

falling into disrepair in the 19th century. In 1927 the cantilevered balconies that had once hung over the gorge were rebuilt, and in 1966 the painter Fernando Zóbel decided to create (inside the houses) the world's first museum devoted exclusively to abstract art. The works he gathered—by such renowned names as Carlos Saura, Eduardo Chillida, Lucio Muñoz, and Antoni Tàpies—are primarily by exiled Spanish artists who grew up under Franco's regime. The museum has free smartphone audio guides that can be downloaded from the website. A plan to build a fine-dining restaurant within one of the historic houses was approved in 2019, but as of 2020, local officials are still squabbling over funding and management. ⊠ *Calle de los Canónigos* ☎ *96/921–2983* ⊕ *www.march.es/arte/ cuenca* ⊠ *Free.*

Catedral de Cuenca
RELIGIOUS SITE | This cathedral looms large and casts an enormous shadow in the evening throughout the adjacent Plaza Mayor. Built during the Gothic era in the 12th century atop ruins of a conquered mosque, the cathedral's massive triptych facade lost its Gothic character in the Renaissance. Inside are the tombs of the cathedral's founding bishops, an impressive portico of the Apostles, and a Byzantine reliquary. There's also a museum in what was once the cellar of the Bishop's Palace containing a jewel-encrusted Byzantine diptych of the 13th century, a Crucifixion by the 15th-century Flemish artist Gerard David, a variety of carpets from the 16th through 18th centuries, and two small El Grecos. An excellent audio guide is included in the price of admission. ⊠ *Pl. Mayor* ☎ *96/922–4626* ⊕ *www.catedralcuenca.es* ⊠ *€8 (free 1st Mon. of month).*

★ Puente de San Pablo
BRIDGE/TUNNEL | The 16th-century stone footbridge over the Huécar gorge was fortified with iron in 1903 for the convenience of the Dominican monks of San

Cuenca's precarious Casas Colgadas (Hanging Houses) are also home to the well-regarded Museum of Abstract Art.

Pablo, who lived on the other side. If you don't have a fear of heights, cross the narrow bridge to take in the vertiginous view of the river and equally thrilling panorama of the Casas Colgadas. It's by far the best view of the city. If you've read the popular English novel *Winter in Madrid,* you'll recognize this bridge from the final scene. ✉ *Cuenca.*

🍴 Restaurants

Much of Cuenca's cuisine is based on wild game, but farm-raised lamb, rabbit, and hen are ubiquitous on menus. Trout from the adjacent river (and, increasingly, from farms) is the fish of choice, and it turns up in entrées and soups. In almost every restaurant you'll find *morteruelo,* Cuenca's pâté of *jabalí* (wild boar), rabbit, partridge, hen, liver, pork loin, and spices, as well as *gazpacho manchego* (aka *galiano*), a meat stew thickened with dry flatbread—a remnant of the Sephardic culinary canon. For dessert, try *alajú,* a hard sugar candy containing honey, almonds, and lemon, or *torrijas,* bread slices dipped in milk, fried until custardy, and sprinkled with cinnamon-sugar.

Figón del Huécar

$$$$ | SPANISH | This family-run white-tablecloth restaurant serves updated Castilian classics in an airy dining room set in a medieval stone house overlooking the old city (ask for an outdoor table when booking). Specialty dishes include Manchegan *migas* (fried pork and breadcrumbs), *ajoarriero* (pounded potatoes, garlic, egg, and olive oil), and veal with potatoes *al montón* (fried with garlic). **Known for:** breathtaking views; scrumptious desserts; elegant dining room. [$] *Average main: €35* ✉ *Ronda de Julián Romero 6* ☎ *96/924–0062, 62/906–3366* 🌐 *www.figondelhuecar.es* 🕓 *Closed Mon. No dinner Sun.*

★ La Ponderosa

$$ | TAPAS | La Ponderosa is a quintessential yet elevated Castilian bar where locals mingle at high volume while tossing back local wine and munching on well-priced seasonal delicacies like griddled wild asparagus, suckling lamb chops, and seared wild mushrooms. It's a stand-ing-room-only joint, so if you want to sit, you'll have to come early and find a place on the terrace. **Known for:** hidden-gem local wines; simple and delicious vegetable dishes; buzzy atmosphere. $ *Average main: €15* ⊠ *Calle de San Francisco 20* 🕾 *96/921–3214* 🕘 *Closed Sun., and July.*

Trivio
$$$$ | SPANISH | The punchy, artfully presented dishes at Trivio—think wild game tartare and house-pickled vegetables—are an anomaly in a region known for its stodgy country fare. Choose from three well-priced tasting menus in the dining room, or opt for a more casual experience in the Bistró-Bar. **Known for:** bold tasting menus; award-winning croquettes; pretty plating. $ *Average main: €30* ⊠ *Calle Colón 25* 🕾 *96/903–0593* ⊕ *www.restaurantetrivio.com* 🕘 *Closed Mon. No dinner Sun.*

Hotels

Cueva del Fraile
$ | HOTEL | FAMILY | Surrounded by dramatic landscapes, this family-friendly three-star lodging occupies a 16th-century building on the outskirts of town. **Pros:** beautiful interior garden terrace; outdoor swimming pool and tennis courts; good value. **Cons:** location 7 km (4½ miles) from town; no a/c in some rooms; some rooms have leaky showers. $ *Rooms from: €50* ⊠ *Ctra. Cuenca–Buenache, Km 7* 🕾 *96/921–1571* ⊕ *www.hotelcuevadelfraile.com* 🕘 *Closed Jan.* ⇆ *75 rooms* ⦿❶ *No meals.*

Hostal Cánovas
$ | B&B/INN | Near Plaza de España, in the heart of the new town, this quirky inn is one of Cuenca's best bargains, and though the lobby's not impressive, the inviting rooms more than compensate. **Pros:** low prices even during high season; spacious digs; clean rooms. **Cons:** uphill trek to the old quarter; thin walls; slightly sunken beds with plastic mattress

Enchanted City

Not a city at all, the Ciudad Encantada ("Enchanted City"), 35 km (22 miles) north of Cuenca, is a series of large, fantastic mushroom-like rock formations erupting in a landscape of pines. It was formed over thousands of years by the forces of water and wind on limestone rocks, and you can see it in under two hours. See if you can spot formations named "Cara" (Face), "Puente" (Bridge), "Amantes" (Lovers), and "Olas en el Mar" (Waves in the Sea). Rent a car or arrange a visit with Ecotourism Cuenca (⊕ *www.ecoturismocuenca.com*).

protectors. $ *Rooms from: €55* ⊠ *Calle Fray Luis de León 38* 🕾 *96/921–3973* ⊕ *www.hostalcanovas.com* ⇆ *17 rooms* ⦿❶ *No meals.*

★ Parador de Cuenca
$$$ | HOTEL | The rooms are luxurious and serene at the exquisitely restored 16th-century convent of San Pablo, pitched on a precipice across a dramatic gorge from Cuenca's city center. **Pros:** great views of the hanging houses and gorge; spacious rooms; consistently good restaurant. **Cons:** expensive breakfast not always included in room rate; secure garage parking not always available; calls to reception sometimes go unanswered. $ *Rooms from: €180* ⊠ *Subida a San Pablo* 🕾 *96/923–2320* ⊕ *www.parador.es* ⇆ *63 rooms* ⦿❶ *No meals.*

★ Posada de San José
$ | B&B/INN | FAMILY | This family-friendly inn, housed in a centuries-old convent, clings to the top of the Huécar gorge in Cuenca's old town. **Pros:** cozy historical rooms; stunning views of the gorge;

well-prepared local food. **Cons:** built to 17th-century proportions, some doorways are low; certain rooms are cramped; sloping floors can be vertiginous when lying in bed. [$] *Rooms from: €50* ✉ *Calle Julián Romero 4* ☎ *96/921–1300, 63/981–6825* 🌐 *www.posadasanjose.com* 🛏 *31 rooms* 🍴 *Free breakfast.*

Almagro

215 km (134 miles) south of Madrid.

The center of this noble town contains the only preserved medieval theater in Europe. It stands beside the ancient Plaza Mayor, where 85 Roman columns form two colonnades supporting green-frame 16th-century buildings. Enjoy casual tapas—such as pickled baby eggplant ("berenjenas de Almagro"), a hyperlocal specialty known the country over—and rustic Manchegan wines in the bars lining the square. Near the plaza are granite mansions emblazoned with the heraldic shields of their former owners and a splendid parador in a restored 17th-century convent.

GETTING HERE AND AROUND

Almagro can be reached by train from Madrid, with one scheduled departure per day departing from Atocha or Chamartín stations for the 2½-hour journey, but it's probably best to rent a car or book a Blablacar rideshare. The drive south from the capital takes you across the plains of La Mancha, where Don Quixote's adventures unfolded.

VISITOR INFORMATION Almagro. ✉ *Pl. Mayor 1* ☎ *92/686–0717* 🌐 *www.ciudad-almagro.com.*

👁 Sights

★ Corral de Comedias
ARTS VENUE | Appearing almost as it did in 1628 when it was built, this theater has wooden balconies on four sides and the stage at one end of the open patio. During the golden age of Spanish theater—the time of playwrights Pedro Calderón de la Barca, Cervantes, and Lope de Vega—touring actors came to Almagro, once a burgeoning urban center for its mercury mines and lace industry. Forego the tourist-oriented spectacles unless you're a Spanish theater buff: poor acoustics and archaic Spanish scripts make it difficult to understand what's going on. ✉ *Pl. Mayor 18* ☎ *92/686–1539* 🌐 *www.corraldecomedias.com* 🎟 *From €4.*

★ Museo Etnográfico Campo de Calatrava
MUSEUM | For a window into what agrarian life was like in this area in centuries past, pop into this tiny museum presided over by the passionate historian who amassed the (mostly obsolete) curiosities on display. A guided tour, in Spanish, takes a little less than an hour and is well worth it. ✉ *Calle Chile 6* ☎ *65/701–0077* 🌐 *www.museodealmagro.com* 🎟 *€5.*

Museo Nacional del Teatro
MUSEUM | This museum displays models of the Roman amphitheaters in Mérida (Extremadura) and Sagunto (near Valencia), both still in use, as well as costumes, pictures, and documents relating to the history of Spanish theater. Kids love handling the antique instruments previously used for sound effects during productions. ✉ *Calle del Gran Maestre 2* ☎ *92/626–1014, 92/626–1018* 🌐 *museoteatro.mcu.es* 🎟 *€3 (free Sat. afternoon and Sun. morning)* 🕒 *Closed Mon.*

🛏 Hotels

★ Parador de Almagro
$$$ | **HOTEL** | Five minutes from the Plaza Mayor of Almagro, this parador is a finely restored 16th-century Franciscan convent with cells, cloisters, and patios. **Pros:** pretty indoor courtyards; outdoor pool; ample parking. **Cons:** occasionally untidy public areas; double-bed rooms smaller than normal rooms; inconsistent restaurant. [$] *Rooms from: €135* ✉ *Ronda*

de San Francisco 31 ☎ *92/686–0100*
⊕ *www.parador.es* ↵ *54 rooms* ❚◎❚ *Free breakfast.*

Salamanca

212 km (132 miles) northwest of Madrid.

Salamanca's radiant sandstone buildings, proportion-perfect Plaza Mayor, and meandering river make it one of the most majestic and beloved cities in Spain. For centuries, its eponymous university has imbued the city with an intellectual verve, a stimulating arts scene, and—in recent decades—raging nightlife to match. You'll see more foreign students here per capita than anywhere else in Spain.

If you approach from Madrid or Ávila, your first glimpse of Salamanca will be of the city rising on the northern banks of the wide and winding Tormes River. In the foreground is its sturdy, 15-arch Roman bridge; soaring above it is the combined bulk of the old and new cathedrals. Piercing the skyline to the right is the Renaissance monastery and church of San Esteban. Behind San Esteban and the cathedrals, and largely out of sight from the river, extends a stunning series of palaces, convents, and university buildings that culminates in the Plaza Mayor. Despite enduring considerable damage over the centuries, Salamanca remains one of Spain's greatest cities architecturally, a showpiece of the Spanish Renaissance.

GETTING HERE AND AROUND

You'll probably feel rushed if you try to visit Salamanca from Toledo in an out-and-back day trip. To fully enjoy its splendor, plan on an overnight. Approximately 13 trains depart Madrid for Salamanca daily, several of which are high-speed ALVIA itineraries that take just over an hour and a half. Avanza buses leave from the Estación Sur de Autobuses; Blablacar

rideshares (about 2 hours and 15 minutes) are faster and more affordable.

Once in town, Salamanca de Transportes runs 64 municipal buses equipped with lifts for passengers with disabilities on routes throughout the city of Salamanca. You may opt to take a bus in order to reach the train and bus stations on the outskirts of the city.

INTRACITY BUS CONTACT Salamanca de Transportes. ☎ *92/319–0545* ⊕ *www.salamancadetransportes.com.*

VISITOR INFORMATION Salamanca Municipal Tourist Office. ✉ *Pl. Mayor 32* ☎ *92/321–8342* ⊕ *www.salamanca.es.* **Salamanca Regional Tourist Office.** ✉ *Rúa Mayor s/n* ☎ *92/326–8571, 90/220–3030* ⊕ *www.salamanca.es.*

◉ Sights

★ **Casa de Las Conchas** (*House of Shells*)
HOUSE | This house, whose facade is covered in scallop shell carvings, was built around 1500 for Dr. Rodrigo Maldonado de Talavera, a chancellor of the Order of St. James, whose symbol is the shell. Among the playful plateresque details are the lions over the main entrance, engaged in a fearful tug-of-war with the Talavera crest. The interior has been converted into a public library. Duck into the charming courtyard, which has an intricately carved upper balustrade that imitates basketwork. ✉ *Calle Compañía 2* ☎ *92/326–9317* ▧ *Free.*

★ **Catedrals Vieja and Nueva**
RELIGIOUS SITE | Nearest the river stands the **Catedral Vieja** (Old Cathedral), built in the late 12th century and one of the most riveting examples of the Spanish Romanesque. Because the dome of the crossing tower has strange, plumelike ribbing, it's known as the Torre del Gallo (Rooster's Tower). The much larger **Catedral Nueva** (New Cathedral) was built between 1513 and 1526 under the late-Gothic architect Juan Gil de

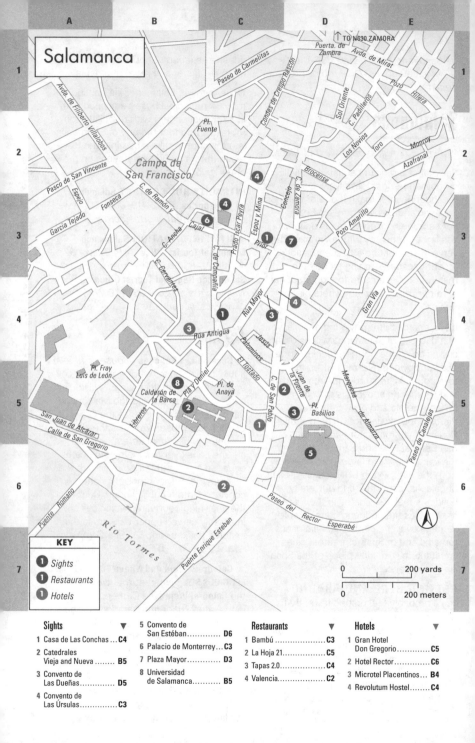

Hontañón. The two cathedrals are part of the same complex, though they have different visiting hours, and you need to enter the new one to get to the Old Cathedral. Take a moment to marvel at the west facade, dazzling in its sculptural complexity. ✉ *Pl. de Anaya and Calle Cardenal Pla y Deniel* ☎ *92/321–7476, 92/328–1123* ⊕ *www.catedralsalamanca. org* 🖃 *Catedral Nueva free, Catedral Vieja €5 (free Tues. 10–noon).*

★ **Convento de Las Dueñas** (*Convent of the Dames*)
RELIGIOUS SITE | Founded in 1419, this convent hides a 16th-century cloister that is the most fantastically decorated in Salamanca, if not in all of Spain. The capitals of its two superimposed Salmantine arcades are crowded with a baffling profusion of grotesques that can absorb you for hours. Don't forget to look down: the interlocking diamond pattern on the ground floor of the cloister is decorated with the knobby vertebrae of goats and sheep. It's an eerie yet perfect accompaniment to all the grinning, disfigured heads sprouting from the capitals looming above you. The museum has a fascinating exhibit on Spain's little-known slavery industry. And don't leave without buying some sweets—the nuns are excellent bakers. ✉ *Pl. del Concilio de Trento* ☎ *92/321–5442* 🖃 *€2.*

Convento de Las Úrsulas (*Convento de la Anunciación*)
RELIGIOUS SITE | Archbishop Alonso de Fonseca I lies here, in this splendid Gothic-style marble tomb created by Diego de Siloe during the early 1500s on the outskirts of the historic center. Magnificent Churrigueresque altarpieces depicting scenes in the life of Jesus were restored in 2014. The cloister is closed to the public as the convent is still active. ✉ *Calle de las Úrsulas 2* ☎ *92/321–9877* 🖃 *€3.*

Fonseca's Mark

Nearly all of Salamanca's outstanding Renaissance buildings bear the five-star crest of the all-powerful and ostentatious Fonseca family. The most famous of them, Alonso de Fonseca I, was the archbishop of Santiago and then of Seville; he was also a notorious womanizer and a patron of the Spanish Renaissance.

★ **Convento de San Estéban** (*Convent of St. Stephen*)
RELIGIOUS SITE | The convent's monks, among the most enlightened teachers at the university in medieval times, introduced Christopher Columbus to Isabella (hence his statue in the nearby Plaza de Colón, back toward Calle de San Pablo). The complex was designed by one of the monks who lived here, Juan de Álava. The massive west facade, a thrilling plateresque work in which sculpted figures and ornamentation are piled up to a height of more than 98 feet, is a gathering spot for tired tourists and picnicking locals, but the crown jewel of the structure is a glowing golden sandstone cloister with Gothic arcading punctuated by tall, spindly columns adorned with classical motifs. The church, unified and uncluttered but also dark and severe, allows the one note of color provided by the ornate and gilded high altar of 1692. An awe-inspiring baroque masterpiece by José Churriguera, it deserves five minutes of just sitting and staring. You can book free guided tours on the website. ✉ *Pl. Concilio de Trento 1* ☎ *92/321–5000* ⊕ *www.conventosanesteban.es* 🖃 *€4* ⊘ *Museum closed Mon.*

Palacio de Monterrey
CASTLE/PALACE | Built in the mid-16th century by Rodrigo Gil de Hontañón and one of the most stunning Renaissance palaces in Spain, this lavish abode was

Did You Know?

Salamanca's "new" cathedral was built in the 16th century to help reinforce the deteriorating "old" cathedral, which dates to the 12th. Today you can see both, entering the new to get to the old.

meant for an illegitimate son of Alonso de Fonseca I. The building is flanked by towers and has an open arcaded gallery running the length of the upper level. Such galleries—often seen on the ground floor of palaces in Italy—were intended to provide privacy for the women of the house and to cool the floor below during the summer. Following years of renovations and much anticipation, the palace finally opened to the public in 2018; tours, which cost €5 per person, are by appointment only (inconveniently, reservations must be made in person at the Plaza Mayor tourist office). Feast your eyes on seldom-before-seen Titians, Coellos, and other masterpieces presided over by the Alba family. ✉ *Pl. de las Agustinas* ⊕ *www.fundacioncasadealba. com* ✉ *€5 tour.*

★ Plaza Mayor

PLAZA | Built in the 1730s by Alberto and Nicolás Churriguera, Salamanca's Plaza Mayor is one of the largest and most beautiful squares in Spain. The lavishly elegant, pinkish **ayuntamiento** dominates its northern side. The square and its arcades are popular gathering spots for Salmantinos of all ages, and its *terrazas* are the perfect spot for a coffee break. At night, the plaza swarms with students meeting "under the clock" on the plaza's north side. *Tunas* (strolling musicians in traditional garb) often meander among the cafés and crowds, playing for smiles and applause rather than tips (though the latter are always appreciated). The plaza was in the news in 2017, when, after decades of controversy, the infamous medallion portraying Franco was removed from one of its capitals. ✉ *Salamanca.*

Universidad de Salamanca

COLLEGE | The university's walls, like those of the cathedral and other structures in Salamanca, often bear large ocher lettering recording the names of famous university graduates. The earliest names are said to have been written in the blood of the bulls killed to celebrate the successful completion of a doctorate (call it medieval graffiti!). The elaborate facade of the **Escuelas Mayores** (Upper Schools) dates to the early 16th century; see if you can spy the eroded "lucky" frog that's become the symbol of the city—legend has it that students who spot the frog on their first try will pass all their exams. ✉ *Calle Libreros* ☎ *92/329–4400, 95/222–2998* ⊕ *www.usal.es* ✉ *Free to view facade, €10 to enter (free Mon. morning).*

🍴 Restaurants

Bambú

$$ | TAPAS | Bambú is two restaurants in one: there's a jovial basement tapas bar serving gargantuan tapas and beers to hungry locals, and then there's the far more sedate white-tablecloth dining room, whose *nueva cocina* (new cuisine) menu is subtler, fussier, and more expensive. Both are worthwhile options; go with the vibe that suits you best. **Known for:** free tapas with every drink at the bar; sedate nueva cocina dining room; friendly collegiate ambience. $ *Average main: €12* ✉ *Calle Prior 4* ☎ *92/326–0092* ⊕ *www.restaurantebambu.es.*

★ La Hoja 21

$$$$ | SPANISH | Just off the Plaza Mayor, this upscale restaurant has a glass facade, high ceilings, butter-yellow walls, and minimalist art—a welcome relief from the dime-a-dozen Castilian *mesones.* Savor traditional fare with a twist, such as ibérico pork ravioli and langoustine-stuffed trotters at dinner, or spring for the €16 lunch prix fixe, an absolute steal served Tuesday through Thursday. **Known for:** nuanced yet unpretentious modern fare; phenomenally affordable menú del día (prix fixe); romantic, low-key atmosphere. $ *Average main: €30* ✉ *Calle San Pablo 21* ☎ *92/326–4028* ⊕ *www.lahoja21.com* ⊗ *Closed Mon. No dinner Sun.*

Salamanca's Plaza Mayor once hosted bullfights.

★ Tapas 2.0

$$ | TAPAS | Decidedly modern, dependably delicious, and shockingly cheap, Tapas 2.0 might pull you back for a second meal. The cool *ensaladilla rusa* (potato salad mixed with tuna), a specialty, is one of the best in Spain; then there are more substantial dishes, like "Momofuku-style" fried chicken and saucy lamb meatballs, all complemented by a wine list featuring unexpected wines like German Riesling. **Known for:** ensaladilla rusa; uncommon wines; the best tapas in town. [$] *Average main: €14* ✉ *Calle Felipe Espino 10* ☎ *92/321–6448.*

★ Valencia

$$$ | SPANISH | Despite its Mediterranean name, this traditional, family-run restaurant serves up Castilian specialties like garlic soup, partridge salad, local river trout, white asparagus, and suckling lamb. The tiny front bar is decorated with black-and-white photos of local bullfighters, and is usually packed with locals (as is the back room). **Known for:** hidden-gem local hangout; soul-warming Castilian fare; outdoor seating. [$] *Average main: €20* ✉ *Calle Concejo 15* ☎ *92/321–7868* 🌐 *www.restaurantevalencia.com* 🕒 *Closed Mon. Nov., Tues. Sept.–May, and Sun. June–Aug.*

🛏 Hotels

Grand Hotel Don Gregorio

$$$$ | HOTEL | This upscale boutique hotel has spacious, contemporary rooms in a building with roots in the 15th century. **Pros:** chic, contemporary facilities; complimentary cava upon arrival; spa and in-room massages. **Cons:** restaurant is expensive—the more casual cafeteria is a better bet; no outdoor space for lounging; some receptionists speak poor English. [$] *Rooms from: €220* ✉ *Calle San Pablo 80–82* ☎ *92/321–7015* 🌐 *www.hoteldongregorio.com* 🛏 *17 rooms* 🍴 *Free breakfast.*

★ Hotel Rector

$$$ | HOTEL | From the stately entrance to the high-ceiling guest rooms, this lovely hotel offers a fairy-tale European experience. **Pros:** terrific value for a luxury hotel; personal service; good location. **Cons:** parking costs extra; no balconies; breakfast could be more ample. [$] *Rooms from: €160* ✉ *Paseo Rector Esperabé 10* ☎ *92/321–8482* 🌐 *www.hotelrector.com* 🛏 *13 rooms* 🍴 *No meals.*

★ Microtel Placentinos

$$ | B&B/INN | This is a cheap-and-cheerful B&B tucked down a quiet pedestrian street in Salamanca's historic center, near the Palacio de Congresos convention center and a short walk from the Plaza Mayor. **Pros:** some rooms have whirlpool baths; quirky decor; short walk to bus station. **Cons:** rooms by interior staircase can be noisy; some accommodations are cramped; boring breakfast buffet. [$] *Rooms from: €90* ✉ *Calle Placentinos 9* ☎ *92/328–1531* 🌐 *www.microtelplacentinos.com* 🛏 *9 rooms* 🍴 *Free breakfast.*

Revolutum Hostel

$ | HOTEL | Embodying the swiftly growing lodging category of "designer hostel," this is the best modern budget hotel in Salamanca. **Pros:** breakfast included; all rooms have private bathrooms; special rates for families and longer stays. **Cons:** deposit required for towels; you have to make your own bed in some rooms; small bathrooms in some rooms. [$] *Rooms from: €49* ✉ *Calle Sánchez Barbero 7* ☎ *92/321–7656* 🌐 *www.revolutumhostel.com* 🛏 *20 rooms* 🍴 *Free breakfast.*

🍸 Nightlife

Particularly in summer, Salamanca sees the greatest influx of foreign students of any city in Spain: by day they study Spanish, and by night they fill Salamanca's bars and clubs.

BARS AND CAFÉS

★ The Doctor Cocktail Bar

BARS/PUBS | This petite, unpretentious *coctelería* off the Plaza Mayor serves an enormous breadth of drinks, from colorful tiki numbers (some with pyrotechnics) to Prohibition-era classics, until 1:30 am daily. ✉ *Calle Doctor Pinuela 5* ☎ *92/326–3151.*

Gran Café Moderno

BARS/PUBS | After-hours types end the night here, snacking on churros dipped in chocolate to ward off the next day's hangover. Gran Café Moderno is also a fine spot to loosen up before hitting the rowdier nightclubs and to recharge in the afternoon—choose from a wide variety of coffee drinks with or without booze. ✉ *Gran Vía 75–77* ☎ *63/753–8165, 92/326–0147.*

🎫 Performing Arts

Teatro Liceo

ARTS VENUE | This 732-seat theater, 40 yards from Plaza Mayor, got a face-lift in 2002, but traces of the old 19th-century theater, built over an 18th-century convent, remain. It hosts classic and modern performances of opera, dance, and flamenco as well as film festivals. ✉ *Calle del Toro 23* ☎ *92/328–0619* 🌐 *www.ciudaddecultura.org.*

👜 Shopping

El Rastro

OUTDOOR/FLEA/GREEN MARKETS | On Sunday, this flea market—named after the larger one in Madrid—is held just outside Salamanca's historic center. It has some 400 stalls. Buses leave from Plaza de España. ✉ *Av. de Aldehuela.*

Isisa Duende

CRAFTS | If you have a car, skip the souvenir shops in Salamanca's center and instead take a joyride 35 km (22 miles) through the countryside along the SA300 road to Isisa Duende, a wooden crafts workshop run by a charming husband-and-wife team. Their music boxes, photo frames, and other items are carved with local themes, from the *bailes charros,* Salamanca's regional dance, to the floral

designs embroidered on the hems of provincial dresses. Because the store has limited hours (primarily weekends only), it's best to call ahead to schedule a free, personal tour; if you're pressed for time, you can buy some of their wares in the tourist office on the Plaza Mayor. ⊠ *Calle San Miguel 1, Ledesma* ☎ *62/651–0527, 62/533–6703* ⊕ *www.isisa-duende.es.*

★ **Luis Méndez**

JEWELRY/ACCESSORIES | Luis and his two brothers are independent third-generation jewelers whose work is distinguished by intricate filigree. The most stunning specimens—costing more than €1,000—are fashioned out of gold and pearls, but there are more affordable options made from silver and semiprecious stones. Visit their boutique, or purchase from the online catalog. ⊠ *Calle Meléndez 8, Bajo 2* ☎ *92/326–0725, 92/344–9111* ⊕ *www.luismendez.net.*

★ **Mercado Central**

FOOD/CANDY | **FAMILY** | At Salamanca's most historic market you can stock up on local gourmet specialties—such as *farinato* sausages, *jamón ibérico* (Iberian ham), and sheep's cheeses—and round out your shopping spree with a glass of wine at any of the market's traditional tapas counters. The 53 stalls are sure to keep any foodie occupied. ⊠ *Pl. del Mercado* ☎ *92/321–3000* ⊕ *www.mercadocentral-salamanca.com* ☯ *Closed Sun.*

Burgos

243 km (151 miles) north of Madrid on A1.

On the banks of the Arlanzón River, this small city boasts some of Spain's most outstanding Gothic architecture. If you approach on the A1 from Madrid, the spiky twin spires of Burgos's cathedral, rising above the main bridge, welcome you to the city. Burgos's second pride is its heritage as the city of El Cid, the part-historical, part-mythical hero of the so-called Reconquest of Spain. For better and for worse, the city has long been synonymous with both militarism and religion, and even today more nuns fill the streets than almost anywhere else in Spain. Burgos was born as a military camp—a fortress built in 884 on the orders of the Christian king Alfonso III, who was struggling to defend the upper reaches of Old Castile from the constant forays of the Arabs. It quickly became vital in the defense of Christian Spain, and its reputation as an early outpost of Christianity was cemented with the founding of the Royal Convent of Las Huelgas, in 1187, and cemented as it became a place of rest and sustenance for Christian pilgrims on the Camino de Santiago. In 1938, as the Spanish Civil War raged on, soon-to-be-dictator Francisco Franco made Burgos his first seat of government, a testament to the city's conservative leanings. Today Burgos is a modern Spanish city like any other, and happily, its name is far more likely to recall its famous *queso fresco* (quark) and *morcilla* (blood sausage) than it is with its fraught political past.

GETTING HERE AND AROUND

Burgos can be reached by train from Madrid, with 13 departures daily from Chamartín (2½ hours on the fast ALVIA train and 4½ on the regional line) and by bus, with hourly service from various Madrid stations. There are usually several Blablacar rideshares available as well. Once in town, municipal buses cover 45 routes throughout the city, many of them originating in Plaza de España.

VISITOR INFORMATION Burgos Tourist Office. ⊠ *Pl. de Alonso-Martínez 7* ☎ *94/720–3125* ⊕ *www.turismoburgos. org.*

The small city of Burgos is famous for its magnificent Gothic cathedral.

Sights

Cartuja de Miraflores (*Miraflores Charterhouse*)

RELIGIOUS SITE | The plain facade of this 15th-century Carthusian monastery, some 3 km (2 miles) outside the historic center, belies a richly decorated interior. There's an altarpiece by Gil de Siloe that is said to be gilded with the first gold plundered in the Americas. ⊠ *Ctra. Fuentes Blancas* ☎ *94/725–2586* ⊕ *www. cartuja.org* 🎟 *Free.*

★ Catedral de Burgos

RELIGIOUS SITE | Start your tour of the city with the cathedral, which contains such a wealth of art and other treasures that the local burghers lynched their civil governor in 1869 for trying to take an inventory of it—the proud citizens feared that the man was plotting to steal their riches. Just as opulent as what's inside is the sculpted flamboyant Gothic facade. The cornerstone was laid in 1221, and the two 275-foot towers were completed by the middle of the 14th century, though the final chapel was not finished until 1731. There are 13 chapels, the most elaborate of which is the hexagonal Condestable Chapel. You'll find the **tomb of El Cid** (1026–99) and his wife, Ximena, under the transept. El Cid (whose real name was Rodrigo Díaz de Vivar) was a feudal warlord revered for his victories over the Moors; the medieval *Song of My Cid* transformed him into a Spanish national hero.

At the other end of the cathedral, high above the West Door, is the **Reloj de Papamoscas** (Flycatcher Clock), so named for the sculptured bird that opens its mouth as the hands mark each hour. The grilles around the choir have some of the finest wrought-iron work in central Spain, and the choir itself has 103 delicately carved walnut stalls, no two alike. The 13th-century stained-glass windows that once shed a beautiful, filtered light were destroyed in 1813, one of many cultural casualties of Napoléon's retreating troops. You'll learn all of this and more via the free audio guide, which has a

Burgos

KEY

- 1 Exploring Sights
- 1 Restaurants
- 1 Hotels

200 yards

200 meters

Sights
1 Cartuja de Miraflores E2
2 Catedral de Burgos E2
3 Monasterio de
   Santa María la Real
   de las Huelgas A3

4 Museo de la Evolución
   Humana G2
5 Paseo del Espolón F2

Restaurants
1 Casa Ojeda G1

Hotels
1 Hotel Mesón del Cid E2
2 Landa F3

Side Trips from Burgos

Monastery of Santo Domingo de Silos

For a sojourn with masters of the Gregorian chant, head to the monastery where 1994's triple-platinum album *Chant* was recorded in the 1970s and '80s. Located 58 km (36 miles) southeast of Burgos, the monastery has an impressive two-story cloister that's lined with intricate Romanesque carvings. Try to drop in for an evening vespers service. It's a unique experience that's well off the tourist path. Single men can stay here for up to eight days (€42 per night with full board). Guests are expected to be present for breakfast, lunch, and dinner but are otherwise left to their own devices. ⊕ *www.abadiadesilos.es*

Ojo Guareña

If you have a day to spare or are traveling on to Cantabria, stop at this breathtaking hermitage hewn into a karst cliffside surrounded by leafy woodlands situated a mile south of Cueva. A national monument, the cave complex housing the religious structure stretches 90 km (56 miles), and there's rock art throughout the many chambers that depicts the cave as a dwelling for early humans. Archeologists date the site's use from the Middle Palaeolithic to the Middle Ages. A worthwhile guided tour of the hermitage lasts 45 minutes; even more scintillating is the tour of nearby Palomera Cave (by appointment only). ⊕ *www.merindaddesotoscueva.es*

12

Day Trips from Madrid BURGOS

---

kid-friendly option. ⊠ *Pl. de Santa María* ☎ *94/720–4712* ⊕ *www.catedraldeburgos.es* ⧰ *€8.*

Monasterio de Santa María la Real de las Huelgas (*Monasterio de las Huelgas*)
MUSEUM | This convent on the outskirts of town, founded in 1187 by King Alfonso VIII, is still run by Cistercian nuns. There's a small on-site textile museum, but the building's main attraction is its stained-glass panels, some of the oldest in Spain. Admission includes a guided tour (Spanish only) of the monastery which is the only way to view the monastery. The monastery is closed to the public between 1:30 and 4. ⊠ *Calle de Los Compases* ☎ *94/720–1630* ⊕ *www.patrimonionacional.es* ⧰ *€6 (free Wed. and Thurs. afternoon).*

★ Museo de la Evolución Humana
MUSEUM | FAMILY | This airy, modern complex is one of the best natural history museums in the world and traces human evolution from primate to the present day. There are life-size replicas of our

ancient ancestors, plus hands-on exhibits and in-depth scientific explanations (in English) that will fascinate visitors of all ages. Pair with a museum-led visit to the Atapuerca archaeological site (inquire at reception or online to arrange). ⊠ *Paseo Sierra de Atapuerca* ☎ *94/725–7103* ⊕ *www.museoevolucionhumana.com* ⧰ *€6* ⊙ *Closed Mon.*

Paseo del Espolón
PROMENADE | The Arco de Santa María frames the city's loveliest promenade, the Espolón. Shaded with black poplars, it follows the riverbank. ⊠ *Burgos.*

🍴 Restaurants

Casa Ojeda
$$$$ | SPANISH | This centennial restaurant—a Castilian classic—is known for refined Burgos standbys, especially cochinillo (suckling pig) and lamb straight from the 200-year-old wood oven. Wines by the glass are local and reasonable. **Known for:** fall-off-the-bone

lamb; old-school waitstaff; tried-and-true Castilian cuisine. $ *Average main: €32* ⊠ *Calle Vitoria 5* ☎ *94/720–9052* ⊕ *www. restauranteojeda.com* ⊗ *No dinner Sun.*

Hotels

Hotel Mesón del Cid

$ | HOTEL | Once home to a 15th-century printing press, this independently owned hotel and restaurant has been hosting travelers for generations in light, airy guest rooms (ask for one facing the cathedral). **Pros:** cathedral views from upgraded rooms; comfy, clean digs; central location. **Cons:** parking is a tight squeeze; could use a face-lift; some rooms noisy. $ *Rooms from: €80* ⊠ *Pl. Santa María 8* ☎ *94/720–8715* ⊕ *www.mesondelcid.es* ⇄ *55 rooms* ⦿ *No meals.*

Landa

$$$ | HOTEL | FAMILY | If you've ever dreamed of holing up in a luxurious castle, consider booking a room at Landa, a converted 14th-century palace some 5 km (3 miles) from the city center surrounded by lush gardens. **Pros:** stunning indoor-outdoor swimming pool; surprisingly affordable for level of luxury; beautiful lobby. **Cons:** roads to and from town are busy; you'll need your own transportation to get here; inconsistent food quality. $ *Rooms from: €140* ⊠ *Ctra. de Madrid–Irún, Km 235* ☎ *94/725–7777* ⊕ *www. landa.as* ⇄ *37 rooms* ⦿ *No meals.*

ⓨ Nightlife

Due to its student population, Burgos has a lively *vida nocturna* (nightlife) in **Las Llanas,** near the cathedral. House wines and *cañas* (small glasses of beer) flow freely through the crowded tapas bars along Calles Laín Calvo and San Juan, near the Plaza Mayor. Calle Puebla, a small, dark street off Calle San Juan, also gets constant revelers. When you order a drink at any Burgos bar, the bartender plunks down a free *pinchito* (small tapa)—a long-standing tradition.

Bardeblás

CAFES—NIGHTLIFE | This intimate bar stays open until 4:30 on the weekends, inviting you to stay awhile—and you just might, thanks to its strong and affordable drinks and catchy throwback jams. ⊠ *Calle de la Puebla 29* ☎ *94/720–1162.*

Cervecería Flandes

BREWPUBS/BEER GARDENS | With 12 beers on tap that run the gamut from Belgian ales to rare Castilian microbrews, this Burgos stalwart for 20 years attracts a diverse crowd of students, travelers, and beer geeks. Just don't expect any fancy food here—potato chips, nachos, and other sundry snacks are the only grub available. ⊠ *Pl. Huerto del Rey 21* ☎ *65/993–4813* ⊕ *www.cerveceriaflandes.es.*

⬤ Shopping

★ Delicatessen Ojeda

FOOD/CANDY | A food lover's paradise, this pristine, well-lit store carries all the Castilian delicacies you can imagine, from Burgos-style morcilla and cheese to roasted oil-packed peppers and top-quality dried beans and pulses. ⊠ *Calle de Vitoria 5* ☎ *94/720–4832* ⊕ *www.delicatessenojeda.com.*

SEVILLE AND AROUND

Updated by
Joanna Styles

🕓 Sights	🍴 Restaurants	🛏 Hotels	💼 Shopping	🍸 Nightlife
★★★★★	★★★★★	★★★★★	★★★★★	★★★★☆

WELCOME TO SEVILLE AND AROUND

TOP REASONS TO GO

★ **The Real Alcázar:** Drink in the sumptuously decorated patios and halls, the heavenly gold ceiling, ornate tile, and lush gardens dotted with pools, palms, and peacocks.

★ **Tour Catedral de Sevilla:** Tour Spain's biggest cathedral (there are 80 chapels) to see Christendom's largest altarpiece.

★ **Live and breathe flamenco:** Tune into Andalusia's soundtrack at one of Seville's many flamenco *tablaos* or spontaneously on any corner in Santa Cruz or Triana.

★ **Feast on tapas:** Make small plates your staples at myriad taverns, traditional and modern, where fine dining comes paired with local wines including sherry.

★ **Shop for tile:** Learn about the history and process of making Sevillian ceramics in a former factory at the Centro de Cerámica Triana, and shop for beautiful souvenirs.

★ **Linger in the Plaza de España:** Take a leisurely stroll at this magnificent semi-circular plaza located in María Luisa Park.

1 Centro. The heart of the city's commercial life.

2 Santa Cruz. Home to the Real Alcázar and a glorious labyrinth of whitewashed alleys.

3 El Arenal. This area includes the Parque Maria Luisa, the Torre de Oro on the river, and a plethora of picturesque taverns.

4 La Macarena. The city's best churches and convents, pleasant squares, and excellent eateries.

5 Triana. Home to the main workshop for Seville's renowned ceramicists.

6 Italica. Known for the ruins of its Roman city.

7 Córdoba. Home to the stunning Mezquita—a must visit.

8 Ronda. Famous for its dramatic escarpments, views, and gorge.

9 Around Ronda. Caves, mountain villages, and gorges.

10 Arcos de la Frontera. A classic Andalusian pueblo blanco.

11 Jerez de la Frontera. The capital of horse culture and sherry.

12 Cádiz. So old that Julius Caesar once held public office here.

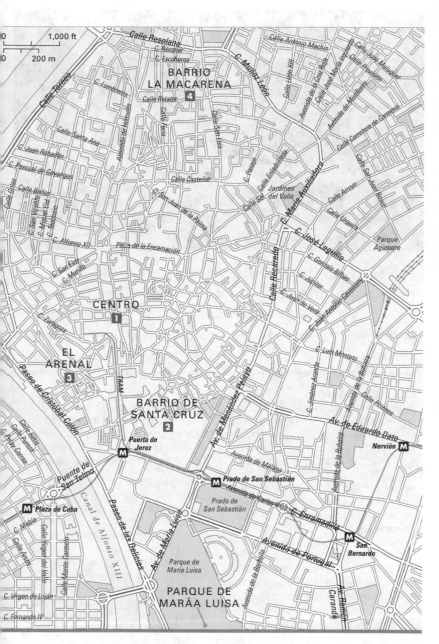

1,000 ft
200 m

Calle Torneo
Calle Resolana
C. Bécquer
C. Escoberos
Calle Antonio Machín
C. Muñoz León
Calle León XIII
Calle José Maluquer
Calle Feria
C. Lumbreras
BARRIO
LA MACARENA 4
Calle Relator
Calle José María Izquierdo
Calle Fray Isla
Avenida de la Cruz Roja
Avenida de Muñagore
Calle Carretera de Carmona
Calle San Juan Bosco
C. Juan Rabadán
Calle Santa Ana
Alameda de Hércules
Calle Feria
Calle San Luis
C. Pascual de Gayangos
Calle Baños
Calle Gravina
C. San Vicente
C. Miguel Cid
C. Redondo
C. Alfonso XII
Calle Castellar
C. San Juan de la Palma
Calle Enladrillada
Calle Sol
Jardines
del Valle
C. Passeo
C. Martín Villa
C. Matías Auxiliadora
Calle Arroyo
Calle Urquita
C. José Laguillo
Parque
Agumore
Plaza de la Encarnación
C. San Eloy
C. Murillo
CENTRO 1
Calle Gonzalo Bilbao
C. Júpiter
C. Zaragoza
Calle Recaredo
C. Juan de Vera
C. Juan-Antonio Cavestany
C. Luis Montoto
EL
ARENAL 3
TRAM
Paseo de Cristóbal Colón
C. Jiménez Aranda
Avenida de la Buhaira
Calle Páramos
BARRIO DE
SANTA CRUZ 2
Av. de Menéndez Pelayo
Av. de Eduardo Dato
Puerta de
Jerez
M
Avenida de Málaga
Nervión M
Prado de San Sebastián M
Puente de
San Telmo
Calle Betis
Calle Pureza
Pelay Correa
M Plaza de Cuba
Canal de Alfonso XIII
Paseo de las Delicias
Av. de María Luisa
Prado de
San Sebastián
Avenida de Carlos V
Avenida de la Buhaira
C. Enramadilla
San
Bernardo M
C. Niebla
Calle Virgen del Valle
Calle Monte Carmelo
Avenida de Portugal
Calle Ardilla
Parque de
María Luisa
Avenida de la Borbolla
Av. Ramón Carandé
C. Virgen de Luján
C. Fernando IV
PARQUE DE
MARÍA LUISA

FLAMENCO

Rule one about flamenco: You don't see it. You feel it. The pain and yearning on the dancers' faces and the eerie voices are real. If the dancers manage to summon the *duende* and allow this soulful state of emotion to take over, then they have done their jobs well.

FLAMENCO 101

Origins: The music is largely Arabic in its beginnings, but you'll detect echoes of Greek dirges and Jewish chants, with healthy doses of Flemish and traditional Castilian thrown in. Hindu sways, Roman mimes, and other movement informs the dance, but we may never know the specific origins of flamenco. The dance, along with the nomadic Gypsies, spread throughout Andalusia and within a few centuries had developed into many variations and styles, some of them named after the city where they were born (such as malaguenas and *sevillanas*) and others taking on the names after people,

emotions, or bands. In all, there are more than 50 different styles (or *palos*) of flamenco, four of which are the stylistic pillars others branch off from—differing mainly in rhythm and mood: *toná, soleá,* fandango, and seguidilla.

Clapping and castanets: The sum of its parts are awe-inspiring, but if you boil it down, flamenco is a combination of music, singing, and dance. Staccato hand-clapping almost sneaks in as a fourth part—the sounds made from all the participants' palms, or *palmas,* is part of the duende—but this element remains more of a connector that all in the performance take part in when their hands are free.

Hand-clapping was likely flamenco's original key instrument before the guitar, *cajón* (wooden box used for percussion), and other instruments arrived on the scene. Perhaps the simplest way to augment the clapping is to add a uniquely designed six-string guitar, in which case you've got yourself a *tablao*, or people seated around a singer and clapping. Dance undoubtedly augments the experience, but isn't necessary for a tablao. These exist all throughout Andalusia and are usually private affairs with people who love flamenco. One needn't be a Gypsy in order to take part in it. But it doesn't hurt. Castanets (or *palillos*) were absorbed by the Phoenician culture and adopted by the Spanish, now part of their own folklore. They accompany other traditional folk dances in Spain and are used pervasively throughout flamenco (though not always present in some forms of dance).

Flamenco now: Flamenco's enormous international resurgence has been building for the past few decades. Much of this revival can be attributed to pioneers like legendary singer Camarón de la Isla, guitarist Paco de Lucía, or even outsiders like Miles Davis fusing flamenco with other genres like jazz and rock. Today the most popular flamenco fusion artists include Rosalía and Fuel Fandango.

FLAMENCO HEAD TO TOE
Wrists rotate while hands move, articulating each finger individually, curling in and out. The trick is to have it appear like an effortless flourish. Facial expression is considered another tool for the dancer, and it's never plastered on but projected from some deeper place. For women, the hair is usually pulled back in touring flamenco performances in order to give the back row a chance to see more clearly the passionate expressions. In smaller settings like tablaos, hair is usually let down and is supposed to better reveal the beauty of the female form overall. The dancer carries the body in an upright and proud manner: the chest is out, shoulders back. Despite this position, the body should never carry tension—it needs to remain pliable and fluid. With professional dancers, the feet can move so quickly, they blur like hummingbird wings in action. When they move slowly, you can watch the different ways a foot can strike the floor. A *planta* is when the whole foot strikes the floor, as opposed to when the ball of the foot or the heel (*taco*) hits. Each one must be a "clean" strike or the sound will be off.

An exploration of Andalusia must begin with Seville, Spain's fourth-largest city and the place where all romantic images of Andalusia, and Spain, spring vividly to life. Known for its steamy-hot summers, delightfully mild winters, its operatic heroine, Carmen, and stunning Game of Thrones settings, Seville is an enchanting city whose fabulous food, extraordinary Mudejar, Gothic, and Renaissance architecture, and exotic flamenco rhythms never fail to seduce and charm.

The layout of the historic center of Seville makes exploring easy. The central zone—Centro—around the cathedral, Calle Sierpes, and Plaza Nueva, is splendid and monumental, but it's not where you'll find Seville's greatest charm. El Arenal, home of the Maestranza bullring, the Teatro de la Maestranza concert hall, and a concentration of picturesque taverns, still buzzes the way it must have when stevedores loaded and unloaded ships from the New World. Just southeast of Centro, the medieval Jewish quarter, Barrio de Santa Cruz, is home to the Real Alcázar and a lovely, whitewashed tangle of alleys. The Barrio de la Macarena to the northeast is rich in sights and authentic Seville atmosphere. The fifth and final neighborhood to explore, on the far side of the Río Guadalquivir, is in many ways the best of all—Triana, the traditional habitat for sailors, bullfighters, and flamenco artists, as well as the main workshop for Seville's renowned ceramicists.

Like all Andalusians, the Sevillanos know how to party. Highlights of the year come in the Feria de abril, a week of colorful and musical festivities to welcome spring, quickly followed by celebrations marking Pentecost when locals take a pilgrimage to El Rocío on the Atlantic Ocean. Religious fervor comes into their own during Holy Week when thousands of devout locals take place in some of Spain's most famous processions.

Side trips from Seville range from half-day excursions to the Roman Itálica and Renaissance Carmona to longer visits to some of Andalusia's finest towns and cities. Nearby Jerez, celebrated for sherry and horses, and Cádiz, a maritime jewel, are both must-sees. Ronda, one of Spain's most beautiful towns merits a full day as does Córdoba whose Moorish mosque ranks as one of the country's most treasured monuments.

Planning

When to Go

Visit Seville in October and November and April and May. It's blisteringly hot in the summer; spend time in the Pedroches of northern Córdoba province if you plan to visit then. Autumn catches the cities going about their business, the temperatures are moderate, and you will rarely see a line form.

December through March tends to be cool, uncrowded, and quiet, but come spring, it's fiesta time, with Seville's Semana Santa (Holy Week, between Palm Sunday and Easter) the most moving and multitudinous. April showcases white-washed Andalusia at its floral best, every patio and facade covered with flowers from bougainvillea to honeysuckle.

Getting Here and Around

AIR
Seville's airport is about 7 km (4½ miles) east of the city. There's a bus from the airport to the center of town every half hour daily (5:20 am–1:15 am; €4 one-way, €6 return). Taxi fare from the airport to the city center is around €23 during the day and €26 at night and on Sunday. A number of private companies operate private airport-shuttle services.

GETTING HERE AND AROUND BUS
Seville has two intercity bus stations: Estación Plaza de Armas, the main one, with buses serving Córdoba, Granada, Huelva, and Málaga in Andalusia, plus Madrid and Portugal and other international destinations; and the smaller Estación del Prado de San Sebastián, serving Cádiz and nearby towns and villages.

Certain routes operate limited night service from midnight to 2 am Monday

through Thursday, with services until 5 am Friday through Sunday. Single rides cost €1.40, but if you're going to be busing a lot, it's more economical to buy a rechargeable multitravel pass, which works out to €0.69 per ride. Special Tarjetas Turísticas (tourist passes) valid for one or three days of unlimited bus travel cost (respectively) €5 and €10. Tickets are sold at newsstands and at the main bus station, Prado de San Sebastián.

CONTACTS Estación del Prado de San Sebastián. ✉ *Calle Vázquez Sagastizábal, El Arenal* ☎ *955/479290.* **Estación Plaza de Armas.** ✉ *Puente Cristo de la Expiración, Centro* ☎ *955/038665* ⊕ *www.autobusesplazadearmas.es.*

CAR
Getting in and out of Seville by car isn't difficult, thanks to the SE30 ring road, but getting around in the city by car is problematic. We advise leaving your car at your hotel or in a lot while you're here.

TAXI
CONTACTS Radio Taxi Sevilla . ☎ *954/580000.*

TRAIN
Train connections include the high-speed AVE service from Madrid, with a journey time of less than 2½ hours.

CONTACTS Estación Santa Justa. ✉ *Av. Kansas City, El Arenal* ☎ *912/320320.*

VISITOR INFORMATION
CONTACTS City of Seville. ✉ *Paseo Marqués de Contador s/n, Barrio de Santa Cruz* ✛ *On waterfront, by Torre de Oro* ☎ *955/471232* ⊕ *www.visitasevilla.es.*

Hotels

Seville has grand old hotels, such as the Alfonso XIII, and a number of former palaces converted into sumptuous hostelries.

In Córdoba, several pleasant hotels occupy houses in the old quarter, close to the mosque. Other than during Holy Week and the Festival de los Patios in May, it's easy to find a room in Córdoba, even without a reservation.

Rental accommodations bookable on portals such as Airbnb are popular in large towns and cities, although quality varies so double-check reviews before you book.

Not all hotel prices include value-added tax (I.V.A.) and the 10% surcharge may be added to your final bill. Check when you book. *Hotel reviews have been shortened. For full information, visit Fodors.com.*

Tours

★ annie b's Spanish Kitchen

SPECIAL-INTEREST | Based in Vejer de la Frontera (Cádiz), Scottish-born Annie B offers food and wine experiences, including sherry tours, tuna *almadraba* (an age-old way of trapping) trips, and cooking classes. ⊠ *Calle Viñas, 11, Vejer de la Frontera* ☎ *620/560649* ⊕ *www.anniebspain.com* ➲ *From €155.*

Azahar Sevilla Tapas Tours

SPECIAL-INTEREST | Local food and wine expert Shawn Hennessey leads guided tours around Seville's best tapas bars (traditional and gourmet). Choose from several different tours, lunch or evening. ⊕ *azahar-sevilla.com/sevilletapas* ➲ *From €75.*

Glovento Sur

AIR EXCURSIONS | Up to five people at a time are taken in balloon trips above Granada, Ronda, and Seville. ⊠ *Placeta Nevot 4, #1A, Granada* ☎ *958/290316* ⊕ *www.gloventosur.com* ➲ *From €165.*

History and Tapas Tour

GUIDED TOURS | Glean local, historical, and culinary knowledge on a variety of tours around sights and tapas bars. ⊕ *www.sevilleconcierge.com* ➲ *From €60.*

Sevilla Bike Tour

BICYCLE TOURS | Guided tours, leaving from the Makinline Shop on Calle Arjona at 10:30 am, take in the major sights of the city and offer interesting stories and insider information along the way. You'll cover about 10 km (6 miles) in three hours. Reservations are required on weekends and recommended on weekdays. ⊠ *Calle Arjona 8, Centro* ☎ *954/562625* ⊕ *www.sevillabiketour.com* ➲ *From €25.*

Sevilla Walking Tours

WALKING TOURS | A choice of three walking tours are conducted in English: the City Walking Tour, leaving Plaza Nueva from the statue of San Fernando; the Alcázar Tour, leaving Plaza del Triunfo from the central statue; and the Cathedral Tour, also leaving from the Plaza del Triunfo central statue. ⊠ *Seville* ☎ *902/158226, 616/501100* ⊕ *sevillawalkingtours.com* ➲ *From €12.*

Your First Flamenco Experience

SPECIAL-INTEREST | Local dancer Eva Izquierdo from Triana teaches you how to clap in time, and take your first dance steps, in authentic costume, all in 1½ hours. ⊠ *Seville* ☎ *626/007868* ⊕ *www.ishowusevilla.com* ➲ *From €28.*

Centro

The Centro area is the heart of Seville's commercial life. It has bustling shopping streets, several of which are pedestrianized, and leafy squares lined with bars and cafés. The residential streets contain some of the best examples of colonial architecture; noteworthy features include fine facades and roof gables topped with local ceramics. Centro is also home to several of the city's most beautiful churches.

Seville's cathedral is the largest and tallest cathedral in Spain, the largest Gothic building in the world, and the third-largest church in the world, after St. Peter's in Rome and St. Paul's in London.

Sights

Calle Sierpes

NEIGHBORHOOD | This is Seville's classy main shopping street. Near the southern end, at No. 85, a plaque marks the spot where the Cárcel Real (Royal Prison) once stood. Miguel de Cervantes began writing *Don Quixote* in one of its cells. ⊠ *Centro.*

★ Catedral de Sevilla

RELIGIOUS SITE | Seville's cathedral can be described only in superlatives: it's the largest and highest cathedral in Spain, the largest Gothic building in the world, and the world's third-largest church, after St. Peter's in Rome and St. Paul's in London. After Ferdinand III captured Seville from the Moors in 1248, the great mosque begun by Yusuf II in 1171 was used as a Christian cathedral. In 1401, Seville pulled down the old mosque, leaving only its minaret and outer courtyard, and built a new cathedral in just over a century. The magnificent *retablo* (altarpiece) in the Capilla Mayor (Main Chapel)

is the largest in Christendom. The Capilla Real (Royal Chapel) is concealed behind a curtain, but duck in if you're quick, quiet, and properly dressed (no shorts or sleeveless tops). Don't forget the Patio de los Naranjos (Courtyard of Orange Trees), where the fountain in the center was used for ablutions before people entered the original mosque. ⊠ *Pl. Virgen de los Reyes, Centro* ☎ *954/214971* ⊕ *www.catedraldesevilla.es* ⌨ *€9 (free Mon. 4:30–6 pm if you book via website).*

Metropol Parasol

ARCHAEOLOGICAL SITE | This huge square, at the west end of Calle Cuna, is home to the world's largest wooden structure, 492 feet long by 230 feet wide. The design, known in the city as "Las Setas" (The Mushroom), actually represents giant trees, reminiscent of Gaudí, and walkways run through the "tree tops" affording great views of the city, especially at sunset. At ground level, there are interesting archaeological remains (mostly Roman) and a large indoor food market. ✉ *Pl. de la Encarnación, Centro* 🖥 *€3 (including a drink).*

★ Palacio de la Condesa de Lebrija

CASTLE/PALACE | This lovely palace has three ornate patios, including a spectacular courtyard graced by a Roman mosaic taken from the ruins in Itálica, surrounded by Moorish arches and fine *azulejos* (painted tiles). The side rooms house a collection of archaeological items. The second floor contains the family apartments and visits are by guided tour only. ■TIP➔ **It's well worth paying for the second-floor tour, which gives an interesting insight into the collections and the family.** ✉ *Calle Cuna 8, Centro* 🕾 *954/227802* 🖥 *€12 (free Mon. 6–6:30 pm, 1st floor only).*

Palacio de las Dueñas

HOUSE | The 15th-century home and official residence of the late 18th Duchess of Alba in Seville is an oasis of peace and quiet in the bustling city. Set around an ornate patio with Mudejar arches and a central fountain, the house includes antiques and paintings, as well as memorabilia relating to the duchess herself. Revered in the city and one of Spain's most important noblewomen and society figures, Cayetana de Alba loved bullfighting, flamenco, and ceramics. The visit (first floor only) also includes the stables, gardens (said to have inspired some of the poet Antonio Machado's most famous early verses), and a Gothic chapel. ✉ *Calle Dueñas 5, Centro* 🕾 *954/214828* 🌐 *www.lasduenas.es* 🖥 *€10 (free Mon. beginning at 4).*

 Restaurants

Casa Morales

$ | TAPAS | Down a side street off the Avenida de la Constitución, this historic bar (formerly a wine store) takes you back to 19th-century Seville, and it is still run by descendents of the same family that established it in 1850. Locals pack the place at lunchtime, when popular

dishes include *menudo con garbanzos* (tripe with chickpeas) and *albóndigas de choco* (cuttlefish croquettes). **Known for:** local atmosphere; wine list; tripe with chickpeas. 💲 *Average main: €8* ✉ *Calle García de Vinuesa 11, Centro* 🕾 *954/221242* 🕙 *Closed Sun.*

Castizo

$$ | SPANISH | True tradition (castizo itself) comes into its own at this busy venue serving regional dishes such as *jabalí con judiones, setas y foie* (braised wild boar with beans, mushrooms and foie) alongside more modern plates like the popular *coliflor toastada con holandesa trufada* (cauliflower cheese with truffle oil) plus daily fish specials and rice dish of the day. The open kitchen gives you a frontline view of your meal in the making. **Known for:** authentic traditional cooking; daily fish and rice specials; open kitchen. 💲 *Average main: €12* ✉ *Calle Zaragoza 6, Centro* 🕾 *955/180562.*

El Pintón

$$ | FUSION | With a privileged spot a block north from the cathedral, this central restaurant offers two dining spaces: on the traditional inside patio, where wood, mirrors, and tasteful lighting create an intimate but airy space, or outside on the pleasant terrace. The cuisine combines Andalusian dishes with a modern touch, with menu items such as bloody gazpacho, *huevo en tempura con parmentier trufado* (egg in batter with truffled potato puree), red tuna tartare, and *solomillo ibérico relleno de setas* (Iberian pork steak filled with mushrooms). **Known for:** attractive interior; value quick bites; Mediterranean dishes. 💲 *Average main: €13* ✉ *Calle Francos 42, Centro* 🕾 *955/075153* 🌐 *elpinton.com.*

★ Espacio Eslava

$ | TAPAS | The crowds gathered outside this local favorite off the Alameda de Hercules may be off-putting at first, but the creative, inexpensive tapas (from €3) are well worth the wait—and so is the house specialty, the Basque dessert *sokoa*. Try delicacies like the *solomillo de pato con pan de queso y salsa de peras al vino* (duck fillet with cheesy bread and pears in wine sauce). **Known for:** tapas; sokoa, a Basque dessert; vegetable strudel. $ *Average main: €12* ⊠ *Calle Eslava 3, Centro* ☎ *954/906568* ⊗ *Closed Mon. No dinner Sun.*

La Azotea

$$ | SPANISH | With a young vibe and a vast and inventive menu (which changes seasonally), this tiny restaurant offers a welcome change from Seville's typical fried fare. The owners' haute-cuisine ambitions are reflected in excellent service and lovingly prepared food—but not in the prices. **Known for:** creative tapas; seasonal menu; local vibe. $ *Average main: €15* ⊠ *Calle Conde de Barajas 13, Centro* ☎ *955/116748* ⊟ *No credit cards* ⊗ *Closed Sun. and Mon.*

★ La Campana

$ | CAFÉ | Under the gilt-edged ceiling at Seville's most celebrated pastry outlet (founded in 1885), you can enjoy the flanlike *tocino de cielo,* or "heavenly bacon." For breakfast, enjoy a traditional feed of toasted bread with tomato and a strong coffee, served at a standing bar. Prices are reasonable despite its popularity. **Known for:** traditional atmosphere; tempting window displays; variety of pastries and desserts. $ *Average main:* ⊠ *Calle Sierpes 1, Centro* ☎ *954/223570* ⊕ *confiterialacampana.com.*

★ La Cata Ciega

$ | SPANISH | Behind an ordinary facade lies one of Seville's best dining spots, a cozy room for just 13 (be prepared for not much elbow room), where owner Alvaro and his nephew serve tapas paired with wine or sherry. You can choose your own or opt for a "blind tasting" as the venue's name suggests in Spanish. **Known for:** house ensaladilla rusa; long wine and sherry lists and food pairings; cash only. $ *Average main: €4* ⊠ *Calle Zaragoza 15, Centro* ☎ *622/843374* ⊗ *Closed Mon. No dinner Sun.* ⊟ *No credit cards*

Hotels

Casa Romana Hotel Boutique

$$$ | HOTEL | Tucked away down a quiet side street in the heart of the Centro district but just 15 minutes' walk from the main sights, this restored 18th-century town house pays homage to the Roman Emperor the street is named for. **Pros:** good location for tapas bars and restaurants; rooftop pool and cocktail bar; classical decor. **Cons:** standard doubles on the small side; sights some distance away; rooms facing patio lack privacy. $ *Rooms from: €150* ⊠ *Calle Trajano 15, Centro* ☎ *954/915170* ⊕ *www.hotelcasa-romana.com* ⇶ *26 rooms* ⦿ *No meals.*

★ Mercer

$$$$ | HOTEL | Housed in a 19th-century mansion, Mercer is one of the city's top boutique hotels, featuring a lofty patio with a fountain, a stunning marble staircase, and a striking geometric chandelier atop a glass gallery. **Pros:** luxury lodging; spacious rooms; rooftop terrace with plunge pool. **Cons:** pricey; a little too prim; patio rooms have no views. $ *Rooms from: €440* ⊠ *Calle Castelar 26, Centro* ☎ *954/223004* ⊕ *www.mercersevilla.com* ⇶ *10 rooms* ⦿ *Free breakfast.*

Nightlife

Jazz Naima

MUSIC CLUBS | This tiny bar off Alameda de Hércules features jazz, blues, or jam sessions every night. It's open from 8 pm till late. ⊠ *Calle Trajano 47, Centro* ☎ *954/382485* Ⓜ *Sevilla–Santa Justa.*

Shopping

Ángela y Adela Taller de Diseño

CLOTHING | Come to this shop for privately fitted and custom-made flamenco dresses. ⊠ *Calle Chapineros 1, Centro* ☎ *954/227186.*

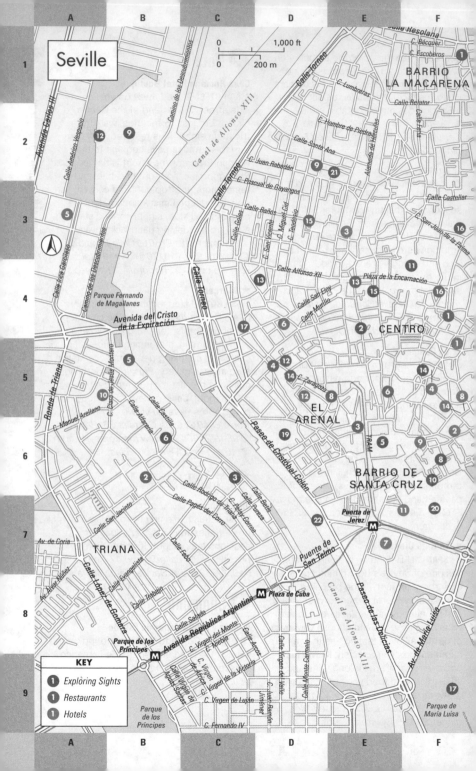

Sights ▼

1 Basílica de la
  Macarena F1
2 Calle Sierpes E4
3 Capilla de los
  Marineros C6
4 Casa de Pilatos G5
5 Catedral de Sevilla E6
6 Centro de Cerámica
  Triana B6
7 Convento de
  Santa Paula G3
8 Hospital de los
  Venerables F6
9 Isla de La Cartuja B2
10 Jewish Quarter F6
11 Metropol Parasol F4
12 Monasterio de
  Santa María de las
  Cuevas A2
13 Museo de
  Bellas Artes D4
14 Museo del
  Baile Flamenco F5
15 Palacio de la
  Condesa de Lebrija E4
16 Palacio de las
  Dueñas................... F3
17 Parque de
  María Luisa............... F9
18 Plaza de España G8
19 Plaza de Toros
  Real Maestranza........ D6
20 Real Alcázar............. F7
21 San Lorenzo y
  Jesús del Gran Poder ... E2
22 Torre del Oro D7

Restaurants ▼

1 Bache San Pedro........ F4
2 Bar Las Golondrinas.... B6
3 Casa Morales E6
4 Castizo D5
5 De la O B5
6 El Pintón E5
7 El Rinconcillo............ G4
8 Enrique Becerra E5
9 Espacio Eslava.......... D2
10 Freiduría Puerta de la
  Carne.................... G6
11 Ispal G7
12 La Azotea D5
13 La Campana E4
14 La Cata Ciega D5
15 La Taberna de
  Panduro Baños D3
16 Palo Cortao.............. F4
17 Vermutería
  Yo Soy Tu Padre.......... C4
18 Vinería San Telmo G6

Hotels ▼

1 Aguilas 5 Sevilla
  Suites F5
2 Casa del Poeta........... F6
3 Casa Romana
  Hotel Boutique E3
4 Corral del Rey F5
5 Eurostars Torre
  Sevilla A3
6 Gran Meliá Colón D4
7 Hotel Alfonso XIII E7
8 Hotel Amadeus
  La Música de Sevilla F5
9 Hotel Casa 1800.......... F6
10 Hotel Monte Triana B5
11 Legado Alcazar E7
12 Mercer.................. D5
13 Palacio de
  Villapanés Hotel......... G4
14 Pensión Córdoba F5

Buffuna

JEWELRY/ACCESSORIES | This shop carries handmade hats and caps for all occasions, especially weddings. ⊠ *Calle Don Alonso el Sabio 8, Centro* ☎ *954/537824* ⊕ *patriciabuffuna.com.*

Lola Azahares

CLOTHING | For flamenco wear, this is one of Seville's most highly regarded stores. ⊠ *Calle Cuna 31, Centro* ☎ *954/222912* ⊕ *www.lolaazahares.es.*

Luisa Perez y Riu

CLOTHING | Flamenco dresses and all the accessories, designed with a modern touch, are sold at this shop between Calles Sierpes and Cuna. ⊠ *Calle Rivero 9, Centro* ☎ *607/817624* ⊕ *www.facebook.com/LuisaPerezLuisaRiu* Ⓜ *Puerta de Jerez.*

Plaza del Duque

CRAFTS | A few blocks north of Plaza Nueva, Plaza del Duque has a crafts market Thursday through Saturday. ⊠ *Centro.*

Barrio de Santa Cruz

The most romantic neighborhood in the city, Santa Cruz offers the visitor quintessential Seville: whitewashed houses with colorful geraniums and bougainvillea cascading down their facades, winding alleyways, and intimate squares scented with orange blossoms in the spring, all lit by old-style lamps at night. This neighborhood is also the busiest and most touristic part of Seville—so stray from the main thoroughfares and lose yourself in the side streets to discover a place where time seems to have stopped and all you hear is birdsong.

Sights

★ Casa de Pilatos

HOUSE | With its fine patio and superb azulejo decorations, this palace is a beautiful blend of Spanish Mudejar and Renaissance architecture and is

Where's Columbus?

Christopher Columbus knew both triumph and disgrace, yet he found no repose—he died, bitterly disillusioned, in Valladolid in 1506. No one knows for certain where he's buried; he was reportedly laid to rest for the first time in the Dominican Republic and then moved over the years to other locations. A portion of his remains can be found in Seville's cathedral.

considered a prototype of an Andalusian mansion. It was built in the first half of the 16th century by the dukes of Tarifa, ancestors of the present owner, the Duke of Medinaceli. It's known as Pilate's House because Don Fadrique, first marquis of Tarifa, allegedly modeled it on Pontius Pilate's house in Jerusalem, where he had gone on a pilgrimage in 1518. The upstairs apartments, which you can see on a guided tour, have frescoes, paintings, and antique furniture. Admission includes an audio guide in English. ⊠ *Pl. de Pilatos 1, Barrio de Santa Cruz* ☎ *954/225298* 🖺 *From €10.*

Hospital de los Venerables

HOSPITAL—SIGHT | Once a retirement home for priests, this baroque building has a splendid azulejo patio with an interesting sunken fountain (designed to cope with low water pressure) and an upstairs gallery, but the highlight is the chapel, featuring frescoes by Valdés Leal and sculptures by Pedro Roldán. The building also houses a cultural foundation that organizes on-site art exhibitions. ⊠ *Pl. de los Venerables 8, Barrio de Santa Cruz* ☎ *954/562696* 🖺 *€10, includes audio guide (free 1st Thurs. of month)* 🕙 *Closed Mon.–Wed.*

Seville's grand alcázar is a UNESCO World Heritage Site and an absolute must-see.

★ Jewish Quarter

NEIGHBORHOOD | The twisting alleyways and traditional whitewashed houses add to the tourist charm of this *barrio*. On some streets, bars alternate with antiques and souvenir shops, but most of the quarter is quiet and residential. On the Plaza Alianza, pause to enjoy the antiques shops and outdoor cafés. In the Plaza de Doña Elvira, with its fountain and azulejo benches, young sevillanos gather to play guitars. Just around the corner from the hospital, at Callejón del Agua and Jope de Rueda, Gioacchino Rossini's Figaro serenaded Rosina on her Plaza Alfaro balcony. Adjoining the Plaza Alfaro, in the Plaza Santa Cruz, flowers and orange trees surround a 17th-century filigree iron cross, which marks the site of the erstwhile church of Santa Cruz, destroyed by Napoléon's general Jean-de-Dieu Soult. ✉ *Barrio de Santa Cruz.*

Museo del Baile Flamenco

MUSEUM | This private museum in the heart of Santa Cruz (follow the signs) was opened in 2007 by the legendary flamenco dancer Cristina Hoyos and includes audiovisual and multimedia displays briefly explaining the history, culture, and soul of Spanish flamenco. There are also regular classes and shows. ✉ *Calle Manuel Rojas Marcos 3, Barrio de Santa Cruz* ☎ *954/340311* ⊕ *www. museoflamenco.com* ✉ *€10 museum only; €26 museum and show.*

★ Real Alcázar

CASTLE/PALACE | The Plaza del Triunfo forms the entrance to the Mudejar palace built by Pedro I (1350–69) on the site of Seville's former Moorish alcázar. Though the alcázar was designed and built by Moorish workers brought in from Granada, it was commissioned and paid for by a Christian king more than 100 years after the Reconquest of Seville. Highlights include the oldest parts of the building, the 14th-century Sala de Justicia (Hall of Justice) and, next to it, the intimate Patio del Yeso (Courtyard of Plaster); Pedro's Mudejar palace, arranged around the beautiful Patio de las Doncellas (Court of the Damsels); the Salón de

Embajadores (Hall of the Ambassadors), the most sumptuous hall in the palace; the Renaissance Palacio de Carlos V (Palace of Carlos V), endowed with a rich collection of Flemish tapestries; and the Estancias Reales (Royal Chambers), with rare clocks, antique furniture, paintings, and tapestries. ✉ *Pl. del Triunfo, Santa Cruz* ☎ *954/502324* 🌐 *www.alcazarsevilla.org* 🎫 *€12 (free 1 hr Mon.: 6–7 pm Apr.–Sept. and 4–5 pm Oct.–Mar.); Cuarto Real €5.*

🍴 Restaurants

Freiduría Puerta de la Carne
$ | **SPANISH** | Fish fried in a delicate tempura and seafood, caught in the Mediterranean or Atlantic Ocean, form a staple in the Andalusian diet, and this venue, first established in 1929, is a firm favorite in Seville to try them. Order your fare by weight—keep an eye on scales as fried fish is surprisingly filling—and take your paper cone to eat in at the cheap and cheerful tables or alfresco in the Jardines de Murillo opposite. **Known for:** fried fish; seafood to go in paper cones; local charm. [$] *Average main: €10* ✉ *Calle Puerta de la Carne 2, Barrio de Santa Cruz* ☎ *954/411159* 🕒 *No lunch July and Aug.*

Ispal
$$$$ | **SPANISH** | At this fine-dining venue near the Prado de San Sebastián bus station, you can taste some of the city's most exciting and innovative menus, using ingredients only from the province of Seville. The tapas tasting menu (€59, €89 paired with wine) includes dishes such as *papas con choco* (potatoes and cuttlefish), and *bacalao con tomate* (cod with tomato). **Known for:** exceptional tapas; regional wine list; suckling pig. [$] *Average main: €59* ✉ *Pl. de San Sebastián 1, Barrio de Santa Cruz* ☎ *954/547127* 🌐 *restauranteispal.com* 🕒 *Closed Mon. No dinner Sun.*

Vermutería Yo Soy Tu Padre
$ | **SPANISH** | Vermouth tasting comes into its own at this tiny venue, home to five home brews created using a secret recipe with a sherry base (manzanilla or fino) and herbs. Take the barman Esteban's advice on which to try and pair it with cold plates such as *trifásico de ahumados* (three types of smoked fish) and nearly two dozen types of cheese. **Known for:** homemade vermouth; authentic atmosphere; pairing tapas. [$] *Average main: €6* ✉ *Calle Gravina 70, Centro* ☎ *619/470784.*

★ Vineria San Telmo
$ | **SPANISH** | Offering dining in a dimly lit dining room or on the street-level terrace, this popular Argentinean-owned restaurant near the touristy alcázar has a menu full of surprises. All dishes—which come as tapas, half portions, or full portions (ideal for sharing)—are superb and sophisticated, especially the eggplant stew with tomato, goat cheese, and smoked salmon; the Iberian pork with potato; and the roast lamb with basil and tarragon. **Known for:** creative tapas; extensive choice of Spanish vinos; Iberian pork with potato. [$] *Average main: €14* ✉ *Paseo Catalina de Ribera 4, Santa Cruz* ☎ *954/410600.*

🛏 Hotels

Aguilas 5 Sevilla Suites
$$$$ | **HOTEL** | If you're looking for a self-catering option in the heart of Santa Cruz, you can't go wrong with at this town house. **Pros:** home-away-from-home vibes; good value for families; central location. **Cons:** could be too basic for some; on pricey side; street can be a little noisy. [$] *Rooms from: €300* ✉ *Calle Aguilas 5, Barrio de Santa Cruz* ☎ *658/628129* 🌐 *www.aguilas5.com* 🛏 *9 rooms* 🍽 *No meals.*

Casa del Poeta
$$$$ | **HOTEL** | Up a narrow alleyway, behind an ordinary facade, a 17th-century palace that was the haunt of Seville's poets at the end of the 19th century is now an oasis of calm. **Pros:** peaceful, central location; authentic palatial atmosphere; rooftop with a view. **Cons:** difficult to reach by car (call shortly before arrival for staff to meet you); could be too traditional for some; service can be a little slow. [$] *Rooms from: €275* ✉ *Calle Don Carlos Alonso Chaparro 3, Santa Cruz* ☎ *954/213868* 🌐 *www.casadelpoeta.es* 🛏 *17 rooms* 🍴 *No meals.*

Corral del Rey
$$$$ | **HOTEL** | Southeast Asian and Moroccan decor fuse to perfection throughout this carefully restored 17th-century palace in the heart of Santa Cruz. **Pros:** private and peaceful setting but easy walk to sights; meticulously restored 17th-century palace with contemporary updates; rooftop terrace with plunge pool. **Cons:** no direct car access; based on both sides of small street and some guests have to cross street for breakfast; some rooms on the small size. [$] *Rooms from: €300* ✉ *Calle Corral del Rey 12, Barrio de Santa Cruz* ☎ *954/227116* 🌐 *www.corraldelrey.com* 🛏 *17 rooms* 🍴 *Free breakfast.*

★ **Hotel Amadeus La Música de Sevilla**
$$$$ | **HOTEL** | With regular classical concerts, a music room off the central patio, and instruments for guests to use, including pianos in some of the soundproofed rooms, this 18th-century manor house is ideal for touring professional musicians and music fans in general. **Pros:** small but charming rooms; roof terrace; friendly service. **Cons:** no direct car access; ground-floor rooms can be dark; layout slightly confusing. [$] *Rooms from: €200* ✉ *Calle Farnesio 6, Santa Cruz* ☎ *954/501443* 🌐 *www.hotelamadeussevilla.com* 🛏 *43 rooms* 🍴 *No meals.*

★ **Hotel Casa 1800**
$$$$ | **B&B/INN** | This classy boutique hotel, in a refurbished 19th-century mansion, is a refuge in bustling Santa Cruz. **Pros:** top-notch amenities; great service; central location. **Cons:** rooms facing the patio can be noisy; no restaurant; on noisy side street. [$] *Rooms from: €275* ✉ *Calle Rodrigo Caro 6, Santa Cruz* ☎ *954/561800* 🌐 *www.hotelcasa1800sevilla.com* 🛏 *33 rooms* 🍴 *No meals.*

Legado Alcázar
$$$$ | **HOTEL** | Nestled next to the alcázar—the monument and hotel share walls—this 17th-century noble house offers a tasteful boutique experience in a very quiet corner. **Pros:** very quiet but central location; historic features; views of the alcázar. **Cons:** no restaurant on-site; room size varies; could be too traditional for some. [$] *Rooms from: €195* ✉ *Calle Mariana de Pineda 18, Barrio de Santa Cruz* ☎ *954/091818* 🌐 *www.legadoalcazarhotel.com* 🛏 *18 rooms* 🍴 *No meals.*

★ **Palacio de Villapanés Hotel**
$$$$ | **HOTEL** | An 18th-century palace with elegant updates and stylish contemporary furnishings, marble-columned patios, high ceilings, and a rooftop with terracotta-rooftop views, a pool, and bar, makes this one of the most chic converted-palace accommodations in Seville. **Pros:** local, off-the-beaten path feel; oozes style and character; tall windows and high ceilings. **Cons:** not the most central location; small spa; small gym. [$] *Rooms from: €300* ✉ *Calle Santiago 31, Centro* ☎ *650/722265* 🌐 *palaciovillapanes.com/en* 🛏 *50 rooms* 🍴 *Free breakfast.*

Pensión Córdoba
$ | **HOTEL** | Just a few blocks from the cathedral, nestled in the heart of Santa Cruz, this small, family-run inn is an excellent value. **Pros:** quiet, central location; friendly staff; rooms have a/c. **Cons:** no entry after 3 am; no breakfast; no elevator to second floor. [$] *Rooms from: €75* ✉ *Calle Farnesio 12, Santa Cruz*

☎ 954/227498 ⊕ www.pensioncordoba.com ⌨ 11 rooms ⏛ No meals.

Nightlife

EME Catedral Hotel
CAFES—NIGHTLIFE | This rooftop terrace has some of the best views of the cathedral in town. Sip your cocktail to the sound of resident DJs most nights. The terrace is open daily beginning at 2 pm. ⊠ Calle Alemanes 27, Barrio de Santa Cruz ☎ 954/560000 ⊕ www.emecatedralhotel.com Ⓜ Puerta de Jerez.

 Performing Arts

FLAMENCO

★ La Casa del Flamenco

THEMED ENTERTAINMENT | Catch an authentic professional performance in the heart of Santa Cruz on the atmospheric patio of a 15th-century house where the excellent acoustics mean there's no need for microphones or amplifiers. Shows start daily at 7 pm and 8:30 pm. ⊠ Calle Ximénez de Enciso 28, Barrio de Santa Cruz ☎ 954/500595 ⊕ www.lacasadelflamencosevilla.com ⌦ €18.

Los Gallos

DANCE | This intimate club in the heart of Santa Cruz attracts mainly tourists. Flamenco performances are entertaining and reasonably authentic. Shows at 8 pm and 10 pm daily. ⊠ Pl. Santa Cruz 11, Santa Cruz ☎ 954/216981 ⊕ www.tablaolosgallos.com ⌦ €35, includes one drink.

Shopping

Pleita

CERAMICS/GLASSWARE | This shop sells ceramics in the traditional Seville blue and white, plus handmade esparto grass accessories and bags. ⊠ Calle Aguilas 14, Barrio de Santa Cruz ☎ 955/091141.

El Arenal and Parque María Luisa

Parque María Luisa is part shady, midcity forestland and part monumental esplanade. El Arenal, named for its sandy riverbank soil, was originally a neighborhood of shipbuilders, stevedores, and warehouses. The heart of El Arenal lies between the Puente de San Telmo, just upstream from the Torre de Oro, and the Puente de Isabel II (Puente de Triana). El Arenal extends as far north as Avenida Alfonso XII to include the Museo de Bellas Artes. Between the park and El Arenal is the university.

Sights

★ Museo de Bellas Artes (Museum of Fine Arts)

MUSEUM | This museum—one of Spain's finest for Spanish art—is in the former convent of La Merced Calzada, most of which dates from the 17th century. The collection includes works by Murillo (the city celebrated the 400th anniversary of his birth in 2018) and the 17th-century Seville school, as well as by Zurbarán, Diego Velázquez, Alonso Cano, Valdés Leal, and El Greco. You will also see outstanding examples of Sevillian Gothic art and baroque religious sculptures in wood (a quintessentially Andalusian art form). In the rooms dedicated to Sevillian art of the 19th and 20th centuries, look for Gonzalo Bilbao's Las Cigarreras, a group portrait of Seville's famous cigar makers. An arts-and-crafts market is held outside the museum on Sunday morning. ⊠ Pl. del Museo 9, El Arenal ☎ 954/542931 ⊕ www.museosdeandalucia.es ⌦ €2 ⊘ Closed Mon.

★ Parque de María Luisa

CITY PARK | Formerly the garden of the Palacio de San Telmo, this park blends formal design and wild vegetation. In the burst of development that gripped

Seville in the 1920s, it was redesigned for the 1929 World's Fair, and the impressive villas you see now are the fair's remaining pavilions, many of them consulates or schools. The old casino holds the Teatro Lope de Vega, which puts on mainly musicals. Note the Anna Huntington **statue of El Cid** (Rodrigo Díaz de Vivar, 1043–99), who fought both for and against the Muslim rulers during the Reconquest. The statue was presented to Seville by the Massachusetts-born sculptor for the 1929 World's Fair. ✉ *Main entrance, Glorieta San Diego, Parque Maria Luisa.*

Plaza de España

PLAZA | **FAMILY** | This grandiose half-moon of buildings on the eastern edge of the Parque de María Luisa was Spain's centerpiece pavilion at the 1929 World's Fair. The brightly colored azulejo pictures represent the provinces of Spain, while the four bridges symbolize the medieval kingdoms of the Iberian Peninsula. In fine weather you can rent small boats to row along the arc-shape canal. To escape the crowds and enjoy views of the square from above, pop upstairs. ✉ *Parque Maria Luisa.*

Plaza de Toros Real Maestranza (*Royal Maestranza Bullring*)

PLAZA | Sevillanos have spent many a thrilling evening in this bullring, one of the oldest and loveliest *plazas de toros* in Spain, built between 1760 and 1763. The 20-minute tour (in English) takes in the empty arena, a museum with elaborate costumes and prints, and the chapel where matadors pray before the fight. Bullfights take place in the evening Thursday–Sunday from April through July and in September. Tickets can be booked online or by phone; book well in advance to be sure of a seat. ✉ *Paseo de Colón 12, El Arenal* ☎ *954/224577 for visits, 954/560759 for bullfights* 🌐 *www.realmaestranza.es for tours, www.plazadetorosdelamaestranza.com for tickets* 🎫 *Tours €8 (free Mon. 3–7).*

Torre del Oro (*Tower of Gold*)

LIGHTHOUSE | Built by the Moors in 1220 to complete the city's ramparts, this 12-sided tower on the banks of the Guadalquivir served to close off the harbor when a chain was stretched across the river from its base to a tower on the opposite bank. In 1248, Admiral Ramón de Bonifaz broke through the barrier, and Ferdinand III captured Seville. The tower houses a small naval museum. ✉ *Paseo Alcalde Marqués de Contadero s/n, El Arenal* ☎ *954/222419* 🎫 *€3.*

🍴 Restaurants

★ Enrique Becerra

$$$ | **SPANISH** | Excellent tapas (try the lamb kebab with dates and couscous), a lively bar, and an extensive wine list await at this restaurant run by the fifth generation of a family of celebrated restaurateurs. The menu focuses on traditional, home-cooked Andalusian dishes, such as cod in a green sauce, pork fillet in whiskey, and *cola de toro guisado con salsa de vino tinto* (stewed oxtail in red wine sauce). **Known for:** traditional Andalusian dishes; fried eggplant stuffed with prawns; stewed oxtail. [$] *Average main: €20* ✉ *Calle Gamazo 2, El Arenal* ☎ *954/213049* 🌐 *enriquebecerra.com.*

🛏 Hotels

Gran Meliá Colón

$$$$ | **HOTEL** | Originally opened for 1929's Ibero-American Exposition, this classic hotel retains many original features, including a marble staircase leading up to a central lobby crowned by a magnificent stained-glass dome and crystal chandelier. **Pros:** good central location; excellent restaurant; some great views. **Cons:** some rooms overlook air shaft; on a busy and noisy street; pricey. [$] *Rooms from: €350* ✉ *Calle Canalejas 1, El Arenal* ☎ *954/505599* 🌐 *www.melia.com* 🔑 *189 rooms* 🍽 *No meals.*

★ Hotel Alfonso XIII

$$$$ | **HOTEL** | Inaugurated by King Alfonso XIII in 1929 when he visited the World's Fair, this grand hotel next to the university is a splendid, historic, Mudejar-style palace, built around a central patio and surrounded by ornate brick arches. **Pros:** both stately and hip; impeccable service; historic surroundings. **Cons:** a tourist colony; expensive; too sophisticated for some. $ *Rooms from: €450* ✉ *Calle San Fernando 2, El Arenal* ☏ *954/917000* ⊕ *www.hotel-alfonsoxiii-seville.com* ⤳ *148 rooms* ❙❍❙ *Free breakfast.*

 Performing Arts

Teatro de la Maestranza

OPERA | Long prominent in the opera world, Seville is proud of its opera house. Tickets go quickly, so book well in advance (online is best). ✉ *Paseo de Colón 22, El Arenal* ☏ *954/223344 for info, 954/226573 for tickets* ⊕ *www. teatrodelamaestranza.es.*

Teatro Lope de Vega

ARTS CENTERS | Classical music, ballet, and musicals are performed here. Tickets are best booked online. ✉ *Av. María Luisa s/n, Parque Maria Luisa* ☏ *954/472828 for info, 955/472822 for tickets* ⊕ *www. teatrolopedevega.org.*

Shopping

Artesanía Textil

TEXTILES/SEWING | You can find blankets, shawls, and embroidered tablecloths woven by local artisans at this textile shop. ✉ *Calle García de Vinuesa 33, El Arenal* ☏ *954/215088.*

El Postigo

CRAFTS | This permanent arts-and-crafts market opposite El Corte Inglés is open every day except Sunday. ✉ *Pl. de la Concordia, El Arenal.*

Barrio de la Macarena

This immense neighborhood covers the entire northern half of historic Seville and deserves to be walked many times. Most of the best churches, convents, markets, and squares are concentrated around the center in an area delimited by the Arab ramparts to the north, the Alameda de Hercules to the west, the Santa Catalina church to the south, and the Convento de Santa Paula to the east. The area between the Alameda de Hercules and the Guadalquivir is known to locals as the Barrio de San Lorenzo, a section that's ideal for an evening of tapas grazing.

Sights

Basílica de la Macarena

RELIGIOUS SITE | This church holds Seville's most revered image, the Virgin of Hope—better known as La Macarena. Bedecked with candles and carnations, her cheeks streaming with glass tears, the Macarena steals the show at the procession on Holy Thursday, the highlight of Seville's Semana Santa pageant. The patron of Gypsies and the protector of the matador, her charms are so great that young sevillano bullfighter Joselito spent half his personal fortune buying her emeralds. When he was killed in the ring in 1920, La Macarena was dressed in widow's weeds for a month. The adjacent museum tells the history of Semana Santa traditions through processional and liturgical artifacts amassed by the Brotherhood of La Macarena over four centuries. ✉ *Calle Bécquer 1, La Macarena* ☏ *954/901800* ⤳ *Basilica free, museum €5.*

★ Convento de Santa Paula

RELIGIOUS SITE | This 15th-century Gothic convent has a fine facade and portico, with ceramic decoration by Nicolaso Pisano. The chapel has some beautiful azulejos and sculptures by Martínez Montañés. It also contains a small museum and a shop selling delicious cakes and jams made by the nuns. ✉ *Calle Santa Paula 11, La Macarena* ☎ *954/536330* 🎟 *€4* 🕒 *Closed Mon.*

San Lorenzo y Jesús del Gran Poder
RELIGIOUS SITE | This 17th-century church has many fine works by such artists as Martínez Montañés and Francisco Pacheco, but its outstanding piece is Juan de Mesa y Velasco's *Jesús del Gran Poder* (*Christ Omnipotent*). ✉ *Pl. San Lorenzo 13, La Macarena* ☎ *954/915672* 🎟 *Free.*

🍴 Restaurants

Bache San Pedro
$ | **SPANISH** | Barack Obama's chosen spot for tapas when he visited the city in April 2019 has outside seating on a small terrace with views of the square or spots inside, where traditional Seville tiles blend perfectly into the sleek industrial vibe. Bringing the taste of Cádiz to Seville, dishes here come as tapas or sharing plates (€3.50–€15) and include *croquetas de puchero* (stew croquettes), a taco of *chicharrones* (pork crackling) with Payoyo goat's cheese, and possibly the spiciest *patatas bravas* (fried potatoes) in town. **Known for:** innovative cuisine; friendly service; delicious desserts. [$] *Average main: €13* ✉ *Pl. Cristo de Burgos 23, Seville* ☎ *954/502934* 🌐 *www.bachesevilla.com* 🕒 *Closed Mon.*

El Rinconcillo
$$ | **SPANISH** | Founded in 1670, this lovely spot serves a classic selection of dishes, such as the *pavía de bacalao* (fried breaded cod), a superb *salmorejo* (a puree consisting of tomato and bread), and espinacas con garbanzos all in generous portions. The views of the Iglesia de Santa Catalina out the front window upstairs are unbeatable, and your bill is chalked up on the wooden counters as you go (tapas are attractively priced from €2). **Known for:** tapas; crowds of locals; views of Iglesia de Santa Catalina. [$] *Average main: €12* ✉ *Calle Gerona 40, La Macarena* ☎ *954/223183* 🌐 *www.elrinconcillo.es.*

Fiesta Time!

Seville's color and vivacity are most intense during Semana Santa, when lacerated Christs and bejeweled, weeping Mary statues are paraded through town on floats borne by often-barefoot penitents. Two weeks later, sevillanos throw Feria de Abril, featuring midday horse parades with men in broad-brim hats and Andalusian riding gear astride prancing steeds, and women in ruffled dresses riding sidesaddle behind them. Bullfights, fireworks, and all-night singing and dancing complete the spectacle.

La Taberna de Panduro Baños
$$ | **SPANISH** | A tavern-style establishment, La Taberna de Panduro Baños is a favorite with locals so expect to find the small restaurant lively and loud. You'll find classic dishes with a modern twist such as squid noodles with *romesco* (tomato) sauce and a deconstructed *ensaladilla rusa* (potato salad), which some claim is the tastiest in Seville. **Known for:** modern twist on traditional dishes; Russian potato salad; white chocolate soup dessert. [$] *Average main: €12* ✉ *Calle Baños 3, La Macarena* ☎ *954/870732* 🕒 *Closed Mon. No dinner Sun.*

Palo Cortao
$ | **SPANISH** | Down an uninspiring side street but with a very quiet terrace with views of San Pedro Church, this bar with stool seating around high tables offers tranquil dining and, most notably, one of the best sherry menus in town. Known as an *abacería* (grocer's store), it serves more than 30 finos, amontillados, and olorosos, plus homemade vermouth on the drinks menu, and each pairs perfectly with a food choice. **Known for:** excellent sherry; pairing menu; ajoblanco (cold garlic soup). [$] *Average main: €5* ✉ *Calle*

Mercedes de Velilla 4, La Macarena
☎ *649/446120* ⊕ *www.palo-cortao.com*
⊙ *Closed Mon. and Tues.*

Triana

Triana used to be Seville's Gypsy quarter. Today, it has a tranquil, neighborly feel by day and a distinctly flamenco feel at night. Cross over to Triana via the **Puente de Isabel II,** an iron bridge built in 1852 and the first to connect the city's two sections. Start your walk in the **Plaza del Altozano,** the center of the Triana district and traditionally the meeting point for travelers from the south crossing the river to Seville. Admire the facade of the Murillo pharmacy here before walking up **Calle Jacinto.** Look out for the fine **Casa de los Mensaque** (now the district's administrative office and usually open on weekday morning), home to some of Triana's finest potters and housing some stunning examples of Seville ceramics. To reach attractions in La Cartuja, take Bus C1.

 ## Sights

Capilla de los Marineros
RELIGIOUS SITE | This seamen's chapel is one of Triana's most important monuments and home to the Brotherhood of Triana, whose Semana Santa processions are among the most revered in the city. There's also a small museum dedicated to the Brotherhood. ⊠ *Calle Pureza 2, Triana* ☎ *954/332645* 🎫 *Free, museum €4.*

Centro de Cerámica Triana (*Ceramics Center*)
MUSEUM | With none of the 40 original ceramists remaining in Triana, this restored factory complete with its original kilns provides an interesting insight into the neighborhood's tile-making past. Downstairs, an exhibition explains the manufacturing process and the story of ceramics while upstairs, there's a selection of tiles on show. Free guided tours in English. ⊠ *Calle Callao 16, Triana* ☎ *954/341582* ⊕ *ceramicatriana.com* 🎫 *€3. Free with regular Alcázar ticket* ⊙ *Closed Mon.*

Isla de La Cartuja
ISLAND | Named after its 14th-century Carthusian monastery, this island in the Guadalquivir River across from northern Seville was the site of the decennial Universal Exposition (Expo) in 1992. The island has the Teatro Central, used for concerts and plays; Parque del Alamillo, Seville's largest and least-known park; and the Estadio Olímpico, a 60,000-seat covered stadium. The best way to get to La Cartuja is by walking across one or both (one each way) of the superb Santiago Calatrava bridges spanning the river. The Puente de la Barqueta crosses to La Cartuja, and downstream the Puente del Alamillo connects the island with Seville. Buses C1 and C2 also serve La Cartuja. ⊠ *Triana.*

Monasterio de Santa María de las Cuevas
(*Monasterio de La Cartuja*)
MUSEUM | The 14th-century monastery was regularly visited by Christopher Columbus, who was also buried here for a few years. Part of the building houses the **Centro Andaluz de Arte Contemporáneo,** which has an absorbing collection of contemporary art. ⊠ *Isla de la Cartuja, Av. Américo Vespucio, Triana* ☎ *955/037070* 🎫 *€2. Free Tues.–Fri. 7–9 pm, Sat.* ⊙ *Closed Mon.*

Restaurants

Bar Las Golondrinas
$$ | SPANISH | Run by the same family for more than 50 years and lavishly decorated in the colorful tiles that pay tribute to the neighborhood's potters, Las Golondrinas is a fixture of Triana life. The staff never change, and neither does the menu—the recipes for the *punta de solomillo* (sliced sirloin), *chipirones* (fried baby squid), and *caballito de jamón* (ham on bread) have been honed to perfection,

and they're served as tapas (€2), or *raciones*, that keep everyone happy. **Known for:** vibrant atmosphere; traditional tapas; good value. $ *Average main: €12 ☒ Calle Antillano Campos 26, Triana ☎ 954/332616.*

De la O

$$ | **SPANISH** | Tucked away on the riverfront in Triana next to Puente Cristo de la Expiración, this modern venue advocates local produce in traditional Andalusian recipes along with a long wine list of Andalusian wines. The long, narrow interior has striking wood-paneled walls with a verdant vertical garden in the middle, while outside dining takes in panoramic views of the river on the intimate terrace. **Known for:** quality local produce; homemade sausages; dishes presented artistically. $ *Average main: €12 ☒ Paseo de Nuestra Señora de la O 29, Triana ☎ 954/339000 ⊕ www.delaorestaurante. com ⊙ Closed Mon. No dinner Sun.*

 Hotels

Eurostars Torre Sevilla

$$$$ | **HOTEL** | Andalusia's highest building, with its 180-meter tower, designed by Cesar Pelli, rises high above the Cartuja area and makes a controversial sight on the city skyline while delivering spectacular views over Seville, Triana, and the river. **Pros:** spectacular views of the city; spacious accommodations; modern amenities. **Cons:** some distance from sights and attractions; limited spa hours during week; indifferent service at times. $ *Rooms from: €200 ☒ Calle Gonzalo Jiménez de Quesada 2, Triana ☎ 954/466022 ⊕ www.eurostarshotels. com ⪫ 244 rooms ⦿l No meals.*

Hotel Monte Triana

$$ | **HOTEL** | Comfortable, squeaky-clean facilities and excellent value for the cost are two key reasons for choosing this hotel to the north of the heart of Triana. **Pros:** good value; private car park; friendly and helpful staff. **Cons:** 20-minute walk

into city center; decor too basic for some; no on-site restaurant. $ *Rooms from: €110 ☒ Calle Clara de Jesús Montero 24, Triana ☎ 954/343111 ⊕ www. hotelesmonte.com ⪫ 114 rooms ⦿l No meals.*

 Performing Arts

FLAMENCO
Lola de los Reyes

DANCE | This venue in Triana presents reasonably authentic shows and hosts "flamenco afternoons" on Saturday—check the website for details. Entrance is free, but there's a one-drink minimum. ☒ *Calle Pureza 107, Triana ☎ 667/631163 ⊕ www.loladelosreyes.es Ⓜ Blas Infante/ Parque de los Principes.*

Teatro Central

ARTS CENTERS | This modern venue on the Isla de la Cartuja stages theater, dance (including flamenco), and classical and contemporary music. Tickets can be bought online or at the ticket office. ☒ *Calle José de Gálvez 6, Triana ☎ 955/542155 for information ⊕ www. teatrocentral.es.*

 Shopping

Potters' District

CERAMICS/GLASSWARE | Look for traditional azulejo tiles and other ceramics in the Triana potters' district, on Calle Alfarería, Calle Antillano Campos, and Calle Callao such as Cerámica Triana (Calle Callao 14) selling a selection of traditional ceramic items. ☒ *Triana.*

Itálica

12 km (7 miles) north of Seville, 1 km (½ mile) beyond Santiponce.

Neighboring the small town of Santiponce, Itálica is Spain's oldest Roman site and one of its greatest, and it is well worth a visit when you're in Seville. If

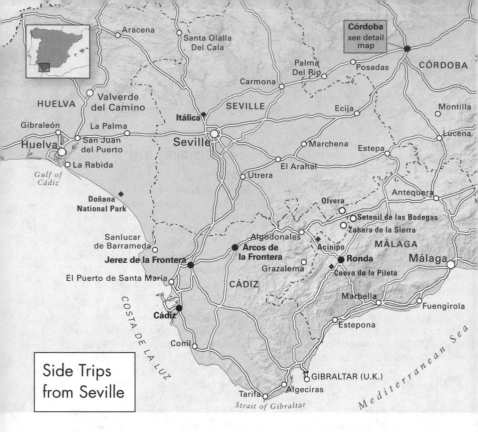

Side Trips
from Seville

you're here during July, try to get tickets for the International Dance Festival held in the ruins (⊕ *www.festivalitalica.es*).

GETTING HERE AND AROUND
The M170A bus route runs frequently (daily 8 am–3:30 pm) between the Plaza de Armas bus station in Seville and Itálica. Journey time is 20 minutes. If you have a rental car, you could include a visit to the ruins on your way to Huelva. Allow at least two hours for your visit.

 Sights

★ **Itálica**
ARCHAEOLOGICAL SITE | One of Roman Iberia's most important cities in the 2nd century, with a population of more than 10,000, Itálica today is a monument of Roman ruins. Founded by Scipio Africanus in 205 BC as a home for veteran soldiers, Itálica gave the Roman world two great emperors: Trajan (AD 52–117) and Hadrian (AD 76–138). You can find traces of city streets, cisterns, and the floor plans of several villas, some with mosaic floors, though all the best mosaics and statues have been removed to Seville's Museum of Archaeology. Itálica was abandoned and plundered as a quarry by the Visigoths, who preferred Seville. It fell into decay around AD 700. The remains include the huge, elliptical **amphitheater**, which held 40,000 spectators, a **Roman theater,** and **Roman baths.** The finale for season 7 of *Game of Thrones* was filmed here in 2018. The small visitor center offers information on daily life in the city. ⊠ *Av. Extremadura 2, Santiponce* ☎ *600/141767* ⊕ *www.juntadeandalucia. es/cultura/museos* ⊠ *€2* ⊙ *Closed Mon.*

Córdoba

166 km (103 miles) northwest of Granada, 407 km (250 miles) southwest of Madrid, 239 km (143 miles) northeast of Cádiz, 143 km (86 miles) northeast of Seville.

Strategically located on the north bank of the Guadalquivir River, Córdoba was the Roman and Moorish capital of Spain, and its old quarter, clustered around its famous Mezquita, remains one of the country's grandest and yet most intimate examples of its Moorish heritage. Once a medieval city famed for the peaceful and prosperous coexistence of its three religious cultures—Islamic, Jewish, and Christian—Córdoba is also a perfect analogue for the cultural history of the Iberian Peninsula.

Córdoba today, with its modest population of a little more than 330,000, offers a cultural depth and intensity—a direct legacy from the great emirs, caliphs, philosophers, physicians, poets, and engineers of the days of the caliphate—that far outstrips the city's current commercial and political power. Its artistic and historical treasures begin with the Mezquita-Catedral (mosque-cathedral), as it is generally called, and continue through the winding, whitewashed streets of the Judería (the medieval Jewish quarter); the jasmine-, geranium-, and orange-blossom-filled patios; the Renaissance palaces; and the two dozen churches, convents, and hermitages, built by Moorish artisans directly over former mosques.

GETTING HERE AND AROUND

BIKE TRAVEL

Never designed to support cars, Córdoba's medieval layout is ideal for bicycles, and there's a good network of designated bicycle tracks.

Rent a Bike Córdoba

Bicycle (electric or manual) rental is available here at reasonable rates (from €6 for 3 hours). The company also offers bike tours around the city and to Medinat Al-Zahra. ⊠ *Calle Maria Cristina 5* ☎ *957/943700* ⊕ *rentabikecordoba.com.*

BUS TRAVEL

Córdoba is easily reached by bus from Granada, Málaga, and Seville. The city has an extensive public bus network with frequent service. Buses usually start running at 6:30 or 7 am and stop around midnight. You can buy 10-trip passes at newsstands and the bus office in Plaza de Colón. A single-trip fare is €1.30.

Córdoba has organized open-top bus tours of the city that can be booked via the tourist office.

CONTACTS Córdoba. ⊠ *Glorieta de las Tres Culturas* ☎ *957/404040* ⊕ *www. estacionautobusescordoba.es.*

CAR TRAVEL

The city's one-way system can be something of a nightmare to navigate, and it's best to park in one of the signposted lots outside the old quarter.

TAXI TRAVEL

CONTACTS Radio Taxi. ☎ *957/764444.*

TRAIN TRAVEL

The city's modern train station is the hub for a comprehensive network of regional trains, with regular high-speed train service to Granada, Seville, Málaga, Madrid, and Barcelona.

CONTACTS Train Station. ⊠ *Glorieta de las Tres Culturas* ☎ *912/320320.*

VISITOR INFORMATION

CONTACTS Tourist Office. ⊠ *Pl. de las Tendillas 5, Centro* ☎ *957/201774* ⊕ *www. turismodecordoba.org.*

Sights

Alcázar de los Reyes Cristianos (*Fortress of the Christian Monarchs*)

CASTLE/PALACE | Built by Alfonso XI in 1328, the alcázar in Córdoba is a Mudejar-style palace with splendid gardens. (The original Moorish alcázar

Córdoba's History

The Romans invaded Córdoba in 206 BC, later making it the capital of Rome's section of Spain. Nearly 800 years later, the Visigoth king Leovigildus took control, but the tribe was soon supplanted by the Moors, whose emirs and caliphs held court here from the 8th to the early 11th century. At that point Córdoba was one of the greatest centers of art, culture, and learning in the Western world; one of its libraries had a staggering 400,000 volumes. Moors, Christians, and Jews lived together in harmony within Córdoba's walls. In that era, it was considered second in importance only to Constantinople; but in 1009, Prince Muhammad II and Omeyan led a rebellion that broke up the caliphate, leading to power flowing to separate Moorish kingdoms.

Córdoba remained in Moorish hands until it was conquered by King Ferdinand in 1236 and repopulated from the north of Spain. Later, the Catholic Monarchs used the city as a base from which to plan the conquest of Granada. In Columbus's time, the Guadalquivir was navigable as far upstream as Córdoba, and great galleons sailed its waters. Today, the river's muddy water and marshy banks evoke little of Córdoba's glorious past, but an old Arab waterfall and the city's bridge—of Roman origin, though much restored by the Arabs and successive generations, most recently in 2012—recall a far grander era.

stood beside the Mezquita, on the site of the present Bishop's Palace.) This is where, in the 15th century, the Catholic monarchs held court and launched their conquest of Granada. Boabdil was imprisoned here in 1483, and for nearly 300 years this alcázar served as the Inquisition's base. The most important sights here are the Hall of the Mosaics and a Roman stone sarcophagus from the 2nd or 3rd century. ✉ *Pl. Campo Santo de los Mártires, Judería* ✛ *Next to Guadalquivir River* ☎ *957/201716* ⊕ *alcazardelosreyescristianos.cordoba.es* 🎟 *€5* ⊘ *Closed Mon.*

★ Calleja de las Flores

NEIGHBORHOOD | A few yards off the northeastern corner of the Mezquita, this tiny street has the prettiest patios, many with ceramics, foliage, and iron grilles. The patios are key to Córdoba's architecture, at least in the old quarter, where life is lived behind sturdy white walls—a legacy of the Moors, who honored both the sanctity of the home and the need to shut out the fierce summer sun. Between the first and second week of May—right after the early-May **Cruces de Mayo** (Crosses of May) competition, when neighborhoods compete at setting up elaborate crosses decorated with flowers and plants—Córdoba throws a **Patio Festival,** during which private patios are filled with flowers, opened to the public, and judged in a municipal competition. Córdoba's tourist office publishes an itinerary of the best patios in town (downloadable from *patios.cordoba.es/ en*)—note that most are open only in the late afternoon on weekdays but all day on weekends. ✉ *Judería.*

★ Madinat Al-Zahra (*Medina Azahara*)

ARCHAEOLOGICAL SITE | Built in the foothills of the Sierra Morena by Abd ar-Rahman III for his favorite concubine, al-Zahra (the Flower), this once-splendid summer pleasure palace was begun in 936. Historians say it took 10,000 men, 2,600 mules, and 400 camels 25 years to erect this fantasy of 4,300 columns in dazzling

Córdoba's stunning Mezquita charts the evolution of Western and Islamic architecture over a 1,300-year period.

pink, green, and white marble and jasper brought from Carthage. A palace, a mosque, luxurious baths, fragrant gardens, fish ponds, an aviary, and a zoo stood on three terraces here, until, in 1013, it was sacked and destroyed by Berber mercenaries. In 1944, the Royal Apartments were rediscovered, and the throne room carefully reconstructed. The outline of the mosque has also been excavated. The only covered part is the Salon de Abd ar-Rahman III (restoration work is due to finish in 2021); the rest is a sprawl of foundations and arches that hint at the original splendor. First visit the nearby museum and then continue with a walk among the ruins. ⊠ Ctra. de Palma del Río, Km 5.5 ✛ 8 km (5 miles) west of Córdoba on C431 ☎ 957/104933 ⊕ www. museosdeandalucia.es ☑ €2 ⊘ Closed Mon.

★ Mezquita (Mosque)
RELIGIOUS SITE | Built between the 8th and 10th centuries, Córdoba's mosque is one of the earliest and most beautiful examples of Spanish Islamic architecture.

Inside, some 850 columns rise before you in a forest of jasper, marble, granite, and onyx. The mezquita has served as a cathedral since 1236, but it was founded as a mosque in 785 by Abd ar-Rahman I. The beautiful **mihrab** (prayer niche) is the mezquita's greatest jewel. In front of the mihrab is the **maksoureh**, a kind of anteroom for the caliph and his court; its mosaics and plasterwork make it a masterpiece of Islamic art. In the 13th century, Christians had the **Capilla de Villaviciosa** built by Moorish craftsmen, its Mudejar architecture blending with the lines of the mosque. Not so the heavy, incongruous Baroque structure of the cathedral, sanctioned in the heart of the mosque by Carlos V in the 1520s. ⊠ Calle de Torrijos, Judería ☎ 957/470512 ⊕ mezquita-catedraldecordoba.es ☑ Mezquita €11, Torre del Alminar €2.

★ Museo de Bellas Artes
MUSEUM | Hard to miss because of its deep-pink facade, Córdoba's Museum of Fine Arts, in a courtyard just off the Plaza del Potro, belongs to a former Hospital

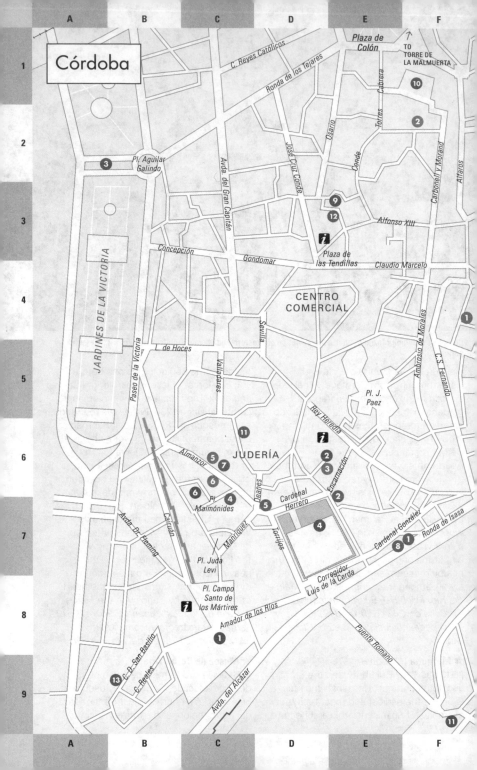

Córdoba

G H I

KEY

1 *Sights*

1 *Restaurants*

1 *Hotels*

i *Tourist Information*

Sights ▼

1 Alcázar de los
  Reyes Cristianos..........**C8**

2 Calleja de las Flores.....**E6**

3 Madinat Al-Zahra.......**A2**

4 Mezquita.................**D7**

5 Museo de
  Bellas Artes **G6**

6 Museo Taurino...........**C6**

7 Palacio de Viana........**G1**

8 Plaza de los Dolores....**G1**

9 Plaza de San Miguel **E3**

10 Plaza Santa Marina **F1**

11 Torre Calahorra **F9**

Restaurants ▼

1 Amaltea...................**F7**

2 Bar Santos...............**E6**

3 Bodegas Campos.......**H6**

4 Casa Mazal...............**C7**

5 Casa Pepe de la
  Judería...................**D7**

6 El Choco **I4**

7 El Churrasco.............**C6**

8 La Regadera.............**E7**

9 La Tinaja **G6**

10 noor **I2**

11 Salón de Té..............**C6**

12 Taberna de
  San Miguel **E3**

13 Taberna La Viuda **B9**

Hotels ▼

1 Casa de los Azulejos **F4**

2 Hospes Palacio
  del Bailio..................**F2**

3 Hotel Balcón
  de Córdoba **E6**

4 Hotel Maestre...........**G6**

5 La Llave de la Judería...**C6**

6 NH Collection
  Amistad Córdoba **C6**

7 Viento 10...................**I5**

de la Caridad (Charity Hospital). It was founded by Ferdinand and Isabella, who twice received Columbus here. The collection, which includes paintings by Murillo, Valdés Leal, Zurbarán, Goya, and Joaquín Sorolla y Bastida, concentrates on local artists. Highlights are altarpieces from the 14th and 15th centuries and the large collection of prints and drawings, including some by Fortuny, Goya, and Sorolla. ⊠ *Pl. del Potro 1, San Francisco* ☎ *957/103659* 🖵 *€2* 🕑 *Closed Mon.*

Museo Taurino (*Museum of Bullfighting*) MUSEUM | Two adjoining mansions on the Plaza Maimónides (or Plaza de las Bulas) house this museum, and it's worth a visit, as much for the chance to see a restored mansion as for the posters, Art Nouveau paintings, bull's heads, suits of lights (bullfighting outfits), and memorabilia of famous Córdoban bullfighters, including the most famous of all, Manolete. To the surprise of the nation, Manolete, who was considered immortal, was killed by a bull in the ring at Linares in 1947. ⊠ *Pl. de Maimónides 1, Judería* ☎ *957/201056* 🖵 *€4* 🕑 *Closed Mon.*

Palacio de Viana
CASTLE/PALACE | This 17th-century palace is one of Córdoba's most splendid aristocratic homes. Also known as the **Museo de los Patios,** it contains 12 interior patios, each one different; the patios and gardens are planted with cypresses, orange trees, and myrtles. Inside the building are a carriage museum, a library, embossed leather wall hangings, filigree silver, and grand galleries and staircases. As you enter, note that the corner column of the first patio has been removed to allow the entrance of horse-drawn carriages. ⊠ *Pl. Don Gomé 2, Centro* ☎ *957/496741* 🖵 *From €5* 🕑 *Closed Mon.*

Plaza de los Dolores
PLAZA | The 17th-century Convento de Capuchinos surrounds this small square north of Plaza San Miguel. The square is where you feel most deeply the city's

languid pace. In its center, a statue of **Cristo de los Faroles** (Christ of the Lanterns) stands amid eight lanterns hanging from twisted wrought-iron brackets. ⊠ *Centro.*

Plaza de San Miguel
NEIGHBORHOOD | The square and café terraces around it, and its excellent tavern, Taberna San Miguel–Casa El Pisto, form one of the city's finest combinations of art, history, and gastronomy. The San Miguel church has an interesting facade with Romanesque doors built around Mudejar horseshoe arches, and a Mudejar dome inside. ⊠ *Centro.*

Plaza Santa Marina
PLAZA | At the edge of the **Barrio de los Toreros,** a quarter where many of Córdoba's famous bullfighters were born and raised, stands a statue of the famous bullfighter Manolete (1917–47) opposite the lovely fernandina church of Santa Marina de Aguas Santas (St. Marina of Holy Waters). Not far from here, on the Plaza de la Lagunilla, is a bust of Manolete. ⊠ *Centro.*

Torre Calahorra
BUILDING | The tower on the far side of the Puente Romano (Roman Bridge), which was restored in 2008, was built in 1369 to guard the entrance to Córdoba. It now houses the **Museo Vivo de Al-Andalus** ("al-Andalus" is Arabic for "Land of the West"), with films and audiovisual guides (in English) on Córdoba's history. Climb the narrow staircase to the top of the tower for the view of the Roman bridge and city on the other side of the Guadalquivir. ⊠ *Av. de la Confederación s/n, Sector Sur* ☎ *957/293929* ⊕ *www. torrecalahorra.es* 🖵 *€5, includes audio guide.*

🍴 Restaurants

Amaltea
$$ | INTERNATIONAL | Satisfying vegetarians, vegans, and their meat-eating friends, this organic restaurant includes

some meat and fish on the menu. There's a healthy mix of Mexican, Asian, Spanish, and Italian-influenced dishes, including salmon steamed in banana leaves, chicken curry with mango and apricots, and couscous. **Known for:** vegetarian food; inviting interior with relaxed vibe; organic options. $ *Average main: €15* ✉ *Ronda de Isasa 10, Centro* ☎ *957/491968* ⊘ *No dinner Sun. Closed Sun. in summer.*

Bar Santos

$ | **TAPAS** | This very small, quintessentially Spanish bar, with no seats and numerous photos of matadors and flamenco dancers, seems out of place surrounded by the tourist shops and overshadowed by the Mezquita, but its appearance—and its prices—are part of its charm. Tapas (from €2.50) such as *albóndigas en salsa de almendras* (meatballs in almond sauce) and *bocadillos* (sandwiches that are literally "little mouthfuls") are excellent in quality and value, while the *tortilla de patata* (potato omelet) is renowned and celebrated both for its taste and its heroic thickness. **Known for:** tortilla de patata; inexpensive tapas; being busy. $ *Average main: €6* ✉ *Calle Magistral González Francés 3, Judería* ☎ *957/488975.*

★ Bodegas Campos

$$$ | **SPANISH** | A block east of the Plaza del Potro, this traditional old bodega with high-quality service is the epitome of all that's great about Andalusian cuisine. The dining rooms are in barrel-heavy rustic rooms and leafy traditional patios (take a look at some of the signed barrels—you may recognize a name or two, such as the former U.K. prime minister Tony Blair). **Known for:** bodega setting; regional dishes; excellent tapas bar. $ *Average main: €22* ✉ *Calle Los Lineros 32, San Pedro* ☎ *957/497500* ⊕ *www.bodegas-campos.com.*

Casa Mazal

$$$ | **ECLECTIC** | In the heart of the Judería, this pretty little restaurant serves a modern interpretation of Sephardic cuisine,

with organic dishes that are more exotic than the usual Andalusian fare. The many vegetarian options include gazpacho with mango, and the *confitura de cordero con espárragos trigueros* (caramelized lamb with baby asparagus) and *siniya* (trout baked in vine leaves with pomegranate and mint) are delicious. **Known for:** traditional Sephardic cuisine; romantic ambience; vegetarian dishes. $ *Average main: €18* ✉ *Calle Tomás Conde 3, Judería* ☎ *957/246304.*

Casa Pepe de la Judería

$$$ | **SPANISH** | Geared toward a tourist clientele, this place is always packed, noisy, and fun, and there is live Spanish guitar music on the roof terrace most summer nights. Antiques and some wonderful old oil paintings fill this three-floor labyrinth of rooms just around the corner from the mosque, near the Judería. **Known for:** traditional Andalusian food; croquetas de jamón; live music on the roof terrace in summer. $ *Average main: €20* ✉ *Calle Romero 1, off Deanes, Judería* ☎ *957/200744.*

★ El Choco

$$$$ | **SPANISH** | The city's most exciting restaurant, which has renewed its Michelin star annually since 2012, El Choco has renowned chef Kisko Garcia at the helm whipping up innovative dishes based on his 10 Commandments to preserve good cooking. One of them is that taste always comes first, and that plays out well during a meal at this minimalist restaurant with charcoal-color walls, glossy parquet floors, and dishes offering new sensations and amazing presentations. **Known for:** creative Andalusian cooking; good value Michelin-star tasting menu; innovative presentation. $ *Average main: €125* ✉ *Compositor Serrano Lucena 14, Centro* ☎ *957/264863* ⊕ *www.restaurantechoco.es* ⊘ *Closed Mon. and Aug. No dinner Sun.*

El Churrasco

$$$ | **SPANISH** | The name suggests grilled meat, but this restaurant in the heart

of the Judería serves much more than that. In the colorful bar try tapas (from €3.50) such as the *berenjenas crujientes con salmorejo* (crispy fried eggplant slices with thick gazpacho), while in the restaurant, opt for the supremely fresh grilled fish or the steak, which is the best in town, particularly the namesake *churrasco ibérico* (grilled pork, served here in a spicy tomato-based sauce). **Known for:** grilled meat; tapas; alfresco dining. $ *Average main: €20* ✉ *Calle Romero 16, Judería* ☎ *957/290819* ⏱ *Closed Aug.*

La Regadera

$$ | SPANISH | It feels as if you could be outside at this bright venue on the river whose fresh interior comes with miniature wall gardens and lots of watering cans (*regaderas*)—there's even a fresh herb garden in the middle. Local produce takes center stage on the menu, where you'll find a mix of traditional and modern dishes including house specials such as wild sea bass ceviche, lamb meatballs with couscous, and cream of lemon. **Known for:** good wine list; gardenlike interior; tuna tartare. $ *Average main: €15* ✉ *Ronda de Isasa 10, Judería* ☎ *957/101400* ⊕ *www.regadera.es* ⏱ *Closed Mon.*

La Tinaja

$$ | SPANISH | On the river to the east of the city, this bodega-bar has kept its original 18th-century-house layout, which means that you can eat in different rooms as well as outside on the pleasant terrace. The food is traditional, with an emphasis on local produce and Córdoba staples such as *mazamorra con atún rojo ahumado* (traditional almond soup with smoked tuna) and *flamenquín* as well as oxtail and salmorejo. **Known for:** grilled meat; riverside terrace; homemade foie gras. $ *Average main: €14* ✉ *Paseo de la Ribera 12, Centro* ☎ *957/047998* ⊕ *latinajadecordoba.com.*

noor

$$$$ | SPANISH | One of the few two Michelin-starred venues in Andalusia, noor offers Andalusí cuisine made exclusively with ingredients that predate the discovery of the New World, so don't expect any potatoes, tomatoes, or chocolate on the menu. Local chef Paco Morales and team create in the open kitchen while diners sit at very modern tables under a dramatic Arabian nights' ceiling. **Known for:** creative, authentic cuisine; destination dining; Arabian nights ambience. $ *Average main: €95* ✉ *Calle Pablo Ruiz Picasso 8, Centro* ☎ *957/964055* ⊕ *noorrestaurante.es* ⏱ *Closed Sun.–Tues. and July and Aug.*

Salón de Té

$ | CAFÉ | A few blocks from the Mezquita, this place is a beautiful spot for tea, with a courtyard, side rooms filled with cushions, and a shop selling Moroccan clothing. It's open daily noon–10 pm. $ *Average main:* ✉ *Calle del Buen Pastor 13, Judería* ☎ *957/487984.*

Taberna de San Miguel

$$ | TAPAS | Just a few minutes' walk from the Plaza de las Tendillas and opposite the lovely San Miguel Church, this popular tapas spot—also known as the Casa el Pisto (Ratatouille House)—was established in 1880. You can choose to squeeze in at the bar and dine on tapas (€2.50) or spread out a little more on the patio decked with ceramics and bullfighting memorabilia, where half and full portions are served. **Known for:** tapas, including pisto; historic ambience; patio with bullfighting memorabilia. $ *Average main: €12* ✉ *Pl. San Miguel 1, Centro* ☎ *957/470166* ⊕ *www.casaelpisto.com* ⏱ *Closed Sun. and Aug.*

Taberna La Viuda

$ | SPANISH | Slightly off the beaten tourist trail and therefore with a local vibe, this lively tavern-style venue specializes in traditional local cuisine such as *salmorejo*, *flamenquín*, and oxtail, but you'll also find

A typical Córdoba patio, filled with flowers

creative touches on the menu in the form of tuna marinated in ginger and venison cold cuts. Most dishes are available as tapas, half or full plates, and all can be paired with local wines. **Known for:** traditional local food; warm welcome; wine pairing. [$] *Average main: €10* ✉ *Calle San Basilio 52, Judería* ☎ *957/296905.*

Hotels

Casa de los Azulejos
$$ | B&B/INN | This 17th-century house still has original details like the majestic vaulted ceilings and, with the use of stunning azulejos—hence the name—it mixes Andalusian and Latin American influences. **Pros:** interesting architecture; generous breakfast buffet; tropical central patio. **Cons:** hyperbusy interior design; limited privacy; plunge pool is only open in summer. [$] *Rooms from: €100* ✉ *Calle Fernando Colón 5, Centro* ☎ *957/470000* 🌐 *www.casadelosazulejos.com* 🛏 *9 rooms* 🍴 *Free breakfast.*

★ Hospes Palacio del Bailío
$$$$ | HOTEL | One of the city's top lodging options, this tastefully renovated 17th-century mansion is built over the ruins of a Roman house (visible beneath glass floors) in the historic center of town. **Pros:** dazzling interiors; impeccable comforts; central location. **Cons:** not easy to access by car; pricey; parking is limited. [$] *Rooms from: €220* ✉ *Calle Ramírez de las Casas Deza 10–12, Plaza de la Corredera* ☎ *957/498993* 🌐 *www.hospes.com/palacio-bailio* 🛏 *53 rooms* 🍴 *No meals.*

★ Hotel Balcón de Córdoba
$$$$ | HOTEL | Located in a tastefully restored 17th-century convent, this boutique hotel has spacious, quiet rooms, and the Mezquita is almost within arm's reach from the rooftop terrace. **Pros:** central location; historic building; rooftop views of the Mezquita. **Cons:** difficult to access by car; very quiet; small breakfast area. [$] *Rooms from: €250* ✉ *Calle Encarnación 8, Judería* ☎ *957/498478*

🌐 *balcondecordoba.com* 🛏 *10 rooms* 🍴 *Free breakfast.*

Hotel Maestre

$ | **HOTEL** | Around the corner from the Plaza del Potro, this is an affordable hotel in which Castilian-style furniture, gleaming marble, and high-quality oil paintings add elegance to excellent value. **Pros:** good location; great value; helpful reception staff. **Cons:** no elevator and lots of steps; ancient plumbing; could be too basic for some. [$] *Rooms from: €65* ✉ *Calle Romero Barros 4–6, San Pedro* ☎ *957/472410* 🌐 *www.hotelmaestre.com* 🛏 *26 rooms* 🍴 *No meals.*

★ **La Llave de la Judería**

$$$ | **B&B/INN** | This small hotel, occupying a collection of houses just a stone's throw from the mezquita, combines enchanting antique furnishings with modern amenities, but its greatest asset is its exceptionally helpful staff. **Pros:** beautiful interiors; rooms are equipped with computers; close to the Mezquita. **Cons:** rooms facing street can be noisy; direct car access is difficult; dark reception area. [$] *Rooms from: €150* ✉ *Calle Romero 38, Judería* ☎ *957/294808* 🌐 *www.lallavedelajuderia.es* 🛏 *9 rooms* 🍴 *No meals.*

NH Collection Amistad Córdoba

$$$ | **HOTEL** | Two 18th-century mansions overlooking Plaza de Maimónides in the heart of the Judería have been melded into a modern business hotel with a cobblestone Mudejar courtyard, carved-wood ceilings, and a plush lounge. **Pros:** pleasant and efficient service; large rooms; central location. **Cons:** parking is difficult; main access via steep steps with no ramp; a little impersonal. [$] *Rooms from: €140* ✉ *Pl. de Maimónides 3, Judería* ☎ *957/420335* 🌐 *www.nh-hoteles.es* 🛏 *108 rooms* 🍴 *No meals.*

Viento 10

$$ | **HOTEL** | Tucked away to the east of the old quarter, but within just 10 minutes' walk of the Mezquita is a quiet, romantic haven, once part of the 17th-century Sacred Martyrs Hospital. **Pros:** quiet location; pillow menu; Jacuzzi and sauna. **Cons:** some walking distance to the main monuments; a little plain; not easy to find. [$] *Rooms from: €120* ✉ *Calle Ronquillo Briceño 10, San Pedro* ☎ *957/764960* 🌐 *www.hotelviento10.es* 🕒 *Closed Jan.* 🛏 *8 rooms* 🍴 *No meals.*

🍸 Nightlife

For nightlife, Córdoba locals hang out mostly in the areas of Ciudad Jardín (the old university area), Plaza de las Tendillas, and the Avenida Gran Capitán.

Bodega Guzman

BARS/PUBS | For some traditional tipple, check out this atmospheric bodega near the old synagogue. Its sherries are served straight from the barrel in a room that doubles as a bullfighting museum. ✉ *Calle de los Judios 6, Judería.*

Café Málaga

MUSIC CLUBS | A block from Plaza de las Tendillas, this is a laid-back hangout for jazz and blues aficionados. There's live music most days and occasional flamenco nights. ✉ *Calle Málaga 3, Centro* ☎ *957/474107.*

🎟 Performing Arts

FLAMENCO

Tablao El Cardenal

DANCE CLUBS | Córdoba's most famous flamenco club offers performances by established artists on a pleasant open-air patio. Admission is €23 (including a drink), and the 90-minute shows take place Monday through Thursday at 8:15 pm and on Friday and Saturday at 9. Book by phone or the website (in Spanish only). ✉ *Calle Buen Pastor 2, Judería* ☎ *619/217922* 🌐 *www.tablaocardenal.es.*

Shopping

Córdoba's main shopping district is around Avenida Gran Capitán, Ronda de los Tejares, and the streets leading away from Plaza Tendillas.

Meryan

SHOES/LUGGAGE/LEATHER GOODS | This is one of Córdoba's best workshops for embossed leather. ⊠ *Calleja de las Flores 2* ☎ *957/475902* ⊕ *www.meryancor.com.*

Ronda

147 km (91 miles) southeast of Seville, 61 km (38 miles) northwest of Marbella.

Ronda, one of the oldest towns in Spain, is known for its spectacular position and views. Secure in its mountain fastness on a rock high over the Río Guadalevín, the town was a stronghold for the legendary Andalusian bandits who held court here from the 18th to the early 20th century. Ronda's most dramatic element is its ravine (360 feet deep and 210 feet across)—known as **El Tajo**—which divides La Ciudad, the old Moorish town, from El Mercadillo, the "new town," which sprang up after the Christian Reconquest of 1485. Tour buses roll in daily with sightseers from the coast 49 km (30 miles) away, and on weekends affluent sevillanos flock to their second homes here. Stay overnight midweek to see this noble town's true colors.

In the lowest part of town, known as El Barrio, you can see parts of the old walls, including the 13th-century Puerta de Almocobar and the 16th-century Puerta de Carlos V. From here, the main road climbs past the Iglesia del Espíritu Santo (Church of the Holy Spirit) and up into the heart of town.

GETTING HERE AND AROUND

The most attractive approach is from the south. The winding but well-maintained A376 from San Pedro de Alcántara,

on the Costa del Sol, travels north up through the mountains of the Serranía de Ronda. But you can also drive here from Seville via Utrera; it's a pleasant drive of a little less than two hours. At least six daily buses run here from Marbella, six from Málaga, and seven from Seville. The Ronda tourist office publishes an updated list (available on the visitor information website).

VISITOR INFORMATION

CONTACTS **Ronda.** ⊠ *Paseo de Blas Infante s/n* ☎ *952/187119* ⊕ *www.turis-moderonda.es.*

Sights

Alameda del Tajo

GARDEN | Beyond the bullring in El Mercadillo, you can relax in these shady gardens, one of the loveliest spots in Ronda. At the end of the gardens, a balcony protrudes from the face of the cliff, offering a vertigo-inducing view of the valley below. Stroll along the cliff-top walk to the Reina Victoria hotel, built by British settlers from Gibraltar at the turn of the 20th century as a fashionable rest stop on the Algeciras–Bobadilla rail line. ⊠ *Paseo Hemingway.*

Baños Arabes (*Arab Baths*)

HOT SPRINGS | The excavated remains of the Arab Baths date from Ronda's tenure as capital of a Moorish *taifa* (kingdom). The star-shape vents in the roof are an inferior imitation of the ceiling of the beautiful bathhouse in Granada's Alhambra. The baths are beneath the Puente Árabe (Arab Bridge) in a ravine below the Palacio del Marqués de Salvatierra. ⊠ *Calle San Miguel* ☎ *656/950937* 🎫 *€4 (free Tues. from 3 pm).*

Juan Peña El Lebrijano

BRIDGE/TUNNEL | Immediately south of the Plaza de España, this is Ronda's most famous bridge (also known as the Puente Nuevo, or New Bridge), an architectural marvel built between 1755 and 1793. The bridge's lantern-lit parapet offers dizzying views of the awesome gorge. Just how many people have met their ends here nobody knows, but the architect of the Puente Nuevo fell to his death while inspecting work on the bridge. During the civil war, hundreds of victims were hurled from it. ✉ *Ronda.*

La Ciudad

NEIGHBORHOOD | This old Moorish town has twisting streets and white houses with birdcage balconies. Cross the Puente Nuevo to enter La Ciudad. ✉ *Ronda.*

Palacio de Mondragón (*Palace of Mondragón*)

HOUSE | This stone palace with twin Mudejar towers was probably the residence of Ronda's Moorish kings. Ferdinand and Isabella appropriated it after their victory in 1485. Today, it's the museum of Ronda and you can wander through the patios, with their brick arches and delicate Mudejar-stucco tracery, and admire the mosaics and *artesonado* (coffered) ceiling. The second floor holds a small museum with archaeological items found near Ronda, plus the reproduction of a dolmen, a prehistoric stone monument. ✉ *Pl. Mondragón* ☎ *952/870818* 🎟 *€3.*

Plaza de Toros

SPORTS VENUE | The main sight in Ronda's commercial center, El Mercadillo, is the bullring. Pedro Romero (1754–1839), the father of modern bullfighting and Ronda's most famous native son, is said to have killed 5,600 bulls here during his long career. In the museum beneath the plaza you can see posters for Ronda's very first bullfights, held here in 1785. The plaza was once owned by the late bullfighter Antonio Ordóñez, on whose nearby ranch Orson Welles's ashes were scattered (as directed in his will)—indeed, the ring has become a favorite of filmmakers. Every September, the bullring is the scene of Ronda's *corridas goyescas,* named after Francisco Goya, whose *tauromaquias* (bullfighting sketches) were inspired by Romero's skill and art. The participants and the dignitaries in the audience don the costumes of Goya's time for the occasion. Seats for these fights cost a small fortune and are booked far in advance. Other than that, the plaza is rarely used for fights except during Ronda's May festival. ✉ *Calle Virgen de la Paz* ☎ *952/871539* 🌐 *www.rmcr.org* 🎟 *€8.*

Santa María la Mayor

RELIGIOUS SITE | This collegiate church, which serves as Ronda's cathedral, has roots in Moorish times: originally the Great Mosque of Ronda, the tower and adjacent galleries, built for viewing festivities in the square, retain their Islamic design. After the mosque was destroyed (when the Moors were overthrown), it was rebuilt as a church and dedicated to the Virgen de la Encarnación after the Reconquest. The naves are late Gothic, and the main altar is heavy with baroque gold leaf. A visit to the rooftop walkway offers lovely views of the town and surroundings. The church is around the corner from the remains of a mosque, Minarete Arabe (Moorish Minaret) at the end of the Marqués de Salvatierra. ✉ *Pl. Duquesa de Parcent* 🎟 *€4.*

🍴 Restaurants

★ Entre Vinos

$ | **TAPAS** | Just off the main road opposite the Hotel Colón, this small and cozy bar has established itself as one of Ronda's best for tapas, wine, and artisan beer. Local Ronda wines are a specialty here—in fact, they're the only ones available, although with more than 100 on the wine list, you'll be spoiled for choice; ask the waiter for recommendations and which tapas to pair them with. **Known for:** Ronda wines; gourmet tapas; bodega (winery) atmosphere. [$] *Average main: €5* ✉ *Calle Pozo 2* ☎ *658/582976* 🕓 *Closed Sun. and Mon.*

Pedro Romero

$$$ | SPANISH | Named for the father of modern bullfighting, this restaurant opposite the bullring is packed with bullfight paraphernalia and photos of previous diners who include Ernest Hemingway and Orson Welles. Mounted bulls' heads peer down at you as you tuck into *choricitos al vino blanco de Ronda* (small sausages in Ronda white wine), *rabo de toro Pedro Romero* (slow-cooked oxtail stew with herbs), or *magret de pato con pera asada* (duck breast with baked pear). **Known for:** traditional Ronda cooking; bullfighting decor; friendly service. $ *Average main: €18* ⊠ *Calle Virgen de la Paz 18* ☎ *952/871110* ⊕ *www.rpedroromero. com.*

 Hotels

Alavera de los Baños

$$ | B&B/INN | Fittingly, given its location next to the Moorish baths, this small, German-run hotel—which was used as a backdrop for the film classic *Carmen*—has an Arab theme throughout. **Pros:** atmospheric and historic; owners speak several languages; first-floor rooms have their own terraces. **Cons:** rooms vary in size; steep climb into town; small bathrooms. $ *Rooms from: €100* ⊠ *Calle San Miguel s/n* ☎ *952/879143* ⊕ *www. alaveradelosbanos.com* ☉ *Closed Dec.– mid-Feb.* ⇥ *11 rooms* ❙◎❙ *Free breakfast.*

Hotel Montelirio

$$$ | B&B/INN | The 18th-century mansion of the Count of Montelirio, perched over the deep plunge to El Tajo, has been carefully refurbished, maintaining some original features, but the highlight is the breathtaking view over the valley. **Pros:** valley views; historic building; Turkish bath and open fireplace make it great for winter. **Cons:** some rooms have windows to the street; parking limited; could be too stuffy for some. $ *Rooms from: €135* ⊠ *Calle Tenorio 8* ☎ *952/873855* ⊕ *www. hotelmontelirio.com* ⇥ *15 rooms* ❙◎❙ *No meals.*

Around Ronda: Caves, Romans, and Pueblos Blancos

This area of spectacular gorges, remote mountain villages, and ancient caves is fascinating to explore and a dramatic contrast to the clamor and crowds of the nearby Costa del Sol.

GETTING HERE AND AROUND

Public transportation is very poor in these parts. Your best bet is to visit by car—the area is a short drive from Ronda.

 Sights

★ Acinipo

ARCHAEOLOGICAL SITE | Old Ronda, 20 km (12 miles) north of Ronda, is the site of this old Roman settlement, a thriving town in the 1st century AD that was abandoned for reasons that still baffle historians. Today it's a windswept hillside with piles of stones, the foundations of a few Roman houses, and what remains of a theater. Views across the Ronda plains and to the surrounding mountains are spectacular. The site's opening hours vary depending on staff availability and excavations—check with the Ronda tourist office by phone before visiting. ⊠ *Ronda* ⊹ *Take A376 toward Algodonales; turnoff for ruins is 9 km (5 miles) from Ronda on MA449* ☎ *951/041452* ⊠ *Free.*

Cueva de la Pileta (*Pileta Cave*)

CAVE | At this site 20 km (12 miles) west of Ronda, a Spanish guide (who speaks some English) will hand you a paraffin lamp and lead you on a roughly 60-minute walk that reveals prehistoric wall paintings of bison, deer, and horses outlined in black, red, and ocher. One highlight is the Cámara del Pescado (Chamber of the Fish), whose drawing of a huge fish is thought to be 15,000 years old. Tours take place on the hour and last around an hour. To book, phone between

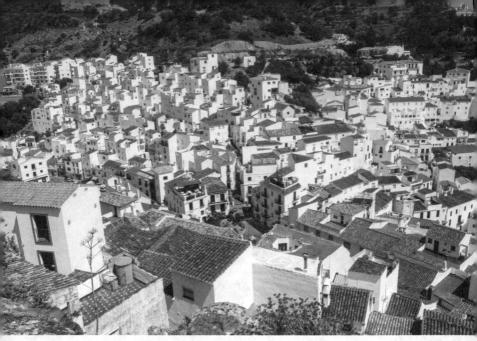

Andalusia's classic pueblos blancos look like Picasso paintings come to life.

10am and 1pm only. ⊠ *Benaoján* ⊹ *Drive west from Ronda on A374 and take left exit for village of Benaoján from where caves are well signposted* ☎ *666/741775* 🚾 *€10.*

Olvera

TOWN | Here, 13 km (8 miles) north of Setenil, two imposing silhouettes dominate the crest of the hill: the 11th-century castle Vallehermoso, a legacy of the Moors, and the neoclassical church of La Encarnación, reconstructed in the 19th century on the foundations of the old mosque. ⊠ *Cádiz.*

Setenil de las Bodegas

TOWN | This small city, in a cleft in the rock cut by the Río Guadalporcín, is 8 km (5 miles) north of Acinipo. The streets resemble long, narrow caves, and on many houses the roof is formed by a projecting ledge of heavy rock. ⊠ *Cádiz.*

Zahara de la Sierra

TOWN | A solitary watchtower dominates a crag above this village, its outline visible for miles around. The tower is all that remains of a Moorish castle where King Alfonso X once fought the emir of Morocco; the building remained a Moorish stronghold until it fell to the Christians in 1470. Along the streets you can see door knockers fashioned like the hand of Fatima: the fingers represent the five laws of the Koran and are meant to ward off evil. ⊠ *Cádiz* ⊹ *From Olvera, drive 21 km (13 miles) southwest to the village of Algodonales, then south on A376 for 5 km (3 miles).*

Arcos de la Frontera

31 km (19 miles) east of Jerez.

Its narrow and steep cobblestone streets, whitewashed houses, and finely crafted wrought-iron window grilles make Arcos the quintessential Andalusian pueblo blanco. Make your way to the main square, the **Plaza de España,** the highest point in the village; one side of the square is open, and a balcony at the edge of the cliff offers views of the Guadalete Valley. On the opposite end is the church of **Santa María de la Asunción,** a fascinating blend of architectural styles—Romanesque, Gothic, and Mudejar—with a plateresque doorway, a Renaissance retablo, and a 17th-century baroque choir. The *ayuntamiento* (town hall) stands at the foot of the old castle walls on the northern side of the square; across is the Casa del Corregidor, onetime residence of the governor and now a parador. Arcos is the westernmost of the 19 pueblos blancos dotted around the Sierra de Cádiz.

GETTING HERE AND AROUND

Arcos is best reached by private car, but there are frequent bus services here from Cádiz, Jerez, and Seville on weekdays. Weekend services are less frequent.

VISITOR INFORMATION

CONTACTS Arcos de la Frontera. ✉ *Cuesta de Belén 5* ☎ *956/702264* 🌐 *www.turismoarcos.com.*

🍴 Restaurants

Gastrobar El Retablo

$$ | **SPANISH** | Traditional Andalusian cuisine comes in generous portions (tapas and sharing plates) at this popular venue with locals. Sit outside on the small terrace opposite the Iglesia de Santa María or inside in the functional bar area or more formal dining room. **Known for:** friendly service; octopus; generous portions. [$] *Average main: €12* ✉ *Calle Dean Espinosa 6* ☎ *856/041614* 🕒 *Closed Tues.*

Restaurante Aljibe

$$ | **FUSION** | Local cooking meets Moroccan cuisine on one of the best fusion menus in the province at this venue with small dining spaces and an Arabian theme. White prawns, *ensalada de higos y payoyo* (fig and goat´s cheese salad) and *alcachofas con almejas* (artichokes with clams) sit perfectly next to *pastela* (game pie) and couscous dishes. **Known for:** Andalusian-Moroccan fusion; good service with a smile; Moroccan sweetmeats for dessert. [$] *Average main: €14* ✉ *Cuesta del Belén 10* ☎ *622/836527* 🕒 *Closed Tues.; no lunch Mon., Wed., Thurs.*

🛏 Hotels

★ El Convento

$ | **B&B/INN** | Perched atop the cliff behind the town parador, this tiny hotel in a former 17th-century convent shares the amazing view of another hotel in town, its swish neighbor (La Casa Grande). **Pros:** picturesque location; intimacy; value. **Cons:** small spaces; lots of stairs; no restaurant. [$] *Rooms from: €70* ✉ *Calle Maldonado 2* ☎ *956/702333* 🌐 *www.hotelelconvento.es* 🕒 *Closed Jan. and Feb.* 🛏 *13 rooms* 🍽 *No meals.*

★ La Casa Grande

$$ | **B&B/INN** | Built in 1729, this extraordinary 18th-century mansion encircles a central patio with lush vegetation and is perched on the edge of the 400-foot cliff to which Arcos de la Frontera clings. **Pros:** attentive owner; impeccable aesthetics; amazing views. **Cons:** inconvenient parking; long climb to the top floor; interior is a little dark. [$] *Rooms from: €100* ✉ *Calle Maldonado 10* ☎ *956/703930* 🌐 *www.lacasagrande.net* 🛏 *7 rooms* 🍽 *No meals.*

Parador Casa del Corregidor

$$$ | **HOTEL** | Expect a spectacular view from the terrace, as this parador clings to the cliffside, overlooking the rolling valley of the Río Guadalete. **Pros:** gorgeous views from certain rooms; elegant interiors; good restaurant. **Cons:** public areas a little tired; expensive bar and cafeteria; not all rooms have views. [$] *Rooms from: €130* ✉ *Pl. del Cabildo s/n* ☎ *956/700500* 🌐 *www.parador.es* 🛏 *24 rooms* 🍽 *No meals.*

Jerez de la Frontera

97 km (60 miles) south of Seville.

Jerez, world headquarters for sherry, is surrounded by vineyards of chalky soil, producing palomino and Pedro Ximénez grapes that have funded a host of churches and noble mansions. Names such as González Byass, Domecq, Harvey, and Sandeman are inextricably linked with Jerez. The word "sherry," first used in Great Britain in 1608, is an English corruption of the town's old Moorish name, Xeres. Both sherry and thoroughbred horses (the city was European Capital of Horses in 2018) are the domain of Jerez's Anglo-Spanish aristocracy, whose Catholic ancestors came here from England centuries ago. At any given time, more than half a million barrels of sherry are maturing in Jerez's vast aboveground cellars.

GETTING HERE AND AROUND

Jerez is a short way from Seville with frequent daily trains (journey time is around an hour) and buses (1 hour 15 minutes), fewer on weekends. If you're traveling to the city by car, park in one of the city-center lots or at your hotel as street parking is difficult. Jerez Airport is small and served by a number of flights to destinations in northern Europe and within Spain.

AIRPORT Jerez de la Frontera Airport . ⊠ *Ctra. N-IV, Km 628.5* ☎ *956/150000* ⊕ *www.aena.es.*

BUS STATION Jerez de la Frontera. ⊠ *Pl. de la Estación* ☎ *956/149990.*

TAXI CONTACT Tele Taxi. ☎ *956/344860, 956/350537.*

TRAIN STATION Jerez de la Frontera. ⊠ *Pl. de la Estación s/n, off Calle Diego Fernández Herrera* ☎ *912/320320.*

VISITOR INFORMATION
CONTACTS Jerez de la Frontera. ⊠ *Edificio Los Arcos, Pl. del Arenal* ☎ *956/338874* ⊕ *www.turismojerez.com.*

 Sights

Alcázar
CASTLE/PALACE | Once the residence of the caliph of Seville, the 12th-century alcázar in Jerez de la Frontera and its small, octagonal **mosque** and **baths** were built for the Moorish governor's private use. The baths have three sections: the *sala fría* (cold room), the larger *sala templada* (warm room), and the *sala caliente* (hot room) for steam baths. In the midst of it all is the 17th-century **Palacio de Villavicencio,** built on the site of the original Moorish palace. A camera obscura, a lens-and-mirrors device that projects the outdoors onto a large indoor screen, offers a 360-degree view of Jerez. ⊠ *Calle Alameda Vieja* ☎ *956/149955* 🎟 *From €5.*

Álvaro Domecq
WINERY/DISTILLERY | This is Jerez's oldest *bodega* (winery), founded in 1730. Aside from sherry, Domecq makes the world's best-selling brandy, Fundador. Harveys Bristol Cream is also part of the Domecq group. Visits must be booked in advance by phone or email. ⊠ *Calle San Ildefonso 3* ☎ *956/339634* ⊕ *www.alvarodomecq. com* 🎟 *From €13.*

★ Bodegas Tradición
WINERY/DISTILLERY | Tucked away on the north side of the old quarter and founded in 1998, this is one of the youngest bodegas, but it has the oldest sherry. The five types sit in the casks for at least 20 years and most are older. Visits (book in advance by phone or email) include a tour of the winery, a lesson in how to pair each sherry type, and a tour of the unique Spanish art collection that includes works by El Greco,

Zurburán, Goya, and Velázquez. ✉ *Pl. de los Cordobeses 3* ☎ *956/168628* ⊕ *www. bodegastradicion.es* 🎟 *€35.*

Catedral de Jerez
RELIGIOUS SITE | Across from the alcázar and around the corner from the González Byass winery, the cathedral has an octagonal cupola and a separate bell tower, as well as Zurbarán's canvas *La Virgen Niña Meditando* (*The Virgin as a Young Girl*). ✉ *Pl. de la Encarnación* ☎ *956/169059* 🎟 *From €6 (includes visit to church of San Miguel).*

González Byass
WINERY/DISTILLERY | Home of the famous Tío Pepe, this is one of the most commercial bodegas. The tour, which is in English, is well organized and includes La Concha, an open-air aging cellar designed by Gustave Eiffel. ✉ *Calle Manuel María González* ☎ *956/357016* ⊕ *www.gonzalezbyass.com* 🎟 *From €19.*

Museo Arqueológico
MUSEUM | Diving into the maze of streets that form the scruffy San Mateo neighborhood east of the town center, you come to one of Andalusia's best archaeological museums. The collection is strongest on the pre-Roman period, and the star item, found near Jerez, is a Greek helmet dating from the 7th century BC. ✉ *Pl. del Mercado s/n* ☎ *956/149560* 🎟 *From €5 (free 1st Sun. of month)* ⏱ *Closed Mon.*

★ Plaza de la Asunción
PLAZA | Here on one of Jerez's most intimate squares you can find the Mudejar church of **San Dionisio,** patron saint of the city, (open 10–noon Monday–Thursday) and the ornate *cabildo municipal* (city hall), with a lovely plateresque facade dating to 1575. ✉ *Jerez de la Frontera* 🎟 *Church free* ⏱ *Church closed for touring Fri.–Sun.*

★ Real Escuela Andaluza del Arte Ecuestre (*Royal Andalusian School of Equestrian Art*)
SPORTS VENUE | FAMILY | This prestigious school operates on the grounds of the Recreo de las Cadenas, a 19th-century palace. The school was masterminded by Álvaro Domecq in the 1970s, and every Tuesday and Thursday (Thursday only in January and February) as well as each Friday in August through October, the Cartujana horses—a cross between the native Andalusian workhorse and the Arabian— and skilled riders in 18th-century riding costume demonstrate intricate dressage techniques and jumping in the spectacular show *Cómo Bailan los Caballos Andaluces* (roughly, *The Dancing Horses of Andalusia*). ■TIP→ **Reservations are essential.** The price of admission depends on how close to the arena you sit; the first two rows are the priciest. At certain other times you can visit the museum, stables, and tack room and watch the horses being schooled. ✉ *Av. Duque de Abrantes* ☎ *956/318008 for information* ⊕ *www.realescuela.org* 🎟 *From €21.*

San Miguel
RELIGIOUS SITE | One block from the Plaza del Arenal, near the alcázar, stands the church of San Miguel. Built over the 15th and 16th centuries, its interior illustrates the evolution of Gothic architecture, with various styles mixed into the design. ✉ *Pl. de San Miguel* ☎ *956/343347* 🎟 *€2 (included in Cathedral admission)* ⏱ *Closed Sun.*

Sandeman
WINERY/DISTILLERY | The Sandeman brand of sherry is known for its dashing man-in-a-cape logo. Tours of the sherry bodegas in Jerez give you some insight into his history and let you visit the cellars. Some visitors purchase tapas to have with their sherry tastings. There is also a museum and shop on-site. ✉ *Calle Pizarro 10* ☎ *675/647177* ⊕ *www.sandeman.com/ visit-us/jerez/sherry-bodegas* 🎟 *From €10.*

Winery Tours in Jerez 🍴

On a bodega visit, you'll learn about the *solera* method of blending old wine with new, and the importance of the *flor* (yeast that forms on the wine as it ages) in determining the kind of sherry.

Phone ahead for an appointment to make sure you join a group that speaks your language. Admission fees start at €10 (more for extra wine tasting or tapas), and tours, which last 60–90 minutes, go through the aging cellars, with their endless rows of casks. (You won't see the actual fermenting and bottling, which take place in more modern, less romantic plants outside town.) Finally, you'll be invited to sample generous amounts of pale, dry fino, nutty amontillado, rich, deep oloroso, and sweet Pedro Ximénez and, of course, to purchase a few robustly priced bottles in the winery shop.

Yeguada de la Cartuja

FARM/RANCH | This farm just outside Jerez de la Frontera specializes in Carthusian horses. In the 15th century, a Carthusian monastery on this site started the breed for which Jerez and the rest of Spain are now famous. Visits include a full tour of the stables and training areas and a show. Book ahead. ✉ *Finca Fuente El Suero, Ctra. Medina–El Portal, Km 6.5* ☎ *956/162809* 🌐 *www.yeguadacartuja.com* 🎟 *From €17.*

Zoobotánico

ZOO | **FAMILY** | Just west of the town center, the Jerez zoo is set in lush botanical gardens where you can usually spy up to 33 storks' nests. Primarily a place for the rehabilitation of injured or endangered animals native to the region, the zoo also houses white tigers, elephants, a giant red panda, and the endangered Iberian lynx (the only place where you can see the lynx in captivity). ✉ *Calle Madreselva* ☎ *956/149785* 🌐 *www.zoobotanicojerez.com* 🎟 *€10* 🕒 *Closed Mon. mid-Sept.–mid-June.*

🍴 Restaurants

★ Albores

$$ | **SPANISH** | Opposite the city hall, this busy restaurant with swift service has pleasant outdoor seating under orange trees and a modern interior with low lighting, and serves innovative, modern dishes with a traditional base. The menu is extensive and changes often, although must-try staples include *barriga de atún con salsa de soja y mermelada de tomate* (tuna belly with soy sauce and tomato jam) and *lomo de ciervo* (venison steak). **Known for:** tuna cooked any which way; generous portions (sharing is encouraged; half portions are also available); desserts like crème brûlée with white chocolate and a house apple pie. [$] *Average main: €15* ✉ *Calle Consistorio 12* ☎ *956/320266* 🌐 *www.restaurantealbores.com.*

Bar Juanito

$ | **SPANISH** | Traditional bars don't come more authentic than Bar Juanito, which has been serving local dishes for more than 70 years and pairs everything, of course, with sherry. You can eat standing at the bar or seated in the pleasant patio restaurant, where there's often live music on Saturday. **Known for:** tapas (52 on the menu); artichoke dishes in season (early spring); pork-based stew. [$] *Average main: €10* ✉ *Calle Pescadería Vieja 8–10* ☎ *956/342986.*

Riders fill the streets during Jerez's Feria del Caballo (Horse Fair) in early May.

★ La Carboná

$$ | **SPANISH** | In a former bodega, this eatery has a rustic atmosphere with arches, wooden beams, and a fireplace for winter nights, and in summer you can often enjoy live music and sometimes flamenco dancing while you dine. The chef has worked at several top restaurants, and his menu includes traditional grilled meats as well as innovative twists on classic dishes, such as foie gras terrine with pear and cardamom or *mero con curry de palo cortado* (grouper fish with sherry curry). **Known for:** multiple-course sherry-tasting menu; bodega setting; innovative dishes. [$] *Average main: €22* ✉ *Calle San Francisco de Paula 2* ☎ *956/347475* ⏲ *Closed Tues. and July.*

Mesón del Asador

$ | **SPANISH** | Just off the Plaza del Arenal, this rustic meat restaurant is always packed with young locals who crowd around the bar for cheap and generous tapas (from €3). Oxtail stew, fried chorizo, black pudding, and pig's-cheek stew come in huge portions, resulting in an incredibly inexpensive meal. **Known for:** grilled meats; generous portions; inexpensive tapas. [$] *Average main: €11* ✉ *Calle Remedios 2–4* ☎ *952/322658.*

Venta Esteban

$$ | **SPANISH** | **FAMILY** | This restaurant is slightly off the beaten track, but well worth seeking out for traditional Jerez cuisine in a pleasant setting. Choose tapas in the bar or à la carte in the spacious and airy dining rooms. **Known for:** seafood; traditional stews; homemade custard. [$] *Average main: €16* ✉ *Colonia de Caulina C.11–03* ✥ *Just off Seville hwy. exit* ☎ *956/316067* 🌐 *www.restauranteventaesteban.es.*

Hotels

★ Casa Palacio Maria Luisa

$$$$ | **HOTEL** | Once home to Jerez's gentlemen's club (known as the Casino) and something of a symbol of the city's sherry heyday, this restored 19th-century mansion is arguably the most comfortable luxurious hotel in town and the only

Just about the whole city turns out for Jerez's Feria del Caballo, and traditional Andalusian costumes are a common sight.

five-star grand-luxe one. **Pros:** beautifully designed, uber-comfortable rooms; excellent service; lovely outside terrace. **Cons:** might be too grandiose for some. [$] *Rooms from: €300* ✉ *Calle Tornería 22* ☎ *956/926263* 🌐 *casapalaciomarialuisa.com* 🛏 *21 rooms* 🍴 *No meals.*

Hotel Doña Blanca

$ | **HOTEL** | Slightly off the main tourist route but still within easy walking distance to attractions, this traditional town-house hotel offers spacious accommodations with some of the best prices in the city. **Pros:** private terrace in some rooms; great value; generously sized rooms. **Cons:** cold breakfast choices only; not right in the city center; might be too basic for some. [$] *Rooms from: €60* ✉ *Calle Bodegas 11* ☎ *956/348761* 🌐 *www.hoteldonablanca.com* 🛏 *30 rooms* 🍴 *No meals.*

Hotel Villa Jerez

$$$ | **B&B/INN** | Tastefully furnished, this hacienda-style hotel offers luxury on the outskirts of town. **Pros:** elegant gardens; Italian restaurant on-site; saltwater swimming pool. **Cons:** outside of town center; some areas need updating; breakfast is average. [$] *Rooms from: €130* ✉ *Av. de la Cruz Roja 7* ☎ *956/153100* 🌐 *www.hace.es* 🛏 *15 rooms* 🍴 *No meals.*

Hotel YIT Casa Grande

$ | **HOTEL** | This cozy hotel, right in the city center with all the main attractions on its doorstep, comes complete with its original 1920s Art Nouveau design and period antiques. **Pros:** central location; personalized service; roof terrace. **Cons:** no pool; decor might not appeal to everyone; some rooms have street noise. [$] *Rooms from: €80* ✉ *Pl. de las Angustias 3* ☎ *956/345070* 🌐 *www.hotelcasagrande-jerez.com* 🛏 *15 rooms* 🍴 *No meals.*

La Fonda Barranco

$ | **HOTEL** | A block away from the cathedral and behind the police station, this typical Jerez town house has been restored to its full bourgeois glory, preserving original tiled floors, beamed ceilings, and a light central patio. **Pros:** personalized attention; central location;

good value. **Cons:** some rooms are dark; no elevator; no breakfast available. $ *Rooms from: €60* ✉ *Calle Barranco 12* ☎ *956/332141* ⊕ *www.lafondabarranco. com* ⇌ *8 rooms, 2 apartments* ⊗ *No meals.*

Cádiz

32 km (20 miles) southwest of Jerez, 149 km (93 miles) southwest of Seville.

With the Atlantic Ocean on three sides, Cádiz is a bustling town that's been shaped by a variety of cultures and has the varied architecture to prove it. Founded as Gadir by Phoenician traders in 1100 BC, Cádiz claims to be the oldest continuously inhabited city in the Western world. Hannibal lived in Cádiz for a time, Julius Caesar first held public office here, and Columbus set out from here on his second voyage, after which the city became the home base of the Spanish fleet. In the 18th century, when the Guadalquivir silted up, Cádiz monopolized New World trade and became the wealthiest port in Western Europe. Most of its buildings—including the cathedral, built in part with wealth generated by gold and silver from the New World—date from this period. The old city is African in appearance and immensely intriguing—a cluster of narrow streets opening onto charming small squares. The golden cupola of the cathedral looms above low white houses, and the whole place has a slightly dilapidated air. Spaniards flock here in February to revel in the carnival celebrations, and ever more cruise ships visit the harbor, but in general it's not too touristy.

GETTING HERE AND AROUND

Every day, around 15 local trains connect Cádiz with Seville, Puerto de Santa María, and Jerez. The city has two bus stations. The main one, run by Comes, serves most destinations in Andalusia and farther afield; the other, run by Socibus, serves Córdoba and Madrid. There are buses to and from Sanlúcar de Barrameda (14 on weekdays), Arcos de la Frontera (9 daily), and the Costa del Sol (via Seville, 4 daily). Cádiz is easy to get to and navigate by car. Once there, the old city is easily explored by foot.

BUS STATION Cádiz–Estación de Autobuses Comes. ✉ *Pl. de Sevilla* ☎ *956/807059.* **Cádiz-Estación de Autobuses Socibus.** ✉ *Av. Astilleros s/n* ☎ *956/257415.*

TAXI CONTACT Radiotaxi. ☎ *956/212121.*

TRAIN STATION Cádiz. ✉ *Pl. de Sevilla s/n* ☎ *912/320320.*

VISITOR INFORMATION

CONTACTS Local Tourist Office. ✉ *Paseo de Canalejas* ☎ *956/241001* ⊕ *www.turismo.cadiz.es.* **Regional Tourist Office.** ✉ *Av. Ramón de Carranza s/n* ☎ *956/203191* ⊕ *www.cadizturismo.com.*

◉ Sights

Begin your explorations in the Plaza de Mina, a large, leafy square with palm trees and plenty of benches. Look out for the ornamental facade on the Colegio de Arquitectos (College of Architects), on the west side of the square.

Cádiz Cathedral

RELIGIOUS SITE | Five blocks southeast of the Torre Tavira are the gold dome and baroque facade of Cádiz's cathedral, which offers history as well as views from atop the Clock Tower (Torre del Reloj)—making the climb to the top worth it. The building's structure was begun in 1722, when the city was at the height of its power. The Cádiz-born composer Manuel de Falla, who died in 1946 at the age of 70, is buried in the **crypt.** The **museum,** on Calle Acero, displays gold, silver, and jewels from the New World, as well as Enrique de Arfe's processional cross, which is carried in the annual Corpus Christi parades. The cathedral is known as the New Cathedral because it supplanted the original, neighboring, 13th-century structure, which was destroyed by the British in 1592, rebuilt, and rechristened the church of **Santa Cruz** when the New Cathedral came along. ☒ *Pl. Catedral* ☎ *956/286154* ☒ *€6, includes crypt, museum, tower, and church of Santa Cruz.*

Gran Teatro Manuel de Falla

ARTS VENUE | Four blocks west of Santa Inés is the Plaza Manuel de Falla, overlooked by this amazing neo-Mudejar redbrick building. The classic interior is impressive as well—try to attend a performance. ☒ *Pl. Manuel de Falla* ☎ *956/220828.*

Museo de Cádiz (*Provincial Museum*)

MUSEUM | On the east side of the Plaza de Mina is Cádiz's provincial museum. Notable pieces include works by Murillo and Alonso Cano as well as the *Four Evangelists* and a set of saints by Zurbarán. The archaeological section contains two extraordinary marble Phoenician sarcophagi from the time of this ancient city's birth. ☒ *Pl. de Mina* ☎ *856/105023* ☒ *€2* ⊙ *Closed Mon. and weekend afternoons.*

Museo de las Cortes

MUSEUM | Next door to the Oratorio de San Felipe Neri, this small but pleasant museum has a 19th-century mural depicting the establishment of the Constitution of 1812. Its real showpiece, however, is a 1779 ivory-and-mahogany model of Cádiz, with all of the city's streets and buildings in minute detail, looking much as they do now. ☒ *Calle Santa Inés 9* ☎ *956/221788* ☒ *Free* ⊙ *Closed Mon. and weekend afternoons.*

Oratorio de la Santa Cueva

RELIGIOUS SITE | A few blocks east of the Plaza de Mina, next door to the Iglesia del Rosario, this oval 18th-century chapel has three frescoes by Goya. On Good Friday, the *Sermon of the Seven Words* is read and Haydn's *Seven Last Words*

played. ☒ *Calle Rosario 10* ☎ *956/222262* ☒ *€4 (free Sun.)* ⊙ *Closed Mon.*

Oratorio de San Felipe Neri

RELIGIOUS SITE | A walk up Calle San José from the Plaza de Mina will bring you to this church, where Spain's first liberal constitution (known affectionately as La Pepa) was declared in 1812. It was here, too, that the Cortes (Parliament) of Cádiz met when the rest of Spain was subjected to the rule of Napoléon's brother, Joseph Bonaparte (more popularly known as Pepe Botella, for his love of the bottle). On the main altar is an *Immaculate Conception* by Murillo, the great Sevillano artist who in 1682 fell to his death from a scaffold while working on his *Mystic Marriage of St. Catherine* in Cádiz's Chapel of Santa Catalina. ☒ *Calle Santa Inés 38* ☎ *662/642233* ☒ *€4 (free Sun.)* ⊙ *Closed Mon.*

Roman Theater

ARCHAEOLOGICAL SITE | Next door to the church of Santa Cruz are the remains of a 1st-century-BC Roman theater, one of the oldest and largest in Spain. The stage remains unexcavated (it lies under nearby houses), but you can visit the entrance and large seating area as well as the visitor center. ☒ *Campo del Sur s/n, Barrio del Pópulo* ☒ *Free* ⊙ *Closed 1st Mon. of month.*

★ Torre Tavira

BUILDING | **FAMILY** | At 150 feet, this watchtower is the highest point in the old city. More than a hundred such structures were used by Cádiz ship owners to spot their arriving fleets. A camera obscura gives a good overview of the city and its monuments; the last show is a half hour before closing time. ☒ *Calle Marqués del Real Tesoro 10* ☎ *956/212910* ⊕ *www.torretavira.com/en* ☒ *€7.*

Cádiz's majestic cathedral, as seen from the Plaza de la Catedral

🍽 Restaurants

★ Casa Manteca

$ | SPANISH | Cádiz's most quintessentially Andalusian tavern is in the neighborhood of La Viña, named for the vineyard that once grew here. *Chacina* (Iberian ham or sausage) and *chicharrones de Cádiz* (cold pork) served on waxed paper and washed down with manzanilla (sherry from Sanlúcar de Barrameda) are standard fare at the low wooden counter that has served bullfighters and flamenco singers, as well as dignitaries from around the world, since 1953. The walls are covered with colorful posters and other memorabilia from the annual carnival, flamenco shows, and ferias. **Known for:** atmospheric interior; delicious cold cuts; manzanilla. $ *Average main: €10* ⊠ *Corralón de los Carros 66* ☎ *956/213603.*

Código de Barra

$$$$ | SPANISH | Local produce comes under the Dutch microscope at one of the most innovative dining venues in Cádiz, under the direction of chef Léon Griffioen and earmarked by the *New York Times.* With only a few tables, and in minimalist surroundings, the restaurant, decked in black and gray, offers a tasting menu (€35 for 7 dishes, €47.50 for 10; pairing options available) that comes with several surprises including an "olive" and long, thin tortillitas de camarones—it is one explosion of flavor after another. **Known for:** creative take on traditional local cuisine; an excellent-value tasting menu; good and long wine list (ask the staff for pairing suggestions). $ *Average main: €35* ⊠ *Pl. Candelaria 12* ☎ *635/533303* 🕐 *Closed Sun.*

El Faro

$$ | SPANISH | This famous fishing-quarter restaurant near Playa de la Caleta is deservedly known as one of the best in the province. From the outside, it's one of many whitewashed houses with ocher details and shiny black lanterns; inside, it's warm and inviting, with half-tile walls, glass lanterns; oil paintings, and photos of old Cádiz. **Known for:** fresh fish; rice dishes; tapas. $ *Average main: €22* ✉ *Calle San Felix 15* ☎ *956/211068* ⊕ *www.elfarodecadiz.com.*

La Candela

$ | **SPANISH** | A block north of Plaza Candelaria and on one of Cádiz's narrow pedestrian streets, La Candela is a good place to try local fare with a modern twist. The salmorejo comes baked with pork loin tartare, the red tuna comes in a variety of ways, and several dishes have Asian touches, served tempura style or with wasabi sauce such as the fried anchovy with pea wasabi. **Known for:** tapas; homemade cheesecake; Spanish-Asian fusion food. $ *Average main: €10* ✉ *Calle Feduchy 1* ☎ *956/221822.*

 Hotels

Hotel Argantonio

$$ | **HOTEL** | This small, family-run hotel in the historic center of town combines traditional style and modern amenities. **Pros:** friendly and helpful staff; great location; good-size bathrooms. **Cons:** rooms in the original building on the small side; street-facing rooms can be noisy; not easy to find. $ *Rooms from: €120* ✉ *Calle Argantonio 3* ☎ *956/211640* ⊕ *www.hotelargantonio.com* ⮍ *17 rooms* ❖ *No meals.*

Hotel Patagonia Sur

$$ | **HOTEL** | With a handy central location just two blocks from the cathedral, this modern hotel offers functional and inexpensive lodging, especially during low season. **Pros:** central location; good value; top-floor rooms have a private terrace. **Cons:** small rooms; street noise can be intrusive; five-night minimum stay in summer. $ *Rooms from: €120* ✉ *Calle Cobos 11* ☎ *856/174647* ⊕ *www.hotelpatagoniasur.es* ⮍ *16 rooms* ❖ *No meals.*

Parador de Cádiz

$$$$ | **HOTEL** | With a privileged position overlooking the bay, this parador has spacious public areas and large modern rooms, most with balconies facing the sea. **Pros:** great views of the bay; pool; bright and cheerful. **Cons:** expensive parking; very quiet in the off season; lacks historic appeal of other paradores. $ *Rooms from: €200* ✉ *Av. Duque de Nájera 9* ☎ *956/226905* ⊕ *www.parador. es/en/paradores/parador-de-cadiz* ⮍ *124 rooms* ❖ *No meals.*

Chapter 14

GRANADA AND AROUND

Updated by
Joanna Styles

👁 Sights	🍴 Restaurants	🛏 Hotels	🛍 Shopping	🍸 Nightlife
★★★★★	★★★★☆	★★★★☆	★★★★☆	★★★★☆

WELCOME TO GRANADA AND AROUND

TOP REASONS TO GO

★ **Be seduced by the Alhambra:** Marvel at this extraordinary Moorish delight, a fortress-palace whose patios, courtyards, halls, baths, and gardens rank among the most magnificent in the world.

★ **Lose yourself in time:** Stroll the cobbled alleyways of the Albayzín, the ancient Arab quarter with its whitewashed facades, churches, convents, and simply stunning views to the Alhambra and the snow-capped Sierra Nevada beyond.

★ **Admire their resting places:** Visit the Capilla Real with the tombs of Spain's greatest monarchs, Isabella and Ferdinand, under whose watch modern day Spain was born and the New World discovered.

★ **Experience the real thing:** Tour the colorful Gypsy caves in Sacromonte and take in a finger-clicking, foot-tapping flamenco show.

★ **Taste the tapas:** Enjoy a complimentary tapa with your drink at any bar in Granada, often more of a minimeal than a mere mouthful.

Granada is compact and easy to navigate with the exception of the Albayzín whose charm lies in losing yourself in the maze of alleyways. Outside the center, prepare for some serious walking in hilly terrain (often on cobbled streets) or take taxis or buses.

1 La Alhambra. Perched on a verdant hill and home to Spain's greatest monument, La Alhambra stands tall over the city, offering panoramic views plus some fine hotels.

2 Realejo. Beneath La Alhambra, narrow cobbled streets and pleasant squares are home to fine palaces and mansions as well as bustling bars and restaurants.

3 Sacromonte. Hilly and riddled with caverns, Sacromonte is the heart of Granada's Gypsy community and its flamenco spirit.

4 Albayzín. Occupying the hillside opposite La Alhambra, the ancient Moorish quarter offers a labyrinth of white-washed alleyways, churches, squares with panoramic views, and boutique hotels and restaurants.

5 Centro. Flat and bustling, the center houses commercial Granada with its main shopping streets, leafy squares and fine architecture including the Cathedral and Capilla Real.

6 Priego de Córdoba. An olive farming town famous for its mansions and baroque churches.

7 Baeza. One of the best-preserved old towns in Spain.

8 Ubeda. Slightly larger than Baeza, this town is known for its architecture, artisan crafts, and olive groves. Shop for all your souvenirs here.

9 The Sierra Nevada. You'll find stunning mountain views and Europe's southernmost ski resort about 45 minutes from Granada.

10 The Alpujarras. The southern slopes of the Sierra Nevada have long been loved by artists and writers for their remoteness and stunning views.

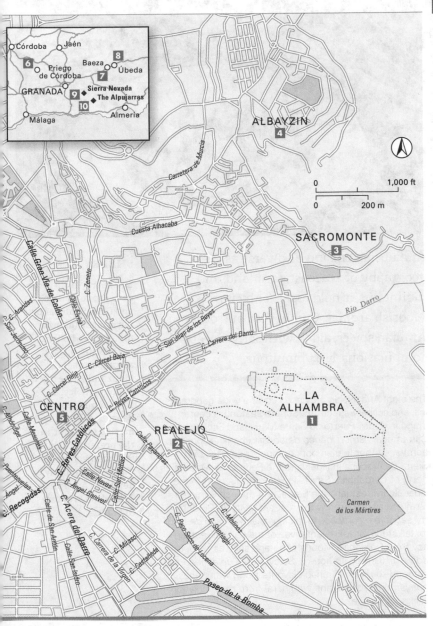

Córdoba   Jaén
6   Priego   Baeza   8
de Córdoba   Úbeda
GRANADA   7
9   Sierra Nevada
10   The Alpujarras
Málaga   Almería

Carretera de Murcia

Cuesta Alhacaba

ALBAYZIN
4

SACROMONTE
3

Río Darro

0   1,000 ft
0   200 m

Calle Gran Vía de Colón

C. Zenete

C. Argüelles

C. San Jerónimo

C. Elvira

C. San Juan de los Reyes

C. Carrera del Darro

C. Cárcel Baja

C. Cárcel Baja

C. Reyes Católicos

CENTRO
5

C. Reyes Católicos

REALEJO
2

LA
ALHAMBRA
1

Calle Pavaneras

Carmen
de los Mártires

Calle Mesones

C. Alhóndiga

C. Reyes Católicos

Calle Navas

Calle San Matías

C. Angel Ganivet

C. Angel

C. Recogidas

Puentezuelas

C. Acera del Darro

Calle de San Antón

C. Carrera de la Virgen

C. Mirasol

C. Castañeda

C. Molinos

C. Santiago

C. Paseo Salón de Lucena

Paseo de la Bomba

EATING AND DRINKING WELL IN ANDALUSIA

A bowl of gazpacho, with accompaniments to be added as desired.

Andalusian cuisine, as diverse as the geography of seacoast, farmland, and mountains, is held together by its Moorish aromas. Cumin seed and other Arabian spices, along with salty-sweet combinations, are ubiquitous.

The eight Andalusian provinces cover a wide geographical and culinary spectrum. Superb seafood is center stage in Cádiz, Puerto de Santa María, and Sanlúcar de Barrameda. *Jamón ibérico de bellota* (Iberian acorn-fed ham) and other Iberian pork products rule from the Sierra de Aracena in Huelva to the Pedroches Mountains north of Córdoba. In Seville look for products from the Guadalquivir estuary, the Sierra, and the rich Campiña farmland all prepared with great creativity. In Córdoba try *salmorejo cordobés* (a thick gazpacho), *rabo de toro* (oxtail stew), or representatives of the salty-sweet legacy from Córdoba's Moorish heritage such as *cordero con miel* (lamb with honey). Spicy *crema de almendras* (almond soup) is a Granada favorite along with *habas con jamón* (broad beans with ham) from the Alpujarran village of Trevélez.

SHERRY

Dry sherry from Jerez de la Frontera (fino) and from Sanlúcar de Barrameda (manzanilla), share honors as favorite tapas accompaniments. Manzanilla, the more popular choice, is fresher and more delicate, with a slight marine tang. Both are the preferred drinks at Andalusian *ferias* (fairs), particularly in Seville in April and Jerez de la Frontera in May.

COLD VEGETABLE SOUPS

Spain's most popular contribution to world gastronomy after paella may well be gazpacho, a simple peasant soup served cold and filled with scraps and garden ingredients. Tomatoes, cucumber, garlic, oil, bread, and chopped peppers are the ingredients, and side plates of chopped onion, peppers, garlic, tomatoes, and croutons accompany, to be added to taste. Salmorejo cordobés, a thicker cold vegetable soup with the same ingredients but a different consistency, is used to accompany tapas.

MOORISH FLAVORS

Andalusia's 781-year sojourn at the heart of Al-Andalus, the Moorish empire on the Iberian Peninsula, left as many tastes and aromas as mosques and fortresses. Cumin-laced *boquerones en adobo* (marinated anchovies) or the salty-sweet cordero con miel are two examples, along with coriander-spiked *espinacas con garbanzos* (spinach with garbanzo beans) and *perdiz con dátiles y almendras* (partridge stewed with dates and almonds). Desserts especially reflect the Moorish legacy in morsels such as *pestiños,* cylinders or twists of fried dough in anise-honey syrup.

Fried calamari with lemon.

Crispy fried fish are an Andalusian delicacy.

FRIED FISH

Andalusia is famous for its fried fish, from *pescaito frito* (fried whitebait) to *calamares fritos* (fried squid rings). Andalusians are masters of deep-frying techniques using very hot olive and vegetable oils that produce peerlessly crisp, dry *frituras* (fried seafood); much of Andalusia's finest tapas repertory is known for being served up piping hot and crunchy. Look for *tortillita de camarones,* a delicate lacework of tiny fried shrimp.

STEWS

Guisos are combinations of vegetables, with or without meat, cooked slowly over low heat. Rabo de toro is a favorite throughout Andalusia, though Córdoba claims the origin of this dark and delicious stew made from the tail of a fighting bull. The segments of tail are cleaned, browned, and set aside before leeks, onions, carrots, garlic, and bay leaves are stewed in the same pan. Cloves, salt, pepper, a liter of wine, and a half liter of beef broth are added to the stew with the meat, and they're all simmered for two to three hours until the meat is falling off the bone and thoroughly tenderized. *Alboronía,* also known as *pisto andaluz,* is a traditional stew of eggplant, bell peppers, and zucchini.

Nestling below the perennially snow-capped Sierra Nevada and rising majestically from a vast fertile place, Granada proudly offers visitors two jewels in Andalusia's crown: the Alhambra and the tomb of the Catholic Monarchs. The two aesthetics, Moorish and Christian pervade the entire city in its architecture, cuisine, handicrafts, and people.

The kingdom of Granada dates back to 1013 when it was founded by the Moorish Nasrid dynasty under whose reign, the city prospered as one of the richest in Spain for over four centuries. In 1491, split by internal squabbles, Boabdil, the "Rey Chico" (Boy King) gave Ferdinand of Aragón his opportunity to claim Granada for Castille. Spurred by Isabella's religious fanaticism, he laid siege to the city for seven months, and on January 2, 1492, Boabdil was forced to surrender the keys of the city.

Granada perches on three hills: the reddish-golf Alhambra palaces dominates the trio and the city skyline; on the opposite side across the small Darro River sprawls the Albayzín, Granada's historic Moorish quarter while time seems to have come to a standstill; and on the third hill sits the Sacromonte, studded with ancient caves and home to the city's Gypsies and flamenco.

All three areas are well worth exploring. The Alhambra ranks as the top must-see and merits a whole day of your visit. If your stay is longer, aim to tour the palace at night too. The Albayzín is an area best appreciated by a leisurely stroll and Sacromonte is an interesting detour before you descend the hills to the historic center below.

The maze of streets that make up the center harbor a bustling hub of commercial activity, yet another legacy of Granada's Moorish past. The main shopping streets, centering on the Puerta Real, are the Gran Vía de Colón, Reyes Católicos, Zacatín, and Recogidas. Most antiques shops are on Cuesta de Elvira and Alcaicería—off Reyes Católicos. Cuesta de Gomérez, on the way up to the Alhambra, also has several handicrafts shops and guitar workshops. Handicrafts have a distinct Moorish air, present in the ceramics, marquetry (especially the *taraceas*, wooden boxes with inlaid tiles on their lids), woven textiles, and silver-, brass-, and copper-ware.

Side trips from Granada give you the chance to experience some of the finest towns in eastern Andalusia. In the rolling olive groves and high mountains, you'll find gems such as Priego de Córdoba, home to some of the region's most impressive Baroque churches; Baeza and Úbeda, both with exceptional examples of Renaissance architecture; the Sierra Nevada, a paradise for mountain walkers and climbers; and the Alpujarras, one of Andalusia's most scenic mountain regions, dotted with white villages.

Planning

When to Go

The best months to go are October and November and April and May. It's blisteringly hot in the summer; if that's your only chance to come, plan on visiting Granada's Sierra Nevada to beat the heat. Autumn catches the cities going about their business, the temperatures are moderate, and you will rarely see a line form.

Getting Here and Around

AIR
Four daily flights connect Granada with Madrid and three connect it with Barcelona.

CONTACTS Aeropuerto de Granada. (*Aeropuerto Federico García Lorca*) ☎ *902/404704.*

BUS
Granada's main bus station is at Carretera de Jaén, 3 km (2 miles) northwest of the center of town beyond the end of Avenida de Madrid. Most buses operate from here, except for buses to nearby destinations such as Fuentevaqueros, Viznar, and some buses to Sierra Nevada, which leave from the city center's Plaza del Triunfo near the RENFE station. Luggage lockers (*la consigna*) are available at the main bus and train stations, and you can also leave your luggage at City Locker (Placeta de las Descalzas 3) and Plaza Nueva Lockers (Calle Imprenta 2).

Autocares Bonal operates buses between Granada and the Sierra Nevada. **ALSA** buses run to and from Las Alpujarras (3 times daily), Córdoba (9 times daily), Seville (9 times daily), Málaga (20 times daily), and Jaén, Baeza, Úbeda, Cazorla, Almería, Almuñécar, and Nerja (several times daily).

In Granada, **airport** buses (€3) run between the center of town and the airport, leaving roughly every hour 7 am–8:45 pm from the Palacio de Congresos and making a few other stops along the way to the airport. Times are listed at the bus stop.

Granada has an extensive public bus network within the city. You can buy 5-, 10-, and 20-trip discount passes on the buses and at newsstands. The single-trip fare is €1.40. Granada Cards include bus trips plus guaranteed tickets for the Alhambra and other main monuments (without having to wait in lines). The card costs from €40, saving at least a third on regular prices. You can purchase the cards at the municipal tourist office, but it's best to buy them online via (⊕ *www. granadatur.com/granada-card*) in advance of your visit; you can download them on your cell phone, or print at home or the tourist office.

CONTACTS ALSA. ☎ *902/422242* ⊕ *www. alsa.es.* **Granada Bus Station.** ⊠ *Ctra. Jaén, Granada* ☎ *902/422242.*

CAR
With the exception of parts of the Alpujarras, most roads in this region are smooth, and touring by car is one of the most enjoyable ways to see the countryside. Local tourist offices can advise about scenic drives. One good route heads northwest from Seville on the A66 passing through stunning scenery; turn northeast on the A461 to Santa Olalla de Cala to the village of Zufre, dramatically set at the edge of a gorge. Backtrack and continue on to Aracena. Return via the Minas de Riotinto (signposted from

Aracena), which will bring you back to the A66 heading east to Seville.

TAXI

Taxis are plentiful and may be hailed on the street or from specified taxi stands. Fares are reasonable, and meters are strictly used; the minimum fare is about €4. You are not required to tip taxi drivers, although rounding off the amount is appreciated. Uber is available in Granada and Baeza.

Expect to pay around €20–€25 for cab fare from the airport to the city center.

CONTACTS Taxi Genil. ☎ *958/132323*. **Tele Radio Taxi.** ☎ *958/280654*.

TRAIN

There are regular trains from Seville and Almería, but service from Málaga and Córdoba is less convenient, necessitating a change at Antequera. A new AVE high-speed fast track entered operation in mid-2019; it reduced journey times considerably (50 minutes to Málaga and 90 minutes to Seville). There are a couple of daily trains from Madrid, Valencia, and Barcelona.

CONTACTS Train Station. ✉ *Av. de los Andaluces, Granada* ☎ *912/320320*.

Hotels

The Parador de Granada, next to the Alhambra, is a magnificent way to enjoy Granada. Hotels on the Alhambra hill, especially the parador, must be reserved far in advance. Lodging establishments in Granada's city center, around the Puerta Real and Acera del Darro, can be unbelievably noisy, so if you're staying there, ask for a room toward the back. Though Granada has plenty of hotels, it can be difficult to find lodging during peak tourist season (Easter through late October).

Rental accommodations bookable on portals such as Airbnb are popular in large towns and cities, although quality varies so double-check reviews before you book.

Not all hotel prices include value-added tax (I.V.A.) and the 10% surcharge may be added to your final bill. Check when you book. *Hotel reviews have been shortened. For full information, visit Fodors. com.*

Restaurants

Eating out is an intrinsic part of the Andalusian lifestyle. Whether it's sharing some tapas with friends over a prelunch drink or a three-course à la carte meal, many Andalusians eat out at some point during the day. Unsurprisingly, there are literally thousands of bars and restaurants throughout the region catering to all budgets and tastes.

At lunchtime, check out the *menús del día* (daily menus) offered by many restaurants, usually three courses and excellent value (expect to pay €8–€15, depending on the type of restaurant and location). Roadside restaurants, known as *ventas,* usually provide good food in generous portions and at reasonable prices. Be aware that many restaurants add a service charge (*cubierto*), which can be as much as €3 per person, and some restaurant prices don't include value-added tax (*impuesto sobre el valor añadido/I.V.A.*) at 10%. Note also that restaurants with tasting menus (*menús de degustación*) usually require everyone at the table to have the menu.

Andalusians tend to eat later than their fellow Spaniards: lunch is 2–4 pm, and dinner starts at 9 pm (10 pm in the summer). In cities, many restaurants are closed Sunday night, and fish restaurants tend to close on Monday; in inland towns and cities, some restaurants close for all of August.

Restaurant reviews have been shortened. For full information, visit Fodors. com.

What It Costs in Euros			
$	$$	$$$	$$$$
RESTAURANTS			
under €12	€12–€17	€18–€22	over €22
HOTELS			
under €90	€90–€125	€126–€180	over €180

Tours

Cabalgar Rutas Alternativas
EXCURSIONS | This is an established Alpujarras equestrian agency that organizes horseback riding in the Sierra Nevada. ⊠ *C. Ermita, Bubión* ☎ *958/763135* ⊕ *www.ridingandalucia.com* ✉ *Rides from €25, tours from €795.*

Cycling Country
BICYCLE TOURS | For information about cycling tours around Granada (Andalusia and Spain), 1–10 days long, contact this company, run by husband-and-wife team Geoff Norris and Maggi Jones in a town about 55 km (33 miles) away. ⊠ *Calle Salmerones 18, Alhama de Granada* ☎ *958/360655* ⊕ *www.cyclingcountry. com* ✉ *From €40.*

Glovento Sur
AIR EXCURSIONS | Up to five people at a time are taken in balloon trips above Granada, Ronda, and Seville. ⊠ *Placeta Nevot 4, #1A, Granada* ☎ *958/290316* ⊕ *www.gloventosur.com* ✉ *From €165.*

Granada Tapas Tours
GUIDED TOURS | Long-time British resident Gayle Mackie offers a range of tapas tours lasting up to three hours. ⊠ *Granada* ☎ *619/444984* ⊕ *www.granadatapastours.com* ✉ *From €40, including 6 tapas.*

Nevadensis
GUIDED TOURS | Based in the Alpujarras, Nevadensis leads guided hiking, climbing, and skiing tours of the Sierra Nevada. Note that prices are per group. ⊠ *Pl. de la Libertad, Pampaneira* ☎ *958/763127* ⊕ *www.nevadensis.com* ✉ *From €150.*

Visitor Information

CONTACTS Municipal Tourist Office. ⊠ *Pl. del Carmen 9, Centro* ☎ *958/248280* ⊕ *www.granadatur.com.* **Provincial Tourist Office.** ⊠ *Calle Cárcel Baja 3, Centro* ☎ *958/247128* ⊕ *www.turgranada.es.*

La Alhambra

Sights

★ Alhambra
CASTLE/PALACE | With more than 2.7 million visitors a year, the Alhambra is Spain's most popular attraction. This sprawling palace-fortress was the last bastion of the 800-year Moorish presence on the Iberian Peninsula. Composed of royal residential quarters, court chambers, baths, and gardens, surrounded by defense towers and massive walls, the Alhambra is an architectural gem. The courtyards, patios, and halls offer an ethereal maze of Moorish arches, columns, and domes containing intricate stucco carvings and patterned ceramic tiling. The heart of the Alhambra, the **Palacios Nazaríes** contain delicate apartments, lazy fountains, and tranquil pools, and are divided into three sections: the *mexuar*, where business, government, and palace administration were headquartered; the *serrallo*, state rooms where the sultans held court; and the harem. The beautiful **Sala de los Abencerrajes** (Hall of the Moors) has a fabulous, ornate ceiling and star-shape cupola reflected in the pool below. ⊠ *Cuesta de Gomérez, Alhambra* ☎ *858/953616 tickets, 958/027971 information* ⊕ *www.alhambra-patronato. es/en* ✉ *From €2, Museo de la Alhambra and Palacio de Carlos V free* ☉ *Museo de Bellas Artes and Museo de la Alhambra closed Mon.*

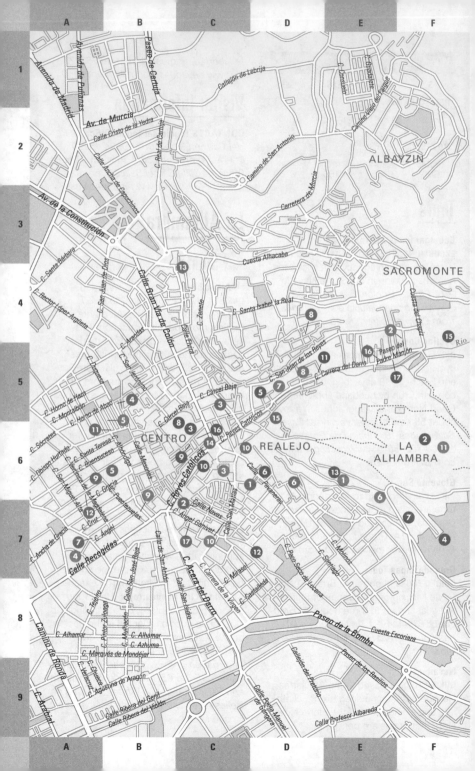

G   H   I

Granada

Sights ▼

1 Abadía del
  Sacromonte I3
2 Alhambra F6
3 Capilla Real.............. C6
4 Carmen de los
  Mártires................... F7
5 Casa de los Pisa D5
6 Casa de los Tiros........ D6
7 Casa-Museo de
  Manuel de Falla.......... F7
8 Cathedral C6
9 Corral del Carbón........ C6
10 Centro José Guerrero... C6
11 El Bañuelo D5
12 El Cuarto Real D7
13 Fundación
   Rodríguez-Acosta/
   Instituto
   Gómez-Moreno E6
14 Museo Cuevas del
   Sacromonte G3
15 Palacio de los
   Córdova F4
16 Palacio Madraza......... C6
17 Paseo Padre Manjón.... E5

Restaurants ▼

1 Alacena de las
  Monjas................... D6
2 Bar Los Diamantes C7
3 Bodegas Castañeda..... C5
4 Café Botánico.......... B5
5 Cunini B6
6 Damasqueros D6
7 El Quinteto A7
8 El Trillo D4
9 La Bodega de
  Antonio................... A6
10 La Brujidera C6
11 Oliver..................... B6
12 Om-Kalsum A6
13 Paprika................... C4
14 Pastelería
   López-Mezquita......... C6
15 Pilar del Toro D5
16 Ruta del Azafrán E5
17 Tinta Fina C7

Hotels ▼

1 Carmen de la
  Alcubilla del Caracol E6
2 Casa Morisca F4
3 Gar Anat Hotel
  Boutique C6
4 Hospes Palacio
  de los Patos A7
5 Hostal Rodri B5
6 Hotel Alhambra
  Palace..................... E6
7 Hotel Casa 1800......... D5
8 Hotel Palacio
  Santa Inés D5
9 Hotel Párraga Siete B7
10 Palacio de los Navas.... C7
11 Parador de Granada..... F6

Calle Siete Cuestas

Camino del Sacromonte

Darro

0   1,000 ft
0   200 m

Camino de la Silla del Moro

Carmen
de los
Mártires

Paseo de la Sabica

Av. Santa María de la Alhambra

Paseo de las Palmas

Carretera de la Sierra

KEY

1 Exploring Sights
1 Restaurants
1 Hotels

G   H   I

Carmen de los Mártires
HOUSE | Up the hill from the Hotel Alhambra Palace, this turn-of-the-20th-century *carmen* (private villa) and its gardens—the only area open to tourists—are like a Generalife in miniature. ✉ *Paseo de los Mártires, Alhambra* ☎ *958/849103* 🎟 *Free.*

Casa-Museo de Manuel de Falla
HOUSE | The composer Manuel de Falla (1876–1946) lived and worked for many years in this rustic house tucked into a charming hillside lane with lovely views of the Alpujarras. In 1986 Granada paid homage to him by naming its new concert hall (down the street from the Carmen de los Mártires) the Auditorio Manuel de Falla—from this institution, fittingly, you have a view of his little white house. Note the bust in the small garden: it's placed where the composer once sat to enjoy the sweeping vista. ✉ *Calle Antequeruela Alta 11, Alhambra* ☎ *958/222189* 🌐 *museomanueldefalla.com* 🎟 *€3* 🕒 *Closed Mon.*

Hotels

★ Carmen de la Alcubilla del Caracol
$$$ | **B&B/INN** | In a traditional granadino villa on the slopes of the Alhambra, this privately run lodging is one of Granada's most stylish hotels. **Pros:** great views; bright, airy rooms; walking distance to the Alhambra. **Cons:** tough climb in hot weather. [$] *Rooms from: €160* ✉ *Calle Aire Alta 12, Alhambra* ☎ *958/215551* 🌐 *www.alcubilladelcaracol.com* 🕒 *Closed mid-July–Aug.* 🛏 *7 rooms* 🍴 *No meals.*

Hotel Alhambra Palace
$$$$ | **HOTEL** | Built by a local duke in 1910, this neo-Moorish hotel is on leafy grounds at the back of the Alhambra hill, and has a very *Arabian Nights* interior (think orange-and-brown overtones, multicolor tiles, and Moorish-style arches and pillars). **Pros:** bird's-eye views; location near the Alhambra; large, warmly decorated rooms. **Cons:** steep climb up from Granada; often packed with business people (it doubles as a convention center); might be too grandiose for some. [$] *Rooms from: €200* ✉ *Pl. Arquitecto García de Paredes 1, Alhambra* ☎ *958/221468* 🌐 *www.h-alhambrapalace.es* 🛏 *126 rooms* 🍴 *No meals.*

★ Parador de Granada
$$$$ | **HOTEL** | This is Spain's most expensive and most popular parador, right within the walls of the Alhambra. **Pros:** good location; lovely interiors; garden restaurant. **Cons:** no views in some rooms; removed from city life; very expensive. [$] *Rooms from: €300* ✉ *Calle Real de la Alhambra, Alhambra* ☎ *958/221440* 🌐 *www.paradorsofspain.com* 🛏 *40 rooms* 🍴 *No meals.*

Realejo

Sights

Casa de los Tiros
MUSEUM | This 16th-century palace, adorned with the coat of arms of the Grana Venegas family who owned it, was named House of the Shots for the musket barrels that protrude from its facade. The stairs to the upper-floor displays are flanked by portraits of miserable-looking Spanish royals, from Ferdinand and Isabella to Felipe IV. The highlight is the carved wooden ceiling in the Cuadra Dorada (Hall of Gold), adorned with gilded lettering and portraits of royals and knights. Old lithographs, engravings, and photographs show life in Granada in the 19th and early 20th centuries. ✉ *Calle Pavaneras 19, Realejo-San Matías* ☎ *600/143175* 🌐 *www.museosdeandalucia.es/web/museocasadelostirosdegranada* 🎟 *€2* 🕒 *Closed Mon.*

El Cuarto Real
BUILDING | Just a block away from Casa de los Tiros is the beautifully restored El Cuarto Real, a 13th-century Nasrid palace

Continued on page 280

ALHAMBRA: PALACE-FORTRESS

 Floating mirage-like on its promontory overlooking Granada, the mighty and mysterious Alhambra shimmers vermilion in the clear mountain air, with the white peaks of the Sierra Nevada rising behind it. This sprawling palace-fortress, named from the Arabic for "red citadel" (*al-Qal'ah al-Hamra*), was the last bastion of the 800-year Moorish presence on the Iberian Peninsula. Composed of royal residential quarters, court chambers, baths, and gardens, surrounded by defense towers and massive walls, the Alhambra is an architectual gem where Moorish kings worked and played—and murdered their enemies.

LOOK UP

Among the stylistic
elements you can see
in the Alhambra are
Arabesque geometrical
designs, and elaborate
Mocárabe arches.

Built of perishable materials, the Alhambra was meant to be forever replenished and replaced by succeeding generations. The Patio de los Leones' (above) has recently been restored to its original appearance.

INSIDE THE FORTRESS

More than 3 million annual visitors come to the Alhambra today, making it Spain's top attraction. Vistors revel in the palace's architectural wonders, most of which had to be restored after the alterations made after the Christian reconquest of southern Spain in 1492 and the damage from an 1821 earthquake. Incidentally, Napoléon's troops commandeered the site in 1812 with intent to level it but their attempts were foiled.

The courtyards, patios, and halls offer an ethereal maze of Moorish arches, columns, and domes containing intricate stucco carvings and patterned ceramic tiling. The intimate arcades, fountains, and light-reflecting pools throughout are identified in the ornamental inscriptions as physical renderings of paradise taken from the Koran and Islamic poetry. The contemporary visitor to this dreamlike space feels the fleeting embrace of a culture that brought its light to a world emerging from medieval darkness.

ARCHITECTURAL TERMS

Arabesque: An ornament or decorative style that employs flower, foliage, or fruit, and sometimes geometrical, animal, and figural outlines to produce an intricate pattern of interlaced lines.

Mocárabe: A decorative element of carved wood or plaster based on juxtaposed and hanging prisms resembling stalactites. Sometimes called *muquarna* (honeycomb vaulting), the impression is similar to a beehive and the "honey" has been described as light.

Mozárabe: Sometimes confused with the Mocárabe, the term Mozárabe refers to Christians living in Moorish Spain. Thus, Christian artistic styles or recourses in Moorish architecture (such as the paintings in the Sala de los Reyes) are also identified as *mozárabe*, or, in English, mozarabic.

Mudéjar: This word refers to Moors living in Christian Spain. Moorish artistic elements in Christian architecture, such as horseshoe arches in a church, also are referred to as Mudéjar.

ALHAMBRA'S ARCHITECTURAL HIGHLIGHTS

Court of the Lions

The **columns** used in the construction of the Alhambra are unique, with extraordinarily slender cylindrical shafts, concave base moldings, and carved rings decorating the upper extremities. The capitals have simple cylindrical bases under prism-shaped heads decorated in a variety of vegetal motifs. Nearly all of these columns support false arches constructed purely for decorative purposes. The 124 columns surrounding the Patio de los Leones (Court of the Lions) are the best examples.

Cursive epigraphy

Cursive epigraphy is used to quote the Koran and Arabic poems. Considered the finest example of this are the Ibn-Zamrak verses that decorate the walls of the Sala de las Dos Hermanas.

Glazed ceramic tiles covered with geometrical patterns in primary colors cover the walls of the Alhambra with a profusion of styles and shapes. Red, blue, and yellow are the colors of magic in Sufi tradition, while green is the life-giving color of Islam.

Ceramic tiles

The **horseshoe arch**, widening before rounding off with lower ends extending around the circle until they begin to converge, was the quintessential Moorish architectural innovation, used not only for aesthetic and decorative purposes but because it allowed greater height than the classical, semicircular arch inherited from the Greeks and Romans. The horseshoe arch also had a mystical significance in recalling the shape of the *mihrab*, the prayer niche in the *qibla* wall of a mosque indicating the direction of prayer and suggesting a door to Mecca or to paradise. Horseshoe arches and arcades are found throughout the Alhambra.

Gate of Justice

The Koran describes paradise as "gardens underneath which rivers flow," and **water** is used as a practical and ornamental architectural element throughout the Alhambra. Whether used musically, as in the canals in the Patio de los Leones or visually, as in the reflecting pool of the Patio de los Arrayanes, water is used to enhance light, enlarge spaces, or provide musical background for a desert culture in love with the beauty and oasis-like properties of hydraulics in all its forms.

Alhambra fountains

The Alcazaba was built chiefly by Nasrid kings in the 1300s.

LAY OF THE LAND

The complex has three main parts: the Alcazaba, the Palacio Nazaríes (Nasrid Royal Palace), and the Generalife. Across from the main entrance is the original fortress, the **Alcazaba**. Here, the watchtower's great bell was once used to announce the opening and closing of the irrigation system on Granada's great plain.

A wisteria-covered walkway leads to the heart of the Alhambra, the **Palacios Nazaríes**. Here, delicate apartments, lazy fountains, and tranquil pools contrast vividly with the hulking fortifications outside. It is divided into three sections: the *mexuar*, where business, government, and palace administration were headquartered; the *serrallo*, a series of state rooms where the sultans held court and entertained their ambassadors; and the *harem*, which in its time was entered only by the sultan, his family, and their most trusted servants, most of them eunuchs. Nearby is the Renaissance **Palacio de Carlos V** (Palace of Charles V), featuring a perfectly square exterior but a circular interior courtyard. Designed by Pedro Machuca, a pupil of Michelangelo, it is where the sultan's private apartments once stood. Part of the building houses the free **Museo de la Alhambra**, devoted to Islamic art. Upstairs is the more modest **Museo de Bellas Artes**.

Over on Cerro del Sol (Hill of the Sun) is **Generalife**, the ancient summer palace of the Nasrid kings.

PALACIO NAZARÍES

ALCAZABA

TO GENERALIFE →

Jardines del Partal

PALACIO DE CARLOS V

TIMELINE

1238 First Nasrid king, Ibn el-Ahmar, begins Alhambra.

1391 Nasrid Palaces is completed.

1492 Boabdil surrenders Granada to Ferdinand and Isabella, parents of King Henry VIII's first wife, Catherine of Aragon.

1524 Carlos V begins Renaissance Palace.

1812 Napoléonic troops arrive with plans to destroy Alhambra.

1814 The Duke of Wellington sojourns here to escape the pressures of the Peninsular War.

1829 Washington Irving lives on the premises and writes Tales of the *Alhambra*, reviving interest in the crumbling palace.

1862 Granada municipality begins Alhambra restoration that continues to this day.

ALHAMBRA'S PASSAGES OF TIME

From Columbus's commissioning to a bloody murder, historic events as well as everyday affairs happened between these walls.

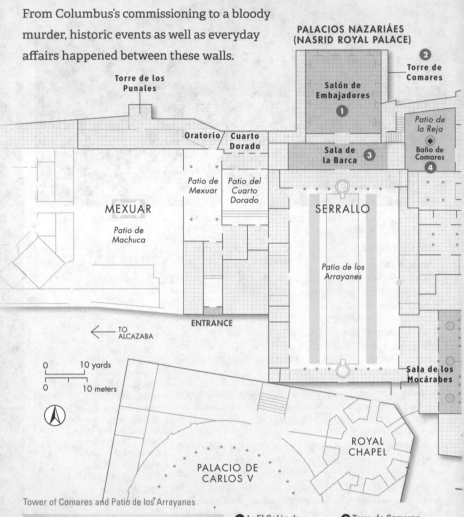

PALACIOS NAZARIÁES (NASRID ROYAL PALACE)

Torre de los Punales

Torre de Comares **2**

Salón de Embajadores **1**

Patio de la Reja

Oratorio / Cuarto Dorado

Sala de la Barca **3**

Baño de Comares **4**

Patio de Mexuar / Patio del Cuarto Dorado

MEXUAR

SERRALLO

Patio de Machuca

Patio de los Arrayanes

ENTRANCE

← TO ALCAZABA

0 ——— 10 yards
0 ——— 10 meters

Sala de los Mocárabes

PALACIO DE CARLOS V

ROYAL CHAPEL

Tower of Comares and Patio de los Arrayanes

1 In El Salón de Embajadores, Boabdil drew up his terms of surrender, and Christopher Columbus secured royal support for his historic voyage in 1492. The carved wooden ceiling is a portrayal of the seven Islamic heavens, with six rows of stars topped by a seventh-heaven cupulino or micro-cupola.

2 Torre de Comares, a lookout in the corner of this hall is where Carlos V uttered his famous line, "Ill-fated the man who lost all this."

3 Mistakenly named from the Arabic word *baraka* (divine blessing), Sala de la Barca has a carved wooden ceiling often described as an inverted boat.

Sala de los Reyes

7 Shhh, don't tell a secret here. In the Sala de los Ajimeces, a whisper in one corner can be clearly heard from the opposite corner.

8 In the Sala de las Dos Hermanas, twin slabs of marble embedded in the floor are the "sisters," though Washington Irving preferred the story of a pair of captive Moorish beauties.

9 In the Patio de Los Leones (Court of the Lions), a dozen crudely crafted lions (restored to their former glory in 2012) support the fountain at the center of this elegant courtyard, representing the signs of the zodiac sending water to the four corners.

10 In the Sala de los Abencerrajes, Muley Hacen (father of Boabdil) murdered the male members of the Abencerraje family in revenge for their chief's seduction of his daughter Zoraya. The rusty stains in the fountain are said to be bloodstains left by the pile of Abencerraje heads.

The star-shaped cupola, reflected in the pool, is considered the Alhambra's most beautiful example of stalactite or honeycomb vaulting. The octagonal dome over the room is best viewed at sunset when the 16 small windows atop the dome admit sharp, low sunlight that refracts kaleidoscopically through the beehive-like prisms.

11 In the Sala de los Reyes, the ceiling painting depicts the first 10 Nasrid rulers. It was painted by a Christian artist since Islamic artists were not allowed to usurp divine power by creating human or animal figures.

The overhead painting of the knight rescuing his lady from a savage man portrays chivalry, a concept introduced to Europe by Arabic poets.

12 The terraces of Generalife grant incomparable views of the city.

Generalife gardens

4 The Baño de Comares is where the sultan's favorites luxuriated in brightly tiled pools beneath star-shape pinpoints of light from the ceiling above.

5 El Peinador de la Reina, a nine-foot-square room atop a small tower was the Sultana's boudoir. The perforated marble slab was used to infiltrate perfumes while the queen performed her toilette. Washington Irving wrote his *Tales of the Alhambra* in this romantic tree-house-like perch.

6 Sultana Zoraya often found refuge in this charming little balcony (Mirador de Daraxa) overlooking the Lindaraja garden.

Map labels:
Peinador de la Reina 5
Apartamientos de Carlos V
Patio de Lindaraja
HAREM
Mirador de Daraxa 6
Sala de los Ajimeces 7
Sala de las Dos Hermanas 8
Patio de los Leones 9
Sala de los Reyes 11
Cistern
Sala de los Abencerrajes 10
TO JARDINES DEL PARTAL, GENERALIFE 12

which has decorations almost identical to the Alhambra. Only the fortified tower remains standing with its exquisite *qubba* (reception room) with stunning walls and ceiling motifs. The adjoining modern extension houses temporary art exhibitions, and the formal gardens make a peaceful place to rest. ✉ *Pl. de los Campos 6, Realejo-San Matías* ☎ *958/849111* 🎟 *Free.*

Fundación Rodríguez-Acosta/Instituto Gómez-Moreno
MUSEUM | This nonprofit organization was founded at the behest of the painter José Marí Rodríguez-Acosta. Inside a typical carmen, it houses works of art, archaeological finds, and a library collected by the Granada-born scholar Manuel Gómez-Moreno Martínez. Other exhibits include valuable and unique objects from Asian cultures and the prehistoric and classical eras. ✉ *Callejón Niños del Rollo 8, Realejo-San Matías* ☎ *958/227497* 🌐 *www.fundacionrodriguezacosta.com* 🎟 *From €5.*

Restaurants

Alacena de las Monjas
$$$ | SPANISH | Just as popular with locals as visitors, this restaurant in the heart of the Realejo district sits on the first floor and basement of a 14th-century convent—you can see the original clay vats that supplied the water downstairs. You can also dine outside in the lovely, quiet square. **Known for:** historic setting; red tuna dishes; steak. [$] *Average main: €20* ✉ *Pl. del Padre Suarez 5, Realejo-San Matías* ☎ *958/229519* 🌐 *www.alacenadelasmonjas.com* ⏲ *Closed Tues. No dinner Mon.*

★ Damasqueros
$$$$ | SPANISH | The modern, wood-paneled dining room and warm lighting form the perfect setting for the creative Andalusian cuisine cooked here by local chef Lola Marín, who learned her trade with some of Spain's top chefs, such as Martín Berasategui. The tasting menu changes weekly and always includes in-season produce in its five courses (cold and hot starters, fish, meat, and dessert). **Known for:** fresh local produce; wine pairing; service. [$] *Average main: €40* ✉ *Calle Damasqueros 3, Realejo-San Matías* ☎ *958/210550* 🌐 *www.damasqueros.com* ⏲ *Closed Mon. No dinner Sun.*

Hotels

Gar Anat Hotel Boutique
$$ | HOTEL | Once a humble hostel on the Granada leg of the Camino de Santiago pilgrimage route, the 17th-century restored palace now offers stylish boutique accommodation. **Pros:** eclectic decor; central location; generous breakfast. **Cons:** street noise can be intrusive; some rooms small and dark; slight challenge to find by car. [$] *Rooms from: €110* ✉ *Placeta de Peregrinos 2, Realejo-San Matías* ☎ *958/225528* 🌐 *www.hotelgaranat.com* 🛏 *15 rooms* 🍴 *No meals.*

Sacromonte

The third of Granada's three hills, the Sacromonte rises behind the Albayzín. The hill is covered with prickly pear cacti and riddled with caverns. The Sacromonte has long been notorious as a domain of Granada's Gypsies and thus a den of thieves and scam artists, but its reputation is largely undeserved. The quarter is more like a quiet Andalusian *pueblo* (village) than a rough neighborhood. Many of the quarter's colorful *cuevas* (caves) have been restored as middle-class homes, and some of the old spirit lives on in a handful of *zambras* (flamenco performances in caves, which are garishly decorated with brass plates and cooking utensils). These shows differ from formal flamenco shows in that the performers mingle with you, usually dragging one or two onlookers onto the floor for an improvised dance lesson. Ask your hotel to book you a spot on a cueva tour, which usually includes a walk through the neighboring Albayzín and a drink at a tapas bar in addition to the zambra.

◉ Sights

Abadía de Sacromonte

CAVE | The caverns on Sacromonte are thought to have sheltered early Christians. In the 15th century, treasure hunters found bones inside and assumed they belonged to San Cecilio, the city's patron saint. Thus, the hill was sanctified—*sacro monte* (holy mountain)—and this abbey was built on its summit. Tours in English are at 2 and 5:30. ✉ *C. del Sacromonte, Sacromonte* ☎ *958/221445* ⊕ *sacromonteabbey.com* ✉ *€5.*

Museo Cuevas del Sacromonte

MUSEUM | The ethnographical museum here shows how people lived in this area, and elsewhere in this interesting complex looks at Granada's flora and fauna. During the summer months, there are live flamenco concerts. ⚠ **It's a steep walk to reach the center, even if you take Bus No. C2 (from Plaza Nueva) to shorten the distance.** ✉ *Barranco de los Negros, Sacromonte* ☎ *958/215120* ⊕ *www.sacromontegranada.com* ✉ *€5.*

Albayzín

Covering a hill of its own, across the Darro ravine from the Alhambra, this ancient Moorish neighborhood is a mix of dilapidated white houses and immaculate carmenes. It was founded in 1228 by Moors who had fled Baeza after Ferdinand III captured the city. Full of cobblestone alleyways and secret corners, the Albayzín guards its old Moorish roots jealously, though its 30 mosques were converted to baroque churches long ago. A stretch of the Moors' original city wall runs beside the ridge called the **Cuesta de la Alhacaba**. If you're walking—the

Bicycling in Granada

At the foot of the Iberian Peninsula's tallest mountain—the 11,427-foot Mulhacén peak—Granada offers challenging mountain-biking opportunities, and spinning through the hairpin turns of the Alpujarras east of Granada is both scenic and hair-raising. For organized cycling tours, contact **Cycling Country**.

best way to explore—you can enter the Albayzín from either the Cuesta de Elvira or the Plaza Nueva. Alternatively, on foot or by taxi (parking is impossible), begin in the Plaza Santa Ana and follow the Carrera del Darro, Paseo Padre Manjón, and Cuesta del Chapíz. One of the highest points in the quarter, the plaza in front of the church of San Nicolás (*€2; open mornings only*)—the **Mirador de San Nicolás**—has one of the finest views in all of Granada: on the hill opposite, the turrets and towers of the Alhambra form a dramatic silhouette against the snowy peaks of the Sierra Nevada. The sight is most magical at dawn, dusk, and on nights when the Alhambra is floodlighted. Take note of the mosque just next to the church—views of the Alhambra from the mosque gardens are just as good as those from the Mirador de San Nicolás and a lot less crowded. Interestingly, given the area's Moorish history, the two sloping, narrow streets of Calderería Nueva and Calderería Vieja that meet at the top by the Iglesia San Gregorio have developed into something of a North African bazaar, full of shops and vendors selling clothes, bags, crafts, and trinkets. The numerous little teahouses and restaurants here have a decidedly Moroccan flavor.

Many of the streets are cobbled so wear sturdy footwear with thick soles.

Sights

Casa de los Pisa

MUSEUM | Originally built in 1494 for the Pisa family, the claim to fame of this house is its relationship to San Juan de Dios, who came to Granada in 1538 and founded a charity hospital to take care of the poor. Befriended by the Pisa family, he was taken into their home when he fell ill in February 1550. A month later, he died there, at the age of 55. Since that time, devotees of the saint have traveled from around the world to this house with a stone Gothic facade, now run by the Hospital Order of St. John. Inside are numerous pieces of jewelry, furniture, priceless religious works of art, and an extensive collection of paintings and sculptures depicting St. John. ✉ *Calle Convalecencia 1, Albaicín* ☎ *958/222144* 🎟 *€3* 🕒 *Closed Sun.*

El Bañuelo (*Little Bath House*)

HOT SPRINGS | These 11th-century Arab steam baths might be a little dark and dank now, but try to imagine them some 900 years ago, filled with Moorish beauties. Back then, the dull brick walls were backed by bright ceramic tiles, tapestries, and rugs. Light comes in through star-shape vents in the ceiling, à la a bathhouse in the Alhambra. ✉ *Carrera del Darro 31, Albaicín* ☎ *958/229738* 🎟 *€5 (ticket includes admission to Dar al-Horra), free Sun.*

Palacio de los Córdova

CASTLE/PALACE | At the end of the Paseo Padre Manjón, this 17th-century noble house today holds Granada's municipal archives and is used for municipal functions and art exhibits. You're free to wander about the large garden, the only area open to visitors. ✉ *Cuesta del Chapiz 4, Albaicín* ☎ *958/180021* 🎟 *Free.*

Paseo Padre Manjón

PROMENADE | Along the Río Darro, this paseo is also known as the Paseo de los Tristes (Promenade of the Sad Ones) because funeral processions once passed this way. The cafés and bars here are a good place for a coffee break. The park, dappled with wisteria-covered pergolas, fountains, and stone walkways, has a stunning view of the Alhambra's northern side. ✉ *Albaicín.*

Restaurants

★ El Trillo

$$$ | **SPANISH** | Tucked away in the warren of alleyways in a restored Albayzín villa, this lovely small restaurant offers perhaps the best food in the area. There's a formal dining room, outside garden with pear and quince trees, plus a roof terrace with Alhambra views. **Known for:** fine dining; views of the Alhambra; rice with wild boar. [$] *Average main: €20* ✉ *Callejón del Aljibe del Trillo 3, Albaicín* ☎ *958/225182* 🌐 *www.restaurante-eltrillo.com.*

Paprika

$$ | **VEGETARIAN** | Inside a pretty brick building and with an informal terrace sprawling over the wide steps of the Cuesta de Abarqueros, Paprika offer unpretentious vegan food. Most ingredients and wines are organic, and dishes include salads, stir-fries, and curries, such as Thai curry with tofu, coconut, and green curry sauce. **Known for:** choice of vegan food; value plate of the day; organic ingredients. [$] *Average main: €12* ✉ *Cuesta de Abarqueros 3, Albaicín* ☎ *958/804785* 🌐 *www.paprika-granada.com.*

Pilar del Toro

$$ | **SPANISH** | This bar and restaurant, just off Plaza Nueva, is in a 17th-century palace with a stunning patio (complete with original marble columns) and peaceful garden. The menu emphasizes meat dishes such as *chuletas de cordero* (lamb chops) and the house specialty, braised *rabo de toro* and giant croquettes known as *croquetón*. **Known for:** atmospheric patio; oxtail; elegant upstairs restaurant. $ *Average main: €16* ✉ *Calle Hospital de Santa Ana 12, Albaicín* ☎ *958/225470* ⊕ *pilardeltoro.es.*

Ruta del Azafrán

$$ | SPANISH | A charming surprise nestled at the foot of the Albayzín by the Darro—this sleek contemporary space in the shadow of the Alhambra offers a selection of specialties. The menu is interesting and diverse and includes dishes like chicken pastela, tuna *tataki* (a method of pounding fish in Japanese cuisine) with pineapple, and several different coucous dishes. **Known for:** wide choice of dishes; views of the Alhambra, especially at night; tasting menus. $ *Average main: €16* ✉ *Paseo de los Tristes 1, Albaicín* ☎ *958/226882* ⊕ *rutadelazafran.com.*

 Hotels

★ **Casa Morisca**

$$$ | B&B/INN | The architect who owns this 15th-century building transformed it into a hotel so distinctive that he received Spain's National Restoration Award for his preservation of original architectural elements, including barrel-vaulted brickwork, wooden ceilings, and the original pool. **Pros:** historic location; award-winning design; easy parking. **Cons:** stuffy interior rooms; no full restaurant on-site; slightly out of the town center. $ *Rooms from: €140* ✉ *Cuesta de la Victoria 9, Albaicín* ☎ *958/221100* ⊕ *www.hotelcasamorisca.com* ⇆ *14 rooms* ◯ *Free breakfast.*

Hotel Casa 1800

$$$ | HOTEL | A stone's throw from the Paseo de los Tristes, this restored 17th-century mansion has a fine, tiered patio. **Pros:** historic building; deluxe suite has balcony with views of the Alhambra; walking distance to most sights. **Cons:** on a street that doesn't permit cars; rooms are small (but comfortable); no bar.

$ *Rooms from: €165* ✉ *Calle Benalua 11, Albaicín* ☎ *958/210700* ⊕ *www. hotelcasa1800granada.com* ⇆ *25 rooms* ◯ *No meals.*

Hotel Palacio Santa Inés

$$$ | HOTEL | It's not often you get to stay in a 16th-century palace—and this one has a stunning location in the heart of the Albayzín. **Pros:** perfect location for exploring the Albayzín; quirky interiors; some rooms have Alhambra views. **Cons:** can't get there by car; some rooms rather dark; breakfast is average. $ *Rooms from: €140* ✉ *Cuesta de Santa Inés 9, Albaicín* ☎ *958/222362* ⊕ *www.palaciosantaines.es* ⇆ *35 rooms* ◯ *No meals.*

 Performing Arts

FLAMENCO
Cueva de la Rocío

DANCE | This is a good spot for authentic flamenco shows, staged nightly at 9, 10, and 11. ✉ *C. del Sacromonte 70, Albaicín* ☎ *958/227129* ⊕ *cuevalarocio.es.*

El Tabanco

MUSIC CLUBS | In the heart of the Albayzín, this small venue is an art gallery by day and live music venue (mostly flamenco and jazz) by night. Book in advance to be sure of a seat. ✉ *Cuesta de San Gregorio 24, Albaicín* ☎ *662/137046* ⊕ *www. eltabanco.com.*

El Templo del Flamenco

DANCE | Slightly off the beaten track (take a taxi to get here) and less touristy because of it, this venue has shows at 8 and 10 daily. ✉ *Calle Parnaleros Alto 41, Albaicín* ☎ *622/500052* ⊕ *templodelflamenco.com.*

Eshavira Club

MUSIC CLUBS | At this dimly lighted club you can hear sultry jazz. There's also flamenco at 11 pm on Friday. Admission fee includes a drink. ✉ *Calle Postigo de la Cuna 2, Albaicín* ☎ *958/290829.*

Jardines de Zoraya

DANCE | This show doesn't take place in a cave, but the music and dance are some of the most authentic available. Daily flamenco shows are at 8 and 10:30 pm, and at 3 pm on weekends. ⊠ *Calle Panaderos 32, Albaicín* ☎ *958/206266* ⊕ *www.jardinesdezoraya.com.*

Peña La Platería

DANCE | This private club in the Albayzín is devoted to flamenco. Performances are usually on Thursday and Saturday evenings—check the club's Facebook page for details (⊕ *www.facebook.com/plateriaflamenco*). ⊠ *Calle Plazoleta de Toqueros 7, Albaicín* ☎ *958/210650.*

Centro

Sights

Capilla Real (*Royal Chapel*)

RELIGIOUS SITE | Catholic monarchs Isabella of Castile and Ferdinand of Aragón are buried at this shrine. When Isabella died in 1504, her body was first laid to rest in the Convent of San Francisco. The architect Enrique Egas began work on the Royal Chapel in 1506 and completed it 15 years later, creating a masterpiece of the ornate Gothic style now known in Spain as Isabelline. In 1521, Isabella's body was transferred to the Royal Chapel crypt, joined by that of her husband, Ferdinand, and later her daughter, Juana la Loca (Joanna the Mad); son-in-law, Felipe el Hermoso (Philip the Handsome); and Prince Felipe of Asturias. The **crypt** containing the coffins is simple, but it's topped by elaborate marble tombs showing Ferdinand and Isabella lying side by side. The **altarpiece** comprises 34 carved panels depicting religious and historical scenes. The **sacristy** holds Ferdinand's sword, Isabella's crown and scepter, and a fine collection of Flemish paintings once owned by Isabella. ⊠ *Calle Oficios, Centro* ☎ *958/227848* ⊕ *www.capillarealgranada.com* ☜ *€5.*

Cathedral

RELIGIOUS SITE | Carlos V commissioned the cathedral in 1521 because he considered the Capilla Real "too small for so much glory" and wanted to house his illustrious late grandparents someplace more worthy. Carlos undoubtedly had great intentions, as the cathedral was created by some of the finest architects of its time: Enrique Egas, Diego de Siloé, Alonso Cano, and sculptor Juan de Mena. Alas, his ambitions came to little, for the cathedral is a grand and gloomy monument, not completed until 1714 and never used as the crypt for his grandparents (or parents). Enter through a small door at the back, off the Gran Vía. Old hymnals are displayed throughout, and there's a museum, which includes a 14th-century gold-and-silver monstrance given to the city by Queen Isabella. ⊠ *Gran Vía, Centro* ☎ *958/222959* ☜ *€5 (including audio guide)* ⊗ *Closed Sun. morning.*

Centro José Guerrero

MUSEUM | Just across a lane from the cathedral and Capilla Real, this building houses colorful modern paintings by José Guerrero. Born in Granada in 1914, Guerrero traveled throughout Europe and lived in New York in the 1950s before returning to Spain. The center also runs excellent temporary contemporary art shows. ⊠ *Calle Oficios 8, Centro* ☎ *958/225185* ⊕ *www.centroguerrero.es* ☜ *Free* ⊗ *Closed Mon.*

Corral del Carbón (*Coal House*)

HOUSE | This building was used to store coal in the 19th century, but its history is much longer. Dating to the 14th century, it was used by Moorish merchants as a lodging house, and then by Christians as a theater. It's one of the oldest Moorish buildings in the city and the only Arab structure of its kind in Spain. ⊠ *Calle Mariana Pineda, Centro* ☜ *Free.*

Palacio Madraza

CASTLE/PALACE | This building conceals the Islamic seminary built in 1349 by Yusuf I.

The intriguing baroque facade is elaborate; inside, across from the entrance, an octagonal room is crowned by a Moorish dome. It hosts occasional free art and cultural exhibitions. ✉ *Calle Zacatín, Centro* ☎ *958/241299* ⧫ *€2.*

🍴 Restaurants

Bar Los Diamantes

$$ | TAPAS | This spit and sawdust bar is a big favorite with locals and draws crowds whatever the time of year. Specialties include fried fish and seafood—try the *surtido de pescado* (assortment of fried fish) to sample the best—as well as *mollejas fritas* (fried lambs' brains). **Known for:** fried fish; communal tables; busy atmosphere. $ *Average main: €14* ✉ *Calle Navas 28, Centro* ☎ *958/222572* ⊕ *www.barlosdiamantes.com.*

Bodegas Castañeda

$$$ | SPANISH | A block from the cathedral across Gran Vía, this is a delightfully typical Granada bodega with low ceilings and dark wood furniture. In addition to the wines, specialties here are plates of cheese, pâté, and *embutidos* (cold meats). **Known for:** tapas; atmospheric bar; Spanish tortilla with creamy aioli. $ *Average main: €18* ✉ *Calle Almireceros 1–3, Centro* ☎ *958/215464.*

★ Café Botánico

$$ | TAPAS | Southeast of Granada's cathedral, this is a modern hot spot, a world apart from Granada's usual traditional tapas bar. Here you'll find a bright-orange-and-beige interior and an eclectic crowd of students, families, and businesspeople. **Known for:** international menu; good-value lunch deal; homemade desserts. $ *Average main: €15* ✉ *Calle Málaga 3, Centro* ☎ *958/271598.*

Cunini

$$$$ | SPANISH | Around the corner from the cathedral, this is one of Granada's longest-established fish restaurants. Catch-of-the day fish and shellfish, fresh from the boats at Motril, are displayed in the window at the front of the tapas bar, adjacent to the cozy wood-paneled dining room. **Known for:** fresh seafood; the only place in town serving angulas (glass eels); outdoor dining. $ *Average main: €22* ✉ *Pl. Pescadería 14, Centro* ☎ *958/250777* ⊗ *Closed Mon.*

El Quinteto

$$ | SPANISH | Don't let the rather impersonal modern exterior put you off because behind the bland-coffeeshop-doors lies one of the city's best eateries. The gluten-free establishment is known for several dishes on the menu although the *cochinillo confitado* (glazed suckling pig) and braised oxtail are established local favorites. **Known for:** suckling pig; gluten-free choices; traditional and modern tapas. $ *Average main: €15* ✉ *Calle Solarillo de Gracia 4, Centro* ☎ *958/264815* ⊕ *www.facebook.com/ elquintetogranada* ⊗ *Closed Sun. and Mon.*

La Bodega de Antonio

$$ | SPANISH | Just off Calle Puentezuelas, this authentic patio complete with original pillars provides a cozy vibe. Specials include the house cod (with prawns and clams) and Galician-style octopus, best enjoyed with a *cerdito* (a "little pig" ceramic jug of sweet white wine, so named for its snout pourer). **Known for:** generous portions; tapas; Galician-style octopus. $ *Average main: €12* ✉ *Calle Jardines 4, Centro* ☎ *958/252275* ⊗ *Closed Wed. and Aug.*

★ La Brujidera

$$ | TAPAS | Also known simply as Casa de Vinos (Wine House), this place, up a pedestrian street just behind Plaza Nueva, is a must for Spanish wine lovers. The cozy interior is reminiscent of a ship's cabin, with wood paneling lining the walls, along with bottles of more than 150 Spanish wines. **Known for:** long wine list; meat and cheese boards; vermouth and sherries on tap. $ *Average main: €12* ✉ *Monjas del Carmen 2, Centro* ☎ *958/222595* ⊗ *Closed 1 wk in Feb.*

Oliver

$$ | **SPANISH** | The interior may look a bit bare, but whatever this fish restaurant lacks in warmth it makes up for with the food. Less pricey than its neighbor Cunini, it serves simple but high-quality dishes like grilled mullet, dorado baked in salt, prawns with garlic, and monkfish in saffron sauce. **Known for:** tapas bar; fresh fish; migas (fried bread crumbs). [$] *Average main: €16* ✉ *Pl. Pescadería 12, Centro* ☎ *958/262200* 🌐 *restauranteoliver.com* 🕒 *Closed Sun.*

Om-Kalsum

$ | **MOROCCAN** | The Moroccan tapas at this small and bustling venue make a pleasant change from the traditional local fare. Tagine, couscous, and kefta are all menu staples where you'll also find a selection of Middle Eastern dishes, also available in vegetarian versions. **Known for:** Moroccan tapas; selection of tapas; lively atmosphere. [$] *Average main: €8* ✉ *Calle Jardines 17, Centro.*

Pastelería López-Mezquita

$ | **SPANISH** | Sweet and savory treats come into their own at this family-owned business in the city center. Top of the specialty list are *piononos* (sponge bites filled with caramel and custard) and pastela (Moroccan chicken pie). **Known for:** piononos (sponge bites with custard); cakes and cookies; pastela. [$] *Average main: €5* ✉ *Calle Reyes Católicos 39, Centro* ☎ *958/221205.*

Tinta Fina

$$$ | **SPANISH** | Underneath the arches just off Puerta Real, this modern bar and restaurant has a reputation for being one of Granada's most chic venues. This trendy spot is especially known for fresh seafood, including oysters and red shrimp. **Known for:** seafood; cocktail and G&T menus; chic atmosphere. [$] *Average main: €20* ✉ *Calle Angel Ganivet 5, Centro* ☎ *958/100041* 🌐 *www.tintafinarestaurante.com.*

Hotels

Hospes Palacio de los Patos

$$$$ | **HOTEL** | This beautifully restored palace is unmissable, sitting proudly on its own in the middle of one of Granada's busiest shopping streets. **Pros:** central location; historic setting; great spa and restaurant. **Cons:** expensive parking; some street noise; basement rooms are dark. [$] *Rooms from: €200* ✉ *Calle Solarillo de Gracia 1, Centro* ☎ *958/535790* 🌐 *www.hospes.es* 🛏 *42 rooms* 🍴 *No meals.*

★ Hostal Rodri

$ | **HOTEL** | This very comfortable and quiet hostel lies conveniently off Plaza de la Trinidad near the cathedral and is a good option for cheaper lodging in a city with so many upscale accommodations. **Pros:** central location; clean, comfortable rooms; value. **Cons:** some rooms on small side; no direct car access; could be too basic for some. [$] *Rooms from: €55* ✉ *Calle Laurel de las Tablas 9, Centro* ☎ *958/288043* 🌐 *www.hostalrodri.com* 🛏 *10 rooms* 🍴 *No meals.*

Hotel Párraga Siete

$ | **HOTEL** | This family-run hotel in the heart of the old quarter within easy walking distance of sights and restaurants offers excellent value and amenities superior to its official two-star rating. **Pros:** central, quiet location; good on-site restaurant; easy nearby parking. **Cons:** difficult to access by car; interiors might be too sparse for some; no historic character. [$] *Rooms from: €80* ✉ *Calle Párraga 7, Centro* ☎ *958/264227* 🌐 *www.hotelparragasiete.com* 🛏 *20 rooms* 🍴 *No meals.*

Palacio de los Navas

$$ | **B&B/INN** | In the center of the city, this palace was built by aristocrat Francisco Navas in the 16th century and it later became the Casa de Moneda (the Mint); its original architectural features blend well with modern ones. **Pros:** great location; peaceful oasis during the day;

rooms are set around a beautiful interior patio. **Cons:** can be noisy at night; breakfast uninspiring. [$] *Rooms from: €120* ✉ *Calle Navas 1, Centro* ☎ *958/215760* 🌐 *www.hotelpalaciodelosnavas.com* 🛏 *19 rooms* 🍴 *Free breakfast.*

Nightlife

Bohemia Jazz Café
MUSIC CLUBS | This atmospheric jazz bar has piano performances and occasional live bands. ✉ *Pl. de los Lobos 11, Centro.*

Shopping

Artesanías González
CRAFTS | Not far from La Alhambra, this is one of the best and longest-established places to buy taracea on handmade chessboards, boxes, side tables, and coasters. ✉ *Cuesta de Gomérez 12, Centro* ☎ *858/122382.*

Espartería San José
CRAFTS | For wicker baskets and esparto-grass mats and rugs, head to this shop off the Plaza Pescadería. ✉ *Calle Jáudenes 3, Centro* ☎ *958/267415.*

Outskirts of Granada

Sights

Casa-Museo Federico García Lorca
MUSEUM | Granada's most famous native son, the poet Federico García Lorca, gets his due here, in the middle of a park devoted to him on the southern fringe of the city. Lorca's onetime summer home, **La Huerta de San Vicente,** is now a museum (guided tours only)—run by his niece Laura García Lorca—with such artifacts as his beloved piano and changing exhibits on specific aspects of his life. ✉ *Parque García Lorca, Virgen Blanca, Arabial* ☎ *958/258466* 🌐 *www.huertadesanvicente.com* 🎟 *€3 (free Wed.)* 🕒 *Closed Mon.*

Monasterio de la Cartuja
RELIGIOUS SITE | This Carthusian monastery in northern Granada (2 km [1 mile] from the center of town and reached by Bus No. N7) was begun in 1506 and moved to its present site in 1516, though construction continued for the next 300 years. The exterior is sober and monolithic, but inside are twisted, multicolor marble columns; a profusion of gold, silver, tortoiseshell, and ivory; intricate stucco; and the extravagant sacristy—it's easy to see why it has been called the Christian answer to the Alhambra. Among its wonders are the trompe l'oeil spikes, shadows and all, in the Sanchez Cotan cross over the *Last Supper* painting at the west end of the refectory. If you're lucky, you may see small birds attempting to land on these faux perches. ✉ *C. de Alfacar, Cartuja* ☎ *958/161932* 🎟 *€5.*

Parque de las Ciencias (*Science Park*)
MUSEUM | **FAMILY** | Across from Granada's convention center and easily reached on Bus No. C4, this museum (one of the most visited in Andalusia) has a planetarium and interactive demonstrations of scientific experiments. The 165-foot observation tower has views to the south and west. ✉ *Av. del Mediterráneo s/n, Zaidín* ☎ *958/131900* 🌐 *www.parqueciencias.com* 🎟 *From €7* 🕒 *Closed Mon.*

Restaurants

Restaurante Arriaga
$$$$ | **BASQUE** | Run by Basque chef Álvaro Arriaga, this restaurant sits on the top floor of the Museo de la Memoria de Andalucía just outside the city (it's well worth the taxi drive) and enjoys panoramic views of Granada with the Sierra Nevada behind. Choose from two tasting menus (€55 for six dishes and €70 for nine dishes), both with one surprise after another. À la carte specialties include *arroz de perdiz* (rice with partridge), slow-cooked (40 hours) beef, and hake cheeks in traditional green sauce. **Known for:** tasting menus; culinary surprises (the menu

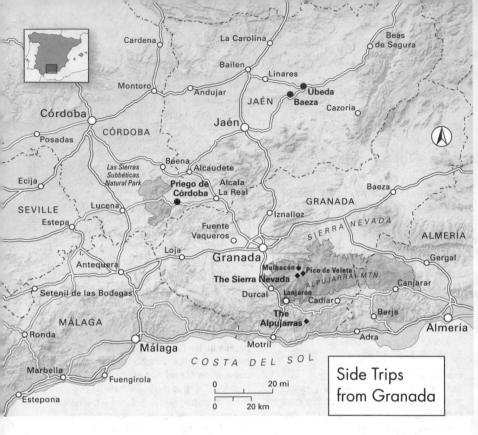

Side Trips
from Granada

starts with dessert!); panoramic views of Granada. $ *Average main: €28* ✉ *Av. de las Ciencias 2, Armilla* ☎ *958/132619* ⊕ *www.restaurantearriaga.com* ⊗ *Closed Mon., no dinner Sun. or Tues.*

Priego de Córdoba

103 km (64 miles) southeast of Córdoba, 25 km (15 miles) southeast of Zuheros.

The jewel of Córdoba's countryside is Priego de Córdoba, a town of 23,500 inhabitants at the foot of Monte Tinosa. Wander down Calle del Río, opposite the town hall, to see 18th-century mansions, once the homes of silk merchants. At the end of the street is the Fuente del Rey (King's Fountain), with some 130 water jets, built in 1803. Don't miss the lavish baroque churches of La Asunción and La Aurora or the Barrio de la Villa, an old Moorish quarter with a maze of narrow streets of white-walled buildings. If you plan to visit several monuments, buy the Bono turístico (€5) to save on admission prices.

GETTING HERE AND AROUND

Priego has reasonable bus service from Córdoba (2½ hours) and Granada (1½ hours), although your best bet is to visit by car en route to either of these cities. Once there, it's perfect for pedestrian exploration.

VISITOR INFORMATION

CONTACTS Priego de Córdoba. ✉ *Pl. de la Constitución 3* ☎ *957/700625* ⊕ *www. turismodepriego.com.*

Restaurants

La Pianola (*Casa Pepe*)
$ | SPANISH | Expect cheap, cheerful, and lively dining at this small venue, a couple of blocks south of the castle and usually packed with locals. On the menu are usual Córdoba staples including oxtail, but the specialties here are the *saquito de boletus* (mushroom pastry) and *carrillada de cerdo* (roast pork cheek). **Known for:** value dining; good tapas; delicious French toast for dessert. $ *Average main: €9* ✉ *Calle Obispo Caballero 6* ☎ *957/700409* ☾ *Closed Mon.*

🛏 Hotels

Hotel-Museo Patria Chica
$ | HOTEL | This charming hotel opened in 2017, housed in a fully restored 19th-century mansion, and is complete with a pretty interior patio and peaceful private garden. **Pros:** central location; period furnishings; pool and restaurant on-site. **Cons:** quiet; slightly out of the town center; some rooms face the street. $ *Rooms from: €75* ✉ *Carrera de las Monjas 47* ☎ *957/058385* ⊕ *www.hotelpatriachica.com* 🛌 *15 rooms* 🍴 *Free breakfast.*

La Posada Real
$ | B&B/INN | In the heart of Priego's Barrio de la Villa, this restored basic town house has two sections, each with geranium-decked balconies and typical Andalusian touches. **Pros:** friendly owner; traditional town house; center of town. **Cons:** rooms on the small side; car access difficult; slightly basic facilities. $ *Rooms from: €60* ✉ *Calle Real 14* ☎ *957/541910* 🛌 *7 rooms* 🍴 *No meals.*

Baeza

48 km (30 miles) northeast of Jaén on N321.

The historic town of Baeza, nestled between hills and olive groves, is one of the best-preserved old towns in Spain. Founded by the Romans, it later housed the Visigoths and became the capital of a Moorish taifa, one of some two dozen mini-kingdoms formed after the Ummayad Caliphate was subdivided in 1031. Ferdinand III captured Baeza in 1227, and for the next 200 years it stood on the frontier of the Moorish kingdom of Granada. In the 16th and 17th centuries, local nobles gave the city a wealth of Renaissance palaces.

GETTING HERE AND AROUND
Frequent buses (16 per day on weekdays, 10 per day on weekends; *ALSA* ☎ *902/422242* ⊕ *www.alsa.es*) connect Baeza with Jaén (45 minutes) and Úbeda, although a private car is the best option given the remoteness of the town and that you may want to explore nearby Úbeda on the same day. Baeza is small and flat, and with its sights clustered around the very center it's very easy to explore on foot.

TOURS
Semer Guided Tours
GUIDED TOURS | Two-hour guided tours around Baeza (in English, minimum two people, Tuesday–Sunday) recount the history, culture, and traditions of the town. Tours of Úbeda are also available, with a discount for combined tours of both towns. ✉ *Baeza* ☎ *953/757916* ⊕ *www.semerturismo.com* ☞ *From €11.*

VISITOR INFORMATION
CONTACTS Baeza. ✉ *Pl. del Pópulo* ☎ *953/779982.*

Sights

Ayuntamiento (*Town Hall*)
GOVERNMENT BUILDING | Baeza's town hall was designed by cathedral master Andrés de Vandelvira. The facade is ornately decorated with a mix of religious and pagan imagery. Look between the balconies for the coats of arms of Felipe II, the city of Baeza, and the magistrate Juan de Borja. Ask at the tourist office about visits to the *salón de plenos,* a meeting hall with painted, carved woodwork. ✉ *Pl. Cardenal s/n.*

Baeza Cathedral
RELIGIOUS SITE | Originally begun by Ferdinand III on the site of a former mosque, the cathedral was largely rebuilt by Andrés de Vandelvira, architect of Jaén's cathedral, between 1570 and 1593, though the west front has architectural influences from an earlier period. A fine 14th-century rose window crowns the 13th-century Puerta de la Luna (Moon Door). Don't miss the baroque silver monstrance (a vessel in which the consecrated Host is exposed for the adoration of the faithful), which is carried in Baeza's Corpus Christi processions—the piece is kept in a concealed niche behind a painting, but you can see it in all its splendor by putting a coin in a slot to reveal the hiding place. Next to the monstrance is the entrance to the clock tower, where a small donation and a narrow spiral staircase take you to one of the best views of Baeza. The remains of the original mosque are in the cathedral's Gothic cloisters. ✉ *Pl. de Santa María* ☎ *953/744157* 🎫 *€4.*

Casa del Pópulo
HOUSE | Located in the central paseo—where the Plaza del Pópulo (or Plaza de los Leones) and Plaza de la Constitución (or Plaza del Mercado Viejo) merge to form a cobblestone square—this graceful town house was built around 1530. The first Mass of the Reconquest was supposedly celebrated on its curved balcony; it now houses Baeza's tourist office. ✉ *Pl. del Pópulo.*

Convento de San Francisco
RELIGIOUS SITE | This 16th-century convent is one of Vandelvira's religious architectural masterpieces. The building was spoiled by the French army and partially destroyed by a light earthquake in the early 1800s, but you can see its restored remains. ✉ *Calle de San Francisco.*

Museo de Baeza
MUSEUM | Tucked away behind the tourist office, the Baeza Museum is in itself a museum piece. Housed in a 15th-century noble palace, the facade and interiors are home to an interesting display of Baeza's history, from Roman remains to more recent religious paintings. ✉ *Calle Casas Nuevas* ☎ *953/741582* 🎫 *€2* 🕐 *Closed Mon.*

Restaurants

Palacio de Gallego
$$$ | **SPANISH** | With a special location next to the cathedral, this is one of the best restaurants in town, known most of all for its barbecue dishes. Red tuna steak stars on the *asados* (roasted dishes) menu, but you can also try meat, including game, as well as *almejas* (clams). **Known for:** barbecue; red tuna steak; outdoor terrace. [$] *Average main: €20* ✉ *Calle Santa Catalina* ☎ *667/760184* 🕐 *Closed Tues. No lunch Wed.*

Hotels

Hotel Puerta de la Luna
$$ | **HOTEL** | This beautifully restored 17th-century palace, one of Baeza's best accommodation options, is centered on two patios—one with a pond and views of the cathedral tower, the other with a small pool. **Pros:** stunning architecture; central location; good food on-site. **Cons:** difficult to find; basic breakfast; a bit too quiet. [$] *Rooms from: €100* ✉ *Calle Canónigo Melgares Raya 7* ☎ *953/747019*

⊕ www.hotelpuertadelaluna.com ↩ 44 rooms ¶◯◀ No meals.

Úbeda

9 km (5½ miles) northeast of Baeza on N321.

Úbeda's *casco antiguo* (old town) is one of the most outstanding enclaves of 16th-century architecture in Spain. It's a stunning surprise in the heart of Jaén's olive groves, set in the shadow of the wild Sierra de Cazorla mountain range. For crafts enthusiasts, this is Andalusia's capital for many kinds of artisan goods. Follow signs to the Zona Monumental, where there are countless Renaissance palaces and stately mansions, though most are closed to the public.

GETTING HERE AND AROUND

Frequent buses (16 weekdays, 10 weekends; *ALSA* ☎ *902/422242 ⊕ www.alsa. es*) connect Úbeda with Jaén (one hour) and Baeza, although a private car is the best option given the remoteness of the town and that you may want to explore nearby Baeza in the same day. Úbeda's sights are all within easy reach of the center so exploring on foot is easy.

TOURS
Semer Guided Tours
Two-hour guided tours around Úbeda (in English, minimum two people, Tuesday through Sunday) recount the history, culture, and traditions of the town. Tours of Baeza are also available, with a discount on combined tours of both towns. *⊠ Calle Juan Montilla 3 ☎ 953/757916 ⊕ www.semerturismo.com ☞ From €11.*

◉ Sights

Ayuntamiento Antiguo (*Old Town Hall*)
BUILDING | Begun in the early 16th century but restored as a beautiful arcaded baroque palace in 1680, the former town hall is now a conservatory of music. From the hall's upper balcony, the town council

watched celebrations and autos-da-fé ("acts of faith"—executions of heretics sentenced by the Inquisition) in the square below. You can't enter the town hall, but on the north side you can visit the 13th-century church of San Pablo, with an Isabelline south portal. *⊠ Pl. Primero de Mayo ⊹ Off Calle María de Molina ☎ 953/750637 ☜ Church free ⊘ Closed Mon.*

Hospital de Santiago
HOSPITAL—SIGHT | Sometimes jokingly called the Escorial of Andalusia (in allusion to Felipe II's monolithic palace and monastery outside Madrid), this is a huge, angular building in the modern section of town and yet another one of Vandelvira's masterpieces in Úbeda. The plain facade is adorned with ceramic medallions, and over the main entrance is a carving of Santiago Matamoros (St. James the Moorslayer) in his traditional horseback pose. Inside are an arcaded patio and a grand staircase. Now a cultural center, it holds many of the events at the International Spring Dance and Music Festival (*⊕ festivaldeubeda.com*). *⊠ Av. Cristo Rey ☎ 953/750842 ☜ Free ⊘ Closed Sun. in July, and weekends in Aug.*

Sacra Capilla de El Salvador
RELIGIOUS SITE | The Plaza Vázquez de Molina, in the heart of the casco antiguo, is the site of this building, which is photographed so often that it's become the city's unofficial symbol. It was built by Vandelvira, but he based his design on some 1536 plans by Diego de Siloé, architect of Granada's cathedral. Considered one of the masterpieces of Spanish Renaissance religious art, the chapel was sacked in the frenzy of church burnings at the outbreak of the civil war, but it retains its ornate western facade and altarpiece, which has a rare Berruguete sculpture. *⊠ Pl. Vázquez de Molina ☎ 609/279905 ☜ €5 (free Mon.–Sat. 9:30–10, Sun. 6–7).*

★ Sinagoga del Agua

RELIGIOUS SITE | This 13th-century synagogue counts among Úbeda's most amazing discoveries. Entirely underground and known as the Water Synagogue for the wells and natural spring under the mikvah, it comprises seven areas open to visitors, including the main area of worship, mikvah, women's gallery, and rabbi's quarters. During summer solstice the sun's rays illuminate the stairway, providing the only natural light in the synagogue. ✉ *Calle Roque Rosas* ☎ *953/758150* 🌐 *www.sinagogadelagua.com* 🎟 *€5.*

🍴 Restaurants

Asador de Santiago

$$$ | **SPANISH** | At this adventurous restaurant just off the main street, the chef prepares both Spanish classics, like white shrimp from Huelva or suckling pig from Segovia, and innovative dishes like *ensalada de queso de cabra en hojaldre con calabaza* (salad with goat's cheese pastry and pumpkin) and *lomo de ciervo en escabeche* (venison steak in pickled sauce). The candle-filled interior is more traditional than the bar and has terra-cotta tiles, dark wood furnishings, and crisp white linens. **Known for:** fine dining; Spanish classics; roast meats. [$] *Average main: €20* ✉ *Av. Cristo Rey 4* ☎ *953/750463* 🌐 *asadordesantiago.com* 🕒 *No dinner Sun.*

Cantina La Estación

$$$ | **SPANISH** | Meals at one of Úbeda's top restaurants are served in a train-carriage interior decorated with railway memorabilia, while tapas reign at an outside terrace and at the bar. Highly rated by locals who flock here on weekends, this distinctive eatery serves creative dishes like *humus con berenjenas, pimientos rojos y anchoas* (eggplant hummus with red peppers and anchovies), *bombón de foie envuelto en oro y queso de cabra* (gold-glazed foie gras with goat's cheese), and *bacalao confitado* (caramelized cod). **Known for:** extensive and reasonably priced wine menu; value tasting menu; fun interior. [$] *Average main: €18* ✉ *Cuesta de la Rodadera 1* ☎ *687/777230* 🕒 *Closed Wed. No dinner Tues.*

Taberna Misa de 12

$$$ | **SPANISH** | This small bar has the best position on the leafy square, one block from the Plaza del Ayuntamiento, and the pleasant outside terrace is the best place to enjoy the tapas. Despite the tiny kitchen, the menu stretches long and includes homemade croquettes in a selection of flavors and roasted peppers, red tuna tartare, and Iberian pork cuts. **Known for:** tapas; wine list; outdoor dining. [$] *Average main: €18* ✉ *Pl. Primero de Mayo 7* ☎ *622/480049* 🌐 *www.misade12.com* 🕒 *No dinner Mon.*

🛏 Hotels

★ Palacio de la Rambla

$$ | **B&B/INN** | In old Úbeda, this stunning 16th-century mansion has been in the same family since it was built—it still hosts the Marquesa de la Rambla when she's in town—and eight of the rooms are available for overnighters. **Pros:** central location; elegant style; all rooms have access to the garden. **Cons:** little parking; grandiosity not for everyone; some areas a little tired. [$] *Rooms from: €125* ✉ *Pl. del Marqués 1* ☎ *953/750196* 🌐 *www.palaciodelarambla.com* 🕒 *Closed July and Aug.* 🔑 *8 rooms* 🍽 *Free breakfast.*

★ Parador de Úbeda

$$$ | **HOTEL** | Designed by Andrés de Vandelvira, this splendid parador is in a 16th-century ducal palace in a prime location on the Plaza Vázquez de Molina, next to the Capilla del Salvador. **Pros:** elegant surroundings; perfect location; excellent restaurant. **Cons:** parking is difficult; church bells in the morning; could be too formal for some. [$] *Rooms from: €130* ✉ *Pl. Vázquez de Molina s/n*

☎ *953/750345* ⊕ *www.parador.es* ⤴ *36 rooms* ❏⊘ *No meals.*

🛍 Shopping

Alfarería Góngora
CERAMICS/GLASSWARE | All kinds of ceramics are sold here. ✉ *Calle Cuesta de la Merced 32* ☎ *953/754605.*

Alfarería Tito
CERAMICS/GLASSWARE | The extrovert Juan Tito can often be found at the potter's wheel in his rambling shop, which is packed with ceramics of every size and shape. ✉ *Pl. del Ayuntamiento 12* ☎ *953/751302* ⊕ *www.alfareriatito.com.*

Melchor Tito
CERAMICS/GLASSWARE | You can see classic green-glazed items—the focus of Melchor Tito's work—being made in his workshops in Calle Valencia and Calle Fuenteseca 17, which are both also shops. ✉ *Calle Valencia 44* ☎ *953/753692.*

Pablo Tito
CERAMICS/GLASSWARE | Clay sculptures of characters from *Don Quixote,* fired by Pablo Tito in an old Moorish-style kiln, are the specialty of this studio and shop. There is also a museum (Monday through Saturday 8–2 and 4–8, Sunday 10–2) on the premises. ✉ *Calle Valencia 22* ☎ *953/751496.*

The Sierra Nevada

Village of Pradollano: 38 km (24 miles) southeast of Granada.

The drive southeast from Granada to Pradollano along the A395—Europe's highest road, by way of Cenes de la Vega—takes about 45 minutes. It's wise to carry snow chains from mid-November to as late as April or even May. The mountains here make for an easy and worthwhile excursion, especially for those keen on trekking.

👁 Sights

Mulhacén
MOUNTAIN—SIGHT | To the east of Granada, the mighty Mulhacén, the highest peak in mainland Spain, soars to 11,427 feet. Legend has it that it came by its name when Boabdil, the last Moorish king of Granada, deposed his father, Abul Hassan Ali, and had the body buried at the summit of the mountain so that it couldn't be desecrated. For more information on trails to the two summits, check the National Park Service's site (⊕ *www.nevadensis.com*). ✉ *Sierra Nevada.*

Pico de Veleta
MOUNTAIN—SIGHT | Peninsular Spain's second-highest mountain is 11,125 feet high. The view from its summit across the Alpujarras to the sea at distant Motril is stunning, and on a very clear day you can see the coast of North Africa. When the snow melts (July and August) you can drive or take a minibus from the Albergue Universitario (Universitario mountain refuge) to within around 400 yards of the summit—a trail takes you to the top in around 45 minutes. ■**TIP➔ It's cold up there, so take a warm jacket and scarf, even if Granada is sizzling hot.** ✉ *Sierra Nevada.*

🏃 Activities

SKIING
Estación de Esquí Sierra Nevada
SKIING/SNOWBOARDING | **FAMILY** | Europe's southernmost ski resort is one of its best equipped. At the Pradollano and Borreguiles stations, there's good skiing from December through April or May; each has a special snowboarding circuit, floodlighted night slopes, a children's ski school, and après-ski sun and swimming in the Mediterranean less than an hour away. In winter, buses to Pradollano leave Granada's bus station three times a day on weekdays and four times on weekends and holidays. Tickets are €9 round-trip. As for Borreguiles, you can get

there only on skis. There's an information center (🌐 *sierranevada.es*) at Plaza de Andalucía 4. ✉ *Sierra Nevada.*

The Alpujarras

Village of Lanjarón: 46 km (29 miles) south of Granada.

A trip to the Alpujarras, on the southern slopes of the Sierra Nevada, takes you to one of Andalusia's highest, most remote, and most scenic areas, home for decades to painters, writers, and a considerable foreign population. The Alpujarras region was originally populated by Moors fleeing the Christian Reconquest (from Seville after its fall in 1248, then from Granada after 1492).To this day, the Galicians' descendants continue the Moorish custom of weaving rugs and blankets in the traditional Alpujarran colors of red, green, black, and white, and they sell their crafts in many of the villages. Be on the lookout for handmade basketry and pottery as well.

Houses here are squat and square; they spill down the southern slopes of the Sierra Nevada, bearing a strong resemblance to the Berber homes in the Rif Mountains, just across the Mediterranean in Morocco. If you're driving, the road as far as Lanjarón and Orgiva is smooth sailing; after that come steep, twisting mountain roads with few gas stations. Beyond sightseeing, the area is a haven for outdoor activities such as hiking and horseback riding. Inquire at the **Information Point** at Plaza de la Libertad, at Pampaneira.

Sights

Lanjarón and Nearby Villages
TOWN | The western entrance to the Alpujarras is some 46 km (29 miles) from Granada at Lanjarón. This spa town is famous for its mineral water, collected from the melting snows of the Sierra Nevada and drunk throughout Spain. **Orgiva,** the next and largest town in the Alpujarras, has a 17th-century castle. Here you can leave the A348 and follow signs for the villages of the Alpujarras Altas (High Alpujarras), including **Pampaneira, Capileira,** and especially **Trevélez,** which lies on the slopes of the Mulhacén at 4,840 feet above sea level. Reward yourself with a plate of the local jamón serrano. Trevélez has three levels—the Barrio Alto, Barrio Medio, and Barrio Bajo—and the butchers are concentrated in the lowest section (Bajo). The higher levels have narrow cobblestone streets, whitewashed houses, and shops.

Hotels

Hotel Alcadima
$ | **HOTEL** | **FAMILY** | One of the best-value hotels in the area, this pleasant if unfancy hotel in the rustic spa town of Lanjarón makes a good base for exploring the lower part of the Alpujarras. **Pros:** swimming pool; excellent restaurant; two-bedroom suites are ideal for families. **Cons:** Lanjarón isn't the prettiest village in the area; could be too plain for some; down an unattractive side street. [$] *Rooms from: €60* ✉ *Calle Francisco Tarrega 3, Lanjarón* ☎ *958/770809* 🌐 *www.alcadima.com* 🛏 *45 rooms* 🍴 *No meals.*

Los Tinaos
$ | **RENTAL** | Located on the way to Trevélez in the pretty whitewashed village of Bubión that almost clings to the mountainside, these comfortable apartments (for two or four people) come squeaky-clean, with open log fires as well as central heating, and sweeping views across the valley. **Pros:** valley views; a short walk from Pitres; bar serving locally produced wine. **Cons:** steep walk down. [$] *Rooms from: €60* ✉ *Calle Parras 2, Bubión* ☎ *958/763217* 🌐 *www.lostinaos.com* 🛏 *10 rooms* 🍴 *No meals.*

Index

Photo Credits

Fodor's MADRID

Publisher: Stephen Horowitz, *General Manager*

Editorial: Douglas Stallings, *Editorial Director;* Jill Fergus, Jacinta O'Halloran, Amanda Sadlowski, *Senior Editors;* Kayla Becker, Alexis Kelly, Rachael Roth, *Editors*

Design: Tina Malaney, *Director of Design and Production;* Jessica Gonzalez, *Graphic Designer;* Mariana Tabares, *Design and Production Intern*

Production: Jennifer DePrima, *Editorial Production Manager;* Elyse Rozelle, *Senior Production Editor;* Monica White, *Production Editor*

Maps: Rebecca Baer, *Senior Map Editor;* Mark Stroud (Moon Street Cartography); David Lindroth, *Cartographers*

Photography: Viviane Teles, *Senior Photo Editor;* Namrata Aggarwal, Ashok Kumar, Carl Yu, *Photo Editors;* Rebecca Rimmer, *Photo Intern*

Business and Operations: Chuck Hoover, *Chief Marketing Officer;* Robert Ames, *Group General Manager;* Devin Duckworth, *Director of Print Publishing;* Victor Bernal, *Business Analyst*

Public Relations and Marketing: Joe Ewaskiw, *Senior Director Communications and Public Relations;* Esther Su, *Senior Marketing Manager*

Fodors.com: Jeremy Tarr, *Editorial Director;* Rachael Levitt, *Managing Editor*

Technology: Jon Atkinson, *Director of Technology;* Rudresh Teotia, *Lead Developer;* Jacob Ashpis, *Content Operations Manager*

Writers: Benjamin Kemper, Joanna Styles

Editor: Jacinta O'Halloran

Production Editor: Elyse Rozelle

1st edition

ISBN 978–1–64097–342–8

ISSN 2691–2295

All details in this book are based on information supplied to us at press time. Always confirm information when it matters, especially if you're making a detour to visit a specific place. Fodor's expressly disclaims any liability, loss, or risk, personal or otherwise, that is incurred as a consequence of the use of any of the contents of this book.

SPECIAL SALES
This book is available at special discounts for bulk purchases for sales promotions or premiums. For more information, e-mail SpecialMarkets@fodors.com.

PRINTED IN CANADA

10 9 8 7 6 5 4 3 2 1

MIX
Paper from responsible sources
FSC www.fsc.org FSC® C016245